GLORY
IN THE
HIGHEST

Removing the Influence of
Socrates, Plato, Philo and Greek Philosophy
from Christian Doctrine

Joel W. Hemphill

Trumpet Call Books
P.O. Box 656
Joelton, Tennessee 37080

Trumpet Call Books
P.O. Box 656
Joelton, TN 37080

www.thehemphills.com • www.trumpetcallbooks.com

Glory To God In The Highest

ISBN: 978-0-9825196-1-5

Printed in the United States of America

Cover Photo from Shutterstock Images

Photos of Joel and LaBreeska Hemphill by
Bloodworth Photography – Goodlettsville, TN.

Unless otherwise indicated, all Scripture taken from
"The Holy Bible: King James Version."

*"Scripture taken from the HOLY BIBLE, NEW INTERNATIONAL VERSION.
Copyright © 1973, 1978, 1984 International Bible Society.
Used by permission of Zondervan Bible Publishers."*

*"Scripture taken from the NEW AMERICAN STANDARD BIBLE ®,
Copyright © 1960, 1962, 1963, 1968, 1971, 1972, 1973, 1975, 1977,
1995 by The Lockman Foundation. Used by permission.*
www.Lockman.org

*"Scriptures quoted from The Holy Bible, New Century Version ®,
copyright © 2005 by Thomas Nelson, Inc. Used by permission."*

About The Rainbow:

> *"As the appearance of the bow that is in the cloud in the
> day of rain...This was the appearance of the likeness of the
> glory of the Lord" (Ezekiel 1:28).*

> *"And there was a rainbow round about the throne* [of God],
> *in sight like unto an emerald" (Revelation 4:3).*

Glory To God In The Highest

Table of Contents

Thanks To....

My darling wife LaBreeska for your wise counsel and for standing with me and putting it all on the line for the biblical truths contained in this book. May your reward be great!

Our wonderful secretary Dawn Mansfield for your labor of love in typing and re-typing the manuscript. You are a gift to us from the Father.

Our dear friend Nancy Carter of *Quality DigiPress* for your skillful interior layout and design.

Our dear friend Joy MacKenzie for your diligent work of editing the manuscript. Your help and advice have made this a better book.

Our dear friend Lynsae Harkins of *Lynsae Printing and Design* for the expert cover artwork and design.

~The above are sweet and talented ladies
on whom I lean for help~

To all who have offered prayers and encouragement and have awaited the release of *Glory To God In The Highest.*

Dedication

I dedicate this book to all who have a sincere hunger to know better the one Most High God of the Bible, our Creator and Father. May this book through Scripture increase your knowledge of Him, that we might more perfectly give God the glory, love, and worship that He deserves and demands. My prayer for you is:

*"That **the God** of our Lord Jesus Christ, **the Father** of glory, may give unto you the spirit of wisdom and revelation in the knowledge of **him**: The eyes of your understanding being enlightened; that ye may know what is the hope of **his** calling, and what the riches of the glory of **his** inheritance in the saints, And what is the exceeding greatness of **his** power to us-ward who believe, according to the working of **his** mighty power, **Which he wrought in Christ**, when he raised him from the dead, and set him at **his** own right hand in the heavenly places" (Ephesians 1:17-20).*

Lynn –

you are a very dear friend whom I appreciate –

In Christian love

Todd Hemphill

7

God The Creator's Glory

"Thus saith the Lord, the Holy One of Israel, and his Maker. I have made the earth, and created man upon it: I, even my hands, have stretched out the heavens, and all their host have I commanded.... and there is no God else beside me; a just God and a Saviour; there is none beside me. Look unto me, and be ye saved, all the ends of the earth: for I am God, and there is none else" (Isaiah 45:11-12, 21-22).

"I am the Lord: that is my name; and my glory will I not give to another" (Isaiah 42:8).

"I will not give my glory unto another" (Isaiah 48:11).

"And I saw another angel fly in the midst of heaven, having the everlasting gospel to preach unto them that dwell on the earth... Saying with a loud voice, Fear God, and give glory to him; for the hour of his judgement is come: and worship him that made heaven, and the earth, and the sea, and the fountains of waters" (Revelation 14:6-7).

Jesus' Glory

"....and we beheld his glory, the glory as of the only begotten of the Father" (John 1:14).

"The Son of Man...shall come in his own glory" [Jesus speaking] (Luke 9:26).

"The Son of man shall sit in the throne of his glory" [Jesus speaking] (Matt. 19:28).

"Father...the glory which thou gavest me...that they may behold my glory which thou hast given me" [Jesus speaking] (John 17:21, 22, 24).

[Christ] *"verily was foreordained before the foundation of the world, but was manifest in these last times for you, Who by him do believe in God, that raised him up from the dead, and gave him glory; that your faith and hope might be in God"* (I Peter 1:20-21).

Foreward

Dear Reader:

In my studies I have been astonished to find that according to Edward Gibbon, Will Durant, and other noted historians, Plato was teaching the doctrine of the *divine Logos* and the doctrine of the *Trinity*, at his university called the *Academy* in Athens, Greece, 375 years **before** the birth of Jesus Christ!

It was several hundred years after the death of the last Apostle, before these Platonic doctrines made their way into Christianity, through the Greek *"church fathers,"* followers of Plato who had *"converted."* They were established at two church councils: Nicea *(325 A.D.)* which decided that in addition to the Father, Jesus is the *"second Deity,"* and Constantinople *(381 A.D.)* which proclaimed the Holy Spirit as the third person of God, who *"with the Father and the Son **he** is worshiped and glorified."* This flies in the face of Moses' statement in Deuteronomy 6:4, which was endorsed by Jesus himself in Mark 12:29:

> *"Hear, O Israel: The Lord our God is **one** Lord."*

To deny the conclusions of these councils which were called by the Roman emperors Constantine and Theodosius, was to be punished by banishment or death. As Thomas Jefferson said, *"The Trinitarian idea...grew in the blood of thousands and thousands of martyr's."* These things I will prove in this book.

It is past time to re-examine those doctrines in the light of Holy Scripture!

Joel Hemphill

Joel Hemphill

The Time-Line Of This Book

1491 B.C. God speaks to Moses from the burning bush saying, *"The Lord God...this is my name for ever, and this is my memorial unto all generations" (Ex. 3:15).*

1451 B.C. Moses' final address to Israel in which he says, *"Hear, O Israel: The Lord our God is one Lord" (Deut. 6:4).*

553 B.C. The prophet Daniel sees a vision of Greece as a violent *"he goat"* destroying with *"fury" (Daniel 8:5-8, 21).*

500 B.C. The Greek philosopher Heraclitus introduces the idea that the world is governed by a *"firelike Logos,"* a divine force similar to human reason, that produces the order and pattern in nature.

469 B.C. The Greek philosopher Socrates is born in Athens, Greece.

430 B.C. Socrates begins his diligent search for *"logos"* in human reason, with intense questioning known as the Socratic method.

424 B.C. The Greek philosopher Plato is born in Athens to aristocratic parents and becomes the most dedicated and famous pupil of Socrates.

399 B.C. Socrates is convicted of crimes, (including corrupting the youth of Athens) by a jury of 500 of his peers, and is executed in prison. Plato, embittered by this execution of his teacher, leaves Athens for travel in North Africa and Egypt.

395 B.C. Plato returns to Athens.

386 B.C. Plato founds a university in Athens called the *"Academy,"* dedicated to the *"worship of spirits"* where he begins to teach the doctrines of the *logos* and the *triune God. (Historian Edward Gibbon; The Decline and Fall Of The Roman Empire; Vol. 2; p. 301).*

300 B.C. Zeno founds the first Stoic school, at Athens. The Stoics believe in the **Logos** as the *"divine reason"* and all-pervading *"breath of fire"* as handed down to them by Heraclitus, Socrates and Plato. They strongly promote this idea for the next several centuries.

11

20 B.C.	Philo Judaeus is born in Alexandria, Egypt. He was to become the most prolific writer of pre-Christian Judaism. A follower of Plato, he would promote his idea of the Logos (using the terms *"logos"* or *"divine logos"* some 1400 times in his writings) before Jesus began his ministry in Galilee.
4 B.C.	Jesus is born in Bethlehem of the virgin Mary.
31 A.D.	Spring - Jesus Christ is crucified outside the city of Jerusalem but was resurrected three days later, victorious over death, hell, and the grave, having *"condemned sin in the flesh" (Rom. 8:3).*
53 A.D.	The apostle Paul preaches a sermon in Athens, on Mars hill, regarding *"the unknown God"* who will one day *"judge the world in righteousness by that man* [Jesus] *whom he hath ordained" (Acts 17:31).*
60 A.D.	The apostle Paul warns the Christian elders of Ephesus, Greece that after his death *"grievous wolves"* will enter in and devastate the flock *(Acts 20:29).*
64 A.D.	The apostle Paul writes a letter to the Christians at Colosse warning them to beware of (Greek) philosophy *(Col. 2:8).*
96 A.D.	John, the last surviving Apostle dies, perhaps in Ephesus, Greece.
110 A.D.	The *"church father"* Justin Martyr is born in Flavia Neapolis, Rome. He will come to teach that Jesus is *"God,"* although in *"second place"* to *"the true God himself."* He will also teach that the Greeks Heraclitus and Socrates were *"Christians, for Christ was and is the Logos who dwells in every man."*
150 A.D.	The *"church father"* Clement of Alexandria is born in Athens. He will grow up to love Plato and Greek philosophy, whose doctrines he will mix with his chosen Christian religion. He will teach that Christ's body had only an *"apparent reality"* and that Jesus *"knew neither pain, nor sorrow, nor emotions."* He will speak of *"the Trinity as reflected in Plato's Timaeus."*

160 A.D.	The *"church father"* Tertullian is born in Carthage and in adulthood will become a lawyer in Rome. He will coin over 900 new words including *trinitas* (Trinity) to explain his belief that God is one substantia (substance), manifested by three separate and distinct *personae* (persons). Using Greek sources, he will teach and promote such ideas as the *"divine Logos"* and the Trinity.
185 A.D.	The *"church father"* Origen is born in Alexandria, Egypt. Through the influence of Greek philosophy and his own *"speculations"* regarding God and Christian doctrine, he will come to teach the pre-existence of all souls, the eventual return of all spirits (including the devil) to the Creator, the deification of men, and purgatory. But his doctrine that will be most devastating to the understanding of future Christians is, the *"eternal generation"* of the Son of God, Jesus.
312 A.D.	General Constantine becomes emperor of the Roman empire. Claiming a conversion to Christianity in that year, he will nevertheless continue to preside at pagan functions, mint coins with pagan images, contribute to the construction of pagan temples and will not be baptized until on his deathbed in 335 A.D.
318 A.D.	A controversy erupts in Alexandria, Egypt regarding the person of Jesus Christ, and his relationship to God the Father. This *"Arian Controversy"* between opposing Christian factions leads to violence in the streets.
325 A.D.	The Arian Controversy threatening the peace of the Roman Empire itself, Emperor Constantine convenes a council of 300 bishops at his palace in Nicea (modern Turkey). This Nicean Council, under pressure from Constantine, will formulate a creed stating that Jesus Christ is *"eternally begotten of the Father...God from God, Light from Light, Very God of Very God...of one substance with the Father."*
375 A.D.	Three Christian Platonist theologians from the province of Cappadocia-Basil, Basil's brother Gregory, and Gregory

of Nazianzus-continuing *"the speculative and Platonist tendencies of Clement and Origen"* arrive at the idea that God exists as one substance, made up of three persons, the Father, the Son, and the Holy Spirit-which are co-equal and co-eternal: the Trinity.

379 A.D. The Roman general Theodosius becomes emperor of Rome. A recent convert to Christianity, he is determined to stamp out the still smoldering *Arian Controversy.*

380 A.D. Theodosius declares Christianity the official and only religion of the Roman Empire, and issues a decree that all Roman citizens confess the Nicean Creed or suffer severe punishment.

381 A.D. Emperor Theodosius convenes the *"Council of Constantinople,"* also called *"the Second Ecumenical Church Council,"* in the city for which it is named. The view of the three Cappadocians prevails at this gathering of 186 bishops which affirms both the *"person"* and full *"deity"* of the Holy Spirit with these words, *"We believe in the Holy Spirit, the Lord, the giver of life.... . With the Father and the Son **he** is worshiped and glorified."* Thus Christianity has a *"primitive"* doctrine of the Trinity with much work left to be done.

386 A.D. (Saint) Augustine, born in North Africa *(in 354)*, is converted to Christianity in Milan, Italy, through the influence of Bishop Ambrose, and *"certain books"* by Plato and other Greek philosophers. He will credit these books for helping him understand the Trinity and that Christ is *"equal to"* and *"coeternal with"* God. His writings on the Trinity will greatly impact Christianity for the following 1600 years.

394 A.D. Emperor Theodosius begins punishing pagans who refuse to adopt Catholic Christianity. A riot in the city of Thessalonica causes the death of one of his officials, and in revenge he invites the citizens to be entertained in the city arena, then massacres 7,000 as punishment.

449 A.D.	At the insistence of Pope Leo, the Emperor Marcian convenes the *"Second Council of Ephesus"* to decide if there were two separate natures in Jesus, or a single deified human nature. The 135 bishops will determine that God, as Christ, was born, suffered and died, and that Jesus was *"God crucified."* Since this council contradicted several previous councils, it will come to be known as *"the Council of Robbers,"* or the *"Gangster Synod."*
451 A.D.	*The Council of Chalcedon (Greece)*, or *"the Fourth Ecumenical Council"* is called to resolve the continuing dispute. This gathering of 600 bishops annuls the declaration of the *"Robbers Council,"* affirms Mary as *"mother of God,"* and adopts Pope Leo's view that Christ possessed two natures, both a human and a divine, thus expanding Nicea and Constantinople.
525 A.D.	The Roman philosopher-statesman Boethius comes to prominence in the West. Deeply versed in the philosophy of Plato and Aristotle, he will write four treatises on the doctrine of the Trinity and the person of Jesus Christ, and become for Christianity a major interpreter of the Augustinian tradition of trinitarian thought.
1033 A.D.	Anselm of Canterbury is born. He will attempt to correct heresies about the Trinity and shed rational light on the mystery. Following in the Platonic tradition of Augustine, his views on the Trinity will heavily influence future church councils.
1150 A.D.	Richard of St. Victor continues the work of defining the Trinity, and provides a new way of thinking regarding the unity of the "trinitarian persons".
1215 A.D.	*"The Fourth Latern Council"* is convened to deal with ongoing misunderstandings regarding details of the doctrine of the Trinity.
1225 A.D.	(Saint) Thomas Aquinas is born in Italy. He will become a Dominican friar and under the influence of Plato, Aristotle,

Augustine and others (both Christians and pagans) will make a great trinitarian contribution. For his work regarding the unity and multiplicity of the triune being of God, he will later be declared *"The Angelic Doctor of the Church"* by popes.

1438 A.D. *"The Council of Florence (Italy),* is convened. It will meet for seven years to debate details of the doctrine of the Trinity.

1517 A.D. The young Catholic priest Martin Luther nails his *"Ninety-five Theses"* to the church doors in Wittenberg, Germany, beginning the Protestant Reformation. But he and the other noted reformers, Ulrich Zwingli and John Calvin, will embrace the doctrine of the Trinity "without serious examination".

1553 A.D. Trinitarian Michael Servetus is burned at the stake outside Geneva, Switzerland, at the instigation of John Calvin and other Protestant pastors for being anti-Nicea, and teaching his unorthodox views regarding the Trinity.

2006 A.D. Pope Benedict gives a speech on September 12th at the University of Regensburg, Germany, in which he decries the *"dehellenization of Christianity which is now in progress."* He praises the past combining of *"the Greek spirit and the Christian spirit"* which he says has resulted in *"a mutual enrichment."* He repeatedly uses with favor the terms Platonism, Platonists, and Platonic and quotes the Greek philosopher Socrates, mentioning him with approval several times.

(*Note: Dates are approximate. Those regarding biblical events are based mostly on the work of James Ussher, 17th century authority on Bible chronology.*)

Introduction

In August of 2006 I finished writing and published a book that I had begun the previous November titled, *"To God Be The Glory."* I began the book by telling of an awesome encounter I had in 1986 with the God of Abraham, Isaac, and Jacob, in which He told me to study the Scripture, as He was going to reveal Himself to me in His word. This statement seemed odd from my perspective because I had been saved at the age of ten, and had been in Christian ministry since the age of nineteen. I was raised "Oneness," the belief that Jesus is the human incarnation of God the Father-the God-man, God Himself in human form. (Trinitarians normally believe that Jesus is an incarnation of God the Son, the second person of a triune God, a pre-existent being). I pastored a church of the Oneness persuasion from 1961-1971.

God also told me in 1986 that the day would come when I would *"write a book or books"* about His glory. *"To God Be The Glory"* was the first of these. *"Should We Pray To God the Father or Our Savior Jesus?"* published in the spring of 2009 was the second. *"Is The Holy Spirit A Third Person of God?"* published in August of 2009 was the third, and this book is the fourth.

The thesis of the first book is this: that we Christians, in our sincere desire to exalt the Lord Jesus Christ, have given him in our hearts and worship, the esteem-honor-glory that rightly belongs to the one Eternal, Most-High God, Jesus' Father and ours.

> *"Go to **my brethren**, and say unto them, I ascend unto my Father, and your Father; and to my God, and your God"* (Jesus speaking) *(John 20:17).*

I am a minister of Jesus Christ and I love to talk about *his* glory. He is the supernaturally conceived, virgin-born, sinless Son of God; savior, redeemer, Messiah, and soon coming king, and he has great glory! He said:

> *"They shall see the Son of man coming in the clouds of heaven with power and **great glory**"* (Matt. 24:30).

17

Jesus' glory is so great that he will destroy the Anti-christ *"with the brightness of his coming" (II Thess. 2:8)*. John the beloved apostle who lay his head on Jesus' bosom at the last supper, *"fell at his feet as dead"* when he saw Jesus in his glory in Revelation chapter one.

But Jesus has his own glory!

> *"...when the Son of man shall sit upon the throne of **his glory**, ye also shall sit upon twelve thrones" (Matt. 19:28)*. Please note: These thrones are not in heaven!

> *"When the Son of man shall come in **his glory**...then shall he sit on the throne of **his glory**" (Matt. 25:31)*.

> *"The Son of man...shall come in **his own glory**" (Luke 9:26)*.

> *"Ought not Christ to have suffered these things, and to enter into **his glory**" (Luke 24:26)*.

> *"...and we beheld **his glory**, the **glory as of the only begotten** of the Father" (John 1:14)*. Note: Not the glory *as of God*, or *as of the Father in flesh*, but *"as of the only begotten of the Father."*

> *"This beginning of miracles did Jesus in Cana of Galilee, and manifested forth **his glory**" (John 2:11)*.

God our Father's glory is much greater than Jesus' glory because God's glory is innate, the essence of who He is, and Jesus' glory is a "given glory," given to him by God his Father.

> *"Father...the **glory which thou gavest me**...that they may behold **my glory which thou hast given me**" (John 17:21, 22, 24)*.

(Christ) *"verily was **foreordained** before the foundation of the world, but was manifest in these last times for you, Who by him do believe in **God,** that raised him up from the dead, and **gave him glory**; that your faith and hope might be in **God"** (I Peter 1:20-21).*

"God the Lord" speaks in the first seven verses of Isaiah chapter forty-two of the coming Messiah, *"my servant"* whom He would send, *"for a covenant of the people, for a light of the Gentiles, to open the blind eyes, to bring out the prisoners from the prison."* (Note: Not once in the Bible is Jesus called *"**God the Lord"***). But God says in verse eight:

*"I am the Lord: that is my name; **and my glory will I not give to another."***

He says again in Isaiah 48:11:

*"**I will not give my glory unto another."***

The Lord God our Father is not jealous of His Son, but He is for sure jealous of His glory. Again and again He commands us in Scripture to give Him the glory that He is due. Here are some examples:

*"Give unto the Lord, O ye mighty, give unto the Lord **glory** and strength. Give unto the Lord **the glory due unto his name**; worship the Lord in the beauty of holiness...And in his temple doth every one speak of **his glory** (Ps. 29:1-2, 9).*

*"Sing unto the Lord, bless his name, Declare **his glory** among the heathen, For the Lord is great, and greatly to be praised: he is to be feared above all gods. **Give unto the Lord the glory due unto his name**: O worship the Lord in the beauty of holiness: fear before him, all the earth" (Ps. 96:2-4, 8-9).*

*"**Give glory to the Lord your God**" (Jer. 13:16).*

19

*"If ye will not hear...**to give glory unto my name**, saith the Lord of hosts..." (Mal. 2:2).*

*"To **God only wise**, be glory **through** Jesus Christ for ever. Amen" (Rom. 16:27).* Notice: Not *"**to**"* Jesus Christ, but *"**through**"* Jesus Christ. Note Paul's statement in Romans 6:4, that *"Christ was raised up from the dead **by the glory of the Father.**"*

"Now unto the King (God the *"great King"*) *eternal, immortal, **invisible**, the **only wise God**, be honor and **glory** for ever and ever. Amen" (I Tim. 1:17).* Note: The word *"invisible."* Jesus was not invisible, he was seen by thousands.

*"To the **only wise God** our Savior* (God our ultimate Savior), **be glory**...both now and ever. Amen" (Jude v. 25).*

*"And the same hour was there a great earthquake...and the remnant were affrighted, **and gave glory to the God of heaven**" (Rev. 11:13).*

*"And men...blasphemed the name of **God**, and they repented not to **give him glory**" (Rev. 16:9).*

When the New Testament speaks of giving glory to God our Father, the word *"glory"* in Greek is *"doxa."* It means *"to recognize a person or thing for what it is. It basically refers to the recognition belonging to a person - honor - renown. To recognize, honor, praise."* [1]

To do properly what we have been commanded to do by our God, we must answer this question in our minds: Is Jesus' glory and God our Father's glory the same? The clear biblical answer is, **no!**

> *"But he* [Stephen]*, being full of the Holy Ghost looked up steadfastly into heaven,* **and saw the glory of God***, and Jesus standing on the right hand of God, and said, 'Behold, I see the heavens opened, and the Son of man* [a human being] *standing on the right hand of God' " (Acts 7:55-56).*

Again, what did Stephen see? ***"The glory of God, and Jesus standing on the right hand of God.*** **"** We have Stephen's dying testimony that they are **distinct and separate**, and what God has separated let no man join together.

Note: Peter, who saw Jesus' awesome glory on the Mount of Transfiguration, said God the Father's glory is the greatest glory!

> *"But we saw the greatness of Jesus with our own eyes. Jesus heard the voice of* **God, the Greatest Glory***, when he received* **honor and glory** *from God the Father. The voice said, 'This is my Son...' "(II Peter 1:17 NCV).*

The first Adam reached for God's glory and brought upon mankind all of the sin, suffering, and death that we have known for the past 6000 years; for the tempter said, Eat of the forbidden fruit, ***"and ye shall be as gods"*** *(Gen. 3:5)*. But when Jesus Christ *"the last Adam...the second man" (I Cor. 15:45-47)* was tempted by the devil and offered **"glory***,*** ***"*** he said, *"Get thee behind me Satan" (Luke 4:6, 8)*. Paul says in Philippians 2:6 that *"Christ Jesus...did not regard* **equality with God a thing to be grasped***" (NASB - NIV - ESV - The Scriptures - The Complete Jewish Bible - The New English Bible)*.

Jesus said in John 8:50, *"I seek not mine own glory: there is one* [the Father] *that seeketh and judgeth,"* so if he did not even seek his own glory, it is for sure he did not seek the Father's glory for himself. It is we in our ignorance who have given Jesus, the Son of God, God the Father's glory.

We are told in John 5:23 that *"all men should honor the Son, even as they honor the Father,"* but trust Jesus when he says in verse forty-one, *"I receive not honor from men."* What is that again precious Jesus? *"I receive not honor from men."* In Scripture, Jesus' honor is from the Father, with which he is more than content.

And **we** are learning. We learned from Scripture in my first book that God is **one** entity, being, person.

> *"Hear, O Israel: The Lord our **God** is **one Lord**"* [Moses speaking] *(Deut. 6:4)*. Notice: God is **one Lord**, not three. **God is not a committee!**

> *"Hear, O Israel; The Lord our **God** is **one Lord**"* [Jesus speaking] *(Mark 12:29)*.

> *"For there is **one God**, and there is **none other but he**"* *(Mark 12:32)*.

> *"The **one and only God**...the **Father**"* [Jesus speaking] *(John 5:44 - 45 NASB)*.

> *"**Father**...that they might know thee **the only true God**"* [Jesus speaking] *(John 17:3)*.

> *"Why callest thou me good? There is none good but **one,** that is **God**"* [Jesus speaking] *(Matt. 19:17)*.

> *"To us there is but **one God**, the **Father**"* [Paul speaking] *(I Cor. 8:6)*.

> *"**One God** and **Father** of all who is above all"* *(Eph. 4:6)*.

> *"Have we not all **one father**? Hath not **one God** created us?"* *(Malachi 2:10)*. *"If then I be a **father**, where is mine honor...saith the Lord of hosts?"* *(Malachi 1:6)*.

*"Now a mediator is not a mediator of one, **but God is one**"* *(Gal. 3:20).*

*"For there is **one God**, and **one mediator** between God and men, **the man** Christ Jesus" (I Tim. 2:5).*

*"For there are certain men crept in unawares...**denying the only Lord God**, and our Lord Jesus Christ" (Jude 1:4).* (This is Jude the half brother of Jesus writing, and he never believed that his brother was *"the only Lord God,"* but rather that he is *"our Lord Jesus Messiah").*

We learned that the one Most High God, the **Lord God**, has called angels, the Davidic kings, Israel as a nation, the first Adam, Jesus the Messiah, and we who are Christians, *"Sons of God."*

*"All the **sons of God** [angels at the time of creation] shouted for joy"* [God speaking] *(Job 38:7).*

*"I will be his father, and he shall be **my son**. If he commit iniquity, I will chasten him"* [God to David] *(II Sam. 7:14).*

*"And thou shalt say unto Pharaoh, Thus saith the Lord, Israel is **my son**, even my firstborn" (Ex. 4:22).*

*"When Israel was a child, then I loved him, and called **my son** out of Egypt" (Hosea 11:1).*

*"**Adam**, which was the **son of God**" (Luke 3:38).*

*"Behold, what manner of love **the Father** hath bestowed upon us, that **we** should be called the **sons of God**...Beloved now are **we** the **sons of God**" (I John 3:1-2).*

So when Jesus is called *"Son of God"* again and again in Scripture, does this mean that he is God or God Junior? No way! It is significant to note that in the Bible he is **never** called "God the Son." That is not biblical terminology! The Bible clearly teaches that **God** is **one**, therefore unique *(one and only; single; sole "a unique specimen," having no like or equal; unparalleled)* the only one in the God family. Since God has no relatives, it is not kinship, it is **"position."** In all cases in the Scriptures, when the phrase *"Son of God"* is used, it denotes a relationship position. The clear answer as to why Jesus is called *"Son of God"* can be found in Gabriel's words to the virgin Mary, as recorded in Luke chapter one. **This is so very important!**

> *"Then said Mary unto the angel, How shall this be, seeing I know not a man? And the angel answered and said unto her, The Holy Ghost shall come upon thee, and the power of the Highest shall overshadow thee: **therefore** [Greek dio kai - "for that reason precisely"] also that holy thing which shall be born of thee shall be called the **Son of God"** (Luke 1:34-35).*

Notice, Gabriel did not tell Mary that God the Father, or God the Son, the second person of a triune God, a pre-existent being, was going to move into her womb and come out looking like a baby. This she was not told, and this Mary never believed! She was told and she did believe that the Holy Ghost, the spirit of the Most High God would come over her and through a creative act, **without the aid of a man**, would produce a baby which **"for that reason precisely"** would be called *"the Son of God."* Note: When you see *"Son"* in your Bible, written with a capital *"S,"* it was not written that way in the original, this is a choice made by the editor or publisher and does not affect the meaning of the word *"son."* Consider what Paul says in Galatians 4:4:

> *"When the fullness of the time was come, God sent forth his Son, **made** of a woman, **made** under the law."*

The word *"made"* in this verse is the Greek word *"genomai"* and means to *"generate - to cause to come into being."* So Jesus was generated by the Holy Ghost *(his genesis or beginning)* in the womb of a virgin, and it was a creative act, and not as most of Christianity has taught in error, an incarnation. The *Harper-Collins Bible Dictionary* correctly says:

> [Incarnation] *"refers to the Christian doctrine that the pre-existent Son of God became man in Jesus. None of these writers* [Matthew, Mark, Luke] *deals with the question of Jesus' pre-existence. Paul does not directly address the question of the incarnation... **It is only with the fathers of the church in the third and fourth centuries, that a full-fledged theory of the incarnation develops.**" (p. 452-453).*

Those who believe that Jesus is God Incarnate, God Himself in human flesh, should take a closer look at Luke, chapter two, Jesus' trip to Jerusalem with Mary and Joseph for dedication to God.

> *"And when the days of her purification according to the law of Moses were accomplished* [forty days] *(Lev. 12:2-4), they brought him* [baby Jesus] *to Jerusalem, **to present him to the Lord***" *(Luke 2:22).* Note: They did not present baby Jesus to himself!

To whom did they present the baby Jesus? *"To the Lord* [God]. *"* Now look ahead to verse twenty-five.

> *"And, behold, there was a man in Jerusalem, whose name was Simeon...and it was revealed unto him by the Holy Ghost that he should not see death before he had seen the **Lord's** Christ"* [i.e. *"the Lord's anointed one"* - *"the Lord's Messiah"*] *(Luke 2:25-26).* Notice Revelation 11:15: *"The kingdoms of this world are become the kingdom of our **Lord** [God], and of **his** Christ [Jesus]."*

Back To Simeon

> *"Then took he him up in his arms, and blessed* [praised] *God, and said, 'Lord, now lettest thou thy servant depart in*

*peace, according to **thy word**: For mine eyes have seen thy salvation' " (Luke 2:28-30).* Note: Simeon is not talking to the baby; he is speaking to the Lord God in heaven who had brought forth His Lord Messiah on earth.

Look At Peter's Confession

My serious concern is that we have built our churches on the **mistaken confession** that Jesus Christ is the eternal God, or the second person of a triune God, incarnate. In Matthew chapter sixteen, Jesus promised his disciples that he would build his church, *"and the gates of hell shall not prevail against it."* The Catholic church has taught that Jesus built his church on **Peter**, but we know it is built on the rock of **Peter's confession**. What was Peter's confession?

> *"Thou art the Christ* [Messiah], *the **Son** of the **living God**" (Matt. 16:16).*

> *"Thou art the Christ"* [Messiah - not "God" or "God the Son, second person of a triune God"] *(Mark 8:29).*

> *"The Christ* [Messiah] *of God" (Luke 9:20).*

> *"Then charged he his disciples that they should tell no man that he was Jesus the Christ"* [Messiah - not "God" or "God the Son"] *(Matt. 16:20).*

Distinguishing Between The Father and The Son

Is Jesus "God," or "the Son of God?" Christianity cannot have it two ways. He is either *God*, or *Son of God*; he simply cannot be both. We must begin to make a distinction in our minds and in our worship, between the One True **God** and His Son **Jesus**. The Bible makes this distinction very clearly, but somehow most of us in Christianity have missed it badly. For example look at Hebrews 2:3-4.

> *"How shall we escape, if we neglect so great salvation; which at the first began to be spoken by the Lord* [Jesus],

> *and was confirmed unto us by them that heard him* [Jesus'
> disciples]*; **God also** bearing them witness, both with signs
> and wonders...according to **his own will**.*"

The writer of Hebrews makes a clear distinction between the Lord Jesus in
verse three, and *"**God also**"* in verse four. Now look at Hebrews 12:22-24:

> *"But ye are come unto mount Sion, and unto the city of the
> living God, the heavenly Jerusalem, and to an innumerable
> company of angels, To the general assembly and church of
> the firstborn, which are written in heaven, and **to God the
> Judge of all**, and to the spirits of just men made perfect,
> And **to Jesus the mediator of the new covenant**, and to the
> blood of sprinkling, that speaketh better things than that of
> Abel.*"

In these verses we see eight things that Christians have come to. They are:

1. *"Mount Sion" (Zion).*
2. *"the city of the living God, the heavenly Jerusalem."*
3. *"an innumerable company of angels."*
4. *"the general assembly and church of the firstborn."*
5. *"**to God** the Judge of all."*
6. *"to the spirits of just men made perfect."*
7. *"**to Jesus** the mediator of the new covenant."*
8. *"to the blood of sprinkling."*

Did that inspired writer expect us to combine numbers five and seven and
make them one and the same. No way! Neither did God who inspired the
Holy Bible.

Jesus Has A God

We learned that Jesus himself has a God, a higher power, whom he worships
(Ps. 18:49; John 4:22-23), whom he fears *(Isa. 11:1-5; Heb. 5:7)* and to
whom he prays *(Matt. 26:53; Luke 6:12, 22:44; Heb. 7:25)*. Notice these
Scriptures regarding Jesus and his God.

*"He shall stand and feed in the strength of the Lord, in the majesty of the name of **the Lord his God**" (Micah 5:4).*

*"**My God, my God**, why hast thou forsaken me?" (Matt. 27:46).*

*"I ascend unto...**my God**, and your God" (John 20:17).*

*"Blessed be the **God** and Father of our Lord Jesus Christ, the Father of mercies and God of all comfort" (II Cor. 1:3 NASB).*

*"Blessed be the **God** and Father of our Lord Jesus Christ" (Eph. 1:3).*

*"That the **God** of our Lord Jesus Christ, the Father of glory may give unto you the spirit of wisdom and revelation in the knowledge of **him**" (Eph. 1:17).*

*"Blessed be the **God** and Father of our Lord Jesus Christ" (I Peter 1:3).*

*"Him that overcometh will I make a pillar in the temple of **my God**, and he shall go no more out: and I will write upon him the name of **my God**, and the name of the city of **my God**, which is new Jerusalem, which cometh down out of heaven from **my God**: and I will write upon him my new name" (Rev. 3:12).*

The person speaking in the verse above is the ascended Jesus, who had been in heaven with the Father for some sixty years when the book of Revelation was written, but he still refers to God as *"my God"* four times. It is for sure that Jesus cannot be the Supreme God, while he at the same time has a God to whom he submits.

How did Christianity get its doctrine so wrong as to who the Most High God is? For the answer to that question we looked back to the men who are called the *"early Church fathers,"* and the Council of Nicea. Convened in 325 A.D. by the Roman Emperor Constantine, and under pressure from him, this gathering of three hundred bishops decided that the *"Lord Jesus Christ, the Son of God,"* was ***"eternally** begotten of the Father. That is, from the essence of the Father, God from God, Light from Light, True God from True God, Begotten, **not made**, of one substance with the Father."* The council in saying that the Son was *"of one substance with the Father,"* ascribed deity to the Son. In other words, *"The Son is truly God, just as the Father is truly God."* At the end of the Creed, the Council attached a written condemnation of anyone denying its conclusion, especially those who believed that Christ did not exist in all eternity. However, the Council of Nicea **did not express belief in a triune God.** That was not done until some fifty-six years later *(381 A.D.)* when the Council of Constantinople added the Holy Ghost as the third person of God with these words, *"...and in the Holy Ghost, the Lord and Giver of life,"* thus canonizing the doctrine of the Trinity as it is known today. This became the dogma of the Christian church, and for centuries afterward, to dissent from its teaching was punishable by death. And multiplied thousands did die rather than embrace this error. These Councils, through the friendly attitude and strong arm of the secular power, led directly to the Roman Catholic Church and the unholy "Holy Roman Empire." It is interesting that the *Harper-Collins Encyclopedia of Catholicism* calls the doctrine of the Trinity *"a late-fourth-century Christian doctrine."*

> *"Today scholars generally agree that there is no doctrine of the Trinity as such in either the O.T. or the N.T. It would go far beyond the intention and thought-forms of the O.T. to suppose that a **late-fourth-century** or thirteenth-century Christian doctrine can be found there. Likewise, the N.T. does not contain an explicit doctrine of the Trinity."* [2]

Martin Luther, John Calvin and the other Protestant reformers were no better off than the Catholics in their understanding of who the one true God of the Bible is. The *New International Encyclopedia* says of the Trinity:

> *"The doctrine is not found in its fully developed form in the Scripture. Modern theology does not seek to find it in the O.T. At the time of the Reformation, the Protestant Church took over the doctrine of the Trinity, **without serious examination.**"* [3]

Southern Baptist theologian Millard J. Erickson in the Introduction to his book, *God In Three Persons,* explains why he felt the need to deal with the doctrine of the Trinity:

> *"Another reason for the importance of this doctrine is that it poses a continuing problem. Some doctrines are worked out and thus cease to be major problems. This state has not been attained with respect to the Trinity, however. There is still confusion about just what the doctrine denotes. The formula was worked out quite definitely in the **fourth century**. God is one substance or essence, existing in three persons. The difficulty is that we do not know exactly what these terms mean. It is not really clear that we have made significant progress in understanding the problem. We may not be much closer to being able to articulate just what we mean by this doctrine than were the delegates to the Councils of Nicea and Constantinople. The doctrine of the Trinity is a perennial problem, **like the problem of evil**. It therefore needs our continued attention."* [4]

And the confusion continues almost unchecked until today. A leading evangelical of our time, Charles Swindoll, whose ministry I enjoy, in his book, *Jesus: When God Became Man,* says: *"Here's an amazing thought: the baby that Mary held in her arms was holding the universe in place! Those tiny, clutching fists once flung stars into space and planets into orbit. That infant flesh so fair housed the Almighty God. Do you see the child and the glory, the infant - God? What you are seeing is the Incarnation - God dressed in diapers."* [5] [God dressed in diapers?]

In a similar vein another leading evangelical, Max Lucado, in his book, *God Came Near,* says:

> *"God came near. The hands that first held him were un-manicured, calloused, and dirty.* **Angels watched as Mary changed God's diaper.** *The universe watched with wonder as the Almighty learned to walk."* [The Almighty learned to walk?] [6]

Respected Christian author Philip Yancey, in his award winning book, *The Jesus I Never Knew,* writes of what he learned about God from studying the first Christmas.

> God is *"humble. What seems like an oxymoron: a humble God. Unimaginably, the Maker of all things shrank down, down, down, so small as to become an ovum, a single fertilized egg that would divide and re-divide until a fetus took shape, enlarging cell by cell inside a nervous teenager."*
> He says he learned that *"God is little. The God who roared, who could order armies and empires about like pawns on a chessboard,* **this God emerged in Palestine as a baby who could not speak or eat solid food or control his bladder,** *who depended on a teenager for shelter, food, and love."* [7]

Aren't they confusing God the Creator with His virgin-born son Jesus? This may make good drama but it is not good theology. I love these men but this is gross error! If baby Jesus was really Almighty God in diapers, then Mary really is "the Mother of God," and the Catholic church has been right all along. We should know better! I listened in amazement recently as a nationally known radio preacher described a conversation between *"God the Father and God the Son"* in which the two of them discussed the need for one or the other to come to earth to die for the sins of man, and decided which one would come. I can assure you by the authority of God's Holy Bible that that conversation never took place. The wife of an internationally known minister was on the radio recently inviting people to go with them on a Holy Land trip *"and walk where Almighty God walked."* There is not one verse of Scripture where Jesus is called *"Almighty God."* Best selling author Bruce Feiler has written a popular book titled, *Where God Was Born*. Was God born, or was it the **Son of God** who was born in Bethlehem? The writer C.S. Lewis, in an amazing flight of fantasy said:

> *"The Eternal Being, who knows everything and who created the whole universe, became not only a man but (before that) a baby, and before that a (fetus) inside a woman's body. If you want to get the hang of it, think how you would like to* **become a slug or a crab.**" [8]

Everyone is entitled to his own beliefs, but everyone is not entitled to his own **truth**. There is only one eternal truth regarding the person of God, and we have missed it badly. As a well known humorist of the past said regarding another idea:

> *"The work of many scholars has already thrown much darkness on this subject, and it is likely if they keep working we shall soon know nothing at all."*

But we have learned from the lives of Luther, John Wesley and others that there is nothing as powerful as a truth of God whose time has come.

God told me in 1986, *"As a candle on a candlestick, I am going to use you to light the church."* I am nobody from nowhere, but in November, 2005, He began to open my understanding and I started to see where the darkness is. My wife LaBreeska and I sat down in our home and agreed that if we lost all of our family, friends, and finances, we were required to write and speak what we had seen. As a noted minister said years ago, *"I want to be loved, but I had rather be hated for speaking the truth than loved for speaking a lie."*

Now many others are coming to see the truth as to who the One Most High God is in Scripture. We have heard from scores of ministers, pastors and evangelists who love Jesus Christ and know as I do that **he is the only way to God**, but who now have seen through reading my books and tracts that he is *"the Son of God,"* and not *"God."* (Despite our lack of understanding in the past, these are not interchangeable terms). One Southern Baptist Doctor of Divinity, who is the assistant pastor of a 5,000 member church, and a long-time friend of ours, wrote me upon reading *To God Be The Glory,* *"Joel, this is the truth. People may deny this on tradition, but they cannot deny it on Scripture, and I will take Scripture over tradition every time."* One pastor from the state of Texas wrote, *"I agree with everything you have said. I want God my Father and my Lord Jesus to both receive the glory that they are due."* A well known singer, songwriter, evangelist wrote, *"Joel, you were born to write this book!"*

Encouragement and agreement have come from Baptists, Methodists, Presbyterians, Nazarenes, Independents, Pentecostals, Assemblies of God, Church of God and United Pentecostals; former Trinitarians and Oneness who are now ready to put away their past differences and embrace this truth. Christians in other areas may not be aware of this fact, but in parts of the Southern U.S. there is still a bitter struggle between the Oneness and the Trinitarians over the position of Jesus in the Godhead. This struggle can be heard from pulpits and it spills over onto radio and TV, causing a serious division in the body of Christ. May I say in love that for Oneness and Trinitarians to argue over which one is right is like identical twins arguing over which one is the ugliest, since they both teach **in error** that the birth of Jesus was an incarnation, when in fact, the Bible teaches that it was a supernatural, creative act of the Holy Spirit. A friend of mine who is pastor of a large Assemblies of God church in Louisiana said to me recently, *"I'm afraid you're going to be like the man in the Civil War who wore a blue coat and grey pants; both sides are going to be shooting at you."*

And there has been opposition, some of it harsh and mean spirited. In June of 2007, I received an email from the editor of a religious publication of international scope whose publications go back over seventy-five years, requesting a 1500-word article from me defending the thesis of my *"revolutionary book."* I found his choice of the word *"revolutionary"* interesting because about a year before I wrote the book *To God Be The Glory,* and before I came to this understanding about God, I awoke one morning in Nashville and told my wife, *"The Lord spoke to me in the night and said we would be speaking things revolutionary."* We rejoiced but had no idea what those things were. The same week that I received the editor's email, a religious leader and Bible teacher who is a friend of mine from Tulsa had used this word *"revolutionary"* also while on the phone with me, in agreement with the truth that I have brought forward. I did not know at this time that it would be *"revolutionary"* war! Through a series of emails and phone conversations with the editor of the magazine, a 2000 word article was written, and a beautiful lay-out was done for publication in the July issue. One day the editor said to me on the phone, *"Mr. Hemphill, it may not be a stretch to say that your book is the reason this magazine is here, and the reason I am here as its editor."* But trouble came! I received an email from him letting me know that a meeting had been called by his editor-in-chief, between them and a group of very influential Christians who assist with the publication of the magazine. I was told the meeting would determine whether my article would be published, and whether or not he would keep his job. The article did not appear. He said these Christians' angry response to my book and the article was *"hysterical, and that's not too strong a word."* He said, *"If they could wave a magic wand and you and your book would both disappear they would do it immediately."* He told me one day on the phone, *"Mr. Hemphill, in another day and time, you would have been burned at the stake for writing this book."* An internationally known evangelist said to me recently, *"I believe what you are saying; I just would not want your job."* But this is God's truth, and He has and will continue to empower it. His timing is perfect! And it is time for *this* book!

We As Christians Need To Get Our Worship In Order

*"Thou shalt **worship the Lord thy God**"* [Jesus speaking] *(Luke 4:8)*.

*"But the hour cometh, and now is when the **true worshipers, shall worship the Father** in spirit and in truth: for **the Father seeketh such to worship him**"* [Jesus speaking] *(John 4:23)*.

"Worship God" (Rev. 19:10).

"Worship God" (Rev. 22:9). Please note: There is not one place in Scripture where the word *"worship"* is used in regard to Jesus after his ascension into heaven.

We Need Power In This End-Time For Life and Ministry

*"Verily, verily, I say unto you, He that believeth on me, the works that I do shall he do also; **and greater works than these shall he do**; because I go unto my Father"* [Jesus speaking] *(John 14:12).* Jesus knew who his God and Father was and so must we.

"And such as do wickedly against the covenant shall he [Anti-christ] *corrupt by flatteries: but **the people that do know their God shall be strong, and do exploits"*** [heroic and notable deeds] *(Daniel 11:32).*

We need prayers answered! God our Father has been patient with our lack of understanding in this area, even when we have prayed to Jesus. But as this truth becomes better revealed, I believe He will require us to approach Him in the manner that He has prescribed in His word.

*"Whatsoever ye shall **ask of the Father** in **my name, he may give it you"*** [Jesus speaking] *(John 15:16).*

*"I go to the Father...and in that day ye shall **ask me nothing**. Verily, Verily, I say unto you, Whatsoever ye shall **ask the Father** in my name, **he will give it you**. At that day ye shall **ask in my name"*** [Jesus speaking] *(John 16:16, 23, 26).*

*"But when thou prayest...**pray to thy Father** which is in secret; and **thy Father** which seeth in secret shall reward thee openly. For **your Father** knoweth what things ye have need of, before ye **ask him**. After this manner therefore pray ye: **Our Father** which art in heaven"* [Jesus speaking] *(Matt. 6:6, 8-9).*

> *"If any man be a **worshiper of God...him he heareth"**
> (John 9:31).*

> *"And when they heard that, they lifted up their voice **to God**
> with one accord and said, **Lord, thou art God** which hast
> made heaven and earth....For of a truth against **thy holy
> child Jesus**, whom thou hast anointed...**by the name of thy
> holy child Jesus"** (Acts 4:24, 27, 30).*

A dear minister friend of mine, who has been a pillar of the Assemblies of God, having founded and pastored one of their largest churches in the state of Texas, and who himself writes books, said to me on the phone several weeks ago, *"Brother Hemphill, I did not know that Jesus said so many things about God the Father. Your book has revolutionized my prayer life."* In fact as recorded in the four gospels Jesus spoke of the Father at least 170 times during his ministry on earth. He always pointed us to the Father. He is the perfect revealer of the Father. He is the *"express image"* of the Father. But Jesus is not the Father!

> *"And call no man your father upon the earth: for **one is your
> Father, which is in heaven.** Neither be ye called masters:
> for **one is your Master,** even **Christ"** [Jesus speaking]
> (Matt. 23:9-10).* Who is our Father? God! Who is our
> Master? Christ!

He said *"My Father is greater than I" (John 14:28),* my Father knows things I do not know *(Matt. 24:36),* and, my Father will decide who sits on my right and left hand in my own kingdom, it *"is not mine to give" (Matt. 20:23; Mark 10:40).* What is that again precious Jesus? *"To sit on my right hand and on my left hand in my kingdom **is not mine to give."***

In Revelation chapter fourteen, the apostle John saw a mighty angel flying in the midst of heaven in the last days with a loud voice, *"having the everlasting gospel to preach unto them that dwell on the earth, and to every **nation,** and **tongue,** and **people."*** And what was the angel's awesome message?

> *"**Fear God**, and **give glory to him**; for the hour of his judgement is come: and **worship him** that made heaven, and earth, and the sea, and the fountains of waters" (v. 6-7).*

That is the message of this book!

Some Notes Regarding My Writing Style

Now a few words about my writing style. I have tried to approach the writing of this book with its awesome subjects as humbly as I know how. Sometimes I wrote with tears and several times wept aloud. I understand Paul's statement in Philippians 3:18:

> *"...of whom I have told you often, and now tell you even **weeping**."*

I have used some repetition as I think it is necessary for clear understanding. (King David said 26 times in Psalm 136, *"For his mercy endureth forever")*. I have **bolded** some words and phrases for effect. This emphasis is mine throughout.

When I have spoken **boldly** it is because of the authority that comes by standing solidly on *"Thus saith the word of God!"* I believe as Christian reformer Martin Luther said, *"A simple man with the Scripture has more authority than the Pope or a council."* The Bible is not ambiguous in stating its doctrines and its important lessons are not *implied*.

> *"For if the trumpet give an uncertain sound, who shall prepare himself to the battle? So likewise ye, except ye utter by the tongue words easy to be understood, how shall it be known what is spoken?" (I Cor. 14:8-9).*

> *"But I fear, lest by any means...your minds should be corrupted from the simplicity that is in Christ"* (Paul) *(II Cor. 11:3).*

A Trumpet Of Truth

At the end of W.W. II, with the death of six million Jews in the Holocaust, many Jewish children were housed in orphanages throughout Europe. Most were too young to know whether or not they were Jewish. After the establishment of the state of Israel, May 14, 1948, these children were wanted and needed to populate the new state. Bands of Jewish elders went to these orphanages with shofars because every Jewish child hears them blown in their synagogues from the time they are a few days old. After blowing the shofars the Jews would say, *"If you have ever heard this sound, raise your hand."* And every child who raised his hand, **went home with love to Israel!**

I have been called to sound a shofar of truth to all of my Christian family. God who called me, let me know that not everyone will receive my message, but it is biblical, clear, and distinct. I cannot be distressed or distracted by those who refuse to hear it, however multitudes are hearing!

Chapter One

While Jesus Was On Earth, God The Father Was In Heaven

"Your Father which is in heaven" (Matt. 5:16, 45, 48; 6:1; 7:11; 18:14; 23:9; Mark 11:25, 26).

"My Father which is in heaven" (Matt. 7:21; 10:32, 33; 12:50; 16:17; 18:10, 19).

"A voice from heaven saying..." (Matt. 3:17; Mark 1:11; Luke 3:22; John 12:28).

"He [Jesus] *looked up to heaven and blessed..."* the bread and fish *(Mark 6:41; Luke 9:16).*

"I leave the world and go to the Father" (John 16:28).

Shortly after my first book was published I called a minister friend of mine of many years to discuss it with him. He is an internationally known evangelist, singer, songwriter, and a life-long trinitarian, and I knew my view would run contrary to his understanding of the person of God. He was kind and the discussion went well, but about twenty minutes into the conversation he made a statement that was profound. He said *"Joel, this must relate to what God told me two weeks ago. God spoke to me and said, 'It's what I said that became flesh'."* He added, *"And I've been dealing with that for the past two weeks."* In one of our subsequent visits he told me how this had occurred. He was reading the Bible one day in John the first chapter:

"In the beginning was the Word, and the Word was with God, and the Word was God. The same was in the beginning with God. All things were made by him; and

39

without him was not any thing made that was made. In him was life; and the life was the light of men" (v. 1-4).

*"And the Word was made flesh, and dwelt among us, (and we beheld **his glory**, the glory as of the only begotten of the Father,) full of grace and truth" (v. 14)*

These verses are at the heart of the debate as to Jesus' deity, and the key to a true biblical understanding as to who he is.

Trinitarian scholar Dr. Colin Brown, in his work, *Trinity and Incarnation: In Search of Contemporary Orthodoxy,* truthfully says:

> *"It is a common but patent **misreading** of the opening of John's Gospel to read it as if it said: 'In the beginning was the **Son** and the **Son** was with God and the **Son** was God.' What has happened here is the substitution of Son for Word, and thereby the Son is made a member of the Godhead which existed from the beginning."* [1]

The noted **trinitarian** scholar Professor James Dunn correctly states in his exhaustive study, *Christology In The Making:*

> *"There is no clear indication anywhere in Paul that he ever identified Christ (pre-existent or otherwise) with the Logos (Word) of God" (p. 39). "Similarly in Acts there is no sign of any christology of pre-existence" (p. 51). "In Matthew and Luke, Jesus' divine sonship is traced back specifically to his birth or conception...he was **Son of God** because his conception was **an act of creative power by the Holy Spirit**" (p. 61). "In the earliest period of Christianity 'Son of God' was not an obvious vehicle of a christology of incarnation or pre-existence. **Certainly such a christology cannot be traced back to Jesus himself** with any degree of conviction,...it is less likely that we can find such a christology in Paul or Mark or Luke or Matthew" (p. 64).*

"There is no indication that Jesus thought or spoke of himself as having pre-existed with God prior to his birth or appearance on earth. We cannot claim that Jesus believed himself to be the incarnate Son of God" (p. 254). Only in the Fourth Gospel can we speak of a doctrine of the incarnation" (p. 259). [2]

Similarly, **trinitarian** Millard J. Erickson, research professor of theology at Southwestern [Southern] Baptist Theological Seminary, in his book, *God In Three Persons,* states:

"John is the only evangelist who identifies Jesus as divine" (p. 193). He says again on page 210, *"He is, for example, the only Gospel writer to clearly identify the Son as divine."* [3]

My contention is, that if Jesus, Paul, Matthew, Mark, Luke, and Peter knew nothing of a pre-existence and incarnation, **it did not happen!** John has been misunderstood! And of course, to take the word of only **one** witness would break the biblical rule for establishing truth, as set down by Moses in the Torah and endorsed by Jesus in Matthew 18:16.

*"At the mouth of **two witnesses**, or at the mouth of **three witnesses**, shall the matter be established" (Deut. 19:15).*

As Professor Dunn says also: (Thank God for men who have the courage to say it!)

*"There is of course always the possibility that '**popular pagan superstition**' became **popular Christian superstition**, by a gradual assimilation and spread of belief" (p. 251).*

This is the basic understanding that is set forth in my first book, and without prior knowledge of that fact my minister friend had heard God say, *"It's what I said that became flesh."* Though my writing is totally based on Holy Scripture and not on voices and visions, this was strong confirmation. This man is now a firm supporter of my book and this biblical understanding.

How did John come to be so misunderstood? For the answer to that important question we shall look briefly at history and then to the Bible.

Much of the confusion regarding the word *"Word"* *(*Greek - *logos)* in the first fourteen verses of the Gospel of John can be laid at the feet of an early first-century writer, mystic, philosopher by the name of Philo. He was a Hellenistic Jew from the city of Alexandria, Egypt. A Hellenist was a non-Greek, especially a Jew, who as an imitator of the Greeks, adopted their ideals, language, customs, etc. As such, Philo the Jew was strongly influenced by the teachings of the Greeks-Socrates, Plato, and Aristotle-while at the same time, trying to hold on to his Jewish faith and its teachings of monotheism *(one God)*. He was of the sect of the **Stoics**, a group that had its roots in Greek philosophy and whose religious sentiments were very near to those of the Pharisees. They opposed the apostle Paul in Acts chapter seventeen, and called him a *"babbler"* because *"he preached unto them Jesus and the resurrection"* *(v. 18)*. Because of Philo's conflicting beliefs between Judaism and Hellenism, his writings betray thinking that is often contradictory.

Philo was born about 20 B.C. and lived until about 50 A.D., so he was already a very famous Jewish philosopher before the beginning of the ministries of Jesus, or John, Peter, Paul and the other N.T. writers. At the beginning of the first century, the Jewish people had not heard from God through a prophet for some 400 years, and in their backsliding were wide open to be corrupted by strange doctrines, including Greek and Roman concepts that took them away from the truth of God as set down in their Torah. Jesus and his followers dealt with this problem continually, as recorded throughout the New Testament.

> *"Teaching for doctrines the commandments of men. For laying aside the commandment of God, ye hold the tradition of men...Full well ye reject the commandment of God, that ye many keep your own tradition...Making the word of God of none effect through your tradition"* [Jesus speaking] *(Mark. 7:7-9, 13)*.

> *"Hath not God made foolish the wisdom of this world? For the Jews require a sign, and **the Greeks seek after wisdom**: But we preach Christ crucified, unto the Jews a stumbling block, and unto the Greeks foolishness"* [Paul speaking] *(I Cor. 1:20-23).*

> *"Beware lest any man spoil you through **philosophy** and vain deceit, after the tradition of men, after the rudiments of the world, and not after Christ" (Col. 2:8).*

It is beyond question that much of pre-Christian Jewish thought had been affected by the writings of Philo, including his wrong concepts regarding the Word. He was the chief proponent of the doctrine of the *"divine Logos."* This was a concept that he had borrowed from Greek philosophy and never in any way related it to Jesus of Nazareth, as he wrote well before the beginning of Jesus' ministry. Unlike his contemporary and fellow Jew, the historian Josephus, Philo never once mentioned Jesus or Christianity in his volume of work. He arrived at his *"divine Logos"* doctrine by mixing Judaism with the ideas of **Plato**, written some 400 years before.

For Philo the term *"logos"* seems to have had an inordinate appeal, as he used it more than 1400 times in his extensive writings. Philo often speaks of the Logos as if it were a being distinct from God, who acts as a mediator between God and the world. He writes, *"To his Word, his chief messenger the Father of all has given the special prerogative, to stand on the border and separate the creature from the Creator."* And, *"of necessity was the Logos appointed as judge and mediator, who is called 'angel'."* And he speaks of *"God's firstborn, the Word, who holds the eldership among the angels, their ruler as it were."* But Philo really betrays the extent to which he has departed from his Jewish roots, and a proper understanding of the God of the Old Testament, when he calls the Word *"the **second God**, who is his Logos."* Again, **he is not speaking of Jesus** as there is no indication that he ever heard of Jesus!

Trinitarian Millard Erickson acknowledges the strong influence of Philo on **post** New Testament religious thinking. Regarding the *"Apologists,"* the church fathers of the late period before Nicea *(Justin Martyr, Tatian, Theophilus of Antioch, etc.)* and their attempt to offer a rational explanation of the relationship of Christ, *"the preexistent Son,"* to God the Father, he writes:

> *"In this explanation, they* **drew heavily** *on the concept of the* **divine Logos** *or* **Word***. This concept was at least formally found in John's Gospel.* **It had much wider currency, however.** *It was found in later Judaism and in Stoicism, and* **through the influence of Philo it had become a fashionable cliche'***. The apologists' unique contribution was in drawing out the* **further implication** *of the concept"* *(p. 43)*. Erickson says also: *"Ignatius' references to the Son deriving his sonship* **from the conception in Mary's womb** *should be thought of as simply a* **common usage of theology** *prior to Origen"* *(p. 40)*. [4] Please note: This Southern Baptist theologian says the idea of *"the Son deriving his* **sonship** *from* **the conception in Mary's womb**" was *"a common usage of theology* **prior to Origen**."* After Origen *(A.D. 185-254)* the non-biblical doctrine of Jesus' "eternal sonship" began to be taught. Notice carefully also: *"the concept of the* **divine Logos***...through the influence of* **Philo** *had become a* **fashionable** *cliche,"* before Jesus. Wow! Listen to Erickson, *"the concept of the* **divine Logos***... through the influence of* **Philo** *[before Christ] had become a* **fashionable cliche'**."*

Regarding the teachings of Philo, Professor James Dunn says, *"Philo's thought, not least his concept of the Logos, is what can fairly be described as a unique synthesis* [combining] *of Platonic* [Plato] *and Stoic world-view with Jewish monotheism. The Logos seems to be envisaged as* **a wholly independent being** *who can act as intermediary between God and man."* He refers to Philo as a Jewish writer whose context of thought *"is strange* *and difficult"* and some of his allegories as *"strained and at times confusing or even contradictory."* [5]

Remember, Philo had used the word *"logos"* (word) over 1400 times in his writings before the apostle John had used it **once** in the first chapter of his Gospel. (We should note that after chapter one, verse fourteen, John never used "Word" again in his Gospel). Philo's tainted doctrine, corrupted by Greek philosophy, had already permeated Jewish thinking, and as Jesus warned, the Pharisees' false doctrine was leaven; and a little leaven leavens the whole lump. It is easy to see how such language from the influential Philo as, ***"the mediating Logos,"*** or ***"the second God, who is his Logos"*** developed subsequently into the myth of Jesus as a **pre-existent divine being** distinct from God.

Thus, **Philo of Alexandria** helped to birth the school of thought that later produced **Athanasius of Alexandria** *(295-373 A.D.),* the chief architect and proponent of the error that prevailed at Nicea; the idea that God existed in the form of two persons, *"That the Son is God, just as the Father is God."*

The *Encyclopedia Americana* says of Athanasius:

> ***"His teaching on the Logos furnished the basic ideas for the development of later Christological doctrine."*** [6]

The *Harper Collins Encyclopedia of Catholicism* says:

> *"**Trinitarian** doctrine as such emerged in the **fourth-century**, due largely to the efforts of Athanasius and the Cappadocians."* [7]

Trinitarian Professor Shirley C. Guthrie , Jr. writes in his best selling book *Christian Doctrine:*

> ***"The Bible does not teach the doctrine of the Trinity.*** *Neither the word 'trinity' itself nor such language as 'one-in-three,' 'three-in-one,' 'one essence' (or "substance"), and three 'persons' is biblical language. The language of the*

45

doctrine is the language of the ancient church **taken from
classical Greek philosophy**" (p. 76-77). "**The doctrine of
the Trinity is not found in the Bible**" (p. 80). [8] Again, "...
is the language of the ancient church [not the N.T. church]
taken from classical Greek philosophy."

Listen to these strong words from Thomas Jefferson, third President of the
United States and author of the Declaration of Independence:

"*The Trinitarian idea triumphed in the church's creeds, not
by the force of reason but by* **the words of Athanasius**, *and
grew in the blood of thousands and thousands of martyrs.*" [9]

The strong influence that **Greek philosophy** had on the conclusions of Nicea
is seen in the historical records of that gathering. The Emperor Constantine
who had called the Council of 300 bishops, and who presided over it from
an exalted place on a wrought gold chair, gave an oration to this gathering
in which he spoke with commendation of the Greek philosopher **Plato** *(427-
347 B.C.)* whose teachings Philo followed, as having taught the doctrine
of "*a second God, derived from the Supreme God, and subservient to his
will.*"[10] Since when is Plato someone from whom Christians should derive
their doctrine? And there is more! St. Augustine *(354-430 A.D.)*, who did as
much as any of the so-called "*early Church fathers*" to advance the doctrine
of the Trinity, says in his work *Confessions* that he once considered Christ a
most excellent man and had no suspicion of the word of God being incarnate
in him, or how "*the Catholic faith differed from the error of Photinus*" (a
fourth-century Unitarian), **till he read the books of Plato**; and that he was
later confirmed in his opinion by reading the Scriptures. [11]

Erickson states, "*It is customary to assume that the major philosophical
influence on the Greek* [Church] *fathers was Plato and the Stoics.*" [12]

It is a fact of history that most of these early Greek church fathers did not
read or speak Hebrew, the language in which the Old Testament is written.
Therefore there was a serious disconnect between their understanding and

the clear teaching of the Old Testament regarding the Most High God being **one person**.

Is That What John Meant, "A Second God?"

> *"In the beginning was the Word and the Word was with God, and the Word was God. The same was in the beginning with God" (John 1:1-2).*

First, Lets Look At The Word *"Beginning"*

One thing I have learned in my study of Scripture is, when you see the word *"beginning"* or the word *"end"* you have to ask the question, "Beginning of what?," or the "End of what?" For example, when Jesus said to his disciples, *"Ye have been with me from the beginning,"* he meant the beginning of his ministry, and not the beginning of time. When John says *"the devil sinneth from the beginning" (I John 3:8),* he meant from the **beginning of sin** and not from the devil's own beginning. (At the devil's own beginning he was sinless, *"the anointed cherub...perfect in thy ways from the day that thou was created, till iniquity was found in thee" Ezek. 28:14-15).* The apostle John uses the word *"beginning"* twenty-one times in his writings (10 times in the Gospel of John and 11 times in First and Second John), which is more than it is used by any other New Testament writer. **Not one time** when John uses the word *"beginning"* does he mean eternity past! So when he uses the word beginning in John 1:1, he is not speaking of the beginning of God: **God has no beginning!** He is not speaking of the beginning of eternity: **eternity has no beginning!** What "beginning"? Jesus answers this question himself in Revelation 3:14: *"These things saith the Amen, the faithful and true witness, the beginning of the creation of God."* The Greek word for **beginning** is the same in John 1:1 and Revelation 3:14. It is the Greek word *"arche"* and it means *"a commencement - to commence in order of time."* We need to stop reading John 1:1 as if it says, *"In eternity past was the Word..."* That is a mistaken idea! Jesus is the *"**beginning** of the creation of God,"* **first in order of time!** This agrees with what Paul said in Colossians 1:15: Jesus *"is the **image** of the invisible God, the **firstborn** of every creature,"* and *"the **image** of him (God) that **created him**" (3:10).* Neither John nor Paul nor any other New Testament writer thought or wrote of Jesus as a pre-existent, eternal being, **and certainly not as a "second person of God."**

Now What About The Word *"Word"* That John Used

"In the beginning was the Word, and the Word was with God..." (John 1:1). Remember, this was **not a second God** that was *"with God,"* so what was it?

John uses the Greek word *"logos."* (The Old Testament was written in Hebrew and the New Testament was given to us in **Greek**, which because of the weakness of men, adds to the possibility of mis-understanding. Some **think** they see the doctrine of the Trinity in the New Testament, who would not dare proclaim it from the Old Testament). The Greek word "logos" *(Strong's Concordance #3056)* means *"something said including the thought-motive-intent."* It is an *"utterance."* In the beginning of creation **something was said!** (Remember God's words to my friend, *"It's what I said...").* This agrees with what John wrote also in his epistle of I John:

> *"That which was from the beginning, **which we have heard**...of the **Word** of life; For the life was manifested, and we have seen it, and bear witness, and show you **that eternal life, which was with the Father**, and was **manifested** unto us" (I John 1:1-2).* Do you see the similarity between this and John chapter one?

So John says it was *"eternal life"* that was with the Father at the **beginning of creation** and later manifested for us **through his Son**. Notice I John 5:11:

> *"And this is the record, that God hath given to us **eternal life**, and this life is **in his Son.**"*

> *"The book of life of the Lamb **slain from the foundation of the world" (Rev. 13:8).** That is, in the thought, motive, intent, and utterance of Almighty God. **So in the same reality in which Jesus existed before his birth, he was "slain" before his birth,** in the immutable **plan, purpose** and **foreknowledge** of God.

This is why John wrote the Golden Text of the Bible, John 3:16:

> *"For **God so loved** the world, that **he gave** his only begotten*
> *Son, that whosoever believeth in him should not perish, **but***
> ***have everlasting life."***

It was also John who recorded Jesus' words from his great prayer to the Father in John 17:1-3:

> *"Father...this is **life eternal**, that they might know thee **the***
> ***only true God**, and Jesus Christ whom thou hast sent."*

Jesus and John knew what they wanted us to know: that there is only **one true God**, and no "second God," not even the Messiah *(the anointed one)* himself!

A Biblical Fact

Please see and understand this biblical fact. At the beginning of creation, before He ever created the first Adam whom He knew would fall through sin and take all of creation down with him, God spoke His Son, *"the last Adam...the second man" (I Cor. 15:45-47)*, to redeem all of creation on an old rugged cross and *"condemn sin in the flesh" (Rom. 8:3)*. **This is Jesus' part in creation.** He is redeemer of all of creation, **spoken before time, to come in time.** God not only spoke Jesus' birth, but He spoke his crucifixion, *"before the foundation of the world,"* and our salvation through him *"in the book of life from the foundation of the world." (Rev. 17:8).* (Therefore Jesus could truly say in John 8:58, *"Before Abraham was, I am,"* since he was **spoken and real in the mind and purpose of God** from the "beginning").

> *"For since **by man** came death, **by man** came also the*
> *resurrection of the dead. For as in **Adam** all die, even so*
> *in **Christ** shall all be made alive. But every **man** in his own*
> *order: **Christ** the **firstfruits**; afterward they that are Christ's*
> *at his coming" (I Cor. 15:21-23).* All foreordained by God
> the Creator **before time,** to be manifested **in time.**

*"But now **once** in the end of the world hath he* [Jesus] *appeared to put away sin by the sacrifice of himself" (Heb. 9:26).*

*"But when the **fullness of time was come,** God sent forth his Son, **made** of a woman, **made** under the law" (Gal. 4:4).*

The Council of Nicea declared that Jesus is *"Begotten, **not made**, of one substance with the Father,"* but many Scriptures including the verse above, teach that he was *"made"* by God. We can add this to the list of false concepts to which that group subjected succeeding generations of Christians. (Rabid *anti-Semitism* was another).

How Were The Worlds Created?

*"Through faith we understand that the worlds were framed by the **word of God**,* [something said], *so that things which are seen were not made of things which do appear" (Heb. 11:3).*

*"By the **word of God** [something said], the heavens were of old, and the earth standing out of the water and in the water" (II Peter 3:5).*

*"By the **word of the Lord** [something said] were the heavens made; and all the host of them by **the breath of his mouth**... For **he spoke**, and it was done, **he commanded**, and it stood fast" (Ps. 33:6, 9).* Notice: *"word," "breath of his mouth," "he spoke."*

*"In the **beginning** God created the heavens and the earth" (Genesis 1:1).*

*"And **God said**, Let there be light" (v. 3).*

*"And **God said**, Let there be a firmament"* (v. 6).

*"And **God said**, Let the waters under the heaven be gathered together"* (v. 9).

*"And **God said**, Let the earth bring forth grass"* (v. 11).

*"And **God said**, Let there be lights in the firmament of the heaven"* (v. 14)

*"And **God said**, Let the waters bring forth abundantly the moving creature"* (v. 20).

*"And **God said**, Let the earth bring forth the living creature"* (v. 24).

Properly Understanding John

Now, with this in mind, we should be able to read John 1:1-2 with proper understanding.

"In the beginning was the logos ["something said, including the thought"], *and the **something said** was with God, and the **something said** was God"* [It was *"the breath of His mouth"*] *(Ps. 33:6).*

Now lets look at John 1:3, which says in the King James Version of the Bible, first published in 1611 A.D.:

*"All things were made by **him**; and without **him** was not any thing made that was made."*

Is the word *"him"* in this verse translated properly? First of all it does not fit with a true understanding of the two preceding verses. ("Something said" is not a "him"). Second, it is important to note that of nine prominent English translations that preceded the King James Version, not one used the word *"him."* **Eight** of the nine rendered John 1:3, *"By **it** all things were* made. *Without **it** nothing was made"* (Tyndale Bible, 1535; Matthew, 1535; Tavener, 1539; The Great (Cranmer's) Bible, 1539; Whittingham, 1557; Genera, 1560; Bishop's Bible, 1568; Tomson NT, 1607). **One**, the famous Coverdale Bible of 1550 has *"the same"* rather than "it." **None of these nine say "*him.*"** Why did the King James translators render *"it"* as *"him,"* as if it were a person? (They also gave *"word"* a capital "W" as if it were a person, which many other translators did not do). They were trinitarians and their mistaken doctrine overpowered their sense of scholarship. They had been influenced by Plato, Philo, the Nicean Council, and 1300 years of false Roman Catholic tradition. Their error has helped to lead millions of sincere Christians astray in their understanding of who the one true God is!

What John Meant In John 1:14 (Brethren we must get this right!)
"And the logos [something said] *was made flesh* [Jesus]*, and dwelt among us, (and we beheld **his glory**, the glory as of the only begotten of the Father,) full of grace and truth."* **What God Said Became Flesh.**

With the foregoing in mind, I implore my Christian family to **stop** reading John 1:1 as if it says:
> "In eternity past was the Son, and the Son was with God, and the Son was God."

That is not what it says!

Listen to **trinitarian** scholar Douglas McCready from his work, *He Came Down From Heaven:*
> *"While some have used the title* ['Son of God'] *to denote Jesus' deity, neither the Judaism nor the paganism of Jesus' day understood the title in this way.* **Neither did the early church.**" [13]

Listen to the respected **trinitarian** Evangelical Biblical scholar Professor Charles C. Ryrie writing in his work, *Basic Theology:*
> *"It is fair to say that **the Bible does not clearly teach the***

doctrine of the Trinity. *In fact,* **there is not even one proof text,** *if by proof text we mean a verse or passage that 'clearly' states that there is one God who exists in three persons" (p. 89). "The above illustrations prove the fallacy of concluding that if something is not proof texted in the Bible we cannot clearly teach the results...**If that were so, I could never teach the doctrine of the Trinity or the deity of Christ or the deity of the Holy Spirit.***" [14]

Southern Baptist theologian Millard Erickson writes:

"Another difficulty stems from the categories used by **those who worked out** *the doctrine of the Trinity that the church* **adopted.** *They used* **Greek categories** *such as substance, essence, and person, which had corresponding* **Latin concepts** *when translated into the forms of thinking that characterized the Eastern church. Over the years, questions have been raised regarding those concepts. One contention is that the Trinity is simply a product of those* **ancient Greek** *categories. It is not present in biblical thought, but arose when biblical thought was pressed into this foreign mold. Thus, the doctrine of the Trinity goes beyond and even distorts what the Bible says about God. It is a* **Greek philosophical,** *not a* **Hebraic biblical,** *concept."* [15]

Now back to the statement that is the title of this Chapter: *"When Jesus was on Earth, God the Father was in Heaven."*

When the angel announced to the shepherds near Bethlehem the arrival of the baby Jesus, the supernaturally conceived, virgin-born, sinless Son of God; the savior, redeemer, Messiah and (destined) ruler of the world, the Bible says:

"And suddenly there was with the angel a multitude of the heavenly host **praising God,** *and saying,* **Glory to God in the highest,** *and on earth peace, good will toward men"* (Luke 2:13-14).

Two geographical locations are spoken of here, *"in the highest"* and *"on earth."* So while the precious baby was in the manger *"on earth,"* God was *"in the highest"* (heaven). Later, during the ministry of Jesus *"on earth,"* more proof is found regarding the truth of our beginning statement. Jesus used the phrase *"your Father **which is in heaven"*** nine times as recorded by the Gospel writers. He used the phrase *"My Father **which is in heaven"*** seven times as recorded in the Gospels. On four occasions there was *"a voice **from heaven** saying..."* Twice it is recorded that, *"He looked **up to heaven** and blessed"* the food. In the Sermon on the Mount Jesus mentions the Father seventeen times. In fact the entire sermon is made up of teachings regarding *"**your Father which is in heaven"** (Matt. chapters 5-7).* At the end of his ministry on earth Jesus told his disciples, *"**I leave the world,** and go to the Father."*

Proof In The Book Of Revelation

None of these verses make any sense if Jesus was Almighty God on earth! For final scriptural proof, we should turn to the book of Revelation. In chapter nineteen Jesus is pictured as coming to Earth on a white horse, with his saints, to rule over it from Jerusalem for 1000 years with a *"rod of iron."* The Anti-christ is **cast into Hell** and **Satan is bound and put in prison**, *"the bottomless pit"* for 1000 years. Regarding the saints John says:

> *"They shall be priests of God and of Christ, and shall reign with him a thousand years. And when the thousand years are expired, Satan shall be loosed out of his prison, and shall go out to deceive the nations which are in the four quarters of the earth... . And they went up on the breadth of the earth, and compassed the **camp of the saints** about, and the **beloved city"** (Rev. 20:6-9).*

Please see this picture. Jesus and his saints are reigning over Planet Earth from Jerusalem, and Satan and his followers surround the city. And it is God the Father to the rescue!

> *"**And fire came down from God out of heaven,** and devoured them" (v. 9).*

While Jesus and the saints reign on earth, God still sits on His throne in heaven. Please consider Psalm chapter two, one of the greatest Old Testament prophecies concerning Jesus, called a Messianic Psalm:

> *"Why do the heathen rage, and the people imagine a vain thing? The kings of the earth set themselves ...against* **the Lord** [God], *and against* **his anointed** [Messiah - Christ "the anointed one"], *saying, Let us break their bands asunder, and cast away their cords from us.* **He that sitteth in the heavens** *shall laugh: the Lord shall have them in derision. Then shall he* [God] *speak unto them...yet have I set my King* [Jesus] **upon my holy hill of Zion**. *The Lord hath said unto me,* **Thou art my Son**; *this day have I begotten thee"* (Ps. 2:1-7) (See also Ps. 110:1).

But here is great news. God Himself is coming to Earth!

Look With Me At Revelation Chapter One

> *"Grace be unto you, and peace, from* **him** *which* **is**, *and which* **was**, *and which* **is to come**; *and from the seven spirits which are before* **his throne**" (Rev. 1:4).

> *"And from Jesus Christ, who is the faithful witness..."* (Rev. 1:5).

Who is this *"**him**"* in **verse four**, *"which* **is**, *and which* **was**, *and which* **is to come**?* It is God the Father. It cannot be Jesus, he is in **verse five**, *"**and from Jesus Christ**.*" Please study this closely!

Now look at Revelation chapter four. In verse four, *"**one** sat on the throne."* In verse eight the beasts worship the *one* on the throne, saying:

> *"Holy, holy, holy,* **Lord God Almighty**, *which* **was**, *and is, and* **is to come**" (Rev. 4:8). Note: Jesus is not in chapter four. He appears as the *"Lamb"* in chapter five.

Now please look at chapter eleven.

> *"We give the thee thanks, **O Lord God Almighty**, which **art***
> [are], *and **wast** [was], and **art to come**" (Rev. 11:17).*

So we see that this phrase occurs repeatedly in the book of Revelation and it always refers to God the Father, Lord God Almighty. Now we are better able to understand Revelation 1:8:

> *"I am Alpha and Omega, the beginning and the ending,*
> *saith the Lord, which **is**, and which **was**, and which **is to***
> ***come**, the **Almighty**."*

Please do not be fooled by *red letter* edition Bibles which have the above verse in **red**, as if Jesus Christ is speaking. Some red letter Bibles have it in **black**, because the translators understand that it is God, the *"Almighty,"* speaking. If you still have doubts, give more study to verses four and five of chapter one. Now let's look at Revelation chapter twenty-one.

> *"And I John saw the holy city, new Jerusalem, coming down*
> *from **God** out of heaven... . And I heard a great voice out*
> *of heaven saying, Behold, the tabernacle* [dwelling] *of **God***
> *is with men, and **he** will dwell with them...and **God himself***
> *shall be with them, and be their **God**. And **God** shall wipe*
> *away all tears from their eyes" (Rev. 21:2-4).*

> *"Blessed are the pure in heart: for **they shall see God**"*
> [Jesus speaking, and they had already been blessed to
> see him] *(Matt. 5:8).*

> *"And they shall see **his** [God's] **face**" (Rev. 22:4).*

> *"...**the face of my Father which is in heaven**"* [Jesus
> speaking] *(Matt. 18:10).*

> *"For I know that my redeemer* [God our ultimate Redeemer
> - see *Ps. 78:35; Isa. 41:14; 63:16*] *liveth, and that he shall*

*stand **at the latter day** upon the earth: And though after my skin worms destroy this body, yet in my flesh* [glorified body] ***shall I see God****: Whom I shall see for myself, and mine eyes shall behold...* " [Job speaking] *(Job 19:25-27).*

Glory to God in the highest!

The following terms used frequently in teaching the doctrines of the "Oneness" and "Trinity" are not biblical terminology.

Trinity	Triune	Triad
Blessed Trinity	Holy Trinity	God the Son
2nd person of the Trinity	3rd person of the Trinity	1st person of the Trinity
God the Holy Spirit	The eternal Son of God	Eternally begotten
God incarnate	God in flesh	Incarnation
God-man	Dual nature	Double nature
Two natures	Jehovah Jesus	Very God and very man
Fully God and fully man	Eternally proceeding	The diety of Christ

There is not one verse of Scripture that says that God is "three" of anything! Not:

Three co-equal, co-eternal persons	Three persons of one essence
One God in three persons	Three essences of one person
Three persons of God	God in three persons
Eternal three	Three in one God
Three Gods	Three Spirits
Three divinities	Three persons
Three modes	Three beings
Three substances	Three agents
Three attributes	Three offices
Three entities	Three infinite minds

Chapter Two

It Is Important To Know God Our Father, As Well As Jesus

*"And these things will they do unto you, because they have not **known the Father**, nor me." (John 16:3).*

*"Father...this is **life eternal**, that they might **know thee** the only true **God**, and Jesus Christ, whom thou hast sent" (John 17:1, 3).*

*"No man knoweth the Son, but the Father; neither knoweth any man the **Father**, save the Son, and he to whomsoever the Son will **reveal him**" (Matt. 11:27).*

*O*n that day in March of 1986 when the God of Abraham, Isaac, and Jacob told me to study the Scripture, as He was going to reveal Himself to me in His word, I knew I had missed something very important in my Bible study. I have been an avid Bible reader since I was a small boy, and have been since the age of nineteen, and I remain a minister of Jesus Christ. However, I had done what most of Christianity has done for centuries. I had clearly seen Jesus in Scripture, but I had overlooked God our Father. Jesus is the *"express image"* of the Father *(Heb. 1:3)* but he is not our heavenly Father. An image is *"a representative likeness"* but **it is not the original**. Jesus is the perfect revealer of God, but he is not God. Jesus told Pilate *"for this cause I came into the world, that I should bear witness unto the truth" (John 18:37).* I thought Jesus was God for over 50 years, but when I realized that he, the witness to the truth never said he is God, **I quit saying it!** Paul said *"God"* some 513 times in his New Testament writings and **not one time** can it be proven that he was referring to Jesus.

*"Blessed be the **God and Father** of our **Lord Jesus Christ"**
(Eph. 1:3).* Paul is clearly speaking of two entities here, and he gives no hint that they are the same.

Peter mentions *"God"* forty-six times in his two epistles, and **not once** was he referring to Jesus.

*"Blessed be the **God and Father** of our Lord Jesus Christ"
(I Peter 1:3).* Peter and Paul believed alike.

The apostle James mentions *"God"* seventeen times in his small but powerful epistle and **not one time** was he speaking of Jesus; it was always God the Father.

Since he is the perfect revealer of God *(John 6:46)*, Jesus desires that men should know God **through** himself, not **lose** God **in** himself. Jesus is the only way to the Father, but **he is not the Father!**

*"Jesus knew that his hour was come that he should depart
out of this world **unto the Father"** (John 13:1).*

Jesus is not God, but he is the door by which we get to God. Some have stopped at the door, **but the object is to get to God!**

*"No man cometh **unto the Father**, but by me" (John 14:6).*

*"Wherefore he is able also to save them to the uttermost
that **come unto God** by him" (Heb. 7:25).*

*"For Christ also hath once suffered for sins...that he might
bring us to God" (I Peter 3:18).*

My belief was what is known as **"Oneness"** or "Jesus Only," which means that I saw Jesus to the exclusion of the Father. I believed that Jesus was a **human incarnation** of God the Father. Normally **Trinitarians** believe that Jesus is a human incarnation of God the Son, a pre-existent being. But since I wrote my first book, I have found many people who call themselves

Trinitarians, when actually in belief they are Oneness. Oneness are usually Pentecostal, but I have found Oneness Baptists, Oneness Methodists, Oneness Assemblies of God, etc. People who emailed me and said, *"Jesus is the God who did the sending, he is the Son who came, and the Holy Spirit who was poured out."* Others emailed or wrote and said *"Jesus is the one on heaven's throne, King of the universe,"* or *"Jesus is the only person of God you will ever see."* My friend, call that what you will, but that is classic "Oneness" doctrine, and it is error!

One Southern Baptist pastor of some thirty-five years, for whom we have ministered in two Southern Baptist churches, told me after reading my book, *"Brother Hemphill, I had never in my life looked beyond Jesus and seen God the Father."*

One Baptist minister friend of mine who has a large ministry, and teaches a Bible College by correspondence of over 2300 enrollment, said to me on the phone, *"I did not know it but I was Oneness! One day I was listening to the Bible on C.D. and heard I Corinthians chapter fifteen, where Jesus lays the Kingdom at God the Father's feet, after it is completed, and I saw the truth."* He said *"I went before my Bible study group and read Revelation chapter four, where Almighty God sits on the throne, and I asked, 'Who is that?' They answered, 'God the Father.' Then I read chapter five where the Lamb stands before God who is seated on His throne, and I asked, 'Who is that?' And they answered, 'Jesus'."* He told me, *"We have about gotten all of that doctrine out of here!"* To God be the glory!

You might ask, *"Why bring up this issue? How important is it?"* Well, let me ask you a question. **How important is it to know who our God is?**

It must be very important to God our Father, for he says seventy-seven times in the Old Testament:

> *"Then they shall know that **I am God** [or "the Lord," or "the Lord God"].*

I am reminded that when my *earthly father* said something *twice*, I had better listen!

In the verse at the beginning of this chapter, from John 17:1, 3, Jesus makes it a very important issue!

> *"Father...**this is life eternal**, that they might **know thee the only true God, and** Jesus Christ, whom **thou** hast sent."*

Precious Jesus, did you say it is *"life eternal"* to know God the Father *"**and** [in addition to] Jesus Christ, which thou [God] hast sent?"* In this verse we have **a sender**, God, the *"only true God,"* and **one "sent,"** Jesus Christ! And to know **both**, Jesus said, is *"life eternal."* I do not seek to make this stronger or less strong than Jesus did, but do yourself a favor and study this verse until you see exactly what God wants you to see in it. But, beware that as a noted Christian scholar of the past said, *"If we explain away the **obvious** meaning of the words, then, there is an end of all significance in language, and Scripture is wiped out as a definite testimony to anything."*

Scripture Clearly Teaches That God Can Be Known

There are awesome mysteries pertaining to the Eternal God which I do not pretend to have the answer to, neither will I speculate on them in this book. We should speak where the Bible speaks, and be silent where the Bible is silent, and not struggle with the unknowable.

> *"The **secret things** belong unto the Lord our God: but **those things which are revealed** belong unto us and to our children for ever..." (Deut. 29:29).*

Moses is saying, there are *"**secret things**,"* and there are *"**revealed things**."* The secret things belong to **God** only, but the revealed things belong to **us**. And God does reveal things in His word that were *previously unseen*.

> *"Then opened he their understanding, that they might understand the Scripture" (Luke 24:45).*

> *"When he, the Spirit of truth is come, he will **guide you
> into all truth**...and he will show you things to come" (John
> 16:13).*

Don't struggle with the *"secret things,"* but do grasp the *"revealed things"* and hold onto them tenaciously!

> *"Prove all things; **hold fast** to that which is good" (I Thess.
> 5:21).*

Since God opened my understanding and revealed **Himself** to me in His word, yes, **I see Jesus**; he is our savior, redeemer, and Messiah *(a high and exalted position)*, but **I now see God our Father** on every page of the Bible and He alone is the Supreme God. That is **true** Oneness. If you have questions and a teachable spirit, God has anointed me to help you see **Him** in His word. If you do not my hands are clean. God for sure did not inspire the writing of a Bible, made up of sixty-six books, with 31,000 verses, and fail to reveal **Himself** in it!

God Is Knowable

I hear ministers of different persuasions say *"God is unknowable,"* but that is gross error! Please don't make that mistake. It is an insult to an all-wise God to say that He made us to be His sons and daughters, but did not give us enough intelligence to **know** and understand Him.

> *"But let him that glorieth **glory in this**, that he **understandeth**
> and **knoweth** me, that **I am the Lord** which exercise loving-
> kindness, judgement, and righteousness, in the earth: for in
> these things I delight, saith the Lord" (Jer. 9:24).*

The Lord God is saying two things in the preceding verse:

1. If you boast in **anything** or rejoice over **anything**, boast and rejoice in this; that you *"understand and know me, that I am the Lord!"* That is knowing who your God is! Listen to the cry of God's heart at the beginning of the book of Isaiah:

> *"Hear, O heavens, and give ear, O earth: for the Lord hath*

*spoken, I have nourished and brought up children, and they have rebelled against me. **The ox knoweth his owner**, and the ass his master's crib: but **Israel doth not know, my people** doth not consider" (Isaiah 1:2-3).* God is saying, if the ox has sense enough to know his owner, and the ass his crib, then we should have sense enough to know Him.

If the awesome God of the Bible, God our Father, is unknowable, the great apostle Paul was certainly not aware of it:

*"Because that which may be **known** of God is manifest in them; for **God hath showed it unto them**. For the invisible things of **him** from the creation of the world **are clearly seen**, being **understood** by the things that are made, even **his** eternal power and Godhead; so that they are **without excuse" (Rom. 1:19-20).*

The confusion in Christianity as to the identity of the One Most High Creator God is inexcusable. In the Old Testament over 10,000 **singular** pronouns and verbs are used in reference to Almighty God ("I, Me, He, Him" **never** "We, They, Them"), proving to any reasonably intelligent person that the God of the Old Testament is **one** entity, being, person. In the New Testament there are over 1300 references to *"God"* when the writer is clearly not speaking of Jesus, teaching us that Jesus the Son of God is not the *"God"* of the New Testament.

2.   The second thing that God is saying in Jeremiah chapter nine is this: Rejoice and boast in what you know **about** me:

*"I am the Lord which exercise loving-kindness, judgement, and righteousness, in the earth...**in these things I delight"** (Jer. 9:24).*

Knowing God is one thing and knowing **about Him**, His character, His wonderful, loving, patient, compassionate, forgiving, Divine nature is another. Many books have been written, could and should be written about the latter, but the focus of *this* book is the former, **knowing God**! Yes, teach us **about** God; that is very important. He is the one concerning whom it can be truly said, *"To know Him is to love Him."* He is so kind, and caring, and merciful, and faithful, and loveable! In fact when Jesus was asked what is the greatest commandment, he bypassed the obvious ten and went to the Creed of Israel *(Deut. 6:4)* and claimed it as his Creed as well:

> *"Hear, O Israel; The Lord our God is* **one** *Lord* [not three]*:*
> *And thou shalt* **love the Lord thy God** *with all thy heart,*
> *and with all thy soul, and with all thy mind, and with all thy*
> *strength" (Mark 12:29-30).*

How can we as Christians obey this our greatest commandment, if we have not seen clearly in Scripture who **"the Lord our God"** is? How can we *"worship the Father in spirit and in truth"* as Jesus said He must be worshiped *("worship the* **Father**....*true worshippers shall worship the* **Father**....*the* **Father** *seeketh such to worship* **him**" - *John 4:22-23),* if we do not understand who *"our Father which is in heaven"* is? Many who know the Lord Jesus Christ, have been blinded by Greek philosophy and Catholic tradition as to the identity of God our Father.

> *"I ascend unto* **my Father,** *and* **your Father;** *and to* **my**
> **God,** *and* **your God"** [Jesus speaking] *(John 20:17).*

Since God revealed *Himself* to me in His word, my task has been to help introduce people to their God. Jesus' message to the Jews who believed in God *"the Holy* **one** *of Israel,"* but who did not see Jesus as Messiah, was:

> *"Ye believe in God, believe also in me" (John 14:1).*

As a minister of Jesus, my message to Christianity that believes in Jesus is, **"you believe in Jesus, believe also in God!"** *"And this is life eternal"* [Jesus speaking]. The Jews must learn **who Jesus is,** but Christianity must learn **who God is!**

> *"How can you believe, when you receive glory from one*
> *another and you do not seek the glory that is from the* **one and**
> **only God**...*the* **Father"** [Jesus speaking] *(John 5:44-45 NASB).*
> Take Jesus' word for it, **the Father is** *"the one and only God!"*

The following statements of fact are not meant to offend or to call into question anyone's salvation; that is not my intent. I am by nature **inclusive** and **not exclusive**. I have spent my entire adult life trying to encourage, build up and gather up the body of Christ, but **the truth** is by nature exclusive. There is only one truth regarding who God is!

If you believe that God is a tyrant then you do not **know God**. If you believe that God is inconsistent then you do not **know God**. If you believe that God is an impersonal God- force, an invisible mist that fills the universe and is **in** all things (flowers, grass, trees, etc.), having no form, essence, or substance, then you do not **know God**. That is pantheism and we need to give it back to the Hindus!

If you believe that God was once a baby soiling His diaper, who had to be taught how to walk; or that God moved into the womb of a virgin, similar to you and me becoming a *"slug or a crab,"* then you do not **know God**.

> *"God is not a man....neither the son of man..."* *(Numbers 23:19).*

> *"God is not a man....."* *(I Samuel 15:29).*

> *"For I am God, and not man; the Holy **One** in the midst of thee"* *(Hosea 11:9).*

If you believe that God ever died, then you don't **know God**. One million atomic bombs could not kill God, much less three nails and a sword. He is *"eternal, immortal* [deathless], *invisible, the only wise God"* *(I Tim. 1:17).* *"No man hath seen God at any time,"* but in our glorified bodies we shall behold Him.

> *"Blessed are the pure in heart: for they shall see God"* *(Matt. 5:8).*

> *"And they shall see his face"* *(Rev. 22:4).*

If you believe that God is a committee of three persons, then you don't **know God**. (Please do not be offended. You may know Jesus, but he is not the Eternal God). The universe is a product of **one awesome mind**, that of God our Creator, and any belief other than that is polytheism *(multiple Gods)!*

Nothing in the world that you could know **about** God could come close to being as important as truly **knowing Him**. Many things **about** God fall into place when you **know** Him; His worship, His love, and His fear.

> *"And they shall **know** that **I** am the **Lord their God**, that brought them forth out of the land of Egypt" (Ex. 29:46).*

> *"Solomon, my son, **know** thou the **God** of thy father"* [David speaking] *(I Chron. 28:9).*

> *"Be still, and **know** that I am **God**" (Ps. 46:10).*

> *"All flesh shall **know** that I the **Lord** am thy Savior and Redeemer, the mighty **One** of Jacob" (Isa. 49:26).*

> *"The heathen shall **know** that I am the Lord, the Holy **One** in Israel. Behold, it is come, and it is done, saith the **Lord God**" (Ezek. 39:7-8).*

> *"So the house of Israel shall **know** that **I** am the **Lord their God**" (v. 22).*

> *"Then shall they **know** that **I** am the Lord their God...saith the **Lord God**" (vs. 28-29).*

Moses Met God

Moses knew about God as an Israelite, but through a divine encounter he came to **truly know God**, and spoke to God *"face to face, as a man speaketh unto his friend" (Ex. 33:11).*

> *"And there arose not a prophet since in Israel like unto Moses, **whom the Lord knew face to face**" (Deut. 34:10).*

Born in Egypt at a time when all of the male Hebrew babies were being killed, Moses was rescued by Pharaoh's daughter and brought up in the palace as her son. However, Moses' real mother was hired to help raise him, and so she taught him *about* the God of Israel. This is shown in the fact that when he grew to manhood and killed the Egyptian who was oppressing the Hebrews, *"he supposed his brethren would have understood how that God by his hand would deliver them" (Acts. 7:25).*

So Moses knew about the true God and knew that God had placed a special call upon his life. But one day some forty years later, while tending sheep on the backside of the desert, **Moses met God!**

> *"And the angel of the Lord appeared unto him in a flame of fire out of the midst of a bush. And when the Lord saw that he turned aside to see, **God** called unto him out of the midst of the bush, and said, 'Moses, Moses.' And he said, 'Here am I' " (Ex. 3:2, 4).*

This *"angel of the Lord"* is none other than Almighty God in angel form, and not as some claim, an Old Testament appearance of Jesus Christ. Notice *"God called unto him" (v. 4).*

> *"Moreover he said, I am the God of thy father, the God of Abraham, the God of Isaac, and the God of Jacob. And Moses hid his face; for he was afraid to look upon **God"** (v. 6).*

Please notice verse fourteen:

> *"And God said unto Moses, I am that I am: And he said, Thus shalt thou say unto the children of Israel, I am hath sent me unto you."*

God uses the term *"I am that I am"* and is teaching Moses that He is *"**underived**, the self-consistent"* one. This is God our Father, the one Most High God. It cannot be Jesus, as over and over in the Gospels he states that all he **is, has,** and **does** is **derived** from God the Father. To be **God** is to be

underived, self consistent, and **un-originated**. Jesus originated from the Father, therefore he cannot be the Supreme God. Notice carefully Jesus' strong statements in John chapter five:

> *"Verily, verily, I say unto you, He that heareth my word, **and believeth on him who sent me**, hath everlasting life...for as the Father hath life in himself; so hath he given to the Son to have life in himself...I can of mine own self do nothing"* (v. 24, 26, 30).

Those who try to force a trinitarian view into the Holy Scriptures often go to the several occasions where Jesus said *"I am"* to try and prove that he is God. This is a ridiculous attempt which violates not only the biblical truth but grammar as well.

> *"**I am** the bread of life" (John 6:35).*

> *"**I am** the light of the world" (John 8:12).*

> *"**I am** the good shepherd" (John 10:14).*

Compare these statements with the statements of others in the New Testament and you will see that Jesus' use of *"I am"* is in no way a claim to deity.

> *"**I am** the voice of one crying in the wilderness"* [John the Baptist speaking] *(John 1:23).*

> *"But he said, **I am** he"* [the man who was healed of blindness speaking] *(John 9:9).*

> *"**I am** what **I am**"* [Paul speaking] *(I Cor. 15:10).*

Trinitarian Millard Erickson tries in every way to prove the doctrine of the Trinity in his book, *God In Three Persons,* but he condemns the misuse of Jesus' *"I am"* statements to try to prove his divinity. He quotes Jesus' statements, *"I am the Good Shepherd"* and *"I am the way, the truth, and the life,"* then says:

> *"On this basis, the argument is constructed that these are references back to God's statement in Exodus 3, where he answered Moses' question about his name by saying, 'I am,' or 'I will be.' In my judgement, **this argument** as a whole **is invalid and should not be utilized**. It fails to recognize distinctions among the four uses of the Copula, 'to be.' This is confusing the '**is** of predication for the '**is** of existence.' Even Hebrews certainly knew the difference between describing something as having a **particular quality** and **declaring its existence**."* [Emphasis mine.]

Interpreting the Bible in this manner is what Erickson calls forcing the doctrine of the Trinity into the Scriptures by using verses *"under the greatest strain."* It is what I call trying to force a triangular peg into a round hole!

Back To Exodus Three

> *"And God said moreover unto Moses, Thus shalt thou say unto the children of Israel, The **Lord God** of your fathers, the God of Abraham, the God of Isaac, and the God of Jacob, hath sent me unto you: **this is my name for ever**, and this is my memorial unto **all generations**"* (v. 15).

What is God's *"name for ever?"* What is His *"memorial unto all generations?"* **The Lord God!** God of your fathers! The God of Abraham, the God of Isaac, and the God of Jacob! This is His name for how long? *"Forever...unto all generations."* In Deuteronomy 7:9 God speaks of keeping His covenants *"to a thousand generations."* If one generation is thirty or forty years, God is speaking of thirty or forty thousands years that His name will still be the same. And other Scriptures prove it. When Gabriel came to Mary in Luke 1:32, he said it is the *"Lord God"* who will give unto Jesus *"the throne of his Father David."* Please note: Jesus is not the Lord God! When Peter spoke of God in Acts 3:13 he says:

> *"The God of Abraham, and of Isaac and of Jacob, the God of our fathers, hath glorified his **Son** Jesus."*

When Brother Ananias was sent to Saul of Tarsus (Paul) that he might receive his sight he said, *"The God of our fathers hath chosen thee, that thou shouldest see"* Jesus *(Acts 22:14)*. When God spoke to me in 1986, He said, *"I am the God of Abraham, Isaac, and Jacob, the God of your father, and also your God."* My friend, that is not Jesus Christ. That is God the Father, the one Most High God, Creator of Heaven and Earth! Then who is Jesus? Trust Gabriel when he says in Luke 1:32: *"He shall be great, and shall be called the **Son of the Highest**."* Jesus is the *"Son of the Highest,"* so what spirit is behind all of this effort to make him *"**the Highest**?"* The same spirit that from ages past has sought to rob God Almighty of the glory He alone is due! Please remember that when the precious baby lay in Bethlehem's manger, the heavenly host praised God, saying, ***"Glory to God in the highest"*** *(Luke 2:14)*. God was still *"in the highest!"*

Concluding This Chapter

Listen to God's statement to Moses in Exodus 3:18:

> *"Thou shalt come, thou and the elders of Israel, unto the king of Egypt, and ye shall say unto him, The **Lord God** of the Hebrews **hath met with us**."*

The Lord God met with Moses and Israel on numerous occasions thereafter, and we will discuss some of those awesome encounters in a future chapter. I would like to close this chapter with the same prayer for you, dear reader, that Paul prayed for the saints of Ephesus, in Ephesians chapter one:

> *"That the **God of our Lord Jesus Christ, the Father of glory**, may give unto you the spirit of wisdom and revelation in **the knowledge of him**. The eyes of your understanding being enlightened; that ye may know what is the hope of **his** calling, and what the riches of the glory of **his** inheritance in the saints, And what is the exceeding greatness of **his** power to us-ward who believe, according to the working of **his** mighty power, Which **he** wrought in Christ when **he** raised him from the dead, and set him at **his** own right hand in the heavenly places" (vs. 17-20).*

Glory to God in the highest!

Seeing God The Father

Our Father God is **a person** *(Job 13:8; Heb. 1:3)*, who has **a will** *(Luke 22:42; John 5:30)*, **a personality** *(Zeph. 3:17)*, **a shape** *(Num. 12:8; James 3:9)*, **a face** *(Matt. 18:10; Rev. 22:4)*, **a head** and **hair** *(Daniel 7:9)*, **eyes** *(Deut. 11:12; Prov. 15:3; Ps. 34:15)*, **ears** *(Num. 11:18; Isa. 59:1; James 5:4)*, **a mouth** *(Deut. 8:3; Matt. 4:4)*, **breath** *(Ps. 33:6; Gen. 2:7)*, **a voice** *(Gen. 3:8; Deut. 4:12; Heb. 12:25)*, **hands** *(Gen. 49:24; Ex. 15:17; Isa. 5:12)*, **back parts** *(Ex. 33:23)*, **and feet** *(Ex. 24:10; II Sam. 22:10; Isa. 60:13; Nah. 1:3)*. **He loves, laughs, sings, walks, stands, sits, feels** and **thinks. He is not in any way human**, but he has **a heavenly body** (as do angels - *Ps. 104:4; I Cor. 15:40, 44; Heb. 12:9; I Kings 22:19)*, and we are made in His image! Note: Do not be confused by the Bible verses that make reference to the Almighty's wings. This is speaking figuratively as the nations of Assyria and Moab are also said to have wings *(Isa. 8:8; Jer. 48:9;* and the Messiah, Jesus Christ is promised to *"arise with healing in his wings" Mal. 4:2)*. **Come to know and love God our Father!**

Chapter Three

God The Father Has His Own Name

*"Holy Father, keep through **thine own name** those whom thou hast given me, that they may be one, as we are" (John 17:11).*

*"After this manner therefore pray ye: Our **Father** which art in heaven, Hallowed be **thy name**" (Matt. 6:9; Luke 11:2).*

*"And God said moreover unto Moses, 'Thus shalt thou say unto the children of Israel, the **Lord God** of your fathers, the God of Abraham, the God of Isaac, and the God of Jacob, hath sent me unto you: **this is my name for ever,** and this is my memorial unto **all generations**' " (Ex. 3:15).*

"And the Lord descended in the cloud, and stood with him [Moses] *there and proclaimed **the name of the Lord.** And the Lord passed by before him and proclaimed, '**The Lord, the Lord God**' " (Ex. 34:5-6).*

*"And the **Lord God** shall give unto him* [Jesus] *the throne of his father David"* [the angel Gabriel to Mary] *(Luke 1:32).*

*"Him that overcometh...I will write upon him **the name of my God**...and I will write upon him **my new name**"* [Jesus speaking] *(Rev. 3:12).*

*M*uch of the confusion regarding the distinction between God our Father and His virgin-born Son Jesus, lies in the fact that most of Christianity does not know God's name! In the Oneness Pentecostal church where I grew up, we were taught that God's name in the New Testament is Jesus;

therefore we should not say God too much, but rather call Him by His name, "Jesus." I now know that this is a serious mistake, but I see that it is a widespread belief that is held by people of various denominations.

Names Are So Important

There is hardly anything as important as a name in establishing identity. We name our children and our pets. We name continents, nations, states, and cities. We name books, songs, and works of art. We name stars, trees, flowers, birds, and objects, for the sake of identity.

The first thing that God gave Adam after his creation was a name. The first task that God gave Adam to do was the job of naming all of the other creatures.

> *"God...brought them unto Adam to see what he would call them: and whatsoever Adam called every living creature, that was the name thereof" (Gen. 2:19).*

When Adam's wife was taken from his side by a creative act of God, Adam gave her a name.

> *"And Adam called his wife's name Eve" (Gen. 3:20).*

When their two sons were born they gave them names, *"Cain"* and *"Abel."* And God acknowledged these given names, and when He spoke *about* them or *to* them in Genesis chapter four, He called them *"Cain"* and *"Abel."* And thus it has been through the centuries, people give names to children, and even Heaven recognizes those names. For example when Pharaoh's daughter drew the Hebrew baby from the Nile, *"she called his name Moses" (Ex. 2:10).* Many years later when God spoke to him from the burning bush He addressed him, *"Moses, Moses" (Ex. 3:4).* Exodus 33:17 says:

> *"And the Lord said unto Moses, I will do this thing also that thou hast spoken: for thou hast found grace in my sight, and **I know thee by name.**"*

Jesus said to his disciples in Luke 10:20:

> *"But rather rejoice, because **your names are written in heaven**."* He also said; *"He that overcometh...I will not blot out **his name** out of the book of life, but I will confess **his name** before my Father, and before his angels" (Rev. 3:5).*

Here we should note God's solemn warning to Moses in Exodus 32:33:

> *"Whosoever hath sinned against me, him will I blot out of my book."*

God Sometimes Changes People's Given Names

God, as our Creator and Sovereign **reserves the right to change a person's name** for His own purpose. See for instance Abram:

> *"And Abram fell on his face: and God talked with him, saying...Neither shall thy name any more be called Abram* [father], *but thy name shall be Abraham* [father of a multitude]; *for a father of many nations have I made thee" (Gen. 17:5).*

And Sarai:

> *"As for Sarai thy wife, thou shalt not call her name Sarai, but Sarah shall her name be" (Gen. 17:15).*

And Jacob:

> *"And God said unto him, Thy name is Jacob: thy name shall not be called any more Jacob* [supplanter], *but Israel shall be thy name; and he called his name Israel* [prince - he will rule as God]*" (Gen. 35:10).*

It seems that in the future some saints will be given new names.

> *"To him that overcometh will I give...him a white stone, and in the stone a new **name** written, which no man knoweth saving he that receiveth it" (Rev. 2:17).*

But What Is God's Name?

To begin to answer that most important question, let us go back to Exodus chapter three and the burning bush encounter, where God identified Himself to Moses.

> *"God called unto him out of the midst of the bush and said, Moses, Moses. And he said, Here am I" (v. 4).*

> *"Moreover he said, I am the God of thy father, the God of Abraham, the God of Isaac, and the God of Jacob. And Moses hid his face; for he was afraid to look upon **God**" (v. 6).* Did Moses have any doubt as to who was speaking to him? No way! He knew it was *"God."*

> *"And Moses said unto God, Behold, when I come unto the children of Israel, and shall say unto them, The God of your fathers hath sent me unto you; and they shall say unto me, What is his name? What shall I say unto them?" (v. 13).* Moses knew that even God Himself must have a name for identity purposes.

> *"And God said unto Moses, **I Am That I Am**: And he said, Thus shalt thou say unto the children of Israel, **I Am** hath sent me unto you" (v. 14).*

This is the **one and only time** that Scripture records God using the name *"I Am That I Am,"* which means *"the self-existent one."* God used many names in the Old Testament in His dealings with men, names that denote different facets of His awesome divine nature. But not one Scripture teaches us that *"I am"* is God's eternal name. Some would love to have it so, to justify their taking every occasion where Jesus used the phrase *"I am,"* to say that he was claiming to be God. This is spurious and ridiculous. It is not good scholarship nor good theology. Listen to **trinitarian** scholar and Southern Baptist professor Millard J. Erickson, writing in his book, *God In Three Persons:*

*"One consideration that has frequently been appealed to in evaluating the bearing of John's witness on the doctrine of the Trinity is the 'I' statements of Jesus: 'I am the Good Shepherd;' 'I am the way, the truth, and the life.' On this basis, the argument is constructed that these are references back to God's statement in Exodus 3, where he answered Moses' question about his name by saying, 'I am,' or 'I will be.' If this is the case, then all of the statements constitute claims to deity." "In my judgement, **this argument as a whole is invalid and should not be utilized.** It fails to recognize distinctions among the four uses of the copula, 'to be.' This is confusing the 'is of predication' for the 'is of existence.' Even Hebrews certainly knew the difference between describing something as having a particular quality and declaring its existence" (p. 209).* [Bold emphasis mine]

Trinitarian scholar Professor James Dunn, writing in his exhaustive work, *Christology In The Making,* says of what Jesus knew regarding himself:

"But if we are to submit our speculation to the text [of Scripture] *and build our theology only with the bricks provided by careful exegesis we cannot say with any confidence that Jesus considered himself to be divine, the pre-existent Son of God" (p. 32).* *"There is no indication that Jesus thought or spoke of himself as having pre-existed with God prior to his birth or appearance on earth."* [That is] *"christological thinking which cannot be traced back to Jesus himself.* **We cannot claim that Jesus believed himself to be the incarnate Son of God"** *(p. 254).*

It was Jesus' **critics** who accused him of making himself God, or of claiming equality with God. But he denied it, and it is proven by the Biblical record that he never did! He for sure never said he is the Great *"I Am,"* or used the name *"I Am that I Am!"*

Back to Exodus Three and God's Eternal Name

*"And God said moreover unto Moses, Thus shalt thou say unto the children of Israel, The **Lord God** of your fathers, the God of Abraham, the God of Isaac, and the God of Jacob, hath sent me unto you: **this is my name for ever**, and this is my memorial unto all generations" (Ex. 3:15).* What is God's *"name for ever?"* What is His *"memorial unto all generations?"* It is, *"The **Lord God** of your fathers, the God of Abraham, the God of Isaac, and the God of Jacob."*

In verse sixteen God says to Moses again:

*"Go, and gather the elders of Israel together, and say unto them, The **Lord God** of your fathers, the God of Abraham, of Isaac, and of Jacob, appeared unto me, saying... ."*

God made the above statement to Moses regarding His identity three times in Exodus chapter three, so do you think Moses ever argued with God regarding what His eternal name is? No way! And neither will I! Moses clearly understood what God said to him, for in Exodus 5:1-2, when Moses and Aaron went in before Pharaoh they said:

*"Thus saith the **Lord God** of Israel, Let my people go...And Pharaoh said, Who is the Lord, that I should obey his voice to let Israel go?"* Pharaoh did not know the **Lord God,** but Moses and Aaron certainly did.

Many years later, while on their journey to the promised land, Moses asked God to show him His glory, and God said:

*"And it shall come to pass, while my glory passeth by, that I will put thee in a cleft of the rock, and will cover thee with my hand while I pass by: And I will take away mine hand, and thou shalt see my back parts; but my face shall not be seen. And the Lord descended in the cloud, and **stood with him** there, and **proclaimed the name of the Lord**. And the Lord passed by before him, and proclaimed, **The Lord, The Lord God**" (Ex. 33:22-23; 34:5-6).*

Once again, when God passed by Moses and proclaimed His name, **what did He say? "The Lord, The Lord God!"** A well intentioned minister said to me in the past few days, *"God is not a name, it is a title."* Why don't you tell that to the Creator? Notice what the *"Lord God"* said eight verses later *(Ex. 34:14):*

> *"For thou shalt worship no other god: for the **Lord**, whose name is Jealous, is a jealous **God.**"*

What The Biblical Record Says About God's Name

Let's look at the biblical record, which begins some 2500 years before Moses. The Creator is called *"God"* thirty-two times in Genesis chapter one. He is called *"Lord God"* twenty times in Genesis chapters two and three.

> Noah called Him *"Lord God" (Gen. 9:26).*

> Abraham called Him *"Lord God" (Gen. 15:2, 8).*

> He is called *"Lord God"* **fourteen times** in the book of Joshua.

> Gideon called Him *"Lord God" (Judges 6:22).*

> Samson called Him *"Lord God" (Judges 16:28).*

> King David called Him *"Lord God"* **eight times** in one prayer *(II Sam. 7:18-29).*

> Solomon called Him *"Lord God"* **eight times** in one prayer *(I Kings 8:15; II Chron. 1:9).*

> Elijah called Him *"Lord God" (I Kings 17:1; 18:37).*

> Elisha called Him *"Lord God."* *"Where is the **Lord God** of Elijah?" (II Kings 2:14).*

Hezekiah called Him *"Lord God." "That all the kingdoms of the earth may know that thou art the **Lord God, even thou only"** (II Kings 19:19).*

Nehemiah called Him *"Lord God." "Stand up and bless the Lord your God for ever and ever: and blessed be **thy glorious name**, which is exalted above all blessing and praise. Thou, even thou, art **Lord alone**; thou hast made **heaven**, the heaven of heavens, with all their host, the **earth**, and all things that are therein, the **seas**, and all that is therein, and thou preservest them all; and the host of heaven **worshipeth thee**. Thou art the **Lord God**, who didst choose Abram"* (Neh. 9:5-7).

He is called *"Lord God"* numerous times in Psalms. *"Blessed be the **Lord God** of Israel" (Ps. 41:13).*

He is called *"Lord God"* many times in Isaiah. *"The spirit of the **Lord God** is upon me" (Isa. 61:1).*

He is called *"Lord God"* many times in Jeremiah. *"I am called by **thy name**, O **Lord God** of hosts" (Jer. 15:16).*

God calls Himself *"Lord God"* **over two hundred times** in the book of Ezekiel including these examples:

> *"But I had pity for **my holy name**...Thus saith the **Lord God;** I do not this for your sakes, O house of Israel, but for **mine holy name's** sake...and the heathen shall know that I am the Lord, saith the **Lord God"** (Ezekiel 36:21-23).*

> *"So will I make **my holy name** known in the midst of my people Israel; and I will not let them pollute **my holy name** any more: and the heathen shall know that I am the Lord, the **Holy One** in Israel. Behold it is come, and it is done, saith the **Lord God"** (Ezekiel 39:7-8).*

*"Therefore thus saith the **Lord God**; Now will I bring again the captivity of Jacob...and will be jealous for **my holy name**" (Ezekiel 39:25).* Can you read the above verses and argue with the **Lord God** concerning what His name is? I certainly cannot!

The prophet Daniel called Him *"Lord God" (Daniel 9:3).*

The prophet Hosea called Him *"Lord God" (Hosea 12:5).*

The prophet Amos called Him *"Lord God"* **twenty-two times** in his small but powerful book.

The prophets Obadiah, Micah, Habakkuk, Zephaniah, Zechariah and Malachi called Him *"Lord God"* in their writings.

Could anyone have a doubt at this point in our study what entity, being, person is meant in the Old Testament when the name *"Lord God"* is used? It is the Creator of all, Almighty God, the one Lord God supreme.

The Lord God In The New Testament
Although in the New Testament Almighty God is most often referred to as *"God," "Lord,"* or *"Father;"*

He is called *"the Lord thy God"* **seven times**.

He is called *"the God of Israel"* **three times**.

He is called *"the living God"* **ten times**.

He is called *"the most high God"* **three times**.

He is called *"the God of Abraham, the God of Isaac, and the God of Jacob"* **five times.**

He is called *"the Lord their God"* **one time**.

He is called *"God the Father"* **seventeen times**.

He is called *"one Father even God"* **one time**.

He is called *"God in the highest"* **one time**.

He is called *"the Highest"* **four times**. *"He* [Jesus] *shall be called the Son of the Highest" (Luke 1:32).*

He is called *"the Lord our God"* **one time**.

He is called *"the Lord your God"* **two times**.

He is called *"the God of our fathers"* **four times**.

He is called *"the God of glory"* **one time**.

He is called *"the God of Jacob"* **one time**.

He is called *"God our Father"* **fifteen times**.

He is called *"the God of peace"* **five times**.

He is called *"the God of love and peace"* **one time**.

He is called *"God only wise"* **one time**.

He is called *"the only wise God"* **two times**.

He is called *"God even the Father"* **one time**. *"Blessed be God, even the Father of our Lord Jesus Christ, the Father of mercies, and the God of all comfort" (II. Cor. 1:3).*

He is called *"the **God** and Father of our Lord Jesus Christ"* **three times**. *"The God and Father of our Lord Jesus Christ, which is blessed for evermore, knoweth that I lie not" (II Cor. 11:31).* (See also *Eph. 1:3; I Peter 1:3*).

He is called *"the God of our Lord Jesus Christ"* **one time**. *"That the **God of our Lord Jesus Christ**, the **Father** of glory, may give unto you the spirit of wisdom and revelation in the knowledge of **him**" (Eph. 1:17).*

He is called *"one God and Father of all"* **one time**. *"**One God** and Father of all, who is **above all**, and through all, and in you all" (Eph. 4:6).*

He is called *"God our Saviour"* **five times**.

He is called *"the great God"* **one time**.

He is called *"God the Judge"* **one time**. *"But ye are come... to **God the Judge of all**, and to the spirits of just men made perfect, **and to Jesus** the mediator of the new covenant" (Heb. 12:23-24).*

He is called *"the God of all grace"* **one time**.

He is called *"the everlasting God"* **one time**.

He is called *"my God"* **fifteen times**. *"But **my God** shall supply all your need according to **his riches** in glory **by Christ Jesus**" (Phil. 4:19).*

He is called *"our God"* **three times**. *"Now is come salvation, and strength, and the kingdom of **our God**, and the power of **his** Christ" (Rev. 12:10).*

He is called the *"God of the earth"* **one time**.

He is called the *"God of heaven"* **two times**.

He is called *"Lord God"* **13 times** in the New Testament, including *"Lord God Almighty"* **five times**.

Is there any doubt as to what entity, being, person, is intended when the above names are used in the New Testament? Again, it is the Creator of all, Almighty God, the one **Lord God** Supreme.

What Gabriel Said To Mary

> *"And in the sixth month the angel Gabriel was **sent from God** unto a city of Galilee, named Nazareth, to a virgin espoused to a man whose name was Joseph, of the house of David; and the virgin's name was Mary. And the angel came in unto her, and said, Hail, thou that art highly favoured, the **Lord** is with thee: blessed art thou among women"* (Luke 1:26-28).

Notice verse twenty-six, *"Gabriel was **sent from God.**"* He had told Zechariah, husband of Mary's cousin Elizabeth and father of John *(the Baptist)*, in verse nineteen of this chapter, *"I am Gabriel, that **stands in the presence of God.**"* So he was sent from *"the presence of God,"* by "God," with a message for Mary.

> *"And the angel said unto her, Fear not, Mary: for thou hast found favour with **God**. And, behold, **thou shalt conceive in thy womb**, and bring forth a son, and shalt call his name Jesus"* (Luke 1:28).

So Gabriel tells Mary of a **conception,** and not an incarnation, that is about to take place in her womb. He had just left the *"presence of God"* in heaven, and the message he was sent to give Mary was **definitely not,** "God is about to be incarnated in your womb." Notice: ***"Thou shalt conceive in*** *thy womb."* Did Gabriel know the difference between a conception and an incarnation? Sure he did!

Gabriel spoke to her of another **conception** that had taken place six months prior:

> *"And, behold, **thy cousin Elisabeth, she hath also conceived** a son in her old age: and this is the sixth month with her, who was called barren. For **with God nothing shall be impossible"** (Luke 1:36-37).*

Two conceptions, but Mary's son will be greater!

> *"He shall be great, and shall be called the **Son of the Highest**; and the **Lord God** shall give unto him the throne of his father, **David**: And he shall reign over the house of Jacob for ever; and of his kingdom there shall be no end."*

Gabriel tells Mary that God, *"the **Lord God**,"* shall give unto Jesus the throne of *"his father David"* in Jerusalem *(II Sam. 7:14-18)*. Gabriel did **not** say, "the throne of God in heaven," but *"the throne of his father David."* When God gave David the promise of the **Messiah**, *"thy seed" (II Sam. 7:12)*, some one thousand years before this day, his reply had been:

> *"Who am I, O **Lord God**? And what is my house, that thou hast brought me hitherto? Wherefore thou art great, O **Lord God**: for there is none like thee, **neither is there any God beside thee"** (II Sam. 7:18, 22).*

David was speaking **to** the same *"Lord God"* that Gabriel is speaking **of** to Mary. Gabriel certainly did not tell her of the coming of a *second* God or a human incarnation of the *only* God. Notice:

> *"Then said Mary unto the angel, How shall this be, seeing I know not a man? And the angel answered and said unto her, **The Holy Ghost shall come upon thee, and the power of the Highest shall overshadow thee: therefore** also that holy thing which shall be born of thee shall be called the **Son** of God" (Luke 1:34-35).*

Again, Gabriel on this occasion spoke to Mary of two conceptions, each an awesome miracle in its own way. *"Elizabeth was barren, and they both were now well-stricken in years," (Luke 1:7)*, so her conception by her husband Zechariah was a miracle of God, *"For with God nothing shall be impossible"* [Gabriel to Mary] *(v. 37)*. But Mary's **conception** by an act of the **Holy Ghost** was by far the greatest miracle, for by this act the **Lord God** *(the Holy Ghost is the Spirit of the Lord God),* produced a unique, sinless human being, the last Adam, to be the Lamb of God that taketh away the sin of the world. Notice carefully the word *"therefore"* in verse thirty-five. **"Therefore,"** or "for this reason," *"that holy thing which shall be born of thee shall be called **the Son of God.**"* Not that God the Father shall move into your womb and come out looking like a baby. Not that "God the Son," second person of a triune God shall move into your womb and come out incarnated as a baby. But the **Lord God** *(the Holy Ghost)* will do a creative act in your womb, and you will bring forth a son, the man Christ Jesus.

When the child **John** was born, Zechariah *"praised God" (v. 64),* and prophesied saying:

> *"Blessed be the **Lord God** of Israel; for **he hath visited** and redeemed his people" (Luke 1:68).*

What is God's eternal name? It is for sure not *Jesus.* Although in that beautiful name there is power, healing, salvation, and it is the name at which demons tremble, our Saviour's name will likely not be "Jesus" when we see him. He will have a name change as did Abram, Sarai, Jacob and Saul of Tarsus. We must accept this truth from the words of our Lord Jesus himself, and his apostle John.

> *"Him that overcometh...I will write upon him the **name of my God**, and the name of the city of my God...**and I will write upon him my new name**" (Rev. 3:12).*

> *"His eyes were as a flame of fire, and on his head were many crowns; **and he had a name written, that no man knew,** but he himself" (Rev. 19:12).* It is obvious that millions know the name *"Jesus."*

86

The Lord Messiah's salvation name is Jesus. It is the same as Joshua and means *"the Lord is salvation."*

> *"And she shall bring forth a son, and thou shalt call his name Jesus: for he shall **save** his people from their sins"* [the angel to Joseph] *(Matt. 1:21).*

Jesus' rulership name, when he comes as supreme ruler of this planet for one thousand years, is one of those *"secret things"* that belongs unto God, so we will not belabor it. It is sufficient to see and acknowledge that this is a fact of Scripture.

For another Biblical example of the Father's name as distinct from His Son's name, consider this scene from Revelation chapter fourteen:

> *"And I looked, and lo, a Lamb stood on mount Zion, and with him an hundred forty and four thousand, having **his Father's name** written in their foreheads" (Rev. 14:1).*

The Lamb's name is Jesus. The Lamb's Father's name is the *"Lord God."* The Lamb's song of praise to his Father is recorded in chapter fifteen.

> *"And they sing the song of Moses the servant of God, and the song of the Lamb, saying, Great and marvelous are thy works, **Lord God Almighty**; just and true are thy ways, thou King of saints. Who shall not fear thee, O Lord, and **glorify thy name**? For thou only art holy; for all nations shall come and **worship before thee" (Rev. 15:3-4).*

An Awesome Promise

We will close this chapter with an awesome promise from the Lord God to those who love Him and **know His name**. It is found in Psalm 91:14-16. Notice that the one speaking is identified as *"the most High"* and *"the Almighty"* in verse one:

> *"Because he hath set his love upon me, therefore will I deliver him: I will set him on high, **because he hath known my name**. He shall call upon me, and I will answer him:*

I will be with him in trouble; I will deliver him, and honor him. With long life will I satisfy him, and show him my salvation."

Glory to God in the highest!

"It is fair to say that the Bible does not clearly teach the doctrine of the Trinity, if by clearly one means there are proof texts for the doctrine. In fact, there is not even one proof text...." (p. 89). "The above illustrations prove the fallacy of concluding that if something is not proof texted in the Bible we cannot clearly teach the results.... . If that were so, I could never teach the doctrines of the Trinity or the deity of Christ or the deity of the Holy Spirit" (p. 90).

Trinitarian scholar Charles C Ryrie;

Basic Theology

Chapter Four

God Our Father Is The One
To Whom We Should Pray

*"When thou prayest, enter into thy closet and...pray to **thy Father** which is in secret; and **thy Father** which seeth in secret shall reward thee openly...for **your Father** knoweth what things ye have need of, before ye **ask him**...therefore pray ye: **Our Father** which art in heaven..." (Matt. 6:6, 8-9).*

*"....your fruit should remain, that whatsoever ye shall **ask of the Father in my name, he** may give it you" (John 15:16).*

*"I go to the Father. And in that day ye shall **ask me nothing**. Verily, Verily, I say unto you, Whatsoever ye shall **ask the Father in my name, he** will give it you. At that day ye shall **ask in my name**" (John 16:16, 23, 26).*

*"**Your Father** which is in heaven* (shall) *give good things to them that **ask him**" (Matt. 7:11).*

*M*y awakening as to whom the One Most High God is, began one day as I was reading in the book of Acts, chapter four. The Apostles were arrested and brought before the council for the healing of the lame man in chapter three. After being questioned, threatened, and released they returned to the group of believers to report what had happened to them. Verse 24 says:

*"And when they heard that, they lifted up their voice **to God** with one accord, and said, **Lord, thou art God**, which hast made heaven, and earth, and the sea...Who by the mouth of thy servant David hast said, Why did the heathen rage, and*

*the people imagine vain things? The kings of the earth stood up...**against the Lord**, and **against his Christ**"* [Messiah] *(vs. 24-26).*

They are clearly praying to the **Lord God** and referring to *"thy servant David"* and the Messianic psalm he penned in Psalm two. That psalm pertains to the heathen raging because God had set His King Messiah *"upon my holy hill of Zion."* They understood that this had been fulfilled in part by their recent experience, since *"the rulers were gathered together against the Lord* [God]*, and against his Christ"* [Jesus]. Their prayer continues in verse twenty-seven:

> *"For of a truth against **thy holy child Jesus**, whom thou hast **anointed**, both Herod, and Pontius Pilate, with the Gentiles, and the people of Israel, were gathered together."*
> They were praying to the Lord God and referring to *"thy holy child Jesus."*

The prayer continues:

> *"And now, Lord, behold their threatenings: and grant unto thy servants, that with all boldness they may speak thy word, By stretching forth thine hand to heal; and that signs and wonders may be done by **the name of thy holy child Jesus**"* *(vs. 29-30).*

When I realized that these Apostles who had just seen Jesus ascend to heaven in Acts chapter one, did not pray to him in Acts chapter four, I was astonished! They prayed to the **Lord God** and twice mentioned *"thy holy child Jesus."* While growing up I was taught that Jesus **is** the "Lord God," and in fact for many years I taught that error to others. I had to make some major adjustments in my theology. In and out of Scripture people have always prayed to their God. In the book of Jonah, chapter one, the heathen shipmaster said to Jonah, *"O sleeper, arise, call upon thy God!"* And Jonah said *"I am a Hebrew; and I fear the Lord, the God of heaven, which hath made the seas and the dry land...Then Jonah prayed unto the **Lord His God** out of the fish's belly"* *(Jonah 1:6, 9; 2:1).*

So these Apostles prayed to the **Lord God** as Jonah did, with one notable difference. The Apostles prayed *"by the name of thy holy child Jesus."* What was the Apostles' understanding regarding the relationship between the Lord God and the man Jesus Christ with whom they had just spent three years in ministry? A strong indication is given in the word *"child"* that they used with reference to Jesus when speaking of him to God his Father. The word *"child"* is *"pais"* in the Greek (pronounced *paheece*) *(Strong's #3816)*, and it means *"a servant boy - a minister to a king or God."* So when speaking to God regarding his Son, they called him *"thy servant boy Jesus."* If these disciples had believed that Jesus is *"God"* they surely would not have referred to him as "God's servant boy." Of course this agrees with the Lord God's own references to their Messiah in Scripture.

> *"Behold **my servant,** whom I uphold...I have put my spirit upon him: he shall bring forth judgement to the Gentiles" (Isa. 42:1).*

> *"...by his knowledge shall **my righteous servant** justify many; for he shall bear their iniquities" (Isa. 53:11).*

> *"Behold, I will bring forth **my servant** the BRANCH" (Zech. 3:8).*

Back To Acts Chapters Two and Three

More of the answer as to who the Apostles understood Jesus to be can be found in Acts chapters two and three. Listen to Peter's sermon on the day of Pentecost from Acts chapter two:

> *"Ye men of Israel, hear these words; Jesus of Nazareth, **a man approved of God** among you by miracles and wonders and signs, which **God did** by him in the midst of you...Him being delivered by the determinate counsel and **foreknowledge** of God...**Whom God hath raised up**" (Acts 2:22-24).*

So to the apostle Peter, Jesus who was then in heaven was still *"a man approved of God,"* by whom God did *"miracles and wonders,"* and who when slain *"God hath raised up."* If Peter believed that Jesus is God, he gives no hint of it in these verses (or in any of his other writings). Notice Peter's confession to Jesus:

> *"And Peter answered and said unto him, Thou art the Christ"* [Messiah] *(Mark 8:29).*

> *"But whom say ye that I am? Peter answering said, The Christ* [Messiah] *of God" (Luke 9:20).* My friend, there is a world of difference between "God," and "Messiah of God!" Notice Peter's words in Acts 2:23: *"Him being delivered by the determinate counsel and **foreknowledge of God**.*" This is *"foreknowledge,"* and not pre-existence.

This agrees with what Peter said in I Peter 1:20: Christ *"verily was **foreordained** before the foundation of the world, but was manifest **in these last times** for you, who by him do believe in **God**, that raised him up from the dead and, **gave him glory**; that your faith and hope might be in **God**.*" Again, *"foreordained"* by God, not pre-existent. Whose word are you going to take-Peter's, or the Nicean Council?

Peter Continues In Acts Chapter Two

David *"being a prophet, and knowing that God had sworn with an oath to him, that of the fruit of his loins, according to the flesh, he would raise up Christ* [Messiah] *to sit on his throne" (Acts 2:30).* Notice: It was David's throne in Jerusalem that Jesus Messiah was promised, and **not God's throne** in heaven. There is not one verse in the Bible where Jesus is promised God's throne in heaven! It is we who have done that in our doctrine, to our shame.

*"And the **Lord God** shall give unto him the throne of **his father David**"* [Gabriel to Mary] *(Luke 1:32).*

*"To him that overcometh will I grant to sit with me in **my throne**, even as I also overcame, and am set down with my Father in **his throne**"* [Jesus speaking] *(Rev. 3:21).*

Peter continues regarding David and Christ.

*"He, seeing this before, spoke of the resurrection of Christ, that his soul was not **left in hell**, neither his flesh did see corruption. This Jesus hath **God raised up**...Therefore being by the **right hand of God** exalted, and having received **of the Father** the promise of the Holy Ghost, he [Christ] hath shed forth this, which ye now see and hear. He [David] saith himself, **The Lord** said unto **my Lord**, Sit thou on my right hand, until I make thy foes thy footstool. Therefore let all the house of Israel know assuredly, that **God hath made** that same Jesus, whom ye have crucified, both **Lord** and Christ"* *(Acts 2:31-36).* Notice: *"God hath made that same Jesus...Lord* [Adoni-Master[*and Christ"* [Messiah].

Peter knew what every Christian should know, that in Scripture there are clearly two Lord's spoken of; **our heavenly Father** *"the Lord God,"* and **our Messiah** *"the Lord Jesus Christ."*

*"The **Lord** said unto my **Lord**"* *(Ps. 110:1).*

*"...denying the only **Lord God**, and our **Lord Jesus Christ**"* *(Jude v. 4).*

*"**One Lord**, one faith, one baptism, **one God**, and **Father** of all"* *(Eph. 4:5-6).*

Now To Peter's Sermon In Acts Chapter Three

After the healing of the lame man at the temple, a large crowd gathered wondering by what power this had been done. Peter then preached a sermon similar to the one he had preached to the multitude at Pentecost in Acts chapter two.

> *"The God of Abraham, and of Isaac, and of Jacob, **the***
> ***God of our fathers**, hath glorified his Son Jesus; whom ye*
> *delivered up" (Acts 3:13).*

Peter made a clear distinction between the *"God of Abraham, Isaac, and Jacob, the God of our Fathers"* and *"his Son Jesus."* Why do so many misguided Christians insist on combining the two?

> *"And killed the **Prince of life**, whom **God** hath raised from*
> *the dead" (v. 15).*

Mistaken theology has made Jesus the King of the universe but Peter and the other Bible writers say he is a Prince.
- *"Messiah, the **Prince**" (Dan. 9:25).*
- *"The **Prince** of Peace" (Isa. 9:6).*
- *"The **Prince** of Life" (Acts 3:15).*
- *"A **Prince** and a Savior" (Acts 5:31).*
- *"The **Prince** of the **kings of the earth**" (Rev. 1:5).*

God Almighty is the Supreme ruler, the great King of the universe, and His Son *"the Prince,"* is under Him. *"The head of Christ is God" (I Cor. 11:3).* *"Christ is God's" (I Cor. 3:23).*

> *"Shout unto **God** with the voice of triumph. For the **Lord***
> ***most high** is terrible; he is a **great King** over all the earth"*
> *(Ps. 47:2). (See also Ps. 68:24; 74:12; Dan. 2:47, 4:37;*
> *Matt. 5:35.)*

Peter Continues

*"Repent ye therefore, and be converted, that your sins may be blotted out, when the times of refreshing shall come from the presence of the Lord [God]; And **he** [God] **shall send Jesus Christ**, which before was preached unto you: Whom the heavens must receive until the time of restitution of all things,*

which **God hath spoken** *by the mouth of all his holy prophets since the world begun" (Acts 3:19-21).* Listen to Peter! The God who sent Jesus Christ the first time has promised to send him again at *"the time of restitution of all things."* This is not God sending a "second God"; this is the Lord God sending His Son, *"the man Christ Jesus."* To Peter and the other Apostles, in fact Jesus himself has a God.

> *"Blessed be **the God** and Father **of our Lord Jesus Christ"***
> *(I Peter 1:3).*

> *"Blessed be **the God** and Father **of our Lord Jesus Christ"***
> *(Eph. 1:3).*

Now to Peter's words in verses 22, 23, and 26 of Acts chapter three:

> *"For Moses truly said unto the fathers, **a Prophet** shall the **Lord** your **God** raise up unto you **of your brethren**, like unto me* [a prophet like Moses]; *him shall ye hear....and it shall come to pass, that every soul which will not hear **that Prophet**, shall be destroyed from among the people. Unto you first **God**, having raised up his Son Jesus, **sent him** to bless you" (Acts 3:22-23, 26).*

No wonder these Apostles who had spent three years with Jesus in ministry, did not pray to him in Acts chapter four. To them he was the righteous sacrifice for the sins of the whole world, Messiah, Prince, and a Prophet like Moses sent by God, but he was not himself God. So they prayed to the one who is their God and ours, *("Lord, thou art God, which has made heaven and earth"),* in *"the name of thy holy child Jesus."* We desperately need to learn from their example! We have come to the end of the age, and we need prayers answered. Look how God showed His approval of the manner in which they prayed.

> *"And when they had prayed, the place was shaken where they were assembled together; and they were all filled with the Holy Ghost, and they spoke the word of God with boldness" (v. 31).*

Jesus Himself Was A Man Of Prayer

Prayer is a declaration of dependence upon God, and Jesus prayed always. The Bible records much regarding his prayer life.

> *"And when he had sent the multitudes away, he went up into a mountain apart **to pray**" (Matt. 14:23).*

> *"Then were there brought unto him little children, that he should **put his hands on them, and pray**" (Matt. 19:13).*

> *"Then cometh Jesus with them unto a place called Gethsemane, and saith unto the disciples, Sit ye here, **while I go and pray** yonder" (Matt. 26:36).*

> *"And in the morning, rising up a great while before day, he went out, and departed into a solitary place, **and there he prayed**" (Mark. 1:35).*

> *"Now when all the people were baptized, it came to pass, that Jesus also being baptized, **and praying**, the heaven was opened, and the Holy Ghost descended in a bodily shape like a dove upon him..." (Luke 3:21-22).*

> *"And he withdrew himself into the wilderness, **and prayed**" (Luke 5:16).*

> *"He took Peter and John and James, and went up into a mountain **to pray. And as he prayed**, the fashion of his countenance was altered, and his raiment was white and glistering [glistening]" (Luke 9:28-29).*

Luke's description of Jesus' prayer in the Garden of Gethsemane shows that Jesus' prayers were not just a formality or to set a good example.

> *"And **being in an agony he prayed more earnestly**: and his*

sweat was as it were great drops of blood falling down to
the ground" (Luke 22:44).

To Whom Did Jesus Pray?

Since Jesus is our great example, we would do well to study the Scriptures
with the question in mind, "To whom did Jesus pray?" Was Jesus just a body
full of God (a robot if you please) as some teach, and therefore when he
prayed, it was *"the flesh praying to the Spirit,"* or was this a unique, perfect,
sinless man who prayed to his God? (Remember his words, *"I ascend unto...
my God and your God" John 20:17).* Notice these Scriptures:

> "And it came to pass in those days, that he went into **a
> mountain to pray**, and continued **all night in prayer to
> God**" (Luke 6:12). [Jesus prayed **"to God"**].

> "These words spake Jesus, and **lifted up his eyes to heaven,**
> and said, **Father**, the hour is come; glorify thy Son, that thy
> Son also may glorify thee" (John 17:1).

> "Who in the days of his flesh, when he had offered up **prayers
> and supplications** with strong crying and tears **unto him**
> [God] that was able to save him from death, and was heard
> in that he feared" (Heb. 5:7).

Listen to Jesus' strong cry from the cross:

> "**Father, forgive them;** for they know not what they do"
> (Luke 23:34).

Jesus is not saying, *"I forgive you,"* though he looked upon them with
forgiveness, but his prayer is to God: *"Father you forgive them!"* Compare
this to Paul's words in Ephesians 4:32, *"....**God** for Christ's sake hath
forgiven you,"* and in Acts 20:21, *"....**repentance toward God**, and faith
toward our Lord Jesus Christ."*

Jesus' closest friends knew that while he was on earth he prayed **to God**
for their needs. Look at what Martha said at the tomb of her dead brother

Lazarus:

> *"Then said Martha unto Jesus, Lord, if thou hadst been here, my brother had not died. But I know that **even, now, whatsoever thou wilt ask God, God will give it thee**" (John 11:21-22).*

And he still prays for us in heaven. The inspired writer of Hebrews says that the ministry of Jesus is a continuing ministry:

> *"But now, **hath he obtained a more excellent** ministry, by how much also he **is** the mediator of a better covenant" (Heb. 8:6).*

Part of his continuing ministry is to intercede (*"entreat in favor of"*) for us.

> *"Wherefore he is able to save them to the uttermost that come **unto God by him**, seeing he **ever liveth** to make intercession for them" (Heb. 7:25).*

> *"Who is even at the right hand of God, who also **maketh intercession** for us" (Rom. 8:34).*

> *"....if I go not away, the Comforter will not come unto you" (John 16:7).*

> *"And **I will pray the Father**, and he shall give you another Comforter, that he may abide with you forever" (John 14:16).*

Jesus Taught The Disciples and Us To Pray To The Father

In Matthew chapter nine we are told that *"Jesus went about all the cities and villages, teaching in their synagogues, and preaching the gospel of the kingdom, and healing every sickness and every disease among the people" (v. 35).* As he traveled about seeing the multitudes, he was *"moved with compassion on them, because they fainted, and were scattered abroad, as sheep having no shepherd" (v. 36).* Jesus saw a problem and made a request of his disciples.

Jesus' Prayer Request

> *"Pray ye therefore **the Lord of the harvest** [not himself],*
> *that **he** will send forth labourers into **his** harvest" (Matt.*
> *9:38).*

Jesus gave a prayer request to his disciples. He is saying in the above verse,
"Help me pray to God the Father about this problem." (For another example
of Jesus requesting prayer from his disciples see *Matthew 26:36-43).* Jesus
never claimed to be *"the Lord of the harvest."* Notice his words in John
15:1.

> *"I am the true vine, and **my Father** is the husbandman."*

When Jesus gave the parable of the householder in Matthew twenty-one, he
pictured himself as *"his son,"* the *"heir,"* who is *"sent"* by the householder
(God), and slain by the wicked men. Jesus never claimed to be *"the
Father"* **and** *"the Son."* It is we who have claimed both positions for him.
Note: We are heirs of God **our Father** and co-heirs with Jesus Christ **our
brother**.

Remarkably there is not one occasion recorded in the Gospels where Jesus
taught them (or us) to pray to himself. In fact he clearly taught otherwise,
so why do millions of Christians persist in praying to Jesus. It is significant
that **trinitarian** James McGrath, a professor of religion at Butler University,
states in his book, *The Only True God, **"...it is noteworthy that not even
Jesus is addressed in prayer by the earliest generation of Christians."*** [1]
Consider Jesus' words on this subject.

> *"But thou, when thou prayest, enter into thy closet, and*
> *when thou has shut the door, **pray to thy Father** which is*
> *in secret; and **thy Father** which seeth in secret shall reward*
> *thee openly. Be not ye therefore like unto them: for **your***
> ***Father** knoweth what things ye have need of, before ye **ask***
> ***him. After this manner therefore pray ye: Our Father***
> *which art in heaven, Hallowed be **thy name...**" (Matt. 6:6,*
> *8-9).*

*"Again I say unto you, that if two of you shall agree on earth as touching any thing that they shall ask, it shall be done for them **of my Father** which is in heaven" (Matt. 18:19).*

*"If ye then, being evil, know how to give good gifts unto your children: how much more **shall your heavenly Father give the Holy Spirit to them that ask him**" (Luke 11:13)?* Notice, *"That ask **him**...your heavenly Father."*

*"And shall not **God** avenge his own elect, which **cry** day and night **unto him**, though **he** bear long with them? I tell you that **he** will avenge them speedily" (Luke 18:7-8).*

Origen Regarding Prayer To God

The early Greek Church father Origen *(A.D. 185-255)* made many serious mistakes in his theology but he read these clear verses and got this much right. We are to pray to the Supreme God, and Him alone. Consider these quotes from his writings:

> *"For every prayer, supplication, intercession, and thanksgiving is to be sent up **to the Supreme God** through the High Priest - the living Word and.....it would not permit us to pray with confidence to anyone other than **to the Supreme God**, who is sufficient for all things, **through** our Savior, the Son of God. **We judge it improper to pray to those beings who themselves offer up prayers.** For even they themselves would prefer that we should send up our requests **to the God to whom they pray**, rather than to send them downwards to themselves, or **to apportion our power of prayer between God and them."** [2]*

Origen raises a good question. Why pray to Jesus, Mary, saints, or angels when we are never instructed to do so, and when, in fact, we have been invited into the throne room of Almighty God Himself?

> *"Seeing then that we have **a great high priest**, that is passed*

into the heavens, Jesus the Son of God...Let us therefore **come boldly unto the throne of grace,** *that we may obtain mercy and find grace to help in time of need" (Heb. 4:14, 16).*

"For through him we both [Jews and Gentiles] *have* **access** *by one Spirit* **unto the Father"** *(Eph. 2:18).*

"In whom [Christ] *we have boldness and* **access** *with confidence by the faith of him. For this cause I bow my knees* **unto the Father** *of our Lord Jesus Christ" (Eph. 3:12, 14).*

The Protocol Of Approaching God

The above verses point us to another important subject regarding prayer. That is the protocol of approaching God. When I was a very young man, I learned a good lesson about protocol. An older friend of mine was on trial in federal court on a draft issue, and several members of our church went with him to give moral support. We visited quietly in the courtroom until just before time for the trial to begin, when to our amazement the bailiff entered and escorted everyone from the room who did not have on a coat, including me. I sat outside in the hallway during the trial pondering the protocol of being in federal court in the presence of a federal judge.

In a similar vein I heard on the news recently of a group of ladies who were invited to the White House to see the President. Whether in ignorance or irreverence, the news did not say, but several of the ladies showed up in flip-flops. It caused quite a stir, as you do not go into the Oval Office to meet the President wearing flip-flops. There is a protocol. You honor the President, you honor the office. You go at his invitation, dressed properly, and acting in a proper manner.

Likewise, there is a protocol to approaching the Great King of the Universe! When the Jewish High Priest went into the Holy of Holies, once a year, to meet with the God of Israel, he went only after much careful preparation.

There were prescribed washings, sacrifice and attire. The penalty for breaking this protocol was death. Of course we now approach a *"throne of grace"* so the penalty for not approaching Him as He has instructed **us** is not death, just **unanswered prayers**.

What Is Our Protocol?

Look at the songs recorded in Psalm ninety-two through one hundred. These songs or hymns were written to be sung in the temple, or while approaching the temple, on the sabbath or for high religious festivals. They celebrate God's awesome majesty, righteousness and authority. These hymns of praise and worship were "songs of ascent" that were meant to bring one into the presence of Almighty God. Look closely at Psalm one hundred.

> *"Make a joyful noise unto the Lord, all ye lands. Serve the Lord with gladness:* ***come before his presence with singing. Know ye that the Lord he is God****: it is he that hath made us, and not we ourselves; we are his people, and the sheep of his pasture.* ***Enter into his gates with thanksgiving, and into his courts with praise: be thankful unto him, and bless his name****. For the Lord is good; his mercy is everlasting; and his truth endureth to all generations."*

Thus the Israelites came into the presence of God, by praise, worship and animal sacrifice. Through Jesus Christ, *"the Lamb of God that taketh away the sin of the world,"* we now have *"a new and living way"* to approach God.

> *"Having therefore, brethren, boldness to enter into the* ***holiest*** *by the blood of Jesus, By* ***a new and living way****, which he hath consecrated for us, through the* ***veil****, that is to say,* ***his flesh****; And having an* ***high priest*** *over the house of God;* ***Let us draw near*** *with a true heart in full assurance of faith"* (Heb. 10:19-22).

Praying To God In Jesus' Name

While Jesus was here on earth with his disciples he **functioned** as God in their lives, much as Moses functioned as the God of Egypt for a time *(Ex. 4:16; 7:1)*. He protected them *(Mark 4:35-41)*, healed their sicknesses *(Matt. 8:14-15)*, and supplied their needs *(Matt. 17:24-27)*. But he taught them that God the Father is the source *(John 5:30-31; 6:32; 7:16)*. Early in Jesus' ministry he instructed the disciples to pray to the Father *(Matt. 6:6-9; Luke 11:1-2)*, but he did not tell them to pray in his name. Since a testament *(will)* is not in force until after the death of the testator *(Heb. 9:15-16)*, they were not to invoke Jesus' name in prayer to the Father until after his death on the cross. That's why his name is not included in the prayer we call *"The Lord's Prayer."* But just before his crucifixion, he began to teach them something new. In John 15:15-16 he tells them:

> *"For all things that **I have heard of my Father** I have made known unto you. Ye have not chosen me, but I have chosen you....that your fruit should remain; **that whatsoever ye shall ask of the Father in my name, he may give it you"** (John 15:15-16).*

In the next chapter he teaches them more about praying **to God in his name**. He had begun to talk to them more openly about his coming death and his ascension to the Father, and they were having a hard time grasping these statements. Notice John 16:16-17.

> *"A little while, and ye shall not see me: and again, a little while, and ye shall see me, **because I go to the Father**. Then said some of his disciples among themselves, What is this that he saith unto us, A little while, and ye shall not see me: and again, a little while, and ye shall see me: and, Because I go to the Father?"*

Jesus says this about praying to the Father after he ascends and is no longer with them:

> *"And in that day **ye shall ask me nothing**, Verily, Verily, I say unto you, **Whatsoever ye shall ask the Father in my name, he** will give it you. Hitherto have ye asked nothing **in my name**: ask, and ye shall receive, that your joy may be full."*

> *"These things have I spoken unto you in proverbs: but the time cometh when I shall no more speak unto you in proverbs, but I shall **show you plainly of the Father**. At that day ye shall **ask in my name**: and I say not unto you, that I will pray the Father for you: **For the Father himself loveth you**, because ye have loved me, and have believed that I came out from God. I came forth from the Father, and am come into the world: again, **I leave the world, and go to the Father**. His disciples said unto him, Lo, now speakest thou plainly, and speakest no proverb"* (John 16:23-29).
> [Look at Jesus' words *"at that day"* in the verse above, and realize that this was to be **after he went to the Father**].

No wonder in Acts chapter four, only a few days after Jesus made these statements, these same disciples prayed to *"God,"* the *"Lord,"* **in the name of *"thy holy child Jesus"*** *(Acts 4:24, 27, 30).*

Brethren, how did we miss these clear instructions from Jesus regarding prayer **to God our Father** in **Jesus name**. I am not being critical, but I hear ministers in services and on T.V. praying to Jesus *"in thy name,"* praying to Jesus *"in Christ's name,"* or praying to the Father, and before the prayer is over calling Him *"Jesus,"* and thanking Him for dying for us. When I consider how wrong we have been in our approach to God, I don't wonder why we have not had **more** prayers answered; I wonder how we have had **any** prayers answered.

We should go boldly to the throne of grace in the name of Jesus, through the blood of Jesus, in his righteousness and worthiness, claiming what he purchased for us on the cross *(Isa. 53:5).* The result will be more answered prayers! I recently had lunch with two ministers, one who strongly endorses the understanding of God as taught in my first book, and one who has my book but had only scanned over it briefly. The second minister, who pastors a large Nazarene church, was open to this truth and eager to discuss it. When the subject of prayer came up, he asked, *"Brother Joel, can we pray directly* to God the Father?" When I gave him Scriptures showing that we can, he rejoined. He said, *"I have been praying to Jesus, and the other day I said, 'Jesus will you tell your Father for me how much I love Him'."* He was delighted to learn that we can go directly to God! We returned to my office, and before they left he asked if he could offer a prayer. He prayed the most beautiful and moving prayer to *"God the Father"* in the *"name of Your Son Jesus."* Count him as another Christian who has been set free by the truth.

Other Supporting Scriptures
Since Jesus taught his disciples to pray to God the Father in his name, and we see that they prayed in that manner in Acts chapter four, we should strengthen our understanding of this awesome truth by looking at other supporting Scriptures. One thing that speaks loudly pertaining to this manner of praying is the absence of any biblical account of Jesus' followers praying to him **after his ascension** to the Father. This is not surprising since any such reference would be in direct contradiction to what Jesus taught them in John, chapters fifteen and sixteen. The fact is that the New Testament records occasions of Jesus' disciples speaking to him after his ascension to the Father, only **while in the midst of visions of him**, or **in response to being spoken to by him**.

At this point in our study, for clearer understanding of this subject, it might be helpful to look at what the dictionary says about the words **pray** and **prayer**. *Webster's New Twentieth Century Dictionary* says regarding **pray:** *"1. Originally, to beseech; to entreat; to implore: now seldom used except as the elliptical form of I pray you, as pray tell me."* In this use of the word **pray** it is a plea that is made to any other person. This is the **broadest** sense of the word. But now look at the word **pray** in the **strictest** sense of the word. *Webster's* says: *"to ask earnestly; to make supplication; to say prayers, **as to God.**"* Regarding the word **"prayer"** *Webster's* says: *"humble entreaty addressed **to God;**" "a request made **to God;**" "any spiritual communion **with God.**"* So in the strictest sense of the word, prayer is offered *"to God,"* and again there is not a single scriptural reference to prayer being made to Jesus after his ascension to the Father.

Did Stephen Pray To Jesus?

Look at Acts chapter seven. Some have supposed that Stephen prayed to Jesus at the time of his stoning, but a closer look at this account proves otherwise. The verses in question are verses fifty-nine and sixty.

> *"And they stoned Stephen, **calling upon God**, and saying, Lord Jesus, receive my spirit" (v. 59).*

In this verse Stephen is clearly **praying to his "God,"** and **committing his spirit to his "Lord** [master] *Jesus."* He spoke to both because in his moment of death he was looking at **both.**

> *"Behold, I see the heavens opened, and the **Son of man** standing on the right hand of **God"** (v. 56).*

In his sermon recorded in this chapter, Stephen makes a clear distinction between God and Jesus. He refers to *"God"* nineteen times and not once is he speaking of Jesus. In verse two, **God** is the *"God of glory,"* in verse thirty-two, **He** is the *"God of Abraham, Isaac, and Jacob,"* and in verse forty-eight, **He** is the *"Most High"* God. Stephen refers to **Jesus** in verse thirty-seven as *"a Prophet"* which *"the Lord your God shall raise up unto you of your brethren."* In verse fifty-two **Jesus** is the *"Just One; of whom ye have been now the betrayers and murderers."* So Stephen distinguishes between God and Jesus and gives no hint that to him they are one and the same person. Now look at verse sixty.

> *"And he kneeled down, and cried with a loud voice, Lord, lay not this sin to their charge."*

Now the question , to whom does the word *"Lord"* refer in this verse? Stephen says *"Lord"* five other times in this chapter when he is clearly speaking of the **Lord God.** In verses thirty to thirty-three, He is the "Lord God of Abraham, Isaac and Jacob" who spoke to Moses at the burning bush. In verse thirty-seven He is the *"Lord your God"* who promised to send Jesus as *"a Prophet"* like Moses. In verses forty-nine and fifty he is *"the Lord,"* the Creator of all. Look at the content of Stephen's prayer in verse sixty. *"Lord, lay not this sin to their **charge."*** He is for sure speaking to the **Lord**

God, for he has already said in verse seven that it is God who will **judge**. This agrees with Paul's statement in Acts chapter seventeen, verse thirty-one, that God *"will judge the world in righteousness,"* and Hebrews 12:23 that calls God the *"Judge of all."* Notice the similarity between Stephen's prayer and Paul's statement in Romans 8:33 .

> *"Who shall lay anything to the **charge** of God's elect? It is **God** that justifieth."*

So Stephen prayed to the *"Lord"* God that this awful sin not be laid to their charge, because he knew that the day would come when *"the dead, small and great, shall **stand before God**,"* and the books will be opened *(Rev. 20:12).*

Did John Pray To Jesus In Revelation Chapter Twenty-Two?

Another place in Scripture where some suppose they see a prayer to Jesus after his ascension to heaven, is John the Revelator's words to Jesus in Revelation 22:20, *"Amen. Even so, come, Lord Jesus."* But a closer look at the context in which this statement is made shows that, rather than a prayer, John's words were a **response** to Jesus who was speaking to him. Look at verse sixteen.

> *"I Jesus have sent mine angel to testify unto you these things in the churches."*

And now to verse twenty.

> *"He which testifieth these things saith, Surely I come quickly."* And John's response in the same verse is: *"Amen. Even so, come, Lord Jesus."*

The word *"Amen"* means *"so be it"* and is a term of agreement. So John's words, rather than being seen as a prayer must be seen as agreement with Jesus' statement to him, *"I come quickly."* If this is perceived as a prayer, it is a direct contradiction of Jesus' words as recorded by John himself in John 16:23, *"And in that day ye **shall ask me nothing**,"* and John 16:26, *"**At that day** ye shall ask **in my name**."*

Did Paul Pray To Jesus At The Time Of His Conversion?

In Acts chapter nine Saul of Tarsus *(Paul)* saw the Lord Jesus in a vision and talked with him, but there is nothing in this chapter that indicates that Paul prayed to Jesus, or believed that he had had an encounter with *"God."* Notice Ananias' words to him as recorded in Acts 22:14:

> *"The God of our fathers* [Abraham, Isaac, and Jacob], *hath chosen thee, that thou shouldest know **his will**, and see the **Just One**, and shouldest hear the voice of his* [Jesus'] *mouth."*

Notice, *"God has chosen you to **see Jesus*** [the Just One] *and hear his voice."* Remember Stephen had also called Jesus *"the Just One"* in Acts 7:52. Afterward Paul spoke of seeing **Jesus** *(I Cor. 9:1; 15:8),* but he never in any of his writings indicated that he had seen *"God."* Notice Paul's **first sermon** after his Damascus road encounter.

> *"And straightway he preached Christ in the synagogues, that he is the Son of God"* [not God] *(Acts 9:20).*

How Paul Prayed

In my book *"To God Be The Glory,"* I included a chapter titled *"How Paul Prayed."* In studying Scripture to write this chapter I found that the apostle Paul prayed thirty-four prayers in the book of Acts and his thirteen epistles. According to the scriptural record, **not one of those prayers was prayed to** Jesus. Thirty-two times it specifically says he prayed to *"God,"* *"the Father,"* and *"the Father of our Lord Jesus Christ."* The only verse I could find in any of Paul's writings that even resembles a prayer to Jesus is I Timothy 1:12:

> *"And I thank Christ Jesus our Lord, who hath enabled me, for that he counted me faithful, putting me into the ministry."*

This verse surely denotes an attitude of the heart rather than a prayer, because he says five verses later:

> *"Now unto the **King eternal, immortal, invisible, the only wise God**, be honor and glory for ever and ever. Amen."*

The **"King eternal, immortal, invisible"** is none other than *"the great King,"* the Lord God, God the Father, whom Paul called **"the only wise God."** Note the word *"invisible."* Our Lord Jesus was not invisible; he was seen by thousands.

Look closely at the following verses that tell us clearly to whom Paul prayed.

> *"And at midnight **Paul and Silas prayed, and sang praises unto God**: and the prisoners heard them (Acts 16:25).* They sang and prayed **to God**.

> *"Testifying both to the Jews, and also to the Greeks, **repentance toward God**, and faith toward our Lord Jesus Christ"* (Acts 20:21).

> *"And when he had thus spoken, he took bread, **and gave thanks to God** in presence of them all; and when he had broken it, he began to eat"* (Acts 27:35). Notice, **"to God."**

> *"And from thence, when the brethren heard of us, they came to meet us as far as Appi forum, and the three taverns: whom when Paul saw, **he thanked God, and took courage"*** (Acts 28:15).

> *"He that eateth, eateth to the Lord, for **he giveth God thanks**: and he that eateth not, to the Lord he eateth not, **and giveth God thanks"*** (Rom. 14:6).

> *"For it is written, As I live, saith **the Lord, every knee shall bow to me**, and every tongue shall **confess to God**. So then every one of us shall give account of himself **to God"*** (Rom. 14:11-12).

> *"Now I beseech you, brethren, for the Lord Jesus Christ's sake,....that ye strive together with me in **your prayers to God** for me"* (Rom. 15:30).

*"Judge in yourselves: is it comely that a woman **pray unto God** uncovered"* (I Cor. 11:13)?

*"For he that speaketh in an unknown tongue, speaketh not unto men, **but unto God**"* (I Cor. 14:2).

*"....but if there be no interpreter....let him speak to himself, and **to God**"* (I Cor. 14:28).

*"Being enriched in every thing to all bountifulness, which causeth through us thanksgiving **to God**"* (II Cor. 9:11).

*"For this cause **I bow my knees unto the Father** of our Lord Jesus Christ"* (Eph. 3:14).

*"Giving thanks always for all things **unto God and the Father** in the **name of our Lord Jesus Christ**"* (Eph. 5:20).

*"I thank **my God** upon every remembrance of you, Always in **every prayer of mine** for you all **making request** with joy"* (Phil. 1:3-4).

*"Be careful for nothing; but in every thing by prayer and supplication with thanksgiving **let your requests be made known unto God**. And the peace of **God,** which passeth all understanding, shall keep your hearts and minds **through Christ Jesus"*** (Phil. 4:6-7).

*"But my **God** shall supply all your need according to **his riches** in glory by Christ Jesus"* (Phil. 4:19).

*"We give **thanks to God** and the **Father** of our Lord Jesus Christ, praying always for you"* (Col. 1:3).

*"Withal **praying also** for us, **that God** would open us a door of utterance, to speak the mystery of Christ" (Col. 4:3).*

*"For what **thanks** can we render **to God** again for you, for all the joy wherewith we joy for your sakes **before our God**" (I Thess. 3:9).*

*"I exhort therefore, that, first of all, **supplications, prayers, intercessions,** and **giving of thanks,** be made for all men; For kings, and for all that are in authority; that we may lead a quiet and peaceable life in all godliness and honesty. For this is good and acceptable **in the sight of God our Savior; For there is one God,** and **one mediator between God and men, the man Christ Jesus**" (I Tim. 2:1-3, 5).*

*"I thank **my God**, making mention of thee always **in my prayers**" (Philemon 1:4).*

Notice carefully this statement by Southern Baptist scholar Millard Erickson:

*"Let us now summarize the matter of prayer to and worship of Jesus Christ. In the New Testament we have definite commands to pray to the Father. We also have the example of our Lord himself, as well as the model prayer that he gave his disciples and us. **We do not have such commands with respect to prayer to Jesus. Jesus himself never commanded it, nor did Paul or any of the other New Testament writers**" (p. 321).*

More Supporting Scriptures

Since most of us in Christianity have missed it so badly in the past as to whom we should pray, we need to look at more supporting Scriptures as we close this chapter.

*"...but if any man be **a worshipper of God**, and doeth his will, **him he heareth**" (John 9:31).*

*"Repent therefore of this thy wickedness, and **pray God**, if perhaps the thought of thine heart may be forgiven thee"* [Philip to Simon the Sorcerer] *(Acts 8:22).*

*"For they heard them speak with tongues, and **magnify God**" (Acts 10:46).*

*"If any of you lack wisdom, **let him ask of God**, that giveth to all men liberally and it shall be given him" (James 1:5).*

*"Every good gift and every perfect gift is from above, and cometh down from the **Father** of lights, with whom is no variableness, neither shadow of turning" (James 1:17).*

*"Therewith **bless we God**, even the **Father**" (James 3:9).*

*"And if ye **call on the Father**..." (I Peter 1:17).*

*"Ye also...offer up spiritual sacrifices, acceptable **to God** by **Jesus Christ**" (I Peter 2:5).*

In Conclusion

Since the above verses clearly teach us that the Apostles' view of prayer was that it should be offered to **God the Father**, and since the Bible is clearly void of any reference to a prayer offered to Jesus after his ascension, we must begin to pray in this manner. But you may say, "I have had many prayers answered that were prayed to Jesus." And I would answer, "So have we." We, our family, and friends have seen miracles of salvation, and provision through prayers prayed to Jesus. We have seen people healed of cancer, heart trouble, asthma, Crohn's disease, shingles, and various other sicknesses and diseases through prayer to Jesus. But this is only a testimony to **God the Father's** loving patience with our lack of understanding of Scripture. May I remind you that we do not get our doctrine from our experience, but we must get our doctrine from God's Holy Word and adjust our experience accordingly. Part of giving Him the glory as He has commanded is to offer Him the love, worship and prayers that He desires and deserves. I believe that as the light of this truth shines upon us, God the Father will require us to approach Him in the manner that He has prescribed, in order to see our prayers answered. And why shouldn't we pray to God the Father when James said:

> *"Every good gift and every perfect gift is from above, and* **cometh down from the Father**" *(James 1:17).*

And Paul said:

> *"But **my God** shall supply all your need according to **his riches** in glory **by Christ Jesus**" (Phil. 4:19).*

> *"Giving thanks always for all things **unto God and the Father*** in the name of our Lord Jesus Christ" (Eph. 5:20).*

Glory to God in the highest!

Paul Prayed To God

Location of Prayer in Scripture	To Whom it was Addressed
Acts 16:25	"God"
Acts 27:35	"God"
Acts 28:15	"God"
Romans 1:9-10	"God"
Romans 10:1	"God"
Romans 15:5-6	"God"
Romans 15:13	"God"
Romans 15:30	"God"
Romans 16:25-27	"God"
I Corinthians 1:4-9	"God"
II Corinthians 1:3-5	"God even the Father"
II Corinthians 2:14	"God"
II Corinthians 9:12-15	"God"
II Corinthians 13:7-9	"God"
Ephesians 1:15-23	"God"
Ephesians 3:14-21	"the Father of our Lord Jesus Christ"
Philippians 1:9-11	"God"
Philippians 4:20	"God our Father"
Colossians 1:9-12	"the Father" (God)
I Thessalonians 1:2-4	"God"
I Thessalonians 2:13	"God"
I Thessalonians 3:11-13	"God"
I Thessalonians 5:23-24	"God"
II Thessalonians 1:11-12	"God"
II Thessalonians 2:13-17	"God"
II Thessalonians 3:5	"the Lord...God"
II Thessalonians 3:16	"the Lord of peace"
I Timothy 1:17	"God"
I Timothy 6:13-17	"God" "whom no man hath seen"
II Timothy 1:3	"God"
II Timothy 1:16-18	"The Lord" (God)
II Timothy 4:14-18	"God"
Philemon 4-6	"God"

(For the answer as to why none of these prayers were addressed to Jesus, notice Paul's first sermon after his conversion on the Damascus Road. "And immediately he preached Christ in the synagogues, that he is the Son of God" - Acts 9:20).

Chapter Five

The Holy Spirit Is The Spirit of The Father

*"But when they deliver you up, take no thought how or what ye shall speak: for it shall be given you in that same hour what ye shall speak. For **it is not ye that speak, but the Spirit of your Father** which speaketh in you"* [Jesus speaking] *(Matt. 10:19-20).*

*"But when they shall lead you, and deliver you up, take no thought beforehand what ye shall speak, neither do ye premeditate: but whatsoever shall be given you in that hour, that speak ye: for **it is not ye that speak, but the Holy Ghost**"* [Jesus speaking] *(Mark 13:11).*

*"But when the **Comforter** is come, whom I will send unto you from the Father, even the **Spirit** of truth, **which proceedeth from the Father**, he shall testify of me"* [Jesus speaking] *(John 15:26).*

*"And, behold, I send **the promise of my Father** upon you: but tarry ye in the city of Jerusalem, until ye be endued with **power from on high**"* [Jesus speaking] *(Luke 24:49).*

*"The **spirit of the Lord God** is upon me; because the Lord hath anointed me to preach..."* [prophecy regarding Jesus] *(Isa. 61:1).*

*"The **Spirit of the Lord** is upon me, because **he** [the Lord God] hath anointed me to preach..."* [Jesus speaking] *(Luke 4:18).*

*"And Jesus being **full of the Holy Ghost** returned from Jordan, and was led by **the Spirit** into the wilderness"* *(Luke 4:1).*

I will begin this chapter by saying that I have great reverence for the Spirit of God. I had rather die today than speak one word against the Holy Spirit. I was baptized with the Holy Ghost at the age of ten at an altar of prayer. Throughout over fifty years of ministry I have been anointed, inspired, empowered, guided and protected by the Holy Spirit.

But here is a question worthy of serious consideration by intelligent, God-loving, God-fearing people everywhere. Does the God of the Bible exist as three co-equal, co-eternal persons: God the Father, God the Son, and God the Holy Spirit-the glory equal, the majesty eternal, the blessed Trinity? The clear scriptural answer to that question is a resounding no! The God of the Bible is **one** entity, being, person.

Listen To The Old Testament

"Hear [listen]*, O Israel: The Lord our God is **one Lord***" *(Deut. 6:4).*

*"See now that I, even I, am he, and **there is no god with me**" (Deut. 32:39).*

*"Stand up and bless the Lord your God...Thou even art **Lord alone**...and the host of heaven **worshipeth thee**" (Neh. 9:5-6).*

*"There is none holy as the Lord: for **there is none beside thee:** neither is there any rock like our God" (I Sam. 2:2).*

*"**Thou art God alone**" (Ps. 86:10).*

*"O Lord of hosts, God of Israel...**thou art the God, even thou alone**" (Isa. 37:16).*

*"Whom hast thou reproached and blasphemed? Even against the **Holy One** of Israel" (Isa. 37:23).*

*"Ye are my witnesses, saith the Lord...**before me there was no God formed, neither shall there be after me**. I, even I, am the Lord; and beside me there is no savior"* (Isa. 43:10-11).

*"**Is there a God beside me?** Yea, **there is no God; I know not any**"* (Isa. 44:8).

*"**I am the Lord** that maketh all things; **that stretcheth forth the heavens alone**; that spreadeth abroad the earth **by myself**"* (Isa. 44:24).

*"**I am the Lord, and there is none else, there is no God beside me**...there is **none beside me**. I am the Lord, and there is **none else**"* (Isa. 45:5-6).

*"Thus saith the Lord, the **Holy One** of Israel, **and his Maker. I made the earth**, and created man upon it: I, even my hands, have stretched out the heavens"* (Isa. 45:11-12).

*"**For thus saith the Lord that created the heavens; God himself...I am the Lord; and there is none else**"* (Isa. 45:18).

*"...**there is no God else beside me**; a just God and a Savior; **there is none beside me...I am God, and there** is none else"* (Isa. 45:21-22).

*"I am God and there is **none else**; I am God, and there is **none like me**"* (Isa. 46:9).

*"As for our redeemer, **the Lord of hosts is his name**, the **Holy One** of Israel"* (Isa. 47:4).

*"**But the Lord is the true God**, he is the living God, and everlasting king...**The Lord of hosts is his name**" (Jer. 10:10, 16).*

*"I am the Lord your God, and **none else**" (Joel 2:27).*

*"Have we not all **one father**? Hath not **one God** created us" (Mal. 2:10)?*

With the foregoing Scriptures in mind please pause and ask yourself, what do *"alone," "none else," "by myself"* and *"Holy One"* mean?

Consider Moses' address to Israel as recorded in Deuteronomy 4:33, 35-36:

*"Did ever people hear the voice of God speaking out of the midst of the fire, as thou hast heard, and live? **Unto thee it was shown, that thou mightest know** that the Lord he is God; **there is none else beside him. Out of heaven he made thee to hear his voice**, that he might instruct thee; and **upon earth he showed thee his great fire;** and **thou heardest his words out of the midst of the fire**"* [Moses speaking] *(Deut. 4:33, 35-36).*

Listen To The Apostles

*"Is he the God of the Jews only? Is he not also of the Gentiles? Yes, of the Gentiles also: **Seeing it is one God** which shall justify the circumcision by faith, and the uncircumcision through faith"* [Paul speaking] *(Romans 3:29-30).*

*"**There is none other God but one**...to us there is but **one God, the Father**...and one Lord Jesus Christ" (I Cor. 8:4, 6).*

*"Now a mediator is not a mediator of one, but **God is one**" (Gal. 3:20).*

*"**One God and Father of all, who is above**, and through all, and in you all" (Eph. 4:6).*

*"For there is **one God**, and one mediator between God and men, the man Christ Jesus" (I Tim. 2:5).*

*"**God cannot be tempted**....But every man is tempted...."* *(James 1:13-14)*

[**Jesus**] *"....**being** forty days **tempted** of the devil" (Luke 4:1-2).*

*"Thou believest that there is **one God**; thou doest well: the devils also believe, and tremble"* [James speaking] *(James 2:19).*

*"For **Christ** also hath once suffered for sins, the just for the unjust, that he might **bring us to God**...who is gone into heaven, and is **on the right hand of God**"* [Peter speaking] *(I Pet. 3:18, 22).*

*"...that **God** in all things may be glorified **through** Jesus Christ" (I Pet. 4:11).*

*"**No man hath seen God at any time**"* [John speaking] *(I John 4:12).* Note: Thousands of people saw Jesus.

*"...denying **the only Lord God**, and our Lord Jesus Christ* [Jude speaking] *(Jude v. 4).*

*"Behold, a throne was set in heaven, and **one sat on the throne**...and they* [the beasts] *rest not day and night, saying, Holy, holy, holy, **Lord God Almighty**"* [John the Revelator] *(Rev. 4:2, 8).*

Listen To Our Savior Jesus Himself

> *"And he said unto him, Why callest thou me good? There is none good but **one, that is God**" (Matt. 19:17).*

> *"And call no man your father upon the earth: for **one is your Father, which is in heaven**. Neither be ye called masters: for one is your **Master**, even Christ" (Matt. 23:9-10).*

> *"In that hour Jesus rejoiced in spirit, and said, I thank thee, O **Father, Lord of heaven and earth**" (Luke 10:21).*

> *"And Jesus answered him, The first of all the commandments is, Hear, O Israel; **The Lord our God is one Lord**...And the scribe said unto him, Well, **Master**, thou has said the truth: for there is **one God; and there is none other but he: And when Jesus saw that he answered discreetly, he said unto him, Thou are not far from the kingdom of God**" (Mark 12:29, 32, 34).* [What does that say about those who do not believe that **God is *"one?"***]

> *"You do not seek the glory that is from **the one and only God**...**the Father**" (John 5:44-45 NASB).*

> *"**Father**...this is life eternal, that they might know **thee the only true God**, and Jesus Christ, whom thou hast sent" (John 17:1, 3).*

Yes, the God of the Bible is one entity, being, person. He is none other than the eternal God, God Almighty, the great Creator of all, our heavenly Father! So who or what is the Holy Spirit (or Ghost) that is spoken of so often in Scripture? The Holy Ghost is the spirit of the Father, the power and presence of God in action. Notice the verses quoting Jesus' words at the beginning of this chapter. He tells the disciples in Mark 13:11 not to premeditate what they will say when they are called before the council for their beliefs, *"for it* *is not ye that speak, but **the Holy Ghost***" that was in them. He says the same thing in Matthew 10:19-20, but this time he says it is *"**the Spirit of your Father** which speaketh in you."* Jesus uses the phrases *"the Holy Ghost"* and *"the Spirit of your Father"* interchangeably because **the Holy Ghost is the Spirit of God our Father**.

Notice the accounts of Jesus' water baptism in the four Gospels. Matthew 3:16 says:

> *"...and he saw **the Spirit of God** descending like a dove, and lighting upon him..."*

Luke 3:22 says:

> *"And **the Holy Ghost** descended in a bodily shape like a dove upon him..."*

When Mark and John give their accounts of Jesus' baptism, they just say it was *"**the Spirit**"* descending from heaven like a dove. Now, was it *"the Spirit of God" (Matt. 3:16)*, *"the Holy Ghost" (Luke 3:22)*, or *"the Spirit" (Mark 1:10; John 1:32)* that descended on Jesus like a dove? It was the Spirit of God the Father referred to in the New Testament as the Holy Spirit (Ghost). God is a Spirit, and He is Holy, thus He is *"the Holy Spirit."* When God sent the Holy Spirit on the day of Pentecost, He sent a portion of Himself. **The Bible for sure does not teach that there are two Spirits of God, one called "God the Father," and one called "God the Holy Ghost".**

> *"For by **one Spirit** are we all baptized into one body...and have been all made to drink into **one Spirit**" (I Cor. 12:13).*

> *"For through him* [Christ] *we both have access by **one Spirit** unto the Father" (Eph. 2:18).*

> *"But if **the Spirit of him** [God the Father] *that **raised up Jesus from the dead** dwell in you, **he** that raised up Christ from the dead shall also quicken your mortal bodies by **his Spirit** that dwelleth in you" (Rom. 8:11).*

Listen To Gabriel's Words To Mary In Luke Chapter One

> *"He* [Jesus] *shall be great, and shall be called Son of the* **Highest** [God the Father]*; and the* **Lord God** *shall give unto him the throne of his father David" (v. 32).*

> *"And the angel answered and said unto her* [Mary]*,* **The Holy Ghost** *shall come upon thee, and* **the power of the Highest** *shall overshadow thee:* **therefore** *also that holy thing which shall be born of thee shall be called* **the Son of God***" (v. 35).*

So the Holy Ghost is the Spirit of God the Father, *"the Highest"*, thus it is the power of God. Jesus said regarding the coming of the **Holy Ghost**:

> *"And, behold, I send the promise of my Father upon you: but tarry ye in the city of Jerusalem, until ye be endued with* **power from on high***" (Luke 24:49).*

For more proof from Jesus that the Holy Spirit is the **power of God** and not the third person of a Trinity look at Matthew 12:28:

> *"But if I cast out devils by* **the Spirit of God***, then the kingdom of God is come unto you."*

Now contrast this with his words in Luke 11:20:

> *"But if I with* **the finger of God** *cast out devils, no doubt the kingdom of God is come unto you."*

The phrase *"the finger of God"* is no doubt a reference to Exodus 8:19 where Pharaoh's magicians, after seeing God's power through Moses demonstrated by the plagues, said: *"This is* **the finger of God***."*

The NIV text *notes* say correctly of Exodus 8:19, *"Finger of God: a concise and colorful figure of speech referring to* **God's miraculous power***."* So Jesus was casting out devils, not by the third person of the Trinity, but by *"God's miraculous power."*

The Holy Spirit Proceeds From The Father

Consider Jesus' words as recorded in John 15:26:

> *"But when the Comforter is come, whom I will send unto you*
> ***from the Father**, even the Spirit of truth, which **proceedeth***
> ***from the Father**, he shall testify of me."*

The word *"proceedeth"* in the foregoing verse is very important to our understanding of the Holy Spirit (*"the Comforter," "the Spirit of truth"*). It is the Greek word *ekporeuomai* and means *"to depart, be discharged, proceed - **come forth out of**, go forth out, issue, **proceed out of.**"* It is the same word Jesus used in Matthew 4:4 when he said:

> *"Man shall not live by bread alone, but by every word that*
> ***proceedeth out of the mouth of God.***"

It is also the word that is used in Revelation 11:5 when it says of the two last-day witnesses:

> *"And if any man will hurt them, **fire proceedeth out of their***
> ***mouth**, and devoureth their enemies."*

So instead of the Holy Spirit being pictured in Scripture as a separate and distinct person of God, it is seen as the breath of God Himself, God's Spirit that comes forth out of the Father. For more biblical proof of this fact look at Peter's words in Acts 2:17-18:

> *"And it shall come to pass in the last days, **saith God, I** will*
> *pour out **of** my Spirit upon all flesh....in those days **of** my*
> *Spirit."*

This for sure is not a promise to send the third person of a trinity, but a portion of God's own spirit. Some other Bible translations of Acts 2:17 make this even clearer:

> *"God says, This will happen in the last days: I will pour*
> *upon everyone **a portion** of my spirit" (The New English*
> *Bible).*

123

> *"....says God, that I will pour out **a portion** of **my spirit** on all mankind" (New American Bible).*

> *"....says God, **I will pour from the Spirit** of **me** on all flesh" (The Interlinear Greek-English N.T.)*

> *"....says God, I shall pour out **some of my spirit**" (New World Bible).*

The much respected Dr. Billy Graham, writing in his book titled *The Holy Spirit* states:

> *"Throughout the Bible it is clear that the Holy Spirit is God Himself. This is seen in the attributes which are given to the Holy Spirit. Without exception these attributes are those of God himself" (p. 5).*

The Holy Ghost Is The Father of Jesus Christ

If the Holy Ghost is viewed in our theology as a separate person of God, one of three co-equal, co-eternal entities, this adds untold confusion as to who is really the father of the baby born from the virgin's womb. Was it "God the Father" or "God the Holy Ghost"?

> *"Now the birth of Jesus Christ was on this wise: When as his mother Mary was espoused to Joseph, before they came together, she was found with child **of the Holy Ghost**" (Matt. 1:18).*

What is that again Matthew? Are you telling us that the baby in the womb of Mary had been begotten in her by *"the Holy Ghost"*? Would that not make the baby Jesus the Son of the Holy Ghost? But we are told again and again in the New Testament that he is the *"Son of the Father"* and *"the only begotten of the Father."* On what authority did Matthew make his statement in verse eighteen? Look at verse twenty.

> *"But while he thought on these things, behold, the angel of the LORD appeared unto him in a dream, saying, Joseph,*

> *thou son of David, fear not to take unto thee Mary thy wife:*
> ***for that which is conceived in her is of the Holy Ghost.***"

Through a **creative act** of God's Spirit, the Holy Ghost, Jesus Christ was conceived in the womb of the virgin Mary.

> "*And the angel answered and said unto her, The Holy Ghost shall come upon thee, and the power of the Highest shall overshadow thee: therefore also that holy thing which shall be born of thee shall be called the Son of God*" [Gabriel to Mary] *(Luke 1:35)*. Our conclusion must be that the **Holy Ghost** is the **power of the Highest**, the **Spirit of God**, and the **Father** of Jesus Christ.

There Is No "Trinity"

The preceding Scriptures, properly understood, effectively destroy the so-called "doctrine of the Trinity" as taught in error by most of Christianity for almost seventeen hundred years. The lack of biblical verses supporting the doctrine of the Trinity, compels many modern knowledgeable and sincere **trinitarian** scholars to admit in their writings that it is not a doctrine to be found in Holy Scripture.

Writing as a **trinitarian** in his best selling book, *Christian Doctrine,* Professor Shirley C. Guthrie Jr., makes these strong admissions:

> "***The Bible does not teach the doctrine of the Trinity.***" *(p. 76).* "***The doctrine of the Trinity is not found in the Bible***" *(p. 80).* [1]

Respected **trinitarian,** evangelical biblical scholar Professor Charles C. Ryrie, writing in his well known work, *Basic Theology,* admits:

> "***It is fair to say that the Bible does not clearly teach the doctrine of the Trinity.*** *In fact,* ***there is not even one proof text****, if by proof text we mean a verse or passage that 'clearly' states that there is* ***one God*** *who exists in* ***three persons***" *(p. 89).* "*The above illustrations prove the fallacy*

*of concluding that if something is not proof texted in the Bible we cannot clearly teach the results...**If that were so, I could never teach the doctrine of the Trinity or the deity of Christ or the deity of the Holy Spirit*** (p. 90).* [2]

Trinitarian Millard J. Erickson, research professor of theology at S.W. Baptist Theological Seminary (Southern Baptist) in his book on the Trinity, *God In Three Persons,* is compelled by the biblical evidence to make some strong admissions:

> *"This doctrine in many ways presents strange paradoxes... It is a widely disputed doctrine, which has provoked discussion throughout all the centuries of the church's existence. It was the very first doctrine dealt with systematically by the church, yet is still one of the most misunderstood and disputed doctrines. Further, **it is not clearly or explicitly taught anywhere in Scripture**, yet it is widely regarded as a central doctrine, indispensable to the Christian faith. In this regard, it goes contrary to what is virtually an axiom [a self evident truth] of biblical doctrine, namely, that there is a direct correlation between the Scriptural clarity of a doctrine and its cruciality to the faith and life of the church"* (p. 11-12).* [3]

Erickson goes on to say that some oppose the doctrine of the Trinity because of :

> *"....the **apparent silence** of the Bible on this important subject. This contention notes that **there really is no explicit statement of the doctrine of the Trinity in the Bible**, particularly since the revelation by textual criticism of the **spurious nature of I John 5:7**. Other passages have been seen on closer study to be applicable **only under the greatest strain**. If this is the doctrine that especially constitutes Christianity's uniqueness, how can it be **only implied** in the biblical revelation? In response to the complaint*

that a number of portions of the Bible are ambiguous or unclear, we often hear a statement something like, 'it is the peripheral matters that are hazy or on which there seem to be conflicting biblical materials. The core beliefs are clearly and unequivocally revealed.' This argument would appear to fail us with respect to the doctrine of the Trinity, however. **For here is a seemingly crucial matter where the Scriptures do not speak loudly or clearly. Little direct response can be made to this charge. It is unlikely that any text of Scripture can be shown to teach the doctrine of the Trinity in a clear, direct, and unmistakable fashion.***

Trinitarian Douglas McCready in his work, *He Came Down From Heaven*, states:

"New Testament scholars disagree whether the N.T. directly calls Jesus God. In terms of first century Judaism, it would be understandable if no N.T. writer described Jesus as God because of the difficulty such language would create for early Christians with a Jewish background... **It is important to note that every passage that identifies Jesus as 'theos' can be translated other ways or has variants that read differently***" (p. 51). "In biblical Judaism the term 'messiah' did not necessarily carry any connotation of divine status, and Jews of Jesus' day were not expecting their messiah to be other than human." (p. 55). "While some have used the title* ['Son of God'] *to denote Jesus' deity, neither the Judaism nor the paganism of Jesus' day understood the title in this way.* **Neither did the early church***" (p. 56).* [4]

Trinitarian scholar and famous church historian, Professor Cyril C. Richardson, in his book, *The Doctrine of the Trinity,* says:

"I cannot but think that the doctrine of **the Trinity, far from being established, is open to serious criticism,** *because*

*of both the modern understanding of the Scripture, and inherent confusions in its expression. **Texts were torn from their contexts and misused to no small degree**" (p. 16). "**Much of the defense of the Trinity as a revealed doctrine, is really an evasion of the objections that can be brought against it**" (p. 16). "**It is not a doctrine specifically to be found in the New Testament. It is a creation of the fourth-century Church**" (p. 17).* [5]

Trinitarians Roger Olson and Christopher Hall say of this doctrine in their book, *The Trinity:*

> *"It is understandable that the importance placed on this doctrine is perplexing to many lay Christians and students. **Nowhere is it clearly and unequivocally stated in Scripture.** How can it be so important if it is not explicitly stated in Scripture?"* (p. 1). *"The doctrine of the Trinity developed gradually **after the completion of the N.T.** in the heat of controversy. The **full-blown doctrine of the Trinity** was spelled out in the **fourth century** at two great ecumenical councils: Nicea (325 A.D.) and Constantinople (381 A.D.)"* (p. 1-2). [6]

The Fourth Century Church Councils

Professors Olson and Hall bring us to a subject that we should explore further in this chapter on the Holy Spirit. That is the conclusions of several church councils that were held in the fourth century A.D., which did incalculable damage to the understanding of future Christians as to whom the One Most High God of the Bible is.

The first of these "ecumenical" councils was called in 325 A.D. by the Roman Emperor Constantine at his palace in Nicea, a city in what is now Turkey. It was called to settle a troubling dispute by the Christian theologians of two prominent cities of the empire, Antioch and Alexandria, regarding the person of Jesus Christ and his relationship to God the Father. It consisted of some 300 bishops and was presided over and largely controlled by the emperor himself from his exalted place on a wrought gold chair. In their work, *A Summary of Christian History*, Robert Baker and John Landers write, *"Constantine dominated the council, addressing it when he desired and **determining its doctrinal conclusions.**"* [7]

Many Christians believe that the doctrine of the Trinity can be traced back to the Council of Nicea, but a closer look at the conclusions of that gathering proves that this is not the case. This council mostly dealt with the person of Jesus Christ, and after one month of what were often very contentious deliberations, concluded that Jesus is *"of one substance with the Father.... true God from true God."* The Creed of Nicea reads:

> *"We believe in one God, the Father almighty, maker of all things visible and invisible; And in one Lord Jesus Christ, the Son of God, begotten from the Father, only-begotten, that is, from the substance of the Father, God from God, light from light, true God from true God, begotten not made, of one substance with the Father, through whom all things came into being, things in heaven and things on earth....,* ***and in the Holy Spirit..***" [8]

In making this statement the council was saying in essence, "Jesus is God, just as the Father is God." The question that the Council of Nicea left unresolved was the place of the Holy Spirit in Christian dogma and whether it (he) proceeded from the Father, or Christ, or from both. Several regional councils were held in the ensuing decades to deal with this issue. In 381 A.D. (56 years after Nicea) what is known as the *"Second Ecumenical Council"* was convened in Constantinople by Emperor Theodosius I. It was not truly "ecumenical" as it was attended by only 186 bishops, none from the west, with no representatives of Pope Damasus I. But it acted as if it had the full authority of the universal church. This council reiterated the Council of Nicea's teaching on Christ's equality with God and formulated a new creed that declared the divinity of the Holy Spirit. This new Creed which scholars refer to as *"Nicene-Constantinopolitan"* expanded Nicea and then states:

*"We believe in the Holy Spirit, the Lord, the giver of life,
who proceeds from the Father and the Son. With the Father
and the Son **he** is worshiped and glorified."*

Thus the mistaken idea that the Holy Spirit is the third person of a triune God
came to be a part of Christian dogma. But the subject was by no means laid
to rest. Yale history professor Ramsey MacMullen begins the preface of his
book, *Voting About God in Early Church Councils,* thus:

> ***"How did Christians agree on their definition of the
> Supreme Being, Triune?*** *It was the work of the bishops
> assembled at Nicea in AD 325, made formal and given
> weight by majority vote and supported after much struggle
> by later assemblies, notably at Chalcedon (451) - likewise
> by majority vote. Such was the determining process. Thus
> agreement was arrived at, **and became dogma widely
> accepted down to our own day."*** [9]

He says the number of provincial and so-called ecumenical councils held
between the years 325 A.D. and 553 A.D. cannot have totaled less than
15,000. However, this great number of gatherings, with their countless
hours of contentious debate did not lay to rest the question regarding who
God is. A famous Christian author whom Dr. Billy Graham calls one of his
favorite evangelical writers said in a letter to me recently: *"As you know, the
Trinity was one of the most hotly debated topics of the first five centuries, and
still it has us **scratching our heads.*** " [10]

Dr. Graham himself says, *"When I first began to study the Bible years ago,
the doctrine of the Trinity was one of the **most complex problems** I had to
encounter. **I have never resolved it**, for it contains an aspect of mystery:
Though I do not totally understand it to this day, I accept it as a revelation
of God."* [11] Note: Should we not understand who God is?

Trinitarian professors Roger Olson and Christopher Hall, writing in their
book, *The Trinity,* document the centuries old struggle over the doctrine of

the Trinity. They include this statement:

> *"John of Damascus (650-749 A.D.) added his own trinitarian reflections to the church's treasury, especially in regard to **the Spirit's role** in the Trinity. Phillip Carey notes that John's 'Exact Exposition of the Orthodox Faith'....is the most comprehensive brief statement of **Greek trinitarian doctrine.** John's work demonstrates how **the church's understanding of the Holy Spirit had matured** since Nicea (325) and Constantinople (381). Whereas **the Spirit had appeared almost as a footnote to the Creed of Nicea**, John writes richly of the Spirit's **person** and work."* [12]

This is John of Damascus writing regarding the *"person"* of the Holy Spirit about 700 A.D. when *"the church's understanding had matured."* It seems strange that this John would have known more than the Apostles Paul, Peter, James and John, who wrote in the first century A.D. That should alert us to the fact that there is something terribly wrong with this *"Greek trinitarian doctrine."*

Trinitarian Millard J. Erickson, research professor of theology at S.W. Baptist Theological Seminary (Southern Baptist) in his book on the Trinity, *God In Three Persons,* says:

> *"Another reason for the importance of this doctrine is that it poses a **continuing problem**. Some doctrines are worked out and thus cease to be major problems. This state has not been attained with respect to the Trinity, however. **The doctrine of the Trinity is a perennial problem, like the problem of evil.** It therefore needs our continued attention"* (p. 19). [emphasis mine] [13]

A further comment from Erickson regarding the councils should be noted.

> *"**Placing trust in the Bible supremely** and in each Christian's ability to interpret it under the illumination of the Holy Spirit, such persons do not automatically*

*concede the correctness of the council's conclusions. Thus,
the declaration of the councils must be scrutinized and
evaluated. **Perhaps the councils did not come to correct
and final conclusions. Since some councils overruled and
contradicted earlier ones, in principle not all of them could
have been correct.** It therefore becomes incumbent on us to
scrutinize carefully the creeds formulated by the councils,
to make certain they embody most fully the truth about the
deity."* [14] To which I would add a hearty, "Amen!"

Another creed formulated sometime between Constantinople *(381)* and
Chalcedon *(451)* is the Athanasian Creed. Though it was named for
Athanasius, Bishop of Alexandria, it was probably not written by him, but
has had wide acceptance down through the centuries. This creed is likely the
source of much of the oppression that has accompanied the doctrine of the
Trinity every since its inception. The Athanasian Creed reads in part:

*"Whoever wishes to be saved must, first of all, hold the
Catholic* [universal] *faith, for, unless he keeps it whole and
inviolate, **he will undoubtedly perish for ever.***

*Now this is the Catholic faith: We worship one God in the
Trinity and the Trinity in unity, without either confusing
the persons or dividing the substance; for the person of the
Father is one, the Son's is another, the Holy Spirit's another;
but the Godhead of Father, Son and Holy Spirit is one, their
glory equal, their majesty equally eternal. So there is one
Father, not three Fathers; one Son, not three Sons; one Holy
Spirit, not three Holy Spirits. **And in this Trinity there is no
before or after, no greater or lesser, but all three persons
are equally eternal with each other and fully equal.** Thus,
in all things, as has already been stated above, both unity
in the Trinity and Trinity in the unity must be worshipped.
Let him therefore who wishes to be saved think this of the
Trinity. This is the Catholic faith. **Unless one believes it
faithfully and firmly, he cannot be saved."** [15]*

132

Had the men who formed this creed not read their Bibles?

> *"My Father, which gave them me, **is greater than all***"
> [Jesus speaking] *(John 10:29).*

> *"I go unto the Father: **for my Father is greater than I**"*
> *(John 14:28).*

> *"The head of every man is Christ; and **the head of Christ is**
> **God**" (I Cor. 11:3).*

> *"One God and Father of all, **who is above all**" (Eph. 4:6).*

> *"And ye are Christ's; **and Christ is God's**" (I Cor. 3:23).*

> *"Then cometh the end, when he shall have delivered up the
> kingdom **to God, even the Father;** when he shall have put
> down all rule and all authority and power. And when all
> things shall be subdued unto him, **then shall the Son also
> himself be subject unto him** [God the Father]; **that God may
> be all in all**" (I Cor. 15:24, 28).* Note: The word **"subject"**
> above is the Greek word **"hupotasso"** *(Strong's #5293)* -
> which means *"**subordinate, in an inferior position.**"*

> *"Called of God an high priest....Jesus, **made an high priest
> for ever** after the order of Melchizedek" (Heb. 5:10; 6:20).*

> *"Jesus Christ the same yesterday, and today, and **for ever**"*
> *(Heb. 13:8).*

All of these creeds sought to canonize belief in the full deity of Christ, and
after Nicea, the full deity of the Holy Spirit, as distinct and separate persons
of God. What we see is the birth and hardening in the minds of misguided
or sometimes wicked men of the mistaken, unbiblical doctrine of the Trinity.
(Constantine murdered his relatives to ensure that his three sons would be

his successors. [16] He continued to build pagan temples after his supposed conversion, and it is doubtful that he ever abandoned sun-worship, yet he considered himself the thirteenth Apostle. [17] Christianity can find better heroes). I agree with someone's comment that "the doctrine of the Trinity is like sausage; you think a lot less of it after you see how it was made."

Erickson further states:

> *"In fact, history suggests that the doctrine of the Trinity has been **part of a great doctrinal system that has been used to justify oppression and exploitation.** Whether this doctrine was actually correlated with oppression, **it has certainly accompanied such oppression.**"* [18] [emphasis mine]

Religious Persecution

Have you ever been persecuted for your Christian faith? If you live in so-called Christian America the answer is probably "No." But you can change that immediately. Just let it be known that you believe Jesus Christ is the supernaturally conceived, virgin-born, sinless Son of God-savior, redeemer, Messiah and soon coming king-but that you do not believe that he is the eternal God, or the second person of a Trinity, and your situation will change swiftly. You will be hated, despised, rejected, and called names such as heretic and blasphemer. But Jesus said such persecution pays great dividends.

> *"They shall put you out of the synagogues....and these things will they do unto you, because they have not known **the Father, nor me"** (John 16:2-3).*

> *"**Blessed are ye,** when men shall hate you, and when they shall separate you from their company, and shall reproach you, and cast out your name as evil, for **the Son of Man's sake.** Rejoice ye in that day, and **leap for joy:** for, behold, **your reward is great in heaven"** (Luke 6:22-23).*

Must A Person Believe In The Trinity To Be Saved?

Here is a good question for Christianity. Did Jesus or his Apostles teach that belief in the Trinity was necessary for salvation? Would they have classified someone as an "anti-christ," "blasphemer," "cultist," or "heretic" who did not believe that the One Most High God of the Bible is in reality "three co-equal, co-eternal persons, the glory equal, the majesty equally eternal?" The answer of course is "no." What did they teach that a person must believe in order to be saved?

> *"For God* [the eternal being] *so loved the world, that he gave his only begotten Son* [a virgin-born human being], *that whosoever **believeth in him** should not perish, but have everlasting life" (John 3:16).*

> *"He that heareth my word, and believeth on **him that sent me**, hath everlasting life"* [Jesus speaking] *(John 5:24).*

> *"Jesus cried and said, He that believeth on **me**, believeth not on me, but on **him** that sent me" (John 12:44).*

> *"Father....this is **life eternal**, that they might know **thee** the **only true God**, and Jesus Christ, whom thou has sent"* [Jesus speaking] *(John 17:1, 3).* Notice: There is no mention of a third person in these verses.

> *"Truly our fellowship is with the Father, and with his Son Jesus Christ" (I John 1:3).*

> *"Who is a liar but he that denieth that Jesus is the Christ* [Messiah]*? He is antichrist that denieth **the Father and the Son" (I John 2:22).***

> *"And every spirit that confesseth that Jesus Christ is come in the flesh is of God" (I John 4:2).*

> *"Whosoever shall confess that Jesus is **the Son of God**,* [not "God" or "the second person of the Trinity"]*, God **dwelleth in him, and he in God" (I John 4:15).***

*"Whosoever believeth that Jesus is the **Christ** [Messiah - not "God"] **is born of God**" (I John 5:1).*

*"He that believeth on the Son of God hath the witness in himself: he that believeth not God hath made him a liar; because he believeth not the record that **God gave of his Son**" (I John 5:10).*

No requirement of a belief in a trinity for salvation is even hinted. On the basis of these and every other Scripture in the Bible, the late minister of the gospel and one of my heroes, Adrian Rogers, was sadly mistaken when he said often, *"Define the Trinity and lose your mind, deny the Trinity and lose your soul."* [19]

Please consider these questions. Did Jesus require of the dying thief a belief in the Trinity in order for him to be saved?

> *"And he said unto Jesus, Lord, remember me when thou comest into **thy kingdom**. And Jesus said unto him, Verily I say unto thee, **today shalt thou be with me in paradise**" (Luke 23:42-43).*

Did Peter require a belief in the Trinity for the multitude to be saved at Pentecost?

> *"Jesus of Nazareth, **a man approved of God** among you by miracles and wonders and signs, **which God did by him** in the midst of you...**Repent** and **be baptized** every one of you **in the name of Jesus Christ** for the remission of sins, and ye shall receive the gift of the Holy Ghost" (Acts 2:22, 38).*

Did Philip require a belief in the Trinity of the eunuch for salvation?

> *"And Philip said, if thou believest with all thine heart, thou mayest [be baptized]. **And he answered and said, I believe that Jesus Christ is the Son of God**" [not God] (Acts 8:37).*

Did Paul and Silas require belief in a Trinity of the Philippian jailer for salvation?

> *"And they said, Believe on the Lord Jesus Christ, and thou shalt be saved, and thy house" (Acts 16:31).*

Have you ever heard of an event that was held for the salvation of souls, be it revival, campmeeting , or crusade, where those who responded to the gospel message were met at the altar, or taken to a side room, and had the doctrine of the Trinity or the Incarnation explained to them, **before they were permitted to claim to be saved?** I think not! Then obviously these are not beliefs that are necessary for salvation.

> *"I believe that Jesus Christ is the Son of God"* [the eunuch speaking] *(Acts 8:37).*

> *"And straightway he preached Christ in the synagogues, that **he is the son of God**"* [Paul's first sermon] *(Acts 9:20).*

> **"Whosoever believeth that Jesus is the Christ** [Messiah - anointed one of God] **is born of God"** *(I John 5:1).*

So with the foregoing scriptures and countless others stating otherwise, why would so many Christians consider other people "heretics" who do not believe in the doctrine of the Trinity? Because they are looking through glasses heavily tinted by false tradition.

> *"Thus have ye made the commandment of God of none effect by your **tradition**"* [Jesus speaking] *(Matt. 15:6).*

> *"Beware lest any man spoil you through **philosophy** and vain deceit, after the **tradition** of men....and not after Christ"* [Paul speaking] *(Col. 2:8).*

As a scientist said recently on TV, acknowledging the errors of Darwinism, *"We have looked at science through the philosophy of Darwin, rather than looking at Darwin through proven science."* Do you see how this analogy applies to the doctrine of a trinity? For some seventeen-hundred years, Christianity has looked at Scripture through its theology, rather than holding its theology up to the light of Holy Scripture.

We have served the triune *"God of theology,"* rather than the One Most High God of Holy Scripture and it has left us void of apostolic power. It reminds me of the old preacher who decried the scourge of empty prayer rooms and said, *"We have substituted tea parties, ice cream suppers and chicken dinners, and it has left us as weak as the tea, as cold as the ice cream, and as dead as the chicken."*

But in the last days:
> *"The people that do know **their God** shall be **strong**, and **do exploits"** [mighty deeds] (Daniel 11:32).*

Please Consider These Biblical Facts

Paul never sent greetings from a third person of a trinity called the Holy Spirit.
> *"Grace to you and peace from **God our Father**, and the Lord **Jesus Christ"** (Rom. 1:7).*

> *"Grace be unto you, and peace from **God our Father**, and from the Lord **Jesus Christ"** (I Cor. 1:3).*

> *"Grace be to you, and peace, from **God our Father**, and from the Lord **Jesus Christ"** (II Cor. 1:2).*

> *"Grace be to you, and peace, from **God the Father**, and from the Lord **Jesus Christ"** (Gal. 1:3).*

> *"Grace be to you, and peace, from **God our Father**, and from the Lord **Jesus Christ"** (Eph. 1:2).*

> *"Grace be unto you, and peace, from **God our Father**, and from the Lord **Jesus Christ"** (Phil 1:2).*

"Grace be unto you, and peace, from **God our Father** *and the Lord* **Jesus Christ**. *We give thanks* **to God and the Father** *of our Lord* **Jesus Christ**, *praying always for you"* *(Col. 1:2-3).*

"Unto the church of the Thessalonians which is in **God the Father** *and in the Lord* **Jesus Christ**: *Grace be unto you, and peace, from* **God our Father**, *and the Lord* **Jesus Christ"** *(I Thess. 1:1).* **Where is the much celebrated triune?**

"Unto the church of the Thessalonians in **God our Father** *and the Lord* **Jesus Christ**: *Grace unto you, and peace, from* **God our Father** *and the Lord* **Jesus Christ"** *(II Thess. 1:1-2).*

"Grace, and mercy, and peace, from **God our Father** *and* **Jesus Christ** *our Lord"* *(I Tim. 1:2).*

"Grace, mercy, and peace, from **God the Father** *and* **Christ Jesus** *our Lord"* *(II Tim. 1:2).*

"Grace, mercy, and peace, from **God the Father** *and the Lord* **Jesus Christ** *our Savior"* *(Titus 1:4).*

"Grace to you, and peace, from **God our Father** *and the Lord* **Jesus Christ"** *(Phil. 1:3).*

One Throne Of God In Heaven

It is clear in Scripture that there is one throne of Almighty God in heaven, not three, and when Jesus the Messiah is pictured with Him, he is seated or standing at the right hand of God the Father *(See Ps. 110:1; Daniel 7:9, 13; Mark 16:19; Acts 2:33-34; Acts 7:55-56; I Peter 3:22; Heb. 10:12-13; Heb. 12:2; Rom. 8:34; Col. 3:1).*

> *"A throne was set in heaven, and **one** sat on the throne....*
> *Lord God Almighty" (Rev. 4:2; 8)*

> *"And he* [the Lamb] *came and took the book out of the right*
> *hand of **him that sat upon the throne**" (Rev. 5:7).*

> *"To him that overcometh will I grant to sit with **me in my***
> ***throne, even as I** also overcame, and am set down with **my***
> ***Father in his throne**" (Rev. 3:21) ("And the Lord God shall*
> *give unto him* [Jesus] *the throne of his father David" Luke*
> *1:32).*

Do you know of any place in the Bible that pictures three thrones in heaven, one for each person of a trinity? Is there a verse of Scripture that pictures a third person of a trinity seated at the Father's **left** hand? If there is a third person of God who is co-equal and co-eternal with the Father, where is his throne? Wake up Christianity!

Augustine and The Holy Spirit

According to church history the man who is credited more than any other with defining the place of the Holy Spirit in trinitarian dogma is the bishop of Hippo known as Saint Augustine *(354-430 A.D.)*. Professors Olson and Hall say of him, *"Augustine, the greatest of the Western Church fathers, has made his own unique contribution to the trinitarian thought of the church"* (p. 43). *"**Augustine was influenced by Platonic thought**, which inclined his trinitarian reflections in the direction of the unity of the Godhead. **For him, the Holy Spirit is the third 'person' of the Trinity** as the 'bond of love' that unites Father and Son and proceeds from both of them"* (p. 55). They quote author Colin Gunton thus, *"Augustine's analogies of the Trinity **can be more readily traced to Neoplatonic philosophy** than to the triune economy...."* (p. 45). [20] Since he was born in 354 A.D., did not convert to Christianity until 387 A.D., and became a Catholic priest in 391 A.D., this raises some obvious questions. If the doctrine of the Trinity is a true biblical doctrine, and the Holy Spirit is the **third** person of God, why was that fact not clearly

140

understood until **over 300 years** after the death of the last Apostle? Why
was it still being struggled with in 400 A.D.?

The late trinitarian Professor Cyril C. Richardson was an outstanding
historian of the early church, the period during which the doctrine of the
Trinity was first formulated. He wrote several books on church history, and
there was perhaps no one more informed on this subject than he. In his book,
The Doctrine of The Trinity, he states:

> *"The place of the Spirit in the Trinity has long been
> regarded as one of the difficult aspects of the doctrine. **Not
> until Augustine was there a thorough attempt to find a
> fitting reason for the existence of the Spirit as the third
> term** [person] **of the Godhead.** Long before him, to be sure,
> the Trinity had been affirmed...But it is **first in Augustine**
> that the distinctive nature of the Spirit and his place in the
> Trinity is given classic expression" (p. 44). "The primary
> notion of Spirit in the Bible is that of God's dynamic activity.
> **The Spirit is his breath,** hence his vitality or life" (p. 45).
> "Where the Spirit is given a personal quality as teaching,
> revealing, witnessing, interceding, creating **it is not as an
> entity distinct from God, but as God himself** doing these
> things and yet not compromising his transcendence" (p.
> 53). "**It was not until Augustine that this conception of
> the Spirit,** as the bond of union [in the Trinity] **was fully
> developed.** In him [Augustine] the Spirit finds his place in
> the Godhead as the principle of unity. The question may
> at once be raised whether this third term can properly be
> personified. If it is a term of relationship, **can it be called
> a 'person' in any legitimate sense? This has always been
> a crucial issue in Christian thinking about the Spirit**" (p.
> 101). "The Spirit has more frequently been conceived as
> "it" rather than as "**he**" (p. 102). [21]*

Richardson quotes Augustine as making this statement,

> *"We say three persons, not that we wish to say it, but **that***

141

we may not be reduced to silence" (p. 102). Richardson continues; *"That is the real problem for Augustine. By personalizing the relation in his symbolism, he introduces untold confusion" (p. 103).* *"My conclusion, then, about the doctrine of the Trinity is that it is an artificial construct. It tries to relate different problems and to fit them into an arbitrary and traditional threeness. It produces confusion rather than clarification; and while the problems with which it deals are real ones, the solutions it offers are not illuminating. It has posed for many Christians dark and mysterious statements, which are ultimately meaningless, because it does not sufficiently discriminate in its use of terms. Christian theology might be aided by abandoning such a procedure and by making clear the inadequacy both of the ambiguous terms and of the threeness into which its doctrines have been traditionally forced. There is no necessary threeness in the Godhead" (p. 148-149).* [Thank you Brother Richardson!]

Why The Holy Spirit Is Sometimes Called In Scripture *"The Spirit of Christ"*

At this point in our study we should consider the four places in Scripture where the Holy Spirit is called *"the Spirit of Christ"* or a close variation of that. Please do not be confused by this terminology because a closer study of Scripture will bring clarity to it. For example, Peter refers to the Holy Spirit as *"the Spirit of Christ"* once in I Peter 1:11:

> *"Searching what...the Spirit of Christ which was in them did signify, when it testified beforehand the sufferings of Christ."*

Peter is for sure referring here to the Holy Ghost for he calls it in the next verse *"the Holy Ghost sent down from heaven."* For what reason would the great apostle Peter feel justified in calling the Holy Ghost *"the Spirit of Christ?"* We should let Peter himself explain it. At Pentecost when the multitude of Jews from different nations heard those Galileans who were filled with the Spirit speaking in various languages, *"they were all amazed, and were in doubt, saying one to another, 'what meaneth this'?" (Acts 2:12).*

> *"But Peter, standing up with the eleven, lifted up his voice, and said unto them....this is that which was spoken by the prophet Joel; and it shall come to pass in the last days, **saith God**, I will pour out of **my Spirit** upon all flesh....and on my servants and on my handmaidens I will pour out in those days of **my Spirit**..." (Acts 2:14-18).*

So there is not doubt in Peter's mind that this outpouring of the Holy Ghost is the Spirit of God that He had promised by the prophet Joel. Peter continues:

> *"Ye men of Israel, hear these words; Jesus of Nazareth, **a man approved of God** among you by miracles and wonders and signs, which **God did** by him....Him being delivered by the **determinate counsel and foreknowledge of God**, ye have taken, and by wicked hands have crucified and slain: **Whom God hath raised up...**" (Acts 2:22-24).* Please note: Jesus was then in heaven with the Father, but to Peter he was still *"a man approved of God,"* who when slain *"God hath raised up."*

Now look at verse thirty-three:

> *"Therefore **being by the right hand of God** exalted, and having received of the Father the promise of the Holy Ghost, **he** [Jesus] **hath shed forth this**, which ye now see and hear."*

Consider These Biblical Truths

1. Jesus called the Holy Ghost *"the promise of the Father."*
   > *"But wait for **the promise of the Father**....For John truly baptized with water, but ye shall be baptized with the Holy Ghost not many days hence" (Acts 1:5).*

2.   Jesus said the Father would **give** the Holy Ghost.

> *"How much more shall **your heavenly Father give** the Holy Spirit to them that **ask him**" (Luke 11:13).*

> *"And I will pray the **Father**, and he shall **give** you another comforter..." (John 14:16).*

> *"But the comforter, which is the Holy Ghost, whom the Father will send in my name" (John 14:26).* Note: **The Father is the source**.

3.   Jesus never claimed to be an incarnation of the Holy Spirit. He made a strong distinction between himself and the Holy Spirit in the following verse:

> *"And whosoever shall speak a word **against the Son of man**, it **shall** be forgiven him: but unto him that blasphemest **against the Holy Ghost** it **shall not** be forgiven" (Luke 12:10).*

4.   Jesus said he himself would **send** the Holy Spirit.

> *"And, behold **I send** the **promise of my Father** upon you" (Luke 24:49).*

> *"But when the Comforter is come, whom **I will send** unto you **from the Father**, even the Spirit of truth which **proceedeth from the Father**" (John 15:26).*

5.   Jesus said the Holy Spirit would not be poured out until he went to heaven, received it from the Father and sent it to believers.

> *"Nevertheless I tell you the truth; It is expedient for you that I go away; for if I go not away, the Comforter will not come unto you; but if I depart, I will send him unto you" (John 16:7).*

So the apostle Peter was on solid ground at Pentecost when he told the multitude:

> *"Therefore being by the right hand of God exalted* [exalted to God's right hand], *and **having received of the Father the promise of the Holy Ghost, he** [Jesus] **hath shed forth this, which ye now see and hear"** (Acts 2:33).*

Jesus is for sure the Holy Ghost baptizer:

> *"The next day John seeth Jesus coming unto him, and saith, Behold the Lamb of God...the same is he which baptizeth with the Holy Ghost" (John 1:29, 33).*

Jesus Is The Intermediary

With the foregoing Scriptures in mind please see this picture. Jesus Christ, the supernaturally conceived, virgin-born, sinless Son of God was crucified as the Lamb of God, arose from the grave and ascended to the Father. He offered his righteous blood to God on the altar in the *True Temple* which is above, and it was accepted of the Father for the sins of the whole world. He received from the Father the gift of the same Spirit with which he himself was filled, inspired and empowered, and shed it forth on us. Thus, the Spirit of God, i.e. the Holy Ghost, is rightly called in a few places *"the Spirit of Christ."*

The *NIV text notes* say regarding I Peter 1:11: *"Spirit of Christ. The Holy Spirit is called this because Christ sent him* [it] *and ministered through him."*

So we can conclude from Peter that *"the Spirit of Christ"* is another name for the Holy Ghost, and they are both terms for the **power of God**. Back up a few verses from I Peter 1:11 to verses 2-5 and read:

> *"Elect according to the **foreknowledge of God the Father**, through sanctification of **the Spirit**, unto obedience and sprinkling of the blood of Jesus Christ...Blessed be the **God** and Father of our Lord Jesus Christ...for you who are kept by **the power of God**..."*

Did Paul Have This Same Truth In Mind?

> *"But ye are not in the flesh, but in the Spirit, if so be that the **Spirit of God** dwell in you. Now if any man have not the **Spirit of Christ**, he is none of his. But if the Spirit of **him** [God the Father] that raised up Jesus from the dead dwell in you, **he** that raised up Christ from the dead shall also quicken your mortal bodies by **his Spirit** that dwelleth in you. The **Spirit itself** beareth witness with our spirit, that we are the **children of God**: And if children, then heirs; **heirs of God** [our Father], and joint-heirs with Christ [our brother]" (Rom. 8:9, 11, 16-17).*

> *"And because **ye are sons, God** hath sent forth the Spirit of his Son into your hearts, crying, Abba, **Father**....and if a son, then an **heir of God through** Christ" (Gal. 4:5-6).*

But dear reader, you might ask, "Is there a precedent in the Bible for calling an anointing of God's Spirit by the name of the prophet-person on which it rested previously?" The answer is "Yes." It is found in the beautiful story of Elijah and Elisha recorded in II Kings chapter two.

> *"And it came to pass, when they were gone over, that Elijah said unto Elisha, ask what I shall do for thee, before I be taken away from thee. And Elisha said, I pray thee, let a double portion of **thy spirit** be upon me" (v. 9).*

Now ponder this. Was Elisha in reality asking for a double portion of **Elijah's spirit**, or a double portion of the **Spirit of God that was upon Elijah**, the spirit that inspired, anointed, and empowered him? Of course it was the latter!

Now look at verses fourteen and fifteen.

> *"And he took the mantle of Elijah that fell from him, and smote the waters, and said, Where is the Lord God of Elijah? And when he also had smitten the waters, they parted hither*

*and thither: And Elisha went over. And when the sons of
the prophets which were to view at Jericho saw him, they
said, **the spirit of Elijah** doth rest on Elisha."*

As the "Elijah anointing" from God that was on Elisha was called *"the spirit
of Elijah,"* likewise the "Jesus anointing" from God that is on Christians can
rightly be called *"the Spirit of Christ."*

*"Now there are diversities of gifts, but the **same Spirit**. And
there are diversities of operation, but it is the same **God**
which worketh all in all. But all these worketh that **one and
the selfsame** Spirit" (I Cor. 12:4, 6, 11).*

Yes, we as Spirit-filled believers have the "Jesus anointing," the same Spirit
of the Father with which Jesus was filled at the time of his water baptism
(Mark 1:10-12; Luke 4:1, 14; John 1:32-34). And thus it is called *"the
Spirit of Christ."*

The Transfer Of Moses' Spirit

There is a story regarding Moses in Numbers chapter eleven that is a beautiful
fore-shadowing of this New Testament outpouring of the Holy Spirit. Moses
became weary in his role as prophet, judge and leader of Israel and cried out
to God:

*"I am not able to bear all this people alone, because it is too
heavy for me" (v. 14).*

So God gave Moses a plan:

*"And the Lord said unto Moses, Gather unto me seventy men
of the elders of Israel...and bring them unto the tabernacle
of congregation, that they may stand there with thee. And I
will come down and talk with thee there: and **I will take of
the spirit which is upon thee, and will put it upon them;**
and the Lord came down in a cloud, and spoke unto him,
and **took of the spirit that was upon him**, and gave it unto
the seventy elders: and it came to pass, that when the spirit*

*rested upon them, **they prophesied**, and did not cease" (v.
16-17, 25).*

Can you imagine a more beautiful picture of God the Father taking of the
Spirit that was upon His Son Jesus, and placing it upon believers to empower
us for Christian living and witnessing? Moses strongly typifies Christ in
Scripture.

> *"I will raise them up **a Prophet from among their brethren,
> like unto thee**, and will put my words in his mouth; and
> he shall speak unto them **all that I command him**"* [God's
> promise of the Messiah to Moses] *(Deut. 18:18).*

> *"We have found him, of whom **Moses** in the law, and
> the prophets, did write, **Jesus of Nazareth**"* [Philip to
> Nathanael] *(John 1:45).*

> *"For **Moses** truly said unto the fathers, **a Prophet** shall
> the Lord your God raise up unto you **of your brethren, like
> unto me**"* [Peter, regarding Jesus] *(Acts 3:22).*

> *"This is that **Moses**, which said unto the children of Israel,
> **a Prophet** shall the Lord your God raise up unto of your
> brethren, **like unto me**"* [Stephen, regarding Jesus] *(Acts
> 7:37).*

One final thought from this story about Moses. Some Israelites became
jealous at having others beside Moses prophesying, and asked him to forbid
them. Moses' answer shows great insight regarding God's future plan to
pour out His *"spirit upon all flesh"* [see *Joel 2:28*]:

> *"And Moses said unto him, Enviest thou for my sake? Would
> God that **all the Lord's people were prophets**, and that **the
> Lord would put his spirit upon them!**"* (Numbers 11:29).

148

Who Is Jesus Christ?

It is so important for Christians to know who Jesus is, for unless we see clearly in Scripture who he is, we cannot understand **who we are in him**. Moses was Israel's God anointed, inspired and empowered prophet-leader and a prototype of Jesus Christ. Jesus' words show that he saw himself in the role of a prophet, a prophet filled and empowered by the Spirit.

> *"And they were offended in him. But Jesus said unto them,* ***a prophet*** *is not without honor, save in his own country, and in his own house" (Matt. 13:57; Mark 6:4; Luke 4:24; John 4:44).*

> *"Nevertheless I must walk today, and tomorrow, and the day following: for it cannot be that* ***a prophet*** *perish out of Jerusalem" [Jesus speaking] (Luke 13:33).*

> *"The Spirit of the Lord is* ***upon me***, *because* ***he*** *['the Lord God'- Isa. 61:1] hath anointed me" [Jesus speaking] (Luke 4:18).*

As Moses was a prototype for Jesus, so Jesus is a prototype or pattern for us. Of course we understand that Jesus was more than a prophet; he is the supernaturally conceived, virgin-born, human Son of God. But if we make him the eternal God, the "God-man" or a super being, rather than **a real man full of God** *("the* **man** *Christ Jesus")*, he is not a pattern for us. We are not super beings! We are human beings who need to be filled with the Spirit of God, just as Jesus was filled. We need to have a reverential fear of the Father just as he did *(Isa. 11:2; Heb. 5:7)*. We need to have a great love for the Father just as he did *(John 14:31; Mark 12:30; John 15:10)*.

People, including Christians, live what they believe. If we believe that Jesus was a super being, "the God-man," we tend to cop-out in our minds and say, "sure he could resist temptation and overcome sin, **he was God**." That is non-biblical thinking, and it is the cause of much of the defeat among Christians. No, he was **a man full of God,** just as we should be.

149

"Be filled with the Spirit" (Eph. 5:18).

"....that ye might be filled with all the fullness of God"
(Eph. 3:19).

"Be ye therefore perfect, even as your Father which is in
heaven is perfect" (Matt. 5:48).

"....let us go on unto perfection" (Heb. 6:1).

Yes, Jesus our elder brother set us a high mark of sinlessness in this world, although *"he suffered being tempted" (Heb. 2:18)*, a mark for which we should aim ourselves in living victoriously.

Likewise, if we see Jesus as a *God-man* working miracles and doing the work of the kingdom, we sell ourselves short, as mere men. **Who are we?**

"Behold, what manner of love the Father hath bestowed
upon us, that we should be called the Sons of God....
Beloved, now are we the Sons of God" (I John 3:1-2).

"For it became him [God the Father], *for whom are all*
things, and by whom are all things, in bringing many Sons
unto glory, to make the captain of their salvation [Jesus]
perfect through sufferings" (Heb. 2:10).

"He that believeth on me, the works that I do shall he do
also; and greater works than these shall he do; because
I go unto my Father [Jesus' promise to believers] *(John*
14:12).

"God is love; and he that dwelleth in love dwelleth in
God, and God in him...because as he is, so are we in this
world" (I John 4:16-17). Compare this to Jesus' words in
John 14:11, *"Believe me that I am in the Father, and the*

Father in me." This is a close relationship between Jesus and the Father, but he says that in him **we have this same relationship** with the Father.

(Find yourself in the following words of Jesus' prayer to the Father in John 17:16-23, and be comforted.)

> *"**They** are not of the world, even as I am not of the world. Sanctify them through thy truth: thy word is truth. **As thou hast sent me into the world, even so have I also sent them into the world.** And for **their** sakes I sanctify myself, that **they** also might be sanctified through the truth. Neither pray I for these alone, **but for them also which shall believe on me through their word;** that **they** all may be one; as thou, Father, art in me, and I in thee, **that they also may be one in us:** that the world may believe that thou hast sent me. **And the glory which thou gavest me I have given them:** that they may be one even as we are one: **I in them, and thou in me, that they may be made perfect in one;** and that the world may know that thou hast sent me, and **hast loved them, as thou hast loved me."***

Notice especially Jesus' words, *"and the **glory** which thou gavest me **I have given them."*** What was Jesus' glory?

> *"And we beheld **his glory,** the glory as of the only begotten of the Father"* (John 1:14).

So in Jesus we also are *"**the begotten of the Father.**"* (If God's Bible says it, we can claim it!).

> *"Blessed be the **God and Father** of our Lord Jesus, which according to **his** abundant mercy **hath begotten us** again unto a lively hope **by** the resurrection of Jesus Christ from the dead"* (I Pet. 1:3).

151

"And again, when he [the Father] *bringeth in the **first-begotten** into the world...." (Heb. 1:6).*

*"We know that **whosoever** is **born of God** sinneth not; but he that is **begotten of God** keepeth himself" (I John 5:18).*

*"And from Jesus Christ who is the faithful witness, and the **first begotten**..." (Rev. 1:5).*

*"For I reckon that the sufferings of this present time are not worthy to be compared with **the glory which shall be revealed in us**. For the earnest expectation of the creature* [creation] *waiteth **for the manifestation of the sons of God**" (Rom. 8:18-19).*

We Cry "Abba Father"

At this point in our study, lets look at the words *"Abba Father"* in the Bible. The term *"Abba Father"* is used only three times in Scripture. Once it is Jesus speaking to the Father, and twice they are **our words** to the Father.

"And he [Jesus] *said, Abba Father, all things are possible unto thee" (Mark 14:36).*

*"Ye have received the **Spirit of adoption**, whereby **we cry**, Abba Father" (Rom. 8:15).*

*"And because **ye are sons**, God hath sent the Spirit of his Son into your hearts, crying, Abba Father" (Gal. 4:6).*

Paul for sure understood our place in God, through Christ, and the awesome work of the Holy Spirit (the Spirit of the Father) in bringing us into this place of blessedness.

*"Wherefore thou art no more a servant, but **a son**; and if a son, then an **heir of God** through Christ" (Gal. 4:7).*

The inspired writer of Hebrews said regarding us and our relationship to Jesus:

> *"For which cause he is not ashamed to call them **brethren**....*
> ***in all things** it behooved* [was necessary for] *him to be made*
> *like unto his brethren" (Heb. 2:11, 17).*

Remember, God's promise to Moses regarding the Messiah had been:

> *"I will raise them up **a Prophet from among their brethren**,*
> *like unto thee" (Deut. 18:18).*

When the seventy elders of Israel received from God the "Moses anointing" they prophesied and did not cease, and then instead of only one Moses, there were seventy-one Moseses. Likewise when believers receive from God the "Jesus anointing," the world should have millions of "anointed ones," Spirit inspired and empowered brothers and sisters of Jesus Christ. Consider this: When the mother of James and John brought them to Jesus and asked for a place of honor for them in his kingdom, one on his right and one on his left, Jesus asked them two questions.

> *"Are ye able to drink of the cup* [of suffering] *that I shall*
> *drink of, and to be baptized with the baptism that I am*
> *baptized with" (Matt. 20:22).* When they answered yes
> Jesus said, *"Ye shall indeed drink of my cup, and **be baptized***
> ***with the baptism that I am baptized with**" (v. 23).*

This is another beautiful promise from Jesus of the baptism of the Holy Ghost, *"the baptism that **I am** [present tense] baptized with."*

That is why John 7:37-39 says:

> *"Jesus stood and cried saying, If any man thirst, let him*
> *come unto me and drink. He that believeth on me, as the*
> *scripture hath said, out of his belly shall flow **rivers of***
> ***living water**. But this spoke he of **the Spirit** which they that*
> *believe on him should receive: for **the Holy Ghost** was not*
> *yet given..."*

This is also why Jesus said in John 14:12:

> *"He that believeth on me, **the works that I do shall he do also**; and **greater works than these shall he do**; because I go unto my Father."*

Where Is Our Power As Christians?

You may say in your heart, "...but I have believed on Jesus, been saved and received the Spirit, yet I feel powerless and without victory." If this is your confession, thank God for your honesty, and His word has answers for you. We need to ponder some important things regarding our elder brother Jesus.

1.   He knew who his Heavenly Father was, and was totally submitted to His will for his life *(John 5:30)*.

2.   Jesus was a worshiper of the Father. Consider his words to the woman at the well in John chapter four:

> *"**We know what we worship**....the true worshipers shall **worship the Father**...the **Father** seeketh such to **worship him**" (v. 22-23).*

Our worship must be in order, as Jesus' was, because John 9:31 says:

> *"But if any man be a **worshiper of God**, and doeth his will, **him he heareth**."*

Here are some questions that we should ask ourselves so that we might have the power Jesus had and do the works that he did, and greater!

1.   **Have I confessed and forsaken every known sin in my life?** Listen to Jesus:

> *"Which of you convinceth me of sin?" (John 8:46).*

> *"The prince of this world* [the devil] *cometh, and **hath nothing in me** [no sin]" (John 14:30).*

2.   **How is my prayer life?** Consider Jesus:

> *"And when he had sent the multitudes away, he went up into a mountain apart **to pray** (Matt. 14:23).*

154

*"And in the morning, rising up a great while before day, he went out, and departed into a solitary place, **and there he prayed"** (Mark 1:35).*

*"And he withdrew himself into the wilderness, **and prayed"** (Luke 5:16).*

*"And being in agony **he prayed more earnestly"** (Luke 22:44).*

3.   **Am I harboring unforgiveness?**

"But if ye do not forgive, neither will your Father which is in heaven forgive your trespasses" (Matt. 6:15; Mark 11:26).

[Husbands and wives live peacefully] *"that your prayers be not hindered" (I Pet. 3:7).*

One final word regarding your desire to be like Jesus. Please do not cop out. You can do it by the power of the Holy Spirit!

*"Likewise **the Spirit also helpeth our infirmities**: for we know not what we should pray for as we ought: but the **Spirit itself** maketh intercession for us with groanings which cannot be uttered. And he that searcheth the hearts knoweth what is the mind of the Spirit, because he maketh intercession for the saints according to the **will of God**. And we know that all things work together for good to them that **love God**, to them who are the called according to his purpose. For whom he did foreknow, he also did predestinate **to be conformed to the image of his Son**, that he might be **the firstborn among many brethren" (Rom. 8:26-29).***

More From Paul Regarding The Spirit of God

Since it is Paul that makes the three references to the Holy Spirit that we noted earlier, calling it *"the Spirit of Christ" (Rom. 8:9); "the Spirit of his (God's) Son" (Gal. 4:6),* and *"the Spirit of Jesus Christ" (Phil. 1:19),* we should give this some biblical perspective by stating emphatically that Paul never actually attributes the Spirit to Christ as the one who bestows it on others. We know from John the Baptist and Peter at Pentecost that Jesus is the intermediary between God and those on whom the Holy Ghost is poured out *(John 1:33; Acts 2:33),* but Paul, for his own reasons, always looks to **God** as the source of the Spirit, and always proclaims **God** as the one who gives it.

> *"Now we have received, not the spirit of the world, but the Spirit **which is of God**; that we might know the things that are freely **given to us of God**" (I Cor. 2:12).*

> *"Now he which **stablisheth us** with you in Christ, **and hath anointed us is God**" (II Cor. 1:21).* **See also:** *I Cor. 2:12; 12:6; II Cor. 5:5; Gal. 4:6; Eph. 1:17; I Thess. 4:8; II Tim. 1:7; Titus 3:5.*

To the apostle Paul, the Holy Spirit is for sure **the Spirit of God the Father.**

> *"For this cause **I bow my knees unto the Father** of our Lord Jesus Christ....that He would grant you according to the riches of **his glory**, to be strengthened with might by **his Spirit** in the inner man" (Eph. 3:14, 16).*

> *"For we....**worship God in the spirit**, and rejoice in Christ Jesus" (Phil. 3:3).*

> *"For as many as are lead by the **Spirit of God**....ye have received the Spirit of adoption, whereby we cry, Abba, **Father**" (Rom. 8:14-15).* (**See also:** *Rom. 8:11; I Cor. 2:11, 14; 3:16; 6:11; 7:40; 12:3; II Cor. 3:3, 17; Eph. 4:30).*

The Word "Spirit" In The Original Greek

To more thoroughly prove that the Holy Spirit is the power or breath of

God the Father and not another person distinct from the Father, it should be helpful at this point to study the word "Spirit" as it is seen in the original Greek. It is the Greek word *"pneuma" (Strong's #4151)*, and means *"a current of air, breath, or a breeze."* To signify to his disciples that the Holy Spirit is the breath of God, after his resurrection, but about seven days before the Spirit was poured out, Jesus *"**breathed** on them and said, receive ye the Holy Ghost" (John 20:22).* Earlier when Jesus had spoken to Nicodemus about being born of the Spirit he said:

> *"The **wind** bloweth where it listeth* [chooses], *and thou hearest the sound thereof, but canst not tell whence it cometh, and whither it goeth: **so is every one that is born of the Spirit**" (John 3:8).*

Remember when the Holy Spirit was poured out on Pentecost:

> *"Suddenly there came a sound from heaven **as of a rushing mighty wind**, and it filled all the house where they were sitting" (Acts 2:2).*

The Greek word *pneuma* is the source of our English word pneumatic which pertains to "air." A tire that **contains air** or a tool that **pumps air** is said to be *"pneumatic."* The New Testament writers used the word *pneuma* some 245 times for the Spirit of God, and **only twice** is it capitalized, *(Luke 1:35 and 4:18),* and then because it is the first word in a quotation. Out of reverence we usually capitalize words that pertain to God such as "Father" or "Spirit", and to Jesus, such as "Son" but this was not done in the original Greek. This is a choice made by the writer, editor, or publisher and does not affect the meaning of the word that is capitalized. (Note: The word "Word" in John 1:1-14 is not capitalized in the original and in some older translations). For instance, I have chosen to capitalize the pronouns that pertain to God in this book such as He, His, and Himself. Again this is done out of reverence but does not affect the meaning of the word that is capitalized. However, here is the problem. When English translations capitalize the word spirit, **it can leave the false impression that it is the name of a person** instead of God's breath or power.

The word "holy" in Greek is *"hagios" (Strong's #40)*, and means *"sacred, pure, or blameless."* It is an adjective used with "Spirit" many times in the New Testament, and **in the original Greek is never capitalized.** So if a translator is absolutely true to the original, the words "Holy Spirit" should be translated **"holy spirit."** That is a fact that cannot be disputed! Again, when people who do not know these things, see the words "Holy Spirit" capitalized in an English translation, they take it for granted that these are proper nouns, the name of a person. This is a false assumption and adds to the confusion about what the Holy Spirit is.

Look at the words *"holy child"* in Acts chapter four, and *"holy scripture"* in II Timothy chapter three.

> *"For of a truth against thy* **holy child** *Jesus....the people of Israel were gathered together" (v. 27).*

> *"That signs and wonders may be done by the name of thy* **holy child** *Jesus" (v. 30).*

> *"And that from a child thou hast known the* **holy scriptures** *" (v. 15).*

You will notice that *"holy child"* and *"holy scriptures"* are not capitalized in these verses, but they could be. Like the **holy spirit** they came from God and are divine in that sense. The word "divine" means *"Deity-God," or "given or inspired by God; holy; sacred."* The *"holy child"* and the *"holy scriptures"* are like the *"holy spirit,"* for sure given and inspired by God, but the translators saw no need to capitalize them. Again when you see *"Holy Spirit"* written with capitals in your Bible, it does not denote a third person of God.

Gender and The Word *Pneuma* In Greek

This is a fact of grammar which seems strange to those of us who were brought up in the English language, but many ancient and modern languages when referring to **things, animals,** as well as **people,** use words such as **him** or **her** which denote gender. For example in Greek, **bread** is a *masculine* word and the personal pronouns "he" or "who" are used when referring to bread. But in Greek the words, "love," "sword," and "city" are considered to be *feminine* in gender and are always referred to as "she." The third option in Greek regarding gender is "neuter," neither masculine nor feminine. **Neuter means that the word has no gender.** In English a neuter object is referred to as "it." Words that are neuter in Greek such as "name" and "water" are also referred to as "it". (This should not be hard as every school child knows the difference between "he" or "him," and "it"). [22]

Now, here is an important fact for our study. The Greek word for spirit *(pneuma)*, be it the *spirit* of human, animal, angel, or God's spirit, is **always** *neuter* in gender. And every **adjective, pronoun,** and **verb** that the Apostles and inspired writers of the New Testament chose in reference to the Holy Spirit **is in a neuter form.** They chose "it" over "he" or "him" and "which" over "who" or "whom," **one hundred percent** of the time when the rules of grammar gave them the choice. Were the Apostles trinitarians? Did they believe the Holy Spirit was a "person" distinct from the Father? No way! If they had, they would not have dared to refer to the Spirit as "it!"

The King James Version and The Gender Of The Holy Spirit
In studying the KJV of the Holy Bible one finds that the translators were not very consistent as to whether they referred to the Holy Spirit as "it" or "he." Most of the time they used "he," but there are exceptions.

> "....the Spirit descending from heaven like a dove, and *it* abode upon him" (John 1:32).

> "The Spirit *itself* beareth witness with our spirit...." (Rom. 8:16).

> "But the Spirit *itself* maketh intercession...." (Rom. 8:26).

> "The Spirit of Christ which was in them did signify, when *it* testified...." (I Pet. 1:11).

There are also numerous times when the KJV translators used "which" or "that" instead of "who" or "whom." But more times than not, they committed a grave error! Did these translators and today's modern linguists, know better when they gave a personal pronoun or verb to a Greek word, though a writer of sacred Scripture did not do so? Of course they do! But one must assume that their sense of scholarship and accountability to God are overpowered by their allegiance to some 1700 years of mistaken church tradition. My friend, there is much confusion among Christians regarding who the One Most High God is, and much of the blame can be laid to the charge of some less than courageous Bible translators.

Regarding the above facts of Scripture allow me to make one final statement. In the original Greek of the New Testament, the word for Spirit is *"pneuma"* a neuter noun, and **if the inspired writers had believed the Spirit is a person,** they could have used **a masculine pronoun or verb** form, **but they never once chose to do so!** Thus we have absolute proof that they did not believe the Holy Spirit is a person.

Are We To Pray To The Holy Spirit?

It is remarkable that there is not one place in Scripture where we are instructed to pray to the Holy Spirit and no example of God's people doing do. Yes, we pray "in the Holy Ghost" *(Jude v. 20)*, under the unction and anointing of the Holy Ghost *(Rom. 8:26-27)*, and *"with the spirit" (I Cor. 14:15),* **but there is not a single reference to praying "to the Holy Ghost."** Therefore I do not do it.

Jesus always taught that our prayers should be to the Father. (**See:** *Matt. 6:6, 8-9; Luke 11:2; John 15:16; 16:16, 23, 26).* Paul says that even when someone speaks in tongues **by** the Holy Ghost, he or she is speaking to **God.** (**See:** *I Cor. 14:2, 28).*

Are We To Worship The Holy Spirit?

As it is with praying to the Holy Spirit, so it is in worshiping the Holy Spirit; there is not one scriptural reference. According to Jesus' statements in John chapter four, our worship should be given to the Father. (Trust Jesus!).

> *"....worship the **Father**....the true worshipers shall worship the **Father**....the **Father** seeketh such to worship **him**" (v. 21-23).*

Yes, the Holy Spirit is the breath or power of God, but God the Father has not instructed us to worship His attributes, but rather to *"**worship him**."* A wife is not highly complimented if her husband only adores her attributes (hair, body, etc.), but she is highly complimented if he adores her as a complete person. Likewise the Father desires that we fall in love with **Him**, and give our adoration, fellowship, prayers and worship to Him alone as our One Most High God. *(Deut. 6:4-5; Mark12:29-30).*

Summary

Biblical Fact

Jesus used the terms *"Holy Ghost"* and *"Spirit of your Father"* interchangeably.

Biblical Fact

There are never three thrones pictured in heaven. There is one throne of God Almighty, and Jesus is seated at His right hand. **There is no third person seated at His left**.

Biblical Fact

No place in Scripture are we told to worship or pray to a "person" called the Holy Spirit.

Biblical Fact

Paul sent greetings from *"God our Father **and** the Lord Jesus Christ"* at the beginning of each of his thirteen epistles. He never sent greetings from a third "person" named the Holy Spirit.

Biblical Fact

> Peter quotes God the Father in Acts 2:17 as promising to pour out a portion of His own Spirit upon believers.

Biblical Fact

> In the original Greek the words *"Holy Spirit"* are not capitalized as if it were the name of a person. It is written *holy spirit.*

Biblical Fact

> In the original Greek no inspired writer of the New Testament referred to the Holy Spirit as "he" or "him." When given a choice under the rules of grammar, they always chose the impersonal pronoun "it."

Historical Fact

> The Council of Nicea *(325 A.D.)* did not declare belief in a Trinity, three co-equal, co-eternal persons of God. This was done fifty-six years later at the Council of Constantinople *(381 A.D.)*. Thus the doctrine of the Trinity is rightly called *"a late fourth century Christian doctrine."* [23]

Historical Fact

> The **place of the Holy Spirit** in the doctrine of the Trinity was not clearly defined until Augustine, **around 400 A.D.** That thought does not bother most theologians, but it should be troubling to every truth loving, Bible believing Christian.

What we have found from our study of the Holy Spirit, Holy Ghost, Spirit of God is, that it is the breath or power of God in action; God Himself creating, empowering, inspiring, teaching, revealing, interceding, witnessing, comforting and guiding. Not as an entity distinct from God, but the Father Himself doing these things **for** and **in** His Son and sons, as God in His active relation to the world.

We are required to come to the same conclusion as trinitarian Bible scholar, Professor Charles C. Ryrie, writing in his work, *Basic Theology:*

> *"Many doctrines are accepted by evangelicals as being clearly taught in the Scripture for which there are no proof texts. The doctrine of the Trinity furnishes the best example of this. It is fair to say that the Bible does not clearly teach the doctrine of the Trinity. In fact, there is not even one proof text, if by proof text we mean a verse or passage that 'clearly' states that there is one God who exists in three persons" (p. 89). "The above illustrations prove the fallacy of concluding that if something is not proof texted in the Bible we cannot clearly teach the results....If that were so, I could never teach the doctrine of the Trinity or the deity of Christ or **the deity of the Holy Spirit**" (p. 90).* [24]

Jesus Himself Has A God

Jesus has a God whom he worships *(Ps. 18:49; John 4:22-23)*, whom he fears *(Isa. 11:1-5; Heb. 5:7)*; and to whom he prays *(Matt. 26:53; Luke 6:12, 22:44; Heb. 7:25)*. Notice these Scriptures regarding Jesus and his God.

> *"He shall stand and feed in the strength of the Lord, in the majesty of the name of **the Lord his God**" (Micah 5:4).*

> *"**My God, my God,** why hast thou forsaken me?" (Matt. 27:46).*

> *"I ascend unto...**my God**, and your God" (John 20:17).*

> *"Blessed be the **God** and Father of our Lord Jesus Christ. That the **God** of our Lord Jesus Christ, the Father of glory..." (Eph. 1:3, 17).*

> *"Blessed be the **God** and Father of our Lord Jesus Christ" (I Peter 1:3).*

> *"He that overcometh will I make a pillar in the temple of **my God**...name of **my God**... city of **my God**...down out of heaven from **my God**" (Rev. 3:12).*

This is the ascended Jesus speaking, who had been in heaven with the Father for some sixty years when the book of Revelation was written, but he still refers to God as *"my God."* It is for sure that Jesus cannot be the Supreme God, while he at the same time has a God to whom he submits.

Chapter Six

Jesus Is Speaking. Listen!

"Listen, O Israel; The Lord our God is one Lord" [Jesus speaking] *(Mark 12:29).*

"And why call ye me, Lord, Lord, and do not the things which I say" [Jesus speaking] *(Luke 6:46).*

"Anyone who goes too far and does not abide in the teaching of Christ, does not have God" (II John v. 9) (NASB).

*"We have now sunk to a depth at which **restatement of the obvious** is the first duty of intelligent men." (George Orwell; English writer)*

Once when I was a young man, I was required to be in court on a minor traffic offense. Although I was less than happy to be there, I found some of what went on in the courtroom before I was called up, quite entertaining. For example, in one case the judge was trying to sort out a love triangle between a female of about twenty-two, a male of about twenty-five, and an older man of about fifty-eight.

This was not the first time this African American trio had been before the judge, but this last altercation had involved a knife. And according to the judge, unless it was resolved once and for all, it would *"lead to a killing."*

The older man was put on the stand and the judge asked him a number of questions which he seemed to have no problem hearing and answering. And then came the question, *"Are you living carnally with this girl?"* To which he replied, *"What was that Mister Judge?"* The judge re-framed the question and asked louder, *"Are you having sex with this woman?"* The man looked at the judge blankly and said, *"I'm sorry Mister Judge, but you're gonna have to speak up, 'cause I can't hear you!"* At which time the courtroom erupted with laughter at this humorous display of selective hearing.

But the selective hearing of Christians today is no laughing matter! Our awesome God said:

> *"**My people are destroyed for lack of knowledge:** because thou hast rejected knowledge, **I will also reject thee**" (Hosea 4:6).*

And God says to those who have been involved in the **spiritual fornication** (false doctrines) of **Mystery Babylon** (Rome, built on *"seven mountains"* Rev. 17:9):

> *"**Come out of her my people**, that ye be not partakers of her sins, **and that ye receive not of her plagues**" (Rev. 18:4).*

Looking Back At Mark 12:29

Here is a good question. Why would Jesus Christ, the greatest man who has ever spoken on this planet, speaking the greatest words that ever came from human lips, proclaiming his Father, God Almighty's greatest commandment to man, need to start his statement with, *"Listen"*? (Note: The Hebrew word for *"hear"* is *shema*, and it means *"listen."* Jesus is not just quoting Moses; in his view this is God's greatest commandment). **Hearing** was a problem in Jesus' day, as it is now. Jesus knew the multitudes *"heard"* what he was saying, but most did not truly *"hear."* Notice his words regarding this:

> *"Their ears are dull of hearing"* (Matt. 13:15).

> *"And having ears, hear ye not?"* (Mark 8:18).

> *"He said unto his disciples, Let these sayings **sink down into your ears**"* (Luke 9:44).

Eight times in the Gospels, Jesus says, *"He that hath ears to hear let him hear."* Though Jesus was saddened by it, he never seemed to struggle with the fact that some just absolutely could not *"hear"* his message. He said:

> *"Therefore speak I to them in parables: because they seeing see not; **and hearing they hear not...**" (Matt. 13:13).*

Jesus knew it was a spiritual problem on their part, over which he had no control. He quoted God from the Book of Isaiah:

> *"For this people's heart is waxed gross, **and their ears are dull of hearing**, and their eyes they have closed; lest at any time they should see with their eyes, and hear with their ears,...**and should be converted**, and I should heal them"* *(Matt. 13:15).*

Once, Jesus made an awesome statement that excludes many people who claim to be *"Christian."*

> *"**My sheep hear my voice**, and I know them, **and they follow me**" (John 10:27).*

Jesus Spoke Plainly

There is no record that Jesus ever preached using vague theological terms or complicated theological concepts, but rather he spoke the language of the common people. His reassurance to John the Baptist that he himself was the Messiah, included the fact that *"the **poor** have the gospel preached to them"* *(Matt. 11:5).*

Jesus also spoke with authority and did not *hint, infer, suggest* or *imply.* *"For he taught them as one **having authority**..." (Matt. 7:29).*

After my first book, *To God Be The Glory,* was published in 2006, proclaiming One Eternal God, the Father, who has a supernaturally conceived, virgin-born, human Son, our savior, the Messiah Jesus, someone challenged me with a book titled, *Renewal Theology,* by trinitarian scholar J. Rodman Williams. Chapter four is *The Holy Trinity,* and begins: *"We come now to* the **central mystery** *of the Christian faith - the doctrine of the Holy Trinity, or the doctrine of the Triune God."* This first paragraph ends, *"**The Christian faith is faith in the Triune God.**"*

And on what, according to Brother Williams, is this **foundational** faith of Christianity, *"faith in the Triune God,"* based? He writes:

> *"In the Old Testament there is **no distinct reference** to God as **existing in three persons.** **Hints** of it, however, may be found"* (p. 84). *"Elohim is a plural noun, and though **no clear statement of a trinity is contained**, a plurality of persons may well be **implied**"* (p. 85). *"**No trinity of persons** as such **is declared,** but the **idea of plurality** seems to be definitely **suggested**"* [*"definitely suggested?"*] *(p. 85). "...hence there is the **suggestion** of a **second, alongside God"** (p. 85). "Although these passages **do not specifically depict** one God in three persons, **they point in that direction"** (p. 85). "The Spirit is not here said to be a **person**, though it can be **inferred"** (p. 85). "**It is the Christian claim** that all three of these persons are God" (p. 87). "This unquestionably **implies** divinity for the Son" (p. 87). "There are many other texts that **without directly using the terminology of 'the Son'** speak of Jesus Christ as God" (p. 88). "Although it could be argued that Jesus is not talking about **an eternal procession**, such would seem to be **implied"** (p. 93).* [1]

Is this what the *"foundational"* doctrine of the Trinity is based on? The doctrine which a person must whole-heartedly believe or else be lost? Such words as *"hints," "implied," "suggested," "do not specifically depict," "inferred,"* and *"would **seem to be implied?**"* Shame on those who base their salvation on such nonsense and condemn to hell those who don't!

In all, this trinitarian theologian and doctor of the church uses the words *hints, implied, suggested* or *inferred* (or their derivatives) **nine times** in this one chapter, in an effort to prove the existence of a Triune God. (Remember his statement, *"**The Christian faith is** faith in the **Triune God**."*)

I would not at all question Brother Williams' sound character or good intentions, but his use of such phrases as *"definitely suggested"* and *"unquestionably implies"* is characteristic of Trinitarian and Oneness double-talk in general. Other examples we hear are *"God-man," "God the Son," "One God in three persons," "fully God and fully man,"* and *"triune God."* This reminds me of something from my childhood. When I was a boy, growing up in the 40's and 50's, powerful 100,000 watt radio stations operated just south of the U.S. border in Mexico. (They were later shut down by a treaty between the two countries). They featured all night programming that consisted of Gospel music, both live and recorded, and fiery preaching. These programs were sponsored mostly by the sale, by mail, of products such as vitamins, baby chicks, music recordings, and anointing oil, to mostly rural, unsuspecting, likely poorly educated people. But one of the most successful, longest lasting sponsors was *"The Ring Man,"* who offered a *"gorgeous engagement ring with two carats of **genuine simulated diamonds** for $19.95."* (The wedding ring was added free). Of course, *"genuine simulated diamonds"* was double-speak for worthless cut glass; however the orders poured in. I can still hear the announcer saying, *"Rush your order today! Send nineteen dollars and ninety-five cents; cash, stamps, or money-order to The Ring Man, in care of XEG, Del Rio, Texas."*

And Williams is only one of many trinitarian scholars who use such double-talk and indefinite or vague words in regard to the doctrine of the Trinity. Professor Millard J. Erickson, in his book, *God In Three Persons*, uses words such as *"indications," "trinitarian suggestion," "intimations," "implied,"* and *"inferred"* in trying to prove the doctrine of the Trinity. [2] Come on Christians, let's get real! It is an insult to the character of the eternal God to teach that He has not **explicitly** and **clearly** revealed Himself in Scripture as a **Trinity**, but sound thinking, rational people **must believe it anyway**, through *"hints," "suggestions," "intimations"* and *"inferences,"* or else they are *"heretics," "reprobates"* and *"Anti-christs,"* and are doomed to everlasting punishment! Wake up Christianity!

Please ask yourself these questions. Is God a God who *"hints"*? Does he just *"imply"* regarding serious matters? Are the *Ten Commandments* actually just ten *"suggestions?"* No way! Even the secular world does not operate on such indefiniteness. A traffic light gives clear messages. Red means *"stop,"* green means *"go,"* and yellow means *"caution."* Imagine the chaos if they left people guessing. Our court system operates on definites. A witness swears to *"tell the truth, the whole truth, and **nothing but the truth!"*** A lawyer who brought such ambiguous fluff as *"hints,"* *"suggested,"* *"implied,"* and *"inferred"* before a judge or jury would be laughed out of court!

Darwinism is based on **speculation** and **theory**, and Bible-believing Christians are right to reject it in favor of biblical truth. But the doctrine of the Trinity, which is likewise based on **speculation** and **theory,** without biblical basis, is taught dogmatically by Christians to the exclusion of all those who dare to deny its errors.

The true doctrines of God's Holy Bible are clearly stated. I do not teach the pre-tribulation rapture, replacement theology, the modern "prosperity" message, or "soul sleep" because they are not clearly stated in Scripture. Because these are clearly stated, I do teach one eternal Creator God, Jesus Messiah His human Son, eternal life through Christ only, repentance, water baptism in the name of Jesus Christ, tongues, clean living, and the eternal punishment of the wicked! If the Bible says it, I am authorized to say it. If the Bible does not state it plainly, I am prone to keep silent.

Here is a point to ponder. If Jesus Christ, our example, had taught the existence of a Triune God, it would not have taken Christianity until 381 A.D. *(Constantinople)* to get this doctrine worked out. And modern trinitarian scholars would not have to spend their time turning over leaves and rocks to see where it might be *"hinted!"* Why all of this effort to try and prove the existence of a Trinity? It is an attempt to force a triangular peg into a round hole.

Our God Speaks Clearly and So Does His Son

God despises ambiguity in His serious matters. He *"thundered"* His message at Sinai and spoke in a *"still small voice"* to Elijah, but He always spoke plainly. In Revelation 1:10 and 4:1, John heard *"a great voice, as of a trumpet, Saying...."* Regarding **our** *message,* God inspired the apostle Paul to write:

> *"For if the trumpet give an **uncertain sound**, who shall prepare himself to the battle? So likewise ye, except ye utter by the tongue **words easy to be understood, how shall it be known what is spoken?"** (I Cor. 14:8-9).*

After inspiring the above instructions to us, would God then give us only *"hints"* regarding His *identity*? When He spoke at the water baptism of His Son, *"there came a voice from heaven saying,* **Thou art my beloved Son, in whom I am well pleased,** *"* and no one was left in doubt as to the message that was conveyed! Some did not believe, and rejected him, but I can almost hear God say to them at the judgement, *"I didn't stutter!"*

Listen To Jesus!

There are many voices in the world today! Voices that demand our attention and seek to influence us. Voices that, unless we are very careful, will drown out the words of the *"lone Galilean."* Consequently, there are some 35,000 different Christian denominations, [3] *"teaching for doctrines the commandments of men"* [Jesus] *(Matt. 15:9).* Some even *"speaking perverse things, to draw away disciples after them"* [Paul] *(Acts 20:30).*

According to Revelation 12:9, by the end of the Age, Satan will have deceived *"the whole world."* The only way to straighten it out is to **listen to Jesus**, stop second guessing him, and trying to put words in his mouth! **To agree with Jesus is to agree with God because his words are the words of God.** The Lord God is speaking of His people coming into agreement with Him when He asks the question in Amos 3:3: *"Can two walk together, except they be agreed?"* Israel had rejected His prophets and gone in their error for so long that God says, *"They **hate him** that rebuketh in the gate,*

171

and **abhor him** *that speaketh uprightly" (Amos 5:10).* When Jesus spoke, **he only quoted the Father**. Trust Jesus when he says:

> *"My doctrine **is not mine**, but his that sent me" (John 7:16).*

> *"...I do nothing of myself; but **as my Father hath taught me**, I speak these things" (John 8:28).*

> *"For I have not spoken of myself; but **the Father** which sent me, **he gave me a commandment**, what I should **say**, and what I should **speak" (John 12:49).*

> *"...**the word which ye hear is not mine**, but the **Father's** which sent me" (John 14:24).*

The above are the clear sayings of Jesus. If you do not receive what he said on this subject, then you should no longer claim to be a true follower of Jesus. Listen again to Jesus:

> *"And these are they which are sown on good ground; **such as hear the word, and receive it**, and bring forth fruit..." (Mark 4:20).*

> *"He that rejecteth me, **and receiveth not my words**, hath one that judgeth him" (John 12:48).*

> *"If ye abide in me, **and my words abide in you**, ye shall ask what ye will, and it shall be done unto you" (John 15:7).* Note: This might be the reason we do not have more of our prayers answered.

Please notice Jesus' statement above, *"and my words abide in you."* Now, compare this with John's statement in II John v. 9:

> *"**Anyone who goes too far and does not abide in the teaching of Christ, does not have God" (NASB).***

Do you understand what John is saying? *"Anyone who goes **too far**,"* i.e., goes beyond what Jesus taught *("the teaching of Christ"),* **"does not have God."** And why do people listen to these teachers of error? Notice John's words again:

> *"...many **false prophets** have gone out into the world. By this you know the Spirit of God: every spirit that confesses that Jesus Christ has come in the flesh* [as a human being] *is from God; **They are from the world;** therefore they speak as from the world, and the world **listens to them**" (I John 4:2, 5 NASB).*

Now look at I John, verses seven and nine from Thomas Nelson's, *New Century Verison*:

> *"Many false teachers are in the world now who do not confess that Jesus Christ came to earth **as a human**. **Anyone who does not confess this** is a false teacher and an enemy of Christ. **Anyone who goes beyond Christs' teaching** and does not continue to follow **only his teaching does not have God."**

Notice John's statement above, *"as a human."* John said also:

> *"This is how you can know God's Spirit: Every spirit who confesses that Jesus Christ came to earth **as a human is from God.** And every spirit **who refuses to say this about Jesus is not from God**" (I John 4:2-3 NCV).*

What Did Jesus Teach?

Jesus spoke more words concerning his Father, and his relationship with his Father, than he did anything else (heaven, hell, sin, righteousness, money, etc.). May I ask how many sermons have you heard on Jesus' relationship to his Father? We as Christians need to study what Jesus said concerning this most important subject, come into agreement with him, **and begin to say what he said!** So, what did Jesus teach concerning God, his Father and ours?

God The Father Is A Person Distinct From Jesus

Jesus certainly saw himself as a person separate from the Father. He made these clear statements:

> *"And the Father **himself**, which hath sent me, hath borne witness of me. **Ye have neither heard his voice** at any time, **nor seen his shape"** (John 5:37).*

> *"Not any man hath seen the Father" (John 6:46).*

> *"...**I go unto my Father**; for my Father is greater than I"* (John 14:28). Note: Jesus could not be *"greater"* than himself.

> *"But now have they...hated **both** me and my Father" (John 15:24).* (Notice, Jesus said *"both."*)

> *"And these things will they do unto you, because they have not known the **Father**, nor **me"** (John 16:3).*

Sadly, we have reached a point in Christianity where Jesus is preached to the exclusion of the Father. When we read the Bible verses where Jesus spoke of the Father as *"he,", "his,"* or *"himself,"* our minds seem to insert the words *"me, "my,"* or *"myself."* This is a serious mistake and adds to our confusion regarding the identity of God. Consider Jesus' words:

> *"...pray ye therefore **the Lord of the harvest**, that **he** would send forth laborers into **his** harvest" (Luke 10:2).*

> *"For **he** is not a God of the dead, but of the living: for all live unto **him"** (Luke 20:38).*

> *"Fear **him**, which after **he** hath killed hath power to cast into hell; yea, I say unto you, Fear **him"** (Luke 12:5).*

*"For as the **Father** hath life in **himself**; so hath he given to the **Son** to have life in **himself**" (John 5:26).*

*"He that believeth on **me**, believeth not on **me**, but on **him** that sent me" (John 12:44).*

*"And in that day ye shall ask **me** nothing. ...Whatsoever ye shall ask the Father in **my** name, **he** will give it you" (John 16:23).*

*"For the **Father himself** loveth you, because ye have loved **me**..." (John 16:27).*

*"As **thou** hast sent **me** into the world...And the glory which **thou** gavest **me**..." (John 17:18, 22).*

*"O my **Father**...not as **I** will, but as **thou** wilt. O my **Father**, if this cup may not pass away from **me**, except I drink it, **thy** will be done" (Matt. 26:39, 42).*

*"My God, my God, why hast **thou** forsaken **me**" (Matt. 27:46)?*

Notice that Jesus always spoke of the Father in the third person, which makes no sense if he is himself *"God."* Here is a good question: If Jesus was God on earth, why did he look up toward heaven when he prayed?

*"And Jesus **lifted up his eyes** and said **Father** I thank thee..." (John 11:41).*

*"These words spoke Jesus, **and lifted up his eyes to heaven**, and said, **Father**, the hour is come..." (John 17:1).*

And who was he thanking when he prayed over food? (As George Orwell said, "We are required to re-state the obvious").

*"And he took the cup and **gave thanks**" (Luke 22:17).*

*"...and he took the seven loaves, and **gave thanks**" (Mark 8:6).*

*"And he took the cup and when he had **given thanks**" (Mark 14:23).*

*"And he took bread and **gave thanks**" (Luke 22:19).*

*"...nigh unto the place where they did eat bread, after that the **Lord** had **given thanks**" (John 6:23).*

When Jesus prayed on the cross, *"Father, forgive them; for they know not what they do" (Luke 23:34)*, he for sure was not saying to the crucifying crowd, *"I forgive you."* He was making an appeal to the Father-"Would *you* please forgive them?"

Are not the above words and actions of Jesus sufficient proof that he saw himself as a person distinct from God? Do we really need anyone else to endorse these clear statements from him? Just in case there is someone who thinks so, here are a few. Listen to Paul:

*"But for us also, to whom it shall be imputed, if we believe on **him** that raised up Jesus our Lord from the dead" (Rom. 4:24).*

*"But **God** commendeth **his** love toward us, in that, while we were yet sinners, **Christ** [Messiah] died for us. For if...we were reconciled to **God** by the death of his Son...and not only so, but we also joy in **God** through our Lord Jesus Christ.... For if through the offense of one [Adam] many be dead, much more the grace of **God**, and the gift by grace, which is by **one man,** [Greek - anthropos - "a human being"] **Jesus Christ**" (Rom. 5:8, 10, 11, 15).*

176

*"Knowing that **Christ** being raised from the dead dieth no more... . For in that he died, he died unto sin once: but in that he liveth, **he liveth unto God**. ...but alive **unto** God **through** Jesus Christ our Lord. For the wages of sin is death; but **the gift of God** is eternal life **through** Jesus Christ our Lord"* (Rom. 6:9-11, 23). Hear Paul, *"...he* [Christ] *liveth **unto God**."*

*"That ye may with one mind and one mouth glorify **God, even the Father** of our Lord Jesus Christ. To **God only wise**, be **glory through** Jesus Christ for ever"* (Rom. 15:6; 16:27).

*"Now unto the King **eternal**, immortal, **invisible**, the **only wise God**, be honor and **glory** for ever and ever. Amen"* (I Tim. 1:17). [Note: Jesus was not *"invisible,"* he was seen by thousands. Paul is for sure speaking of God the Father] Notice: *"Giving thanks unto the **Father**...Who hath...translated us into the kingdom of **his** dear **Son**... Who is the **image** of the **invisible God**, the **firstborn of every creature"** (Col. 1:12, 13, 15). [Note: An *"image"* is not the original, it is a *"representative likeness."* Notice also that Paul called Jesus a *"creature."* You can argue with Paul.]

*"For there is **one God**, and **one** mediator between God and men, the man* [again *"anthropos"* - a human being] *Christ Jesus* (I Tim. 2:5).

*"But to us there is but **one God**, the **Father**... ."* (I Cor. 8:6).

*"For this cause I bow my knees unto the **Father** of our Lord Jesus Christ"* (Eph. 3:14).

Listen To Peter

> *"Jesus of Nazareth,* ***a man approved of God*** *among you by miracles and wonders and signs which* ***God did by him****... Whom* ***God hath raised up****.... . This Jesus hath* ***God raised up****.... . Therefore being* ***by the right hand of God*** *exalted... (Acts 2:22, 24, 32, 33).*

> *"And he* [God] *shall* ***send*** *Jesus Christ which before was preached unto you..." (Acts 3:20).* [Note: This is a future event.]

> *"Christ...Who verily was* ***foreordained*** *before the foundation of the world.... . Who by him do* ***believe in God****, that raised him up from the dead, and gave him glory; that your faith and hope might be in* ***God****" (I Peter 1:19-21).*

> [Christ] ***"committed himself to him*** [God] *that judgeth righteously" (I Peter 2:23).*

> *"For he* [Jesus Christ] ***received from God the Father*** *honor and glory" (II Peter 1:17).*

Listen to Jude the half-brother of Jesus:

> *"...to them that are sanctified by* ***God the Father****, and preserved in* ***Jesus Christ****.... . For there are certain men crept in...denying the* ***only Lord God****, and* [in addition to] *our Lord Jesus Christ. Keep yourselves in the love of* ***God****, looking for the mercy of* ***our Lord Jesus Christ*** *unto eternal life" (Jude 1, 4, 21).*

Jesus Taught That God The Father Is Creator Of All

It is a fact that Jesus Christ never claimed to be the Creator. He gave the credit for that awesome act to God his Father. Here are some statements by him to prove it.

*"Wherefore, if **God** so clothe the grass of the field..." (Matt. 6:30).*

*"Have ye not read, that **he** [God] which made them at the beginning..." (Matt. 19:4).*

*"But from the **beginning** of the creation **God made them** male and female" (Mark 10:6).*

*"For in those days shall be affliction such as was not from the **beginning** of creation **which God created**" (Mark 13:19).* [Note: *"In the **beginning God created** the heaven and the earth" Gen. 1:1*]. Please note: Scripture is void of a claim by Jesus that he was present at the original creation, or had any part in it. His part in creation is that he **redeemed it,** by the sacrifice of his sinless blood!

*"Consider the ravens...and **God feedeth them**" (Luke 12:24).*

The Apostles agreed with Jesus on this very important point regarding creation. Notice their prayer in Acts, chapter four:

*"And when they had heard that, **they lifted up their voice to God** with one accord, and said, **Lord, thou art God, which hast made heaven,** and **earth,** and the **sea,** and **all** that in them is" (v. 24).* *"For of a truth against **thy holy child Jesus...**"(v. 27).* *"...by the name of **thy hold child Jesus**" (v. 30).*

Listen to Stephen:

*"Howbeit the **Most High** dwelleth not in temples made by hands; as saith the prophet, Heaven is my throne, and earth is my footstool...**Hath not my hand made all these things**" (Acts 7:48-50)?*

Listen to Paul:

> *"**God** that **made** the world and all things therein, seeing that **he is Lord of heaven and earth**" (Acts 17:24). "I thank thee, O **Father, Lord of heaven and earth**" [Jesus speaking] (Matt. 11:25).*

> *"Now **he** that hath **wrought** [made] us for the selfsame thing is **God**" (II Cor. 5:5).*

> *"...hid in **God, who created all things** by Jesus Christ"* [i.e. with Jesus as the redeemer and heir] *(Eph. 3:9).*

> *"...commanding to abstain from meats, **which God created**" (I Tim. 4:3).*

Listen to Peter:

> *"For this they are willingly ignorant of, that by **the word of God** the heavens were of old, and the earth..." (II Peter 3:5).*

Listen to the *"four beasts"* and the *"four and twenty elders,"* who said to the *"one"* on the throne:

> *"Holy, holy, holy, **Lord God Almighty**...**for thou hast created all things**, and for **thy** pleasure they are and were created" (Rev. 4:8, 11).* Note: The Lamb [Jesus], is not in Revelation chapter four.

The following are some verses by which you can check yourself and see if you are a true follower of Jesus, or a follower of Origen (the disciple of Plato), who taught the *"eternal generation"* of the Son.

> *"These things saith the Amen, the faithful and true witness, **the beginning of the creation of God**"* [Jesus Christ speaking] *(Rev. 3:14).* Note: The word *"beginning"* above is the Greek word *arche',* and it means *"to commence, first in order of time."* **Trust Jesus!**

Paul agreed:

> [Christ] *"who is the image of the invisible God, the **firstborn** of every **creature**" (Col. 1:15).*

> *"And put on the **new man** [Christ], which is renewed in knowledge after the image of **him** [God] **that created him**" (Col. 3:10).* Note: The new man that we *"put on"* is *Christ.*

> *"For as many of you as have been baptized into Christ, have **put on Christ**" (Gal. 3:27). "But **put ye on the Lord Jesus Christ**" (Rom. 13:14).*

The above Scriptures speak for themselves!

Jesus Taught That, Unlike God The Father, He Himself Is A Man
The foregoing Scriptures bring us to a very important subject, where the teachings of modern Christianity diverge from the clear teachings of God's Messiah, that is, the manhood of Jesus.

Jesus Christ is for sure the supernaturally conceived, virgin born, sinless Son of God. He is the *perfect man, unique man, the mirror image* of God, *"the express image of His person" (Heb. 1:3),* **but man nevertheless.** He did not leave us wondering!

> *"But now ye seek to kill me, **a man** that hath told you the truth, **which I have heard of God**" (John 8:40).*

> *"Greater love hath no **man** than this, that **a man** lay down his life for his friends. Ye are my friends... (John 15:13-14).*

> *"If I had not done among them the works that **none other man** did, they had not had sin" (John 15:24).*

No *Oneness* or *Trinitarian* can produce a Scripture where Jesus calls himself *"God"* or a *"God-man,"* as that never came from his lips, but in the three verses above he clearly refers to himself as a *"man."* (Are we followers of Jesus?) It is a fact that Jesus must be either *"God," "angel"* or *"man."* Scripturally, there is no such thing as a *"God-man."* **That idea came from Tertullian about 200 A.D.**

Is Jesus *"God?"* In the Bible there is only **one** who is *God (Deut. 6:4; Mark 12:29).*

> *"Have we not all **one father**? Hath not **one God** created us" (Mal. 2:10).* Note Malachi 1:6: *"If then I be a **father**, where is mine honor...saith the Lord of hosts... ."*

> *"...for **one** is your **Father, which is in heaven"** [Jesus speaking] (Matt. 23:9).*

> *"But to us there is but **one God**, the **Father**..."* [Paul speaking] *(I Cor. 8:6).*

> *"**One God** and **Father** of all, who is above all..."* [Paul speaking] *(Eph. 4:6).*

> *"For there is **one God**, and one mediator between God and men, the man Christ Jesus"* [Paul speaking] *(I Tim.2:5).*

What Does It Mean To Be *God*?

God is *omniscient* (all-knowing) and Jesus was not. Our Lord asked questions to get information *(Mark 9:21, 33; Luke 8:30, 46).* He apparently **did not know** at the Cana marriage that the hour had arrived to begin his miracle ministry *(John 2:4).* He **denied knowing** the time of his second coming.

> *"But of that day and that hour knoweth no man, no, not the angels which are in heaven, **neither the Son**, but the Father" (Mark 13:32).*

182

God is ***omni-present*** (present everywhere) and Jesus was not. Jesus told his disciples that he was not present in Bethany when Lazarus died.

> *"And I am glad for your sakes that **I was not there**" (John 11:15).* [Note: God was there, but Jesus wasn't].

God is ***omnipotent*** (all powerful), and Jesus was not.

> *"The Son can **do nothing** of himself...I can of mine own self **do nothing**" (John 5:19, 30).*

> *"And he could there **do no mighty work**.... And he marveled because of their unbelief" (Mark 6:5-6).*

> *"It is not for you to know the times or the seasons, **which the Father hath put in his own power**" (Acts 1:7).*

God is ***immortal*** (incapable of dying), and Jesus was not.

> *"I give thee charge in the sight of **God...Who only hath immortality**, dwelling in the light which no man can approach unto; **whom no man hath seen, nor can see**"* [Paul] *(I Tim. 6:13, 16).*

> *"And when Jesus had cried with a loud voice, he said, **Father, into thy hands I commend my spirit: and having said thus, he gave up the ghost**" (Luke 23:46).*

Every Christian in the world testifies that Jesus is not *"God,"* because we all say that Jesus died, and **God** is immortal, **incapable of dying**! The word *"mortal"* means ***"appointed to death,"*** and Jesus was a *mortal* man. The inspired writer of Hebrews spoke of Jesus being *"appointed to death."*

> *"And **as it is appointed unto men once to die**...**So Christ** was once offered..." (Heb. 9:27-28).*

> *"...Christ Jesus; Who was faithful to **him** who **appointed** him" (Heb. 3:2).*

God Is Underived, and Jesus Was Not

To be *"God,"* one must be underived or un-originated, which means having no beginning and no source. Jesus clearly taught us that he came forth from the Father, received his very life from the Father, and is the beginning of God the Father's creation. Therefore he cannot be the eternal God. Notice Jesus' words on this subject.

> *"I came forth from the Father, and am come into the world" (John 16:28).*

> *"...they have received them* [his words]*, and have known surely that I came out from thee" (John 17:8).*

> *"...so hath he* [the Father] *given to the Son to have life in himself" (John 5:26).*

> *"These things saith the Amen...the beginning of the creation of God" (Rev. 3:14).*

Origen taught the *"eternal generation"* of the Son, but Jesus taught that he is *"the beginning of the creation of God."* The Nicean Council followed Origen and said that Jesus was *"not made."* Will you follow Origen or Jesus? The apostle Paul was a follower of Jesus. He wrote:

> *"Concerning his Son Jesus Christ our Lord, which was made of the seed of David..." (Rom. 1:3).*

> *"But when the fullness of the time was come, God sent forth his Son, made of a woman, made under the law" (Gal. 4:4).*
> [Note: Paul said Jesus was *"made of a woman,"* not *"made before the woman"*].

The inspired writer of Hebrews agreed with Jesus as well.

> *"Wherefore in all things it behooved* [was necessary for] *him to be made like unto his brethren" (Heb. 2:17).*

Jesus Taught That God Is Invisible [incapable of being seen by men], **and He Himself Is Not**

> *"And the Father himself, which hath sent me...Ye have neither heard his voice at any time, **nor seen his shape**"* *(John 5:37).*

> *"**Not that any man hath seen the Father**" (John 6:46).*

The apostle John agreed:

> *"No **man** hath seen God at any time" (John 1:18).*

> *"No **man** hath seen God at any time" (I John 4:12).*

So did the apostle Paul:

> *"Now unto the King eternal, immortal, **invisible**, the only wise God..." (I Tim. 1:17).*

However, Jesus taught that God the Father is seen by angels.

> *"...**in heaven** their angels do **always behold the face of my Father** which is **in heaven**" (Matt. 18:10).*

And Jesus has promised that someday we (in our glorified bodies) shall see God.

> *"Blessed are the pure in heart: for **they shall see God**" (Matt. 5:8).*

Revelation 22:4 is for sure referring to **God the Father** when it says:

> *"**And they shall see his face**; and his name shall be in their foreheads."* [See Rev. 14:1].

Was or Is Jesus An Angel?

Some teach in error that Jesus was the *"angel of the Lord"* of the Old Testament, or even Michael the archangel, that entered the womb of Mary and came forth as the Lord Jesus Christ. Of course the Bible doesn't even hint this. Those who teach such things should read again the first two chapters of Hebrews and see that Jesus did not come in the *angel family*, but he came in the *human family*. Notice these verses:

> *"But to which of the angels said he [God] at any time, Sit on my right hand, until I make thine enemies thy footstool"* *(Heb. 1:13)?*

> *"But we see Jesus, who was* **made** *a little* **lower than the angels** *for the suffering of death...that he by the grace of God should taste death for every* **man** *" (Heb. 2:9).*

> ***"For unto angels hath he not put in subjection the world to come"*** *(Heb. 2:5).*

Notice carefully the verse above. God has not put *"the world to come"* under angels. He has put it under redeemed *"man."* Jesus, our redeemer, a man, came in the human family; thus he is our **brother** and we are his co-heirs.

> *"Wherefore in all things it behooved him to be made like unto his* **brethren***..." (Heb. 2:17).*

> *"And if children, then heirs;* **heirs of God, and joint-heirs with Christ***" (Rom. 8:17).*

> *"...then* **an heir of God** *through Christ" (Gal. 4:7).*

In spite of the fact that Jesus taught plainly that he is a **"man"** (Greek *"anthropos"*), a member of the species *homo sapien*, this is such a hard concept for people to grasp, we should look at overwhelming biblical support for this truth.

The Old Testament Prophets Agreed

> *"**A man** of sorrows and acquainted with grief" (Isa. 53:3).*

*"David shall never want **a man** to sit upon the throne of the house of Israel" (Jer. 33:17).*

*"Awake, O sword against **the man** that is my fellow" (Zechariah 13:7)* [See Matt. 26:31].

*"And **this man** shall be the peace" (Micah 5:5).*

John The Baptist Agreed

*"After me cometh **a man** who is preferred before me" (John 1:30).*

*"All things that John spoke of **this man** were true" (John 10:41).*

The Apostle Peter Agreed

*"Jesus of Nazareth, **a man** approved of God..." (Acts 2:22).*
[Note: Peter is speaking of the *ascended* Jesus].

The Apostle Paul Agreed

*"Through **this man** is preached unto you the forgiveness of sins" (Acts 13:38).*

[God] *"will judge the world...by **that man** whom he hath ordained" (Acts 17:31).*

*"The gift of grace, which is by **one man**, Jesus Christ" (Rom. 5:15).*

*"**Every man** in his own order: **Christ** the firstfruits"* [in resurrection] *(I Cor. 15:23).*

*"And being found in fashion as **a man**" (Phil. 2:8).*

*"Put on the **new man**"* [Christ] *(Col. 3:10).*

> *"For there is **one God**, and one mediator between God and men, **the man Christ Jesus**" (I Tim. 2:5).*

The Writer Of Hebrews Agreed

> *"For **this man** was counted worthy of more glory than Moses" (Heb. 3:3).*

> *"But **this man**...hath an unchangeable priesthood" (Heb. 7:24).*

> *"It is of necessity that **this man** have somewhat to offer" (Heb. 8:3).*

> *"But **this man**...sat down on the right hand of God" (Heb. 10:12).*

Jesus Is The Last Adam, Not The First God-man

Listen to the apostle Paul:

> *"For since **by man came death**, **by man came also** the resurrection of the dead. For as in **Adam** all die, even so in **Christ** shall all be made alive" (I Cor. 15:21-22).*

> *"The **first man Adam** was made a living soul: the **last Adam** was made a quickening spirit" (I Cor. 15:45). "The **first man**...the **second man**" (v. 47).*

Jesus as *"the **last Adam**"* was genetically equal to the *"**first man Adam**."* Adam was created by God from the dust, in Genesis one. Jesus was created by God (the Holy Ghost) in the womb of the virgin Mary in Matthew one and Luke one *(Matt. 1:20; Luke 1:32, Rev. 3:14; Col. 1:15 & 3:10).* Study carefully Galatians 4:4:

> *"But when the fulness of the time was come, God sent forth his Son, **made of a woman, made** under the law."* The word *"made"* is *"ginomai"* in Greek and means *"to generate -*

cause to come into being". This was a **creative act** of the Holy Spirit and not an incarnation.

Jesus Is A Glorified Man At The Right Hand Of God

*"Behold, I see the heavens opened and **the Son of man** standing on the right hand of God"* [Stephen] *(Acts 7:56).*

*"But **this man**, after he had offered one sacrifice for sins for ever, sat down on the **right hand of God**"* *(Heb. 10:12).*

Jesus Is Coming To Reign On Earth For 1000 Years As A Glorified Man

Again, listen to Jesus:

*"And then shall they see **the Son of man** coming in the clouds with **great power** and glory"* *(Mark 13:26; Matt. 24:30; Luke 21:27).*

*"Nevertheless, when **the Son of man** cometh, shall he find faith on the earth"* *(Luke 18:8).*

And we shall **be like him**, not *"Gods,"* but glorified men who have attained immortality through Jesus' death, burial and resurrection. Notice I John 3:2:

*"Beloved, **now are we the sons of God**, and it doth not yet appear what we shall be: but we know that when he* [Jesus] *shall appear, **we shall be like him**; for we shall see him as he is."*

Note: Jesus referred to himself as *"the Son of man"* in the two verses above. In fact, Jesus is called *"Son of man"* 84 times in the Gospels and it means *"a human being."* The phrase comes from Psalms 8:6 according to Hebrews 2:6. God called Ezekiel *"son of man"* 90 times in the book of Ezekiel. Whatever Ezekiel was as to manhood, Jesus was. Jesus came as a human being. He had a human body, mind, spirit, soul, will and personality. The *"first Adam"* was made with a sinless nature, but as an act of his will he sinned anyway. The *"last Adam"* was made sinless, with blood untainted by

189

the sin of the first Adam, and as an act of his will he *"did no sin, neither was guile found in his mouth" (I Peter 2:22).* He did it, not as a God-man, but as **a man**. Jesus *"condemned sin in the flesh" (Rom. 8:3).* **"Wherefore** [for this specific reason] *God also hath highly exalted him" (Phil. 2:9).*

So, please receive and understand this biblical truth. The rulership of *"the world to come"* will not be under angels, but God has ordained that it will be under His human Son, Jesus, and us his brethren.

> *"What is **man**, that thou art mindful of **him**? Or the **son of man**, that thou visitest **him**? Thou madest him a little lower than the angels; thou **crownedst** him with **glory** and **honor** [* "Jesus...**crowned** with **glory** and **honor**" v. 9*], and didst set him* [man] *over the works of thy hands: Thou hast put all things in subjection under his* [man's] *feet" (Heb. 2:6-8; Ps. 8:4-6).*

A note of warning as we close this section of Chapter Six. If we in our doctrine, remove Jesus from the *human* family, and place him in the *God* family, or *angel* family, he loses his ability to redeem us! We are not *"gods"* or *"angels,"* but *men*. The lesson taught by the entire Book of Ruth, is that Ruth could only be claimed, and **the lost inheritance redeemed**, by a *gaal* (Hebrew), a **"kinsman redeemer."** If Boaz had not been a member of Ruth's family, **he would not have qualified as the redeemer!** Wake up Christianity!

Jesus Taught That Our Worship Should Be Directed To The Father

The Jews to whom Jesus came understood clearly that no one was to be worshiped as God, but the Lord God. Consequently, the Bible only records a few occasions where Jesus spoke directly regarding *worship*. During his temptation in the wilderness, Jesus refused to worship Satan and reminded him that worship must be given to God only.

> *"Get thee hence, Satan: for it is written, **Thou shalt worship the Lord thy God**, and **him only** shalt thou serve" (Matt. 4:10).*

Once, he warned the Jews of *vain worship,* by quoting God the Father's statement to Israel through the prophet Isaiah:

> *"But in vain they do worship me, teaching for doctrines the commandments of men" (Matt. 15:9; Mark 7:7).*

This brings us to the only other occasion where Scripture records Jesus speaking on the subject of *God worship*, that is, his visit with the woman of Samaria at the well, in John chapter four. Since this gives us Jesus' greatest teaching on *"worship,"* it deserves our very close attention. We learn from Jesus that the Samaritans were confused in their worship:

> *"Ye worship ye know not what"* [Jesus speaking] *(John 4:22).*

Jesus had an important lesson to teach her:

> *"We know what **we** worship" (v. 22).*

It is significant that Jesus had used the phrase **"worship the Father"** in verse twenty-one, and now uses the word *"we"* in verse twenty-two. Jesus continues this important lesson:

> *"But the hour cometh, and now is, when **the true worshipers shall worship the Father** in **spirit** and in **truth:** for the Father seeketh such to worship him."*

Notice that Jesus did not say *"worship **me**,"* but rather, *"worship **him!**"* Consider again Jesus' statement in verse twenty-two, *"**we** know what **we** worship,"* and realize that Jesus himself is a worshiper of the Father. Then Jesus says:

> *"God is a Spirit: and they that worship **him** must worship **him** in spirit and in truth" (v. 24).*

Look at the woman's response:

> *"I know that **Messiah** cometh, which is called **Christ**: when he is come, he will tell us all things" (v. 25).*

To which Jesus replied:

> *"I that speak unto thee am he" (v. 26).*

Here is a good question. Did Jesus make a claim to this woman, or even hint, that he is *"God?"* No way! Did he make a bold claim that he is the *"Messiah"* [Christ]? He did for sure! (Question: What is your claim regarding Jesus?)

Secondary Worship

If the Bible teaches anything, it teaches that **God is jealous of His worship**. Therefore, *"worship"* is a very serious thing! However, the Bible also teaches that a lesser form of worship can be given to others besides the Lord God, with His approval. For example, when Solomon was crowned king of Israel, and *"sat on the throne of the Lord"* at Jerusalem, I Chronicles 29:20 says:

> *"And all the congregation blessed the **Lord God** of their*
> *fathers, and bowed down their heads, and worshiped **the***
> ***Lord,** and **the king**."*

Yes, you read that correctly! Israel on this awesome occasion, worshiped the **Lord God** as **God**, and king Solomon, God's *"son"* (II Sam. 7:14) as **the king**, with God's approval. Thus we see two different levels of *"worship"*, *primary worship* to God, and *secondary worship* to another. It is this *secondary worship* that is seen in Revelation 3:9, when Jesus says to the overcoming saints of Philadelphia regarding their enemies:

> *"I will make them to come and **worship before thy feet**... ."*

Jesus also spoke of secondary worship in Luke chapter fourteen, when he gave the lesson regarding taking the lower or humble seat when invited as a guest to a wedding feast. He said it is better to be promoted to a higher seat:

> *"...**then shalt thou have worship** in the presence of them*
> *that sit at meat with thee" (v. 10).*

Now we are better able to understand what occurred on those occasions when Jesus Messiah was *"worshiped."* Here are some examples of Jesus receiving worship:

The wise men from the east, when they found the baby Jesus in Bethlehem, *"fell down and worshipped him" (Matt. 2:11).*

A leper needing healing came and worshiped him and was healed. *(Matt. 8:2)*

A certain ruler needing resurrection for his daughter, came and worshiped him and she was raised. *(Matt. 9:18)*

After Jesus walked on the sea and calmed the storm, those who were in the ship worshiped him. *(Matt. 14:33)*

The mother of James and John came and worshiped him, and made a request of Jesus that her sons be given a place of honor in his kingdom. *(Matt. 20:20)*

Mary Magdalene and the other Mary, when they saw the risen Lord, came and held him by the feet and worshiped him. *(Matt. 28:9)*

The man possessed with a legion of demons in Gadara, when he saw Jesus afar off, ran and worshiped him. *(Mark 5:6)*

The blind man who was healed when he washed mud from his eyes in the pool of Siloam, found Jesus and worshiped him. *(John 9:38)*

But, lets take a closer look at these occasions and see if any of these people were worshiping Jesus as *"God."*

Did the wise men who found the babe in Bethlehem, think they were looking at God? No, they had come to Jerusalem asking, *"Where is he that is born* **King of the Jews"** *(Matt. 2:2).* When Herod had his scribes search the Scriptures to see where Christ would be born they said:

> *"In Bethlehem of Judah: for thus it is written by the prophet,*
> *And thou Bethlehem, in the land of Judah, art not the least*
> *among the princes of Judah: for out of thee* **shall come a**
> **Governor**, *that shall* **rule my people Israel"** *(Matt. 2:5-6).*

So, they were not searching for God, but "a Governor" sent by God. And how did they know he would be *"King of the Jews."* They had *"seen his star,"* but there is no way they could have read all of this in the stars. They had no doubt read it in the chronicles of Babylon, for centuries before, Daniel, a wise man and prophet in Babylon, had seen visions and foretold the coming of Israel's Prince Messiah.

> *"Know therefore and understand, that from the going forth*
> *of the commandment to restore and to build Jerusalem unto*
> *the Messiah the Prince shall be seven weeks, and threescore*
> *and two weeks"* [69 weeks - 483 years] *(Dan. 9:25).* **And**
> **he was right on time!**

Did the disciples who worshiped Jesus in the boat, after he calmed the sea in Matthew 14:32-33, think they were worshiping him as God? Let's see. In chapter 13:37-41, he had taught great lessons in which he twice called himself *"the Son of man,"* a human being. He closes out the teaching by referring to himself as *"a prophet" (Matt. 13:57).* In chapter 14, Jesus comes to the disciples walking on the sea and calms it.

> *"Then they that were in the ship came and worshipped him,*
> *saying, Of a truth thou art the Son of God" (Matt. 14:33).*

Did they think they were worshiping one in the boat with them who was in fact *"God"* or *"God the Son?"* No! They ate with him, slept with him, saw that he grew weary, tired and hungry and had bodily functions as they did, and knew he was **a man**. They had asked among themselves on a previous and similar occasion *"What **manner of man** is this, that even the winds and the sea obey him" (Matt. 8:27)!* **He is the perfect man,** but *"man"* nevertheless. This incident helped their understanding that this man is indeed Messiah, Son of God, proven by his resurrection as well *(Rom. 1:4).* Listen to their words again; *"Of a truth thou art the Son of God."*

Did the mother of James and John believe she was requesting that her sons sit on the right and left hand side of *"God?"* No! As a Hebrew, this mother knew what all Hebrews knew, that no man could be God. But in her heart she believed that the one whom she worshiped and made her request to was

God's promised Messiah. As such, he would soon have a kingdom, and she wanted a special place for her sons.

Jesus' answer is very enlightening:

> *"To sit on my right hand, and on my left, is **not mine to give**, but it shall be given to them **for whom it is prepared of my Father**" (Matt. 20:23).*

His response to her teaches us several things about Jesus. One, there is someone over him, with greater authority than he, who has not told him all of His plan *(Mark 13:32, Rev. 1:1)*. Number two, God had not given everything into his hands. Look at his words again:

> *"**It is not mine to give**, but it shall be given to them for whom **it is prepared of my Father**."*

This agrees with what Jesus said in Acts 1:7 in response to his disciples question, *"Wilt thou at this time restore again the kingdom of Israel" (v. 6)? "And he said unto them, It is not for you to know the times or the seasons, which the Father hath put **in his own power**" (v. 7).*

Jesus made no claim to be God, and would never have accepted God's worship. But he did receive *secondary worship.* God the Father has even decreed this form of worship from His mighty angels for His son Jesus. Look at Hebrews 1:6:

> *"And again, when he [God] bringeth in the first begotten into the world [not before, as he was not there], He saith, and let all the **angels of God** worship him."*

Jesus came as a man *(Matt. 8:20, Luke 9:58, I Tim. 2:5)* and as such **was made**, as are all men, lower than the angels *(Ps. 8:5, Heb. 2:7)*. Hebrews 2:9 says:

> *"But we see Jesus, **who was made a little lower than the angels** for the suffering of death, crowned with glory and honor; that he by the grace of God should taste death for every man."*

195

But by birth he is the Son of God *(Luke 1:35)* and has been exalted by his Father above the angels. Look at Hebrews 1:4-5:

> *"Being made so much better than the angels, as **he hath by inheritance** obtained a more excellent name than they. For unto which of the angels said he at any time, Thou art my Son, this day have I begotten thee? And again, I will be to him a Father, and he shall be to me a son?"*

Yes the angels worshiped him. God commanded it saying, *"Let all the angels of God worship him"* [the Son]. Not as God Almighty, **whose angels they are**, but as God's virgin-born, sinless Son, under whom He has ***"put in subjection the world to come"*** *(Heb. 2:5)*.

Did the angels of God who worshiped him at his birth *(not before his birth)* think they were worshiping God? No! They saw God's face continually in heaven and knew that this baby was not God, but Messiah, Son of God *(Matt. 18:10; Rev. 5:11-13)*. No one in the scriptural accounts worshiped Jesus as the Lord God, and **we must not!** There are several Greek words in the New Testament that are translated *"worship,"* and are pictured as being offered to God, Jesus, a guest at a wedding, the saints of Revelation, and **improperly** to angels *(Col. 2:18)* and idols *(Rev. 9:20)*. But there is one word *"latreuo"* (Strong's #3000) which means *"to minister to God - render religious homage,"* **and is not in Scripture given to Jesus or anyone else but God** *(Acts 24:14; Phil. 3:3; Heb. 10:2)*. To give Jesus the Son, God the Father's place in our hearts and in our worship is to flirt with idolatry. ***"Thou shalt have no other gods*** [plural] ***before me*** [singular]*" (Ex. 20:3)*. Jesus called his Father *"the **only true God**"* in John 17:3, and **He alone should be worshiped as God.** It is important to note that no place can be found in Scripture where anyone *"worshiped"* Jesus after his ascension to heaven, nor where any New Testament writer told us to *"worship"* him. He is now in the presence of God, seated at the right hand of God the Father, and our *"worship"* is to be directed to God.

> *"Now to appear in the presence of God for us" (Heb. 9:24)*.

Twice in Revelation a scene is described where God and the Lamb are present and both receive praise, **but only God is *"worshiped"*** *(Rev. 5:12-14; 7:9-11).*

Jesus never said he was God. In fact he denied that he is *(Matt. 19:17, John 5:19, 30-31).* If he were God he would have told us; he would not have left us wondering about such a serious matter as that.

Solomon, David's *"great son"* and God's *"son"* received worship with God's approval. David's *"greater son"* Jesus Christ (*"Behold a greater than Solomon is here" Matt 12:42)* received worship as ordained by God his Father. Jesus was worshiped as Savior, Redeemer, Messiah, Son of God, but again, there is no scriptural account of Jesus receiving *"worship"* after his ascension to the Father.

> *"Saying with a loud voice,* **Worthy is the Lamb** *that was slain to receive power, and riches, and wisdom, and strength, and honor, and glory, and blessing" (Rev. 5:12).*
> Please note that the word **"worship" is not included.**

A Summary of What Jesus' Words and Actions Teach Us Regarding The Identity Of God

If Jesus said his Father is *"the only true God"* then he himself cannot be God. *(John 17:3).*

If Jesus said *"Why callest thou me good, there is none good but one, that is God,"* he cannot be God *(Matt. 19:17).*

If Jesus said *"I can of mine own self do nothing...If I bear witness of myself, my witness is not true,"* then he cannot be God *(John 5:30-31).*

If Jesus said *"my Father is greater than I,"* he cannot be God *(John 14:28).*

If Jesus said *"I...am set down with my Father in* **his throne"** then he cannot be God *(Rev. 3:21).*

If Jesus said, when Lazarus died in Bethany *"I was not there,"* then he cannot be God, for God is omnipresent *(John 11:15).*

If Jesus claimed the Father as *"my God"* seven times in the N.T., he himself cannot be God *(Matt. 27:46; John 20:17; Rev. 3:12).*

If Jesus claimed to be a *"man"* (Greek - anthropos *"a human being"*), again and again in Scripture, he cannot be God *(John 8:28, 40; 12:23).*

If Jesus was *"driven by the Spirit into the wilderness"* and was *"forty days, tempted of Satan" (Mark 1:12-13)*, then he cannot be God, for *"God cannot be tempted" (James 1:13)*.

If Jesus went to his home town of Nazareth *"and he could there do no mighty work"* because of their unbelief, he cannot be God *(Mark 6:5-6)*.

If Jesus went to a fig tree seeing leaves, but not knowing if it had figs, then he cannot be God *(Mark 11:13)*.

If Jesus did not have the authority to decide who would sit on his right or left hand **in his own kingdom,** then he cannot be God *(Matt. 20:23)*.

If Jesus did not have *"the times or the seasons"* in his power, then he cannot be God *(Acts 1:7)*.

If Jesus left planet earth to go to the Father, not knowing when he would return, then he cannot be God *(Matt. 24:36; Mark 13:32)*.

If Jesus did not know the end-time events as recorded in *Revelation*, until after he ascended to the Father and **God revealed them to him,** then he cannot be God *(Rev. 1:1)*.

Every Christian that says Jesus died on the cross, is saying he is not God because **God cannot die!** God is *"immortal"* which means *"deathless, incapable of dying."* Jesus was mortal, *"appointed to death"* (Heb. 9:27-28).

If the disciples who saw Jesus ascend to heaven in Acts chapter one, **did not pray to him in Acts chapter four,** then he cannot be God *(Acts 4:24-30)*.

If Jesus said *"I am the vine, ye are the branches"* and *"my Father is the husbandman"* [i.e. the farmer, owner of the vineyard], then he himself cannot be God *(John 15:1, 5)*.

If Jesus referred to himself as the *"Amen, the faithful and true witness, **the beginning of the creation of God,"*** then he cannot be God *(Rev. 3:14)*.

*"We know what **we** worship" (John 4:22)*. Jesus joins us in worshiping *"the only true God,"* **his God** and **our God.**

*"...The testimony of Jesus: **Worship God**" (Rev. 19:10)*.

*"...**Worship God**" (Rev. 22:9)*.

Chapter Seven

The Influence Of Greek Philosophy

*"**Beware** lest any man spoil you through **philosophy** and vain deceit, after the **tradition** of men, after the rudiments of the world, and not after Christ" (Colossians 2:8).*

"While Christianity converted the world; the world converted Christianity, and displayed the natural paganism of mankind. Christianity did not destroy Paganism; it adopted it." (Will Durant, Twentieth-century American Historian) [1]

𝒯he first step to my current understanding regarding the One Most High God was when I realized that the doctrine of the Trinity and the Incarnation were not to be found in Holy Scripture. I had believed and taught the *"Oneness"* doctrine (the belief that Jesus is God the Father Himself incarnate) for several decades but came to realize that this doctrine was based on the misinterpretation of a few verses, while ignoring hundreds of others. As the wife of a very prominent minister, pastor, missionary and former Oneness said to me recently, *"Brother Joel, we based our doctrine on a few cliches."* We accepted what we were told without close enough, prayerful consideration of our traditions. As to how we **should** arrive at our beliefs, I strongly agree with what Professor Charles C. Ryrie says in his popular work, *Basic Theology:*

> *"The argument from **church history** seems to rear its head almost every time any doctrine is discussed. **The truth or untruth of any doctrine does not depend on whether or not it was ever taught in church history. Its truthfulness depends solely on whether or not it is taught in the Bible.** ...the Bible, not church history, is the standard against which **all teachings must be measured."** [2]

I also found statements by many scholars, mostly trinitarian, admitting that the doctrine of the Trinity is not to be found in Scripture. Professor Ryrie, himself an avowed **trinitarian** says:

> "**Trinity is, of course, not a biblical word.** *Neither are triunity, triune, trinal, substance, nor essence. Furthermore, this is a doctrine that is* **not explicit in the New Testament** *even though it is often said that it is implicit* [implied] *in the Old Testament and* **explicit** *in the New. But 'explicit' means 'characterized by full, clear expression,* **'an adjective hard to apply to this doctrine'** *" (p. 58).* "**It is fair to say that the Bible does not clearly teach the doctrine of the Trinity**, *if by clear one means there are proof texts for the doctrine.* **In fact there is not even one proof text**" *(p. 89).*

Trinitarian Millard J. Erickson, Southern Baptist theologian, writes in his work, *God In Three Persons:*

> "*We will see the doctrine of the Trinity being developed, layer by layer*" *(p. 33).* "**It is unlikely that any text of Scripture can be shown to teach the doctrine of the Trinity in a clear, direct, and unmistakable fashion**" *(p. 109).* "*We are not coming to the text* [of the O.T.] *with the expectation of finding the doctrine of the Trinity taught therein. We will not even find a full fledged and explicit* [trinity] *doctrine within the New*" *(p. 159).* [3]

Dr. George O. Wood, General Superintendent of the Assemblies of God, in his book, *Living In The Spirit,* acknowledges the lack of biblical support for the doctrine of the Trinity and says:

> "*...the clearest setting forth of the Trinity is the record of Jesus' baptism in which the Son is baptized, the Spirit descends, and the Father speaks. I'll leave it to others to more thoroughly explore this subject*" *(p. 64).* [4]

The *New International Dictionary of New Testament Theology* states:

> "The Bible lacks the express declaration that the Father, the Son, and the Holy Spirit are of equal essence and therefore in an equal sense God himself. And the other express declaration is also lacking, that God is God thus, and only thus, i.e. as the Father, the Son, and the Holy Spirit. **These two express declarations, which go beyond the witness of the Bible, are the twofold content of the Church doctrine of the Trinity. The New Testament does not contain the developed doctrine of the Trinity**" **(Trinitarian** Colin Brown; Gen. Editor). [5]

The *Encyclopedia Britannica* says:

> "Believers in God as a **single person** were at the beginning of the third century **still forming the large majority.**" [6]

The **trinitarian** Methodist, Adam Clarke in his *Adam Clarke's Commentary On The Bible,* makes this strong statement:

> "Here I trust I may be permitted to say, with all due respect for those who differ from me, that the doctrine of the **eternal sonship of Christ** is in my opinion **anti-Scriptural** and **highly dangerous.**" [7]

Theologian James Hastings, a **trinitarian**, in his famous work, *Hastings' Dictionary of The Bible,* states:

> "We must avoid every kind of language which suggests that to Saint Paul the ascension of Christ was a **deification**. To a Jew the idea that a man might come to be God would have been an **intolerable blasphemy**" (p. 707). "It may be that Saint Paul **nowhere names** Christ 'God,' " and verses that seem to infer it *"must be otherwise explained."* Hastings calls this *"one of the most baffling problems of N.T. theology"* (p. 708). [8]

The *Encyclopedia International* says:

> *"The doctrine of the Trinity did not form part of the apostles' preaching as this is reported in the New Testament."* [9]

I highly regard the integrity, sincerity, and scholarship of these Christian men I have quoted, telling us that the doctrine of the Trinity is not biblical, that it, in fact, is not to be found clearly stated in the Old or New Testaments. That being true, the next question is, "Where did it originate, and how did it come to be such a part of modern Christian doctrine?" As we go forward we will listen to Christian scholars as they tell us.

The Origin Of The Doctrine Of The Trinity

Throughout over forty-five years of Christian ministry (evangelism, pastoring, singing, songwriting), I had almost no interest in Greek philosophy or philosophers, and very little understanding as to how they held any importance regarding who I was and what I was called to do. However, that started to change in 2005 when I began to do research for my first book, *To God Be The Glory.*

I found that names such as Socrates, Plato, Aristotle, etc. surfaced again and again in the writings of scholars and historians, both Christian and secular, both ancient and modern, who have chronicled the development of Christian doctrine. Some of the writers considered the influence of these Greeks and their philosophy as a positive thing, or at least not a negative thing, while others saw this influence as a devastating blow to our understanding of biblical truth.

Greek Influence

The influence of Greek culture, customs and language, especially from what is known as the *"Hellenistic Period,"* on Western civilization is a well documented fact of history. Hellenism means, *"imitation of the Greeks in thought, culture, language and customs."* The term comes from Hellen, a man in ancient Greek **lore** whose parents, because of their piety, were saved from a devastating flood that destroyed all of creation. Hellen was believed to be the father of the nations of Greece. In ancient times Greeks were called "Hellenes." *Funk and Wagnalls New Encyclopedia* states:

> *"By the time of Alexander's death* [the Great] *in 323 B.C., the culture of Greece had spread through most of the ancient world. Thus, one of the characteristics of the* **Hellenistic period***, which lasted from the death of Alexander until the acquisition of Greece as a Roman province in 146 B.C. was the deterioration...of Greek political independence as a whole. Nevertheless, the Hellenistic period was marked by the* **triumph of Greece** *as the fountainhead of* **culture***, and its* **way of life was adopted***, as a result of Alexander's conquests,* **throughout most of the ancient world***. So strong was* **Hellenistic** *culture implanted that it became* **one of the most important elements in early Christianity"***. [10]

And today that Greek influence on modern America is beyond our ability to fathom. The noted American historian Will Durant *(1885-1981),* authored *The Story of Civilization,* an exhaustive, eleven-volume work on world history that earned him a Pulitzer Prize. In volume two, *The Life of Greece,* he writes of that powerful Greek influence:

> *"Excepting machinery,* **there is hardly anything secular in our culture that does not come from Greece***. Schools, gymnasiums, arithmetic, geometry, history, rhetoric, physics, biology, anatomy, hygiene, therapy, cosmetics, poetry, music, tragedy, comedy,* **philosophy, theology***, agnosticism, skepticism, stoicism, epicureanism, ethics, politics, idealism, philanthropy, cynicism, tyranny, plutocracy, democracy: these are* **all Greek words** *for cultural forms seldom originated, but in many cases* **first matured for good or evil** *by the abounding energy of the* **Greeks.** *"* [11]

This is amazing! However, the *Greek Influence* that is troubling to me is that which has affected *"theology,"* our beliefs about God. Please study carefully the following quotes:

Trinitarian Professor Shirley C. Guthrie, Jr. in his best selling book, *Christian Doctrine,* says:

> ***"The Bible does not teach the doctrine of the Trinity"*** *(p. 76).* *"The language of the doctrine is the language of the ancient church **taken from classical Greek philosophy"** (p. 77). "The doctrine of the Trinity is not found in the Bible" (p. 80).* [12]

Trinitarian Professor Cyril C. Richardson, an outstanding historian of the early church, especially the period during which the doctrine of the Trinity was first formulated, states in his work, *The Doctrine of The Trinity:*

> *"It is not a doctrine specifically to be found in the New Testament. **It is a creation of the fourth-century church"** (p. 17). "In Paul, to be sure, the problem is not so simple as that, for he never calls the Son of God or Lord (Kyrios) 'God' " (p. 23). "The idea that the **logos** is begotten by God, is his 'first-born', his 'invisible image', plays an important role in **Philo**, and whether directly from him or not, **comes into Christian thinking"** (p. 34). "My conclusion, then, about the doctrine of the Trinity is that it is an artificial construct" (p. 148). **"There is no necessary threeness in the Godhead"** (p. 149).* [13]

Trinitarians Roger Olson and Christopher Hall, writing in their scholarly work, *The Trinity,* make these very revealing statements:

> *"Boethius (circa -525 A.D.) was a major interpreter of the Augustinian tradition of trinitarian thought who sought to use **Aristotelian** categories to explain it" (p. 51). "The medieval mind of the Latin West made little distinction between philosophy and theology. **Scripture, Plato, Aristotle,** and subtle **logic played significant if not equal roles in developing explanations and defenses of doctrines such as the Trinity and the person of Christ"** (p. 52). "Augustine was influenced by **Platonic thought,** which*

inclined his **trinitarian views** in the direction of the unity
of the Godhead" (p. 55). "The philosophy of **Plato** and
Aristotle both found expression in Thomas Aquinas' system
of theology, as did the seemingly competing **trinitarian**
vision of Anselm and Richard of St. Victor" (p. 63). [14]
Note: Thomas Aquinas *(1224-1274 A.D.)* has been declared
"The Angelic Doctor of the Church" by popes. He was
one of the Catholic church's greatest theologians and **an
authority on the doctrine of the Trinity**. Now they tell us
he was influenced in his beliefs by *"Plato and Aristotle."*
Shocking! Olson and Hall refer in their book to *"**Greek
trinitarian doctrine**" (p. 39),* and *"**Greek trinitarian
thought**" (p. 131).*

Trinitarian Millard J. Erickson, Southern Baptist scholar writes:

"He [nineteenth century historian Adolph Harnack] *finds
the Christian community **borrowing heavily from Greek
philosophy**. It was from these **foreign sources**, not
from Jesus himself, that the doctrine of the **Trinity**, the
incarnation, and related conceptions grow" (p. 122).*

Erickson continues:

*"We have also observed that the specific metaphysical
vehicle used to express the classical **doctrine of the Trinity**
was a **Greek metaphysics** that was viable in that time but **no
longer makes a great deal of sense** to most persons today"*
*(p. 211). "While it is customary to assume that the major
philosophical influence on the Greek fathers was **Plato**
and the **Stoics**, [Michael] Durant believes the influence of
Aristotle should not be overlooked" (p. 259).* [15]

Trinitarian D.J. Constantelos, church historian and author writes:

*"**Greek thought served as a preparation for Christian
doctrines**. For example, the **doctrine of God** was formulated*

*on the basis of centuries - old **Greek** intellectual tradition."* **And**: *"When Greek religion and Christianity met, **they were fused**, and after their fusion, **many of the older forms and beliefs reappeared under different forms.**"* **And**: *"It is neither unnatural nor illogical for the Creator to elect some persons such as Noah, Abraham, Moses, Amos, **Socrates, Plato,** or others and use them as special instruments in history."* **And**: *"Nevertheless, the influence of **ancient Greek religion** on Christian religion is apparent in **every major aspect of Christianity**, its **doctrines**, ethics and worship."* **And**: *"To be sure there was* [initial] *hostility to Hellenic thought, religious practices, and culture. But ultimately, it was the **Hellenized school of Christian theology** and the synthesis achieved by the Cappadocian Fathers **that prevailed.**"* [16]

Thomas Jefferson, third President of the United States and author of the *Declaration of Independence* wrote in a letter to a friend on June 26, 1822:

*"The doctrines of Jesus are simple, and tend to the happiness of man. Had the doctrines of Jesus been preached always as pure as they came from his lips, **the whole civilized world would now have been Christian**. I rejoice that in this blessed country of free inquiry and belief...**the genuine doctrine of the one only God is reviving.**"* But he feared that believers in one God would follow *"**Platonizing Christians**"* and *"fall into the fatal error of fabricating formulas of creed and confessions of faith, the engines which so soon destroyed the religion of Jesus, and made of Christendom a mere Aceldama; that they will give up morals for mysteries, and **Jesus for Plato.**"* [17]

The *Encyclopedia Americana* says:

*"**The full development of Trinitarianism** took place in the West, in the scholasticism of the Middle Ages, when an*

> *explanation was undertaken in terms of **philosophy** and*
> ***psychology**, especially of the recovered **Aristotelianism** of*
> *the 13th Century."* [18]

The great nineteenth century historian Adolph Harnack in his work, *History of Dogma,* says the early church father Justin (Martyr) *(100-165 A.D.)* made the assertion that in *"virtue of 'reason' **Socrates** exposed superstition; in virtue of the **same reason**, this was done by the teacher* (Jesus) *whom the Christians follow."* Harnack says Justin *"represents Christ as the **Socrates** of the barbarians, **and consequently makes Christianity a Socratic doctrine"** (Vol. 2; p. 181).* Justin taught that Christ was known by **Socrates** (who died in 399 B.C.), for *"Christ was and is the **Logos** who dwells in every man."* According to Justin, *"it may be asserted that all who have lived with the Logos...were Christians. Among the Greeks this specially applies to **Socrates** and **Heraclitus**."* [19]

This is shocking stuff! No wonder the great apostle Paul gave us the dire warning that is quoted at the beginning of this chapter. Again:

> ***"Beware** lest any man spoil you through **philosophy** and*
> *vain deceit, after the **tradition** of men, after the rudiments*
> *of the world, and not after Christ" (Col. 2:8).*

The word *philosophy* means *"a love for wisdom or knowledge."* But it should be understood that not all wisdom comes from God. Notice these verses:

> *"...my preaching was not with enticing words of **man's***
> ***wisdom**...But we speak the **wisdom of God**"* [Paul] *(I Cor.*
> *2:4, 7).*

> *"For the wisdom of this world is **foolishness with God**" (I*
> *Cor. 3:19).*

> *"This wisdom descendeth not from above, but is **earthly,***
> ***sensual, devilish**" (James 3:15).*

*"Professing themselves to be **wise**, they became **fools**..."*
(Rom. 1:22).

Jesus' Hebrew Roots

Please receive and understand this biblical fact. The church that Jesus Christ founded has its roots firmly planted in Hebrew *(Jewish)* soil; its heritage, religion, culture, customs, etc. The patriarchs Abraham, Isaac and Jacob *(Israel)* were Hebrews, and faithfully served the God of the Hebrews. *(Their descendants are called Jews because of **one** tribe of Israel, Judah).* Every writer of the books of the Old and New Testaments, with the possible exception of Luke, was Hebrew. Moses, Elijah, Isaiah, Jeremiah and Daniel were Hebrews. King David was a Hebrew of the tribe of **Judah**, therefore our Savior Jesus Messiah, David's descendent through the virgin Mary, was a Jew.

"For it is evident that our Lord sprang out of Judah"
(Hebrews 7:14).

Look at the first verse in the New Testament:
"The book of the generation of Jesus Christ, the Son of David, the son of Abraham" (Matt. 1:1).

Jesus was born in Bethlehem, five miles south of Jerusalem, and after Mary and Joseph took him to Egypt for two years to avoid the wrath of Herod, they moved back to their home city of Nazareth. Nazareth is a hill city of *"Upper Galilee,"* and Jesus began his ministry there at the age of thirty. He performed his first miracle *(water to wine)* about three miles from home in the small village of Cana. Jesus preached his first sermon in Nazareth *(Luke chapter four)*, but when they rejected him and his message, he went down to *Lower Galilee,* near the Sea of Galilee, and continued his ministry. There were sixteen fishing villages around the Sea of Galilee *(Capernaum, Gadara, Magdala, etc.)*, and except for brief trips south to Jerusalem, this is where his teaching, preaching and miracles were done.

Galilee, Palestine and Greek Influence

God the Father not only chose the *race* into which Jesus was born, but in His wisdom He chose a *time* and a *place*. Galatians 4:4 says, *"But when the fullness of the time was come, God sent forth his Son... ."* Why this particular time?

It is said that every age has its prevailing mood, and when Jesus was born at the height of the Roman Empire, hope and optimism abounded. The Roman poet Virgil *(70-19 B.C.)* had predicted *"a new order of the ages,"* brought about because *"a new human race is descending from the heights of heaven."* He saw this happening due to *"the birth of a child, with whom the iron age of humanity will end and the golden age begin."* Though Virgil sounds like an Old Testament prophet predicting the coming of the Messiah, this baby of which he spoke was already born. He was none other than Caesar Augustus, called *"the present deity"* and the *"restorer of the world."* My thoughts on these words by Virgil are this: Satan tries to anticipate God's moves, perhaps through his knowledge of prophecy, and de-rail people's faith by producing distracting counterfeits. Of course the birth of the true *"child,"* the *"restorer of the world"* was to happen about twenty-five years after Virgil wrote. Look at these prophecies regarding Jesus, given over 700 years before this time.

> *"For unto us a **child** is born, unto us a son is given..."* (Isa. 9:6).

> *"He shall not fail nor be discouraged till he have set judgement in the earth"* (Isa. 42:4).

> *"Thou shall be called...**The restorer** of paths to dwell in"* (Isa. 58:12).

And Jesus said this kind of deceptive work of Satan will happen again when counterfeit "christs" arise before his **second coming.**

And in Virgil's time, during the reign of Augustus, things did look promising, as he had managed to reunite the Roman empire, after the civil war that was sparked by the assassination of Julius Caesar in 44 B.C. by Brutus and his cohorts. Augustus offered peace and security to all loyal Roman subjects.

Philip Yancey, respected, award-winning author, and editor-at-large for *Christianity Today* magazine, writes of this time in his book, *The Jesus I Never Knew:*

> *"Rome kept peace at the point of a sword, but by and large even the conquered peoples cooperated. **Except in Palestine, that is.** Meanwhile, a **Greek soul** filled the Roman body politic. People throughout the empire dressed like the **Greeks**, built their buildings in the **Greek** style, played **Greek** sports, and spoke the **Greek** language. **Except in Palestine.**"* [20]

Palestine Resists Hellenization

For Rome, the area called Palestine was a different story. The Jews who lived there had been **visited and called out of Egypt** by our Creator, the God of Abraham, Isaac and Jacob, and He had placed within them a resolve that the doctrines of Hellenism and the power of Rome could not subdue. William Barclay describes what happened when Rome and Palestine collided.

> *"It is the simple historical fact that in the thirty years from 67 B.C. to 37 B.C. before the emergence of Herod the Great, no fewer than 150,000 men perished in Palestine in revolutionary uprisings. There was no more explosive and inflammable country **in the world than Palestine.**"* [21]

Regarding the Jews' overall response to Hellenization, Philip Yancey states it well:

> *"Jews resisted Hellenization (imposed Greek culture) as fiercely as they fought the Roman legions. Rabbis kept this aversion alive by reminding Jews of the attempts by a Seleucid madman named Antiochus to **Hellenize** the Jews*

> *more than a century before. Antiochus had compelled young*
> *boys to undergo reverse circumcision operations so they*
> *could appear nude in Greek athletic contests. He flogged*
> *an aged priest to death for refusing to eat pig's flesh, and*
> *butchered a mother and her seven children for not bowing*
> *down to an image. In a heinous act that became known as*
> *the 'abomination of desolation', he invaded the Most Holy*
> *Place of the temple, sacrificed an unclean pig on the altar*
> *in honor of the Greek god Zeus, and smeared the sanctuary*
> *with its blood."* [22]

This was a fore-shadowing of some future day when the Anti-christ will stand in the temple of God in Jerusalem and defile it *(Matt. 24:15; II Thess. 2:3-4)*. But Antiochus IV's campaign failed, driving the Jews to an open revolt led by Judas Maccabeus.

Funk and Wagnalls New Encyclopedia says of this revolt:

> *"When he* [Antiochus IV] *attempted to impose worship*
> *of the* **Greek gods**, *the Jews revolted, and led by Judas*
> *Maccabeus, established an independent Jewish state*
> *relatively* **free of Hellenism**. *In Acts 6:1 and 11:20 the*
> *apostle contrasts Hellenistic ("Grecians") with Hebrews,*
> *Jews who resisted Hellenistic influences."* [23]

For nearly a century the Maccabeans held out against the foreign invaders, until the Roman legions rolled into Palestine. It took thirty years for Rome to put down all Jewish rebellion; then in 37 B.C. Rome installed the local tough guy Herod as their puppet king. By this time the Romans had devastated Palestine, killing men, women and children in their houses, markets, and even in the temple; destruction that left not only Jerusalem, but the entire country, in ruins. Palestine stayed fairly quite under the iron rule of Herod the Great, and he reigned until the birth of Jesus in 4 B.C. However, that period of time was not totally without trouble in Palestine, as a destructive earthquake in 31 B.C. killed 30,000 people and much livestock, and it was

Herod himself who ordered the killing of all boy babies under the age of two in Bethlehem. Ruthless as he was, Herod did one good thing during his reign. Probably as a political move to placate the Jews, he began a major rebuilding and expansion of the temple, **the one that was to know visits by Jesus and Paul**.

Why A Place Called Galilee?
If no other place in the world resisted Roman authority and Greek Hellenization like Palestine, no place in Palestine resisted them like Galilee.

Galilee was an area of Palestine located north of Judea (and Jerusalem), made up of "upper Galilee" in the hills and "lower Galilee" around the Sea of Galilee. The Galilean Jews of Jesus' day lived in small hamlets and fishing villages in the midst of a more modern and alien culture. Nazareth where Jesus grew up, sits on a hillside 1,300 feet above sea level, and was so small and obscure back then that, out of sixty-three towns in Galilee that are named in the Talmud, it is not mentioned.

The Galileans were hardworking, salt-of-the-earth people who fished the sea, toiled in the wheat fields, and gathered in abundance, figs from their fig trees and grapes from their grapevines. Literature of the time portrays the Galileans as bumpkins and the butt of ethnic jokes. The Galileans pronounced Hebrew crudely, and their common language of Aramaic was spoken in such a slipshod way that if spoken down south in Jerusalem, it was a telltale sign of Galilean roots. Notice:

> "Surely thou art one of them: for thou art a Galilean and your speech shows it" [the damsel to Peter] *(Mark 14:70 NKJV)*.

> "Behold, art not all these which speak Galileans" [the multitude at Pentecost] *(Acts 2:7)?*

And Jesus was a native son of Galilee which made big city people suspicious of him.

212

> *"And the multitude said, This is Jesus the prophet of Nazareth **of Galilee**" (Matt. 21:11).*

> *"Can any good thing come out of Nazareth" (John 1:46)?*

> *"Shall Christ come out of Galilee? Search, and look: for out of Galilee ariseth no prophet"* [Jesus' skeptics] *(John 7:41, 52).*

Some people of Jesus' day thought he might be for Rome just another Galilean trouble maker *(Acts 5:36-37)*, and Galilee had produced quite a few. In 4 B.C., about the time of Jesus' birth, a rebel broke into the army arsenal at Sepphoris, three miles north of Nazareth, and looted it to arm his followers. Roman soldiers recaptured the town and **crucified** two thousand Jews who had participated in the uprising. [24]

Ten years later, another rebel named Judas led a revolt, urging Galileans to pay no taxes to the pagan emperor. He helped found the group called the Zealots, and they harassed Rome for the next sixty years. Two of Judas's sons were crucified, and his last son led a group that captured the Roman stronghold Masada, in 66 A.D., and vowed to defend it to the death. Watching for months as the Roman army built a stone and earthen ramp up the hill from the valley below, hope was abandoned, and 960 Jewish men, women, and children committed suicide rather than submit to Rome. Galileans were freedom-lovers to the bone.

The Small Town Ministry Of Jesus
The ministry of our Messiah Jesus thrived in the hamlets and fishing villages of Galilee. His was a simple message to simple people, *"Repent: for the kingdom of heaven is at hand" (Matt. 4:17; Mark 1:12)*, backed up by Holy Spirit anointing and miracles. His first sermon *text*, at his home church in Nazareth, was Isaiah 61:1.

> *"The Spirit of the Lord* [God] *is upon me, because **he** hath anointed me to preach the gospel **to the poor**" (Luke 4:18).*

213

*"And the **common people** heard him gladly" (Mark 12:37).*

Jesus loved all people, but we notice in his ministry that he had problems with educated people who gloried in their education, rich people who despised and neglected the less fortunate, and people with a "religious spirit" who trusted in their good works to bring them favor with God. To them he made this shocking statement:

> *"**Verily I say unto you, that the publicans and the harlots go into the kingdom of God before you**" (Matt. 21:31).*

> *"Blessed are the **poor** in spirit: for **theirs** is the kingdom of heaven" (Matt. 5:3).*

> *"**How hardly shall they that have riches enter into the kingdom of God**. And the disciples were astonished at his words. But Jesus answered **again**, and said unto them, Children, **how hard is it** for them that trust in riches to enter into the kingdom of God. It is easier for a camel to go through the eye of a needle, than for a rich man to enter into the kingdom of God!" (Mark 10:23-25).*

To illustrate the kind of person he (and God) were looking for, he sat a small child in the midst of them and said:

> *"Except ye be converted, and become as little children, **ye shall not enter** into the kingdom of heaven. Whosoever therefore shall **humble himself** as this little child, the same is **greatest** in the kingdom of heaven" (Matt. 18:3-4).*

Part of Jesus' encouraging message to a questioning John the Baptist in prison, was:

> *"...and **the poor** have the gospel preached to them" (Matt. 11:5).*

Except for an occasional visit to Jerusalem, Jesus mostly avoided Romanized and Hellenized big cities. For most of his life, the beautiful city of Sepphoris was being rebuilt after its destruction in 4 B.C. It became once again a thriving Greco-Roman metropolis, with colonnaded streets, a forum, a palace, a bath and gymnasium, and luxurious houses, all constructed in white limestone and colored marble. In the amphitheater that seated 4,000, **Greek** actors called *hypocrites,* entertained the multinational crowds. (Jesus would later borrow this word to describe people who play a false role in public). This thoroughly Hellenized city was the capital of Galilee throughout Jesus' lifetime, and though it was only three miles north of his hometown, **not once** do the Gospels record that Jesus ever visited or mentioned that city! [25]

My wife LaBreeska and I, on more than one occasion, have visited the home of friends and ministered in an auditorium in the large modern city of Tiberius, Galilee. It is situated on the Sea of Galilee, near the other towns where Jesus ministered, and in his day was a thriving big city, and Herod's winter resort town. But we were surprised to find that there is no biblical or historical record that Jesus ever set foot there.

You may ask, what are you suggesting? It is my conclusion that Jesus had little time for Hellenized and Romanized cities and gave them a wide berth. It must be that God the Father who chose Bethlehem as the place of Jesus birth, and Nazareth and Galilee as the places of his upbringing and ministry, did not want the mind and doctrine of His Son, our Messiah tainted by the "Greek spirit." He also ordained that his disciples and early church be free of such influences. (Perhaps you will better understand these statements as we go forward).

Enlightening Visions In Daniel

This is a fact of history. About 586 years before the birth of Jesus, Nebuchadnezzar the King of Babylon had destroyed Jerusalem, burned the Temple of God and taken many captives back with him. Daniel and his friends were among that number. The book of Daniel was written in Babylon, but the books of Ezra and Nehemiah tell the story of those Jews who were sent back to Jerusalem, some seventy years after its destruction to rebuild it.

During this seventy years of Jewish captivity, Babylon had itself been conquered by the Medes and Persians. In Daniel's vision, as told in Daniel chapter eight, that Medo-Persian kingdom is pictured as *"a ram with two horns" (v. 3)*.

The Rise Of Greece

But in this vision Daniel sees a *"he goat"* with one great horn between his eyes, and this goat smote the *"ram with two horns" (vs. 5-7)*, and Daniel writes:

> *"Therefore the **he goat** waxed very **great**: and when he was strong the great horn was **broken**,"* and in its place *"came up four notable ones" (vs. 8-9)*.

When the angel Gabriel explained this vision to Daniel, he said the *"rough goat is the king of Grecia* [Greece]*: and the great horn that is between his eyes is the first king" (Daniel 8:21)*.

This is an amazing prophecy from God to Daniel concerning the overthrow of the Medo-Persian empire by Greece, which happened in about 466 B.C. some one-hundred years after Daniel's vision. The *"first king"* is none other than *Alexander the Great* (he named himself *"the Great"*) for God had said *"the **he goat** waxed very great" (v. 8)*.

But in Daniel's vision *"when he was strong, the great horn was broken"* and *"**four** notable ones"* came up in its place *(v. 8)*. When Alexander the Great had conquered the known world of his day by the age of thirty-three, he despaired of life and died in a drunken binge. History says **four** of his generals took over the nation of Greece and thus it was divided. Infecting the Middle East with its language, culture, customs and *"Greek Spirit,"* Greece continued to rule until 146 B.C. when it was conquered by the Romans. Strife and warfare between two of its main cities, Athens and Sparta, had weakened Greece until it was easily overthrown by what became the Roman Empire.

In his vision Daniel saw this rise of Rome also *(Daniel 8:9-15; 23-25)*. Daniel's response to the events that he saw is described in verse twenty-seven:

> *"And I Daniel **fainted, and was sick certain days**; afterward I rose up...and I was **astonished** at the vision."*

However, this is not the last we read of Greece in the book of Daniel. In Daniel chapter ten, Daniel set out to seek God by fasting and praying for *"three full weeks."* At the end of this period, an angel appeared to Daniel and said he had been sent by God *"the first day"* he had begun to seek. Notice:

> *"But the **prince** of the kingdom **of Persia** withstood me one and twenty days: but, **Michael**, one of the chief princes [angels], came to help me..." (Daniel 10:13).*

Please note. These angels, called princes, that were sent to Daniel are *spirit beings,* messengers of God that do His bidding.

> [God] *"maketh his angels **spirits**, and his ministers a flame of fire" (Heb. 1:7).*

> *"Are they not all ministering **spirits**, sent forth to minister..." (Heb. 1:14).*

> *"Michael, one of the chief princes..." (Daniel 10:13).*

So if these angels (princes) are ministering spirits from God, it would follow that the *"prince of the kingdom of Persia"* is a *demon spirit* sent from the prince of devils, himself: Lucifer, Satan. **Listen to Paul:**

> *"For we **wrestle** not against flesh and blood, but against **principalities**, against **powers**, against the **rulers** of the darkness of this world, against spiritual wickedness **in high places" (Eph. 6:12).*

*"Wherefore we would have come unto you, **even I Paul**, once and again; **but Satan hindered us**" (I Thess. 2:18).*

Listen To Jesus

*"Depart from me ye cursed, into everlasting fire, prepared for **the devil and his angels**" (Matt. 25:41).*

Listen To The Apostle John

*"And there was war in heaven: Michael and his angels fought against the **dragon**; and the **dragon** fought and **his angels**...and the great **dragon** was cast out, that old **serpent**, called the **Devil**, and **Satan**, which **deceiveth the whole world**" (Rev. 12:7, 9).*

The Spirit Of Persia

What is this prince, demon-spirit of Persia? Look at how he is described in Daniel 8:4:

*"I saw the ram **pushing** westward, and northward, and southward; so that no beasts [powers] might stand before him, neither was there any that could **deliver out of his hand**."*

So this is a **pushing, violent spirit,** so strong that he hindered the angel of God from reaching Daniel for twenty-one days, until Michael the Archangel came to assist him *(Daniel 10:13)*. Is that pushing, violent spirit that controls Persia active in the world today? For sure! The modern nation of Iran was named Persia until 1935. Does it have a history of violence? Yes! Is Iran *"pushing"* and promoting violence in the world today? Yes! Iran is pursuing nuclear weapons at the price of poverty and unrest of its people, for one purpose: In the words of their President Ahmadinejad, to *"wipe Israel off the face of the earth."*

We should pause with wonder that an ancient spirit of violence *"the spirit of Persia,"* that opposed **Michael the special angel of Israel,** [*"Michael, the great prince which standeth for the children of thy people"*] *(Daniel 12:1)* some 2550 years ago, is still at work to try to destroy Israel today!

The Prince Of Greece

The angel that came to Daniel in chapter ten, after a twenty-one day struggle with the demon spirit of Persia, let him know that he (the angel) after leaving Daniel, had more battles to fight. Look at verses 20 and 21.

> *"...and now will I return to fight with the prince of Persia: and when I am gone forth, lo **the prince of Grecia shall come..**and...there is none that holdeth with me in these things but Michael your prince."*

Thus Daniel (and we) are introduced to another demon spirit, *"the prince of Grecia."* What is *"the spirit of Grecia?"* Like in Persia, there is for sure a degree of violence *(Daniel 8:7)*, but according to other related verses and history, the *"Greek spirit"* is primarily the pursuit of knowledge, human wisdom, and exalting and **deifying men**, by the development of the body and mind. Today it is called *"humanism."* (The Greeks gave us the Olympics). We will see other characteristics of this *"Greek spirit"* as we go forward.

Nashville, Tennessee, our home for the past thirty-eight years, because of its institutes of learning, both secular and religious, and a life-size replica of the Greek Parthenon, is called the *"Athens of the South."* But, is human knowledge and wisdom the route to virtue and ultimately to God, as Socrates taught?

Listen To The Great Apostle Paul

> *"For after that in the wisdom of God **the world by wisdom knew not God**, it pleased God by the **foolishness of preaching** to save them that believe. For **the Jews require a sign**, and **the Greeks seek after wisdom**: But we preach Christ crucified, unto the Jews a stumbling block, and **unto the Greeks foolishness**" (I Cor. 1:21-23).*

The Church Started Out Jewish

Let's consider Paul. Like all of the original Apostles, he was a Jew. Jesus had chosen twelve Galilean Jews as his Apostles, on which his church is built. **There was not a gentile or Greek in the number**. Jesus' ministry was for and to the Jews. He sent his followers out to preach the gospel of the kingdom with this command:

> *"**Go not into the way of the Gentiles**, and unto any city of the Samaritans enter ye not: But go rather to the lost sheep of the house of Israel"* *(Matt. 10:5-6).*

Peter's sermon on the day of Pentecost had been:

> *"**Therefore let all the house of Israel know...**"* *(Acts 2:36).*

It was about eight years later *(A.D. 41)* when Peter himself was sent by God to preach the first gospel message to the Gentile Cornelius and his household *(Acts 10:1-48)*. In fact it was about that same year when Acts 11:19 records:

> *"Now they which were scattered abroad upon the persecution that arose about Stephen traveled as far as Phoenicia, and Cyprus, and Antioch, preaching the word to **none** but unto **Jews only**."*

Why this action in the wisdom of God to keep the infant church of Jesus Christ *"Jewish"* for the first eight years of its existence? I believe it was to assure that it would be thoroughly grounded in the doctrines of the Old Testament, and the knowledge of the Hebrew God of the Old Testament, **before it could be tainted by outside doctrines and influences.**

Of course, some who see the **later Greek influence** on the doctrines and practices of this **Jewish Christian church** as a good thing, would like to date that influence back to the minds **and beliefs of Jesus and his chosen Galilean Apostles**. There is a French word that adequately sums up my feelings toward that idea. **Baloney!**

Chapter Eight

Enter The Apostle Paul

*W*hen the gospel of Jesus Messiah was more and more rejected by the Jews, and those who preached this gospel persecuted and killed, it was time to take it to the Greek and Roman gentile world. However, God did not choose a Greek or Roman for that task. He reached and "apprehended" Saul of Tarsus a *"Hebrew of the Hebrews."*

> *"Circumcised the eighth day, of the stock of Israel, of the tribe of Benjamin, an Hebrew of the Hebrews" (Phil. 3:5).*

Yes, a Jew like the other twelve, but unlike them, highly educated. Notice Acts 4:13:

> *"Now when they saw the boldness of Peter and John, and perceived that they were unlearned and ignorant men, they marveled; and they took knowledge of them, that they had been with Jesus"* [Unlearned and ignorant in "book learning," but thoroughly taught by Jesus in the art of "fishing for men"].

Now, God needed a man of letters, a man of zeal for God and a love for Israel, a gentle man, but one who could dish it out and take it, an educated Saul of Tarsus. His parents had named him Saul after Israel's first king, head and shoulders taller than other men, King Saul. They gave him the best education available, under the best teachers available. One was the great Gamaliel, a man who when he spoke, other men listened *(Acts 5:34-40)*. Saul's parents had big plans for this boy so they sat him *"at the feet of Gamaliel" (Acts 22:3)*. But God had bigger plans!

> *"Go thy way: for he is a chosen vessel unto me, to bear my name before the Gentiles, **and kings**, and the children of Israel: For I will show him how great things he must suffer for my name's sake"* [Jesus to Ananias] *(Acts 9:15-16)*.

Yes said Ananias, *"The God of our fathers* [Abraham, Isaac and Jacob] *has chosen you to see Jesus, and hear his voice,"* but also to preach to King Herod Agrippa, Governor Festus, Governor Felix (*"Felix trembled" Acts 24:25)*, and some of Caesar's household in Rome whom he would win to Christ. Chosen to write much of the New Testament but also to receive forty stripes five times, be beaten with rods three times, and spend a night and a day on a board floating in the sea *(II Cor. 11:25-26).*

> *"In journeyings often, in perils of waters, in perils of robbers, in perils by mine own countrymen, in perils by the heathen, in perils in the city, in perils in the wilderness, in perils in the sea, in perils **among false brethren**; in weariness and painfulness, in watchings often, in hunger and thirst, in fastings often, in cold and nakedness. The **God and Father** of our Lord Jesus Christ, which is blessed for evermore, knoweth that I lie not" (II Cor. 11:26-27, 31).*

God took an educated man and let him preach to educated men, but not before He had emptied him of all dependence on his own wisdom and strength. And what did it take to do that? A trip into Arabia! Listen to Paul:

> *"But when it pleased **God**...to reveal **his Son** in me, that I might preach him among the heathen; immediately **I conferred not with flesh and blood**: Neither went I up to Jerusalem to them which were apostles before me; but **I went into Arabia**..." (Gal. 1:15-17).*

That is precisely what is wrong with what comes over many Christian pulpits today. There is too much conferring *"with flesh and blood,"* and not enough of the learning that only comes from a trip into the soul's Arabia. Some of us have a diploma from that university! The Arabia of cancer, loss of loved ones, depression, hopelessness, failure, despair, persecution and pain. Arabia is a hot, dry and barren place and it "teaches a dear school."

When Paul returned from that school he counted all he had learned of man's wisdom, including Greek philosophy, but *"loss for Christ."*

*"Yea doubtless, and I count **all things but loss** for the excellency of the **knowledge** of Christ Jesus my Lord: **for whom I have suffered the loss of all things**, and do count them but **dung** that I might win Christ" (Phil. 3:8).*

Paul and Greek Philosophy

Did Paul know Greek philosophy? Of course he did! The Greek teachings of the **Hellenist Philo**, a contemporary of Paul's teacher Rabbi Gamaliel, had permeated practically all of Judaism. And although Paul never spoke good about Greek wisdom and philosophy, he could quote it if need be.

In Acts chapter seventeen, when Paul entered Athens, he encountered another facet of the Greek spirit, and that is a *"a religious spirit."*

Paul In Athens

We are told in Acts chapter seventeen that Paul's missionary travels led him to Athens, Greece, having left Timothy and Silas at Berea. Verse sixteen says:

*"Now while Paul waited for them at **Athens**, his spirit was stirred in him, when he saw **the city wholly given to idolatry**."*

This is the Athens that had known Socrates, Plato, Aristotle and Alexander the Great. This was religious Athens that contained the temples of Zeus, Athena, Aphrodite, Hermes, Olympus and others. It is said that there were more temples and places of worship to the gods in ancient Athens than there are Christian churches in most cities of America today.

Historian Will Durant says:

*"The religious imagination of Greece produced a luxuriant mythology and a populous pantheon. Every object or force of earth or sky, every blessing and every terror, every quality-even the vices-of mankind was personified as a deity, usually in **human form**; no other religion has ever*

been so anthropomorphic [man centered] *as the Greek. Every craft, profession, and art had its divinity, or, as we should say, its patron saint; and in addition there were demons, harpies, furies, fairies, gorgons, sirens, nymphs, almost as numerous as the mortals of the earth. Despite the achievements of philosophy and the attempts of a few to preach a monotheistic creed, the people continued to the end of Hellenic civilization to create myths, and even gods.* "[1]

Primarily the Greeks worshiped **a triad of gods**, made up of the *"cloud-compelling, rain-making, thunder-herding **Zeus**,"* looked upon as *"Father God of all gods, **Poseidon**,* god of the sea (worshiped in port cities and non-port cities alike), and **Hades**, also called Pluto, god of the bowels of the earth. **Consider this unholy trinity!**

Under the above **triad** the Greeks worshiped a swarm of lesser gods that can be divided into seven groups: sky gods, earth gods, fertility gods, animal gods, ancestor or hero gods, and Olympians. Will Durant says:

*"A thousand lesser deities dwelt on the earth, in its waters, or in its surrounding air: spirits of sacred trees, especially the oak; Nereids, Naiads, Oceanids, in rivers, lakes, or the sea; gods gushing forth as wells or springs, or flowing as stately streams like the Maeander or the Spercheus; gods of the wind, like Boreas, Zephyr, Notus, and Eurus, with their master Aeolus; or the great god Pan, the horned, cloven-footed, sensual, smiling Nourisher, god of shepherds and flocks, of woods and the wild life lurking in them, he whose magic flute could be heard in every brook and dell, whose startling cry brought panic to any careless herd, and whose attendants were fauns and satyrs, and those satyrs called "sileni," half **goat** and half **Socrates**. Everywhere in nature there were gods; the air was so crowded with spirits of good and evil that, said an unknown poet, 'There is not one empty chink into which you could push the spike of a blade of corn.'"* [2]

No wonder the Bible verse above *(Acts 17:16)* says of the great apostle Paul, *"his spirit was stirred in him, when he saw the city **wholly given to idolatry**."* Notice the first word in the next verse, *"Therefore."* Therefore Paul began to preach! If a man had an ounce of *"preach"* in him, he would *preach* in Athens, and Paul was full of *"preach."* He preached to the Jews in the synagogue and in the marketplace, and to the philosophers called Epicureans and Stoics whenever he encountered them. And they listened because:

> *"All the Athenians and strangers which were there spent their time in nothing else, but either to **tell** or to **hear** some new thing" (v. 21).*

And the response was mixed. Some said, *"What will this babbler say?"* Others said, *"He seemeth to be a setter forth* [teacher] *of strange gods: because he preached unto them Jesus, and the resurrection" (v. 18).* Then a crowd of these Athenians took Paul to the Areopagus, a rocky hill where the Supreme Court met (northwest of the Parthenon), to an area called *"Mars Hill,"* and said *"preach."* And preach he did!

> *"Then Paul stood in the midst of Mars hill and said, Ye men of Athens, I perceive that in all things ye are too superstitious" (v. 22).*

The use of this word *"superstitious"* took much courage on the part of Paul. It is the Greek word *"**deisidaimonesteros**" (Strong's #1174).* It means *"too religious,"* but more than that it has the root word *"daimon" (Strong's #1142)* in it. *Daimon* is the Greek spelling of *"demon,"* and means *"a demon or supernatural spirit of a bad nature - devil."* So Paul told this crowd of curious Athenians, "You are too demonically religious," or in other words, "Your religion is devilish!"

Now that Paul had them on the ropes, he needed to find some common ground on which to base his message, and here it is.

> *"As I passed by, and beheld your devotion* [literally, "the gods that you worship"], *I found an altar with this inscription, TO THE UNKNOWN GOD. Whom therefore ye ignorantly worship, **him** declare I unto you" (v. 23).*

Isn't it amazing that with all of their hundreds of gods, their worship left them with an empty hunger for the **One True God**. As John Adams, our second President (a Christian) wrote in a letter to his wife Abigail, *"Man is the only animal who is hungry with his belly full."* [3] Paul continues:

> *"God that made the world and all things therein, seeing that*
> *he is Lord of heaven and earth" (v. 24).*

Paul is telling them about God our Creator, the God of Abraham, Isaac and Jacob, the Lord God our Father. Notice, *"Lord of heaven and earth."* This is not Jesus, but Jesus' Father. Listen to the words of Jesus himself, as recorded in Luke 10:21:

> *"In that hour Jesus rejoiced in spirit, and said, I thank thee*
> *O Father, Lord of heaven and earth... ."*

In our mistaken doctrine we have given that position to *"the man Christ Jesus,"* but Jesus and Paul taught that God our Father is *"Lord of heaven and earth,"* the Great King of the universe. Listen to Paul:

> *"For in **him** we live, and move and have our being; as*
> *certain also of **your own poets** have said, For we are also*
> *his offspring" (Acts 17:28).*

Here Paul is quoting two of their Greek poets Epemenides and Aratos. They had that much right, Creator God is our Father.

> *"Have we not all **one father**? Hath not **one God** created*
> *us" (Mal. 2:10).*

Paul agreed with these Greeks as much as possible for common ground on which to relate. It is no surprise that these poets got something right. We have a saying down South, *"Even a blind hog finds an acorn now and then."*

Notice what Paul could have preached that would likely have brought shouts of agreement from them. He did not mention a *"divine Logos doctrine."* This popular doctrine had been taught by Socrates, Plato and their other philosophers for over 400 years. Neither did Paul mention the doctrine of "a second deity" or "a second god," which Plato had taught over 375 years before. He preached to them of **one** entity, being, person; the **Lord God** of heaven and earth! Notice verse thirty:

> *"And the times of this ignorance God winked at; **but now commandeth all men everywhere to repent**."* **Repent!** Not just "believe."

Why?

> *"Because he* [God] *hath appointed a day, in which he* [*"God the judge of all" - Heb. 12:23*] *will judge the world in righteousness **by that man*** [Jesus] *whom he* [God] *hath ordained; whereof he* [God] *hath given assurance unto all men, in that he* [God] *hath raised him* [Jesus] *from the dead"* (v. 31).

It is remarkable that Jesus had been in heaven with the Father for some twenty years when Paul stood on Mars hill, but he still refers to him as *"that man* (i.e. "human being") *whom he* [God] *hath ordained."* Jesus refers to himself several times in Scripture as *"a man."* One example is John 8:40.

> *"But now ye seek to kill me, **a man** that hath told you the truth, which I have heard of **God**."*

The word *"man"* in this verse is the Greek word *anthropos (Strong's #444)* and it has one meaning, *"a human being."* Why do **we** insist on making him "God" or a superbeing? Paul never did that in any of his preaching or writings. If he had believed that Jesus is a *God-man* or *deity,* he would certainly have told these Greeks, for their doctrines and beliefs were rife with *gods as men* and *men as gods.* They were *humanist* and they loved to **deify men!** Remember, Will Durant said, *"Every object or force...was personified as a **deity**, usually in **human form**."* [4] That was *"incarnation"* gone to seed. Listen to these mistaken statements by Tertullian: *"**God** suffers Himself to be conceived in a mother's womb, and awaits the time for birth. And when born, He bears the delay of growing up... . **Was not God crucified**? And, having been really crucified, did He not really die? And, having indeed really* *died, did He not really rise again?" (A Dictionary of Early Christian Beliefs; p. 356).* Harnack says, *"In them (the Greek church fathers) a religious and realistic idea takes place...the **deifying of the human race** through the **incarnation** of the Son of God."* [5] The apostle Paul knew nothing of it! He taught that rather than an effort to make us **"gods,"** God's purpose was to make us **"righteous" men**, through the blood of His dear Son.

Reviewing Paul's Sermon

Let's look again briefly at Paul's sermon in Athens to make sure it agrees with the doctrines we preach and endorse.

1. Paul preached about two entities, our Creator God, **and** *"that man whom he hath ordained."* He did not mention a triad, triune, trinity, or incarnation.

2. Paul preached about a judgement day to come. *(See Rev. 20:11-15).*

3. Paul preached repentance (not just belief). God *"now commandeth **all men** everywhere* [Jew and Gentile] *to **repent**" (Acts 17:30).*

It should be noted that unlike some later *Christian* teachers, Paul saw nothing here in Athens' *"demonic religion"* that he thought would enrich the gospel of God.

The Power Of This Demonic "Greek Spirit"

Since the "Greek spirit" is a powerful demon spirit which Daniel 10:20 calls *"the prince of Grecia,"* and Daniel 8:6 refers to *"the fury of his power,"* there is hardly anything on earth that can withstand its influence. Even powerful Rome that conquered Greece was in turn conquered by this influence. In the wake of Roman soldiers returning home, came a swelling stream of "Greeklings," as the scornful Romans called them: captives, slaves, refugees, traders, travelers, athletes, artist, actors, musicians, teachers, and lecturers, bringing their gods with them. Many of them became tutors in Roman families; some teachers opened schools for instruction in the language and literature of Greece. Some gave instruction and lectures on oratory, literary composition and philosophy. **The Greek conquest of Rome** took.the form of sending Greek religion and comedy to Roman commoners, and Greek morals, philosophy and art to the upper classes.

Roman leaders soon saw how this strong wind was blowing and were alarmed. In 161 B.C. the Senate decreed that *"no philosophers or rhetors shall be permitted in Rome,"* but it was too late. The Roman statesman Cicero said, *"It was no little brook that flowed from Greece into our city, but a mighty river of culture and learning."* As Will Durant says, *"This is the **central stream** in the history of European civilization; all other currents are **tributaries**."* As the Roman poet Horace said, *"Conquered Greece took captive her barbarous conqueror."* [6]

What About Christianity?

After the deaths of God's great Apostles who defended His truth in the first century, **neither did Christianity withstand this powerful *"Greek spirit"* and its false doctrines.**

As Harnack and Durant have so capably documented, the doctrines of Greek Hellenism made their way into the stream of Christianity, perverting its teachings. What are some of these false teachings?

1. **Incarnation** and re-incarnation.
2. Humanism - The pursuit of human knowledge and the deification of man.
3. **A triad of gods**.
4. Purgatory.
5. The purchase of indulgences by the wealthy to release dead loved ones from Purgatory.
6. Prayer to dead heros (saints).
7. Universalism - The belief that all, both good and bad, will find eternal bliss.
8. Eating of the "literal" flesh of gods in order to become divine.
9. The worship of the "great mother deity" Detemer, and her son Triptolemus. Durant says, *"Essentially it was the same myth as that of*

*Isis and Osiris in Egypt, Tammuz and Ishtar in Babylon, Astarie and Adonis in Syria, Cybele and Attis in Phyrgia. The cult of motherhood survived through classical times to take new life in the worship of **Mary the Mother of God.**"* [7]

Reviewing Paul's Ministry To, and Attitude Toward, The Greeks

The apostle Paul loved Greek people, and much of his ministry was directed to them.

Paul and Barnabas preached in Iconium and *"a great multitude both of the Jews and also of the **Greeks** believed" (Acts 14:1).*

Paul and Silas preached in Thessalonica and *"many of them believed; also of honorable women which were **Greeks**, and men, not a few" (Acts 17:12).*

Paul preached in Ephesus for two years, *"so that all they which dwelt in Asia heard the word of the Lord Jesus, both Jews and **Greeks**" (Acts 19:10).*

Paul *"came into **Greece**, and there abode three months" (Acts 20:2-3).*

Paul's ministry to the Greek's was motivated **by what he believed**.
The gospel of Christ *"is the power of God unto salvation to every one that believeth; to the Jew first, **and also the Greek**" (Rom. 1:16).*

*"For there is no difference between the Jew and the **Greek**: for the same Lord over all is rich unto **all** that call upon him" (Rom. 10:12; Gal. 3:28; Col. 3:11).*

Paul's beloved *"son in the gospel"* Timothy was **Greek**, having been born of a Greek father and a Jewish mother *(Acts 16:1-3)*, and his faithful co-worker Silas was also a **Greek** *(Gal. 2:3)*.

Paul, as a Jew, spoke the Hebrew language, and when Jesus spoke to him from above at the time of his conversion **he spoke in Hebrew**. But as an *educated* Jew, Paul also spoke Greek *(Acts 21:37)*.

On at least three occasions Scripture records that Paul quoted ancient Greek poets, **not for doctrine but to make a point** *(Acts 17:28; I Cor. 15:33; Titus 1:12)*.

But Paul was always opposed to and wary of Greek philosophy and doctrine. Shortly after his conversion in Damascus, Barnabas took him to Jerusalem to introduce him to the church, but daily in public places:

> *"He spoke boldly in the name of the Lord Jesus, and disputed **against the Grecians** [not "with" but "against"]: but they went about to slay him" (Acts 9:29).*

At one point Paul left Titus in Crete, a Greek island from which the ancient Grecian people had received much of their art, religion, and character, so Titus could *"set in order the things that are wanting" (Titus 1:5)*. But Paul gave him a strong word of caution regarding some of their personal habits.

> *"One of themselves, even a prophet of their own, said, The Cretians are always liars, evil beasts, slow bellies* [gluttons]. ***This witness is true.*** *Wherefore rebuke them sharply, that they may be sound in the faith"* [i.e. Christian doctrine] *(Titus 1:12-13)*.

These are unusually strong words from Paul, but he knew by experience how insidious and devastating Greek philosophy and doctrine could be. The quotation is from the Greek poet Epemenides (a sixth-century B.C. native of Knossos, Crete), who was held in high esteem by the Cretians and several fulfilled predictions were credited to him. In Greek literature *"to cretanize"* meant to lie, [8] and according to *Webster's* dictionary, the modern word *"cretin"* means *"a very stupid or foolish person."*

231

Of course Paul strongly withstood **all types of erroneous doctrine** wherever he found it, and in the next verses he warns also against false *Jewish* doctrine.

> *"Not giving heed to **Jewish fables**, and commandments of men, that turn from the truth. They profess that they know God; but in works they deny him, being abominable, and disobedient, and unto every good work reprobate. **But speak thou the things that become sound doctrine"** (Titus 1:14, 16; 2:1).*

Paul and The Corinthians

In Paul's day the city of Corinth in many ways was the chief city of Greece. It had a population of about 650,000 (250,000 plus 400,000 slaves) and was a city of typical Greek culture. Its people were interested in **Greek philosophy** and placed a high premium on **wisdom**. It was a very religious city that contained at least twelve temples, including the temple of the goddess Aphrodite. She was the goddess of love, and worship to her included "temple prostitution," and at one time 1000 "sacred prostitutes" served her temple. No wonder the Greek verb *"to Corinthianize"* came to mean *"to practice sexual immorality."* [9]

When writing to a Christian church in this immoral setting, we might expect Paul to open his apostolic letter with a warning against sexual perversion. He did deal with this subject later on, but Paul knew that people live what they believe, and that the "Greek spirit" and their dependence on wisdom and philosophy was the root of the problem. Therefore he opened his great epistle called *First Corinthians* with an attack on **Greek human wisdom**. Please read carefully the following verses from the **heart** and **pen** of Paul.

> *"For Christ sent me...to preach the gospel: not with **wisdom** of words, lest the cross of Christ should be made of none effect. For the preaching of the cross is to them that perish foolishness; but unto us which are saved it is the power of God. For it is written, I will destroy the **wisdom** of the wise, and will bring to nothing the understanding of the prudent. Where is the wise? Where is the scribe? Where is the*

disputer of this world? **Hath not God made foolish the wisdom of this world?** *For after that in the wisdom of God* **the world by wisdom knew not God**, *it pleased God by the foolishness of preaching to save them that believe. For the Jews require a sign, and the* **Greeks seek after wisdom***: But we preach Christ crucified, unto the Jews a stumbling block, and unto the* **Greeks foolishness***; But unto them which are called, both Jews and Greeks, Christ the power of God, and the wisdom of God. Because the foolishness of God is wiser than men; and the weakness of God is stronger than men. For ye see your calling, brethren, how that* **not many wise men** *after the flesh, not many mighty, not many noble, are called: But God hath chosen the* **foolish things** *of the world* **to confound the wise***; and God hath chosen the weak things of the world to confound the things which are mighty; That no flesh should glory in his presence"* (I Cor. 1:17-27, 29).

Can anyone deny that God's man, the great apostle Paul stood firmly against the "Greek spirit" and the "Hellenization" of the doctrine of the church of Jesus Christ? No wonder it did not happen until long after his death! But through the Spirit he saw it coming.

> *"For I know this, that* **after my departing** *shall* **grievous wolves** *enter in among you, not sparing the flock. Also of* **your own selves** *shall men arise, speaking perverse things, to draw away disciples after them.* **Therefore watch...***"* [Paul] *(Acts 20:29-31).*

Again, Paul's Warning!

*"****Beware*** *lest any man spoil you through* **philosophy*** ... ."* Notice the word *beware.* Paul did not use the words "notice," or "caution," or "warning," but he used one of the strongest words of **alert** that there is, *"Beware."* Beware as in "**Beware of dog!**" or, "**Beware of high voltage lines!**" It is the same word of caution that Jesus used when he said to his disciples:

> *"****Beware*** *of the leaven* [doctrine] *of the Pharisees, and of*

the Sadducees" (Matt. 16:12). Note: The doctrine of the Pharisees was similar to the doctrine of the **Greek Stoics,** and according to history the Sadducees had "Hellenized." **Beware! Be on guard!**

Please proceed prayerfully as we seek through Scripture to sort out truth from tradition, and *"thus saith the word of God"* from the doctrines and precepts of man. We have much to learn and unlearn!

Glory to God in the Highest!

"The Bible does not teach the doctrine of the Trinity. Neither the word 'trinity' itself nor such language as 'one-in-three,' 'one essence' (or 'substance'), and **'three persons'** *is biblical language. The language of the doctrine is the language of the ancient church* **taken from classical Greek philosophy."**

Trinitarian professor Shirley C. Guthrie, Jr.
Christian Doctrine

Chapter Nine

The Pope's Speech

I suppose the final straw for me in deciding that I should write a book regarding the influence of Greek philosophy on Christian doctrine was when a friend of mine gave me a printed copy of a speech made by Pope Benedict XVI at the University of Regensburg, Germany, on September 12, 2006. This is the speech that was heard around the world, because in it, Benedict quotes a brief statement made in 1391 A.D. by the Byzantine (Christian) emperor Manual II Paleologus regarding the violence of Mohammed and *"his command to spread by the sword the faith he preached."* The speech brought a firestorm of anger from Muslims, which caused Benedict to issue a statement from the Vatican that was part explanation and part apology.

However, the speech was not primarily about Islam. The speech was part of an ongoing effort by this pope to **stop** the trend toward the *"dehellenization"* of Christianity and Christian doctrine that is evident in our time. In fact he used the words *"hellenism" "hellenization"* or *"dehellenization"* nine times. As previously noted, the word *"hellenism"* means *"imitation of the Greeks in thought, culture, language and customs."* In former times, Greeks were called *"Hellenes."* To *"Hellenize"* means to *"make or become like the Greeks in customs, ideals, form, or language,"* and *"dehellenization"* is the removal of those things.

Pope Benedict is right in one regard. There is a powerful force at work in Christianity today, no doubt ordained by God, to acknowledge and reexamine its Hebrew root. This is the root that the apostle Paul referred to in Romans chapter eleven when he reminded these gentile Christians that they were grafted into *"a good olive tree" (v. 24).* He says in verse eighteen, *"thou bearest not the root, but the root thee."* Now there is a hunger among sincere Christians to see and understand the Jewishness of Jesus and his Apostles.

With this trend in mind, when *Time* magazine published a cover article in its March 12, 2008 issue, titled, *"Ten Ideas That Are Changing The World,"* number ten was *"Re-Judaizing Jesus."* Time says *"This is seismic,"* and includes *"first a brute acceptance that Jesus was born a Jew and did Jewish things; then admission that he and his interpreter Paul saw themselves as Jews even while founding what became another faith."* The article quotes Vanderbilt University New Testament scholar Amy-Jill Levine as saying, *"if you get the* [Jewish] *context wrong, you will certainly get Jesus wrong."* To which I would add a hearty "Amen!"

Pope Benedict for sure sees the *"hellenization of Christianity"* (the wedding of Christian doctrine with Greek philosophy that occurred in the 2nd, 3rd, and 4th centuries) as a good thing. He describes Emperor Manual II whom he quoted, as *"a Byzantine* [Christian] *shaped by Greek philosophy."* He says, *"I believe that here we can see the profound harmony between what is Greek in the best sense of the word and the biblical understanding of faith in God."* He says, *"The encounter between the Biblical message and Greek thought did not happen by chance."* He mentions the vision of Paul in *Acts 16:6-10*, in which a man of Macedonia pleads, *"come over to Macedonia and help us,"* and says this vision showed *"the intrinsic necessity of a reapproachment* [coming together] *between Biblical faith and Greek inquiry."* He says, ***"Biblical faith**, in the Hellenistic period, encountered **the best of Greek thought** at a deep level, resulting in a **mutual enrichment...**"*

He speaks with joy of *"the very heart of Christian faith and...the heart of Greek thought now joined to faith... ."* He decries the fact that *"in the late Middle Ages we find trends in theology which would sunder this synthesis* [combining] *between the **Greek spirit** and the **Christian spirit**."* Question. I know about the *"**Christian spirit**,"* but what is this *"**Greek spirit**"* to which the pope refers to more than once in this speech? He alleges that *"this convergence, with the subsequent addition of the Roman heritage, created Europe and remains the foundation of what can rightly be called Europe."* He states, *"The thesis that the **critically purified Greek heritage forms an integral part of Christian faith** has been countered by the call for a* *dehellenization of Christianity."* He says this *"dehellenization first emerges in...the Reformation of the sixteenth century. Looking at the tradition of scholastic theology, the Reformers* [Luther, Calvin, Wesley, etc.] *thought they were confronted with a faith system **totally conditioned by philosophy... based on an alien system of thought."***

He condemns the *"principle of sola scriptura"* (basing doctrine solely on Scripture) that the Reformers adopted, and the fact that they *"sought faith in its pure, primordial form, as originally found in the Biblical Word."* Of course the Catholic Church falsely teaches that **truth** should be arrived at by **tradition** and **experience, in addition to the Bible**.

I should say at this point that it is highly regrettable that the Reformers, at the time they were endeavoring to rid Christianity of erroneous Catholic dogma, did not take a close and critical look at the Greek originated doctrine of the Trinity. The *New International Encyclopedia* says:

> *"The Trinity doctrine; the Catholic Faith is this: We worship one in trinity...The doctrine is not found in its fully developed form in the Scriptures. Modern theology does not seek to find it in the Old Testament. **At the time of the Reformation the Protestant Church took over the doctrine of the Trinity, without serious examination."*** [1]

Noted Catholic scholar Graham Greene, in defending their doctrine of the Assumption of Mary stated:

> *"Our opponents sometime claim that no belief should be held dogmatically which is not explicitly stated in Scripture...**but the Protestant churches have themselves accepted such dogmas as the Trinity, for which there is no such precise authority in the Gospels."*** [2]

Pope Benedict states that the *"**second stage** in the process of dehellenization"* began in the nineteenth century with the writings of German historian *"Adolf Von Harnack as its outstanding representative."* Harnack wrote an awesome account in the late 1800's chronicling the formation of Christian doctrine by the Greek Church Fathers in the centuries that followed the death of the Apostles of Jesus. It is called *"History of Dogma,"* and a thorough reading of it is devastating to the doctrines of the Trinity and Incarnation. No wonder the pope includes this work as an important step in the *"dehellenization"* of Christianity. He says, *"Harnack's goal was to bring Christianity back into harmony with modern reason, liberating it from seemingly **philosophical** and **theological** elements, **such as faith in Christ's divinity and the triune God.**"* He says Harnack made a *"**distinction** between **the God of the philosopher's and the God of Abraham, Isaac, and Jacob.**"* The pope may see the above as a bad thing, but every God loving, Bible believing Christian should see it as a good thing!

Benedict refers to *"**the third stage of dehellenization, which is now in progress.**"* He continues, *"it is often said nowadays that the synthesis* [coming together] *with Hellenism achieved in the early Church was a preliminary inculturation* [how culture affects doctrine] *which ought not to be binding on other cultures. The latter are said to have the right to return to the **simple message of the New Testament** prior to that* [Greek] *inculturation...**This thesis is not only false; it is coarse** and lacking in precision. The New Testament was written in Greek and bears the imprint of the **Greek spirit**, which had already come to maturity as the Old Testament developed."*

Pope Benedict has a right to be alarmed! Millions of people around the world, but especially in Central and South America, are leaving the Roman Catholic Church with its pagan doctrines and practices. This is causing growth in all fundamentalist faiths, especially those with the simple message of the Gospel and the freedom to worship in the Holy Spirit. Recognizing this trend, *Newsweek* magazine said in an article in its September 21, 2009 edition:

> *"Pentecostalism, **the fastest growing brand of religion in the world,** stresses the gifts of the spirit: healing, and speaking in tongues. In his new book, The Future of Faith,*

> *Harvard professor Harvey Cox calls this new era 'the age*
> *of the spirit'."*

This can be nothing else but a fulfillment of God's promise for the end-times as stated in *Joel 2:28* and *Acts 2:17*, and Pope Benedict nor anyone else can stop it!

> *"And it shall come to pass in the last days, **saith God, I***
> ***will pour out of my Spirit upon all flesh***: *and your sons*
> *and daughters shall prophesy, and your young men shall*
> *see visions, and your old men shall dream dreams."*

Regarding *Newsweek's* use of the term *"Pentecostalism"*, I believe they refer to an *experience* more than just a *label*. I hope so! Since, according to the New Testament, neither the early Church nor any of the Apostles wore the word *"Pentecostal"* as a label, there is very little to be gained by us doing so. There is however, much to be gained by being baptized with the Holy Ghost as they experienced at Pentecost *(Acts 2:4)*. With this *"power from on high,"* the infant church grew on that day from *"about one hundred and twenty"* to about three thousand one hundred and twenty. (May I recommend this Holy Spirit baptism as a *one step program* for church growth?).

Back To Pope Benedict's Speech

Pope Benedict is for sure on the side of Greek philosophy, as defending it is his focus throughout this important speech. He repeatedly uses the terms Platonism (Plato), Platonist, and Platonic. Although in this speech, Jesus is not mentioned by name or quoted, Benedict saw fit to mention Socrates repeatedly and ended with a quote from this strange Greek philosopher. As we go forward, we will understand more clearly how *"hellenized,"* not just Catholicism, but all of Christianity, really is!

Pagan Christianity

Frank Viola and George Barna caused quite a stir in 2008 with the publication of their *"explosive"* and *"unsettling"* book titled, *Pagan Christianity?* Viola is a noted author, having penned eight books, and is a nationally recognized expert on new trends of the Church. Barna is the author of thirty-nine books, but is best known as a "Christian pollster," founder and leader of *The Barna Group*, a research firm that keeps its finger on the pulse of current Christian matters. He has been hailed as *"the most quoted person in the Christian church today,"* and is one of its most influential leaders. *Pagan Christianity?* received the attention of Christian and secular media because it revealed in a well documented manner, the startling degree to which foreign influences, such as Greek philosophy and pagan customs (both Greek and Roman) have made their way into the accepted ideas and *practices* of modern Christianity! (My book deals with how these pagan influences have damaged Christian *doctrine*).

Viola and Barna *"believe the first-century church was the church in its purest form, before it was tainted and corrupted,"* and although Christianity still believes we are *"doing it by the book,"* they are troubled by the effect that paganism has had on it. They see this in *"church services, the education and ordination of clergy, the routines commonly used in youth ministry, the methods of raising funds for the ministry, the ways in which music is used in churches, even the presence and nature of church buildings."* [3]

They write, *"after the Romans destroyed Jerusalem in A.D. 70, Judaic Christianity waned in numbers and power. Gentile Christianity dominated, and the new faith began to absorb Greco-Roman philosophy and ritual."* They continue, *"Strikingly, much of what we do for 'church' was lifted directly out of pagan culture in the postapostolic period* (after 100 A.D.). *Paganism dominated the Roman Empire until the fourth century, and many of its elements were absorbed by Christians...particularly during the Constantinian and early post-Constantinian eras (324 to 600)"* (p. 6). They say *"Constantine's thinking was dominated by superstition and pagan magic"* and *"his story fills a dark page in the history of Christianity"* (p. 17). ***"Fourth-century Christianity was being profoundly shaped by Greek paganism** and Roman imperialism"* (p. 25). ***"Constantine is still living and breathing in our minds"*** *(p. 40).*

Viola and Barna correctly point out that the polluted stream from which Christianity now drinks began centuries before Constantine, in Athens, Greece, with the birth of Greek philosophy. They quote historian Will Durant as saying, *"The Greek mind, dying, came to a transmigrated life in the **theology and liturgy** of the church; the **Greek language**, having reigned for centuries over **philosophy**, became the vehicle of Christian literature and ritual" (p. 52).* They see the influence of Plato in modern Christian architecture, and the influence of Greek rhetoric ('The Greeks were intoxicated with rhetoric'), on modern pulpit oratory. They say that by the third and fourth centuries *"**many pagan orators and philosophers were becoming Christians. As a result, pagan philosophical ideas unwittingly made their way into the Christian community. Many of these men became the theologians and leaders of the early Christian church and are known as the 'church fathers' "** (p. 91).* Again they quote Durant as saying that Christianity *"grew by the absorption of pagan faith and ritual...as Judea had given Christianity ethics and **Greece had given it theology**, so now Rome gave it organization; **all these...entered into the Christian synthesis"** (mix) (p. 119).*

Viola and Barna are trinitarians but make the following shocking statements. *"These (Monastic) schools sent missionaries to uncharted territories after the fourth century. During this stage, the Eastern church fathers became **steeped in Platonic thought.** They held to the misguided view that **Plato** and **Aristotle** were schoolmasters whose techniques could be used to bring men to Christ. Though they did not intend to lead people astray, their heavy reliance on **these pagan philosophers seriously diluted the Christian faith.** Justin Martyr (100-165) believed that **philosophy was God's revelation to the Greeks.** He claimed that **Socrates, Plato, and others** had the same standing for the Gentiles as **Moses had for the Jews" (p. 202).***

What Viola and Barna Call "The Heart Of The Problem"

They continue:

> *"The Greek philosophers Plato and Socrates taught that knowledge is virtue. Good depends on the extent of one's*

knowledge. Hence the teaching of knowledge is the teaching of virtue. Herein lies the root and stem of contemporary **Christian education.** *It is built on the* **Platonic idea** *that knowledge is the equivalent of moral character. Therein lies the great flaw.* **Plato and Aristotle, both disciples of Socrates, are the fathers of contemporary Christian education.** *....present day Christian education, whether it be seminaries or Bible College, is serving food from the wrong tree:* **the tree of the knowledge of good and evil rather than the tree of life"** *(p. 215-216).* [Emphasis mine throughout]

As to Christian **theological** education they conclude, *"**Athens is still in its bloodstream**" (p. 205).*

Although I do not agree with all of the opinions that Viola and Barna state in their book, I do believe *Pagan Christianity?* was ordained of God, and that He is using it and will continue to use it to set some important things straight. Their historical facts and statements are well documented, and I recommend this book to all who love and care about the church that Jesus is building. A book like this will make you throw rocks at The *Da Vinci Code* because the secrets *Pagan Christianity?* uncovers, are treasures of truth, and the intent of the authors is to help to purify Christianity, rather than to further corrupt it.

In Conclusion

I suppose my brethren Viola and Barna failed to see the irony of justifying their intense examination of the heathen influence on Christianity, and the very good book that resulted, by beginning it with a quote (chapter one - page one) from the father of philosophy himself:

"The unexamined life is not worth living" [**Socrates**].

Behold the power of the influence of Greek philosophy!

Chapter Ten

Who Was Socrates?

*"Now the Spirit speaketh **expressly**, that in the latter times some shall depart from the faith, giving heed to **seducing spirits**, and **doctrines of devils**; Speaking **lies** in hypocrisy; having their conscience seared with a hot iron"* [Paul speaking] *(I Tim. 4:1-2).*

*"Christ was known by **Socrates** for Christ was and is the Logos who dwells in every man. It may be asserted that all who have lived with the Logos were Christians. Among the Greeks, this specially applies to **Socrates** and **Heraclitus"** (Justin Martyr; 100-165 A.D.; early Church father).*

*"When the **Greek mind** and the **Roman mind**, instead of the Hebrew mind came to dominate the church, **there occurred a disaster** from which the Church has never recovered, either in doctrine or practice"* (Historian H.L. Goudge).

$\mathcal{T}$he apostle Paul, before his death by the sword at the hands of the Romans (in Rome), never expressed any dread for himself regarding what he was facing. However, he did express strongly the dread and urgency in his spirit, placed there by the Holy Spirit, concerning what he saw ahead for the Church of Jesus Christ after his soon departure. He saw this trouble being brought about through *"grievous wolves"* devastating *"the flock,"* by bringing in *"seducing spirits and **doctrines of devils."*** Please notice again:

> *"**For I know this**, that after my departing shall **grievous wolves** enter in among you, not sparing the flock"* (Acts 20:29).

Perhaps Paul was thinking back to Jesus' warning to his disciples before his own departure, *"Behold, I send you forth as sheep in the midst of wolves"* *(Mark 10:16; Luke 10:3).* Here is a good question. How should sheep behave themselves in *wolf country?* They should stay close to the Shepherd, listen to His words (the Bible), and stay close to each other! Both Jesus and Paul warned us about following *"the doctrines and traditions of men,"* and in the verse at the beginning of this chapter, Paul cautions us regarding **"doctrines of devils."**

I think we are far enough along in our study for me to make this strong statement. The doctrine of the Trinity and the Incarnation, **as taught in modern Christian theology,** is one of the **greatest frauds** that has ever been perpetrated in the history of humanity. I say this for two reasons.

1. These doctrines, since their inception in the second, third, and fourth centuries A.D., have clouded the minds of literally billions of people as to who the One Most High God of the Bible is! Please look with me at Revelation chapter twelve, where John sees a vision of end-time events.

    *"And the great dragon was cast out, that old serpent, the Devil, and Satan, which **deceiveth the whole world"** (v. 9).*

Consider this. The population of the "world" today is about 6½ billion, one third Christian and two-thirds **non-Christian.** But John did not say "two thirds of the world was deceived by Satan," he said, *"Satan which deceiveth the **whole world!"*** I am not saying these Christians are not saved, but I am saying Christianity as a whole has been deceived in some **very important areas.** For example over one billion of these Christians pray to the Virgin Mary and call her "Mother of God," "Queen of Heaven," and "Queen of the Universe." Millions of Christians in South Korea, Japan, and other countries mix *ancestor worship* with their Christianity. Millions of Christians in Haiti (and people of Haitian descent in New Orleans) mix voodoo practices with their Christian religion. Voodooism is a merging of African and Christian beliefs dating back to the 16th century. As a Catholic priest said while standing in the midst of devastation from the recent earthquake: *"If everything is good, they go to church. If something bad is happening to them, they go to the voodoo priest to get help."* He says he *"feels obligated to preach against voodoo, but knows it won't do any good."* He believes **most** Haitian Christians practice voodoo on the side, because *"It is in their blood." (USA Today; January 12, 2010)*

In Jesus' great prophetic discourse, recorded in Matthew chapter twenty-four, he warns repeatedly regarding coming deception:

> *"Take heed that no man **deceive you"** (v. 4).*

> *"And many false prophets shall arise and shall **deceive many"** (v. 11).*

> *"...insomuch that, if it were possible, **they shall deceive the very elect** [Christians] (v. 24).*

Consider with me Jesus' troubling question to his disciples in Luke 18:8:

> *"Nevertheless, when the Son of man cometh, **shall he find faith on the earth?"***

Jesus is not speaking regarding "miracle faith" or "healing faith", he is in essence asking, "When I return shall I find people abiding in the Christian faith?"

But I am optimistic for the church! It is built on the good and godly men in its foundation: Peter, James, John, Matthew, Paul, etc., *"**Jesus Christ** himself being the chief cornerstone,"* (Note: **There are no Greek philosophers in the foundation of Jesus' church**). I am also optimistic because of the awesome promise that Jesus gave!

> *"...upon this rock* [of Peter's confession; *"**Thou art the Christ"*** - not God] *I will build **my church; and the gates of hell shall not prevail against it"** (Matt. 16:18).*

But do not think for a minute that they haven't tried!

Back to my statement regarding the great fraud against humanity!

2.   These doctrines were designed by the master deceiver to take glory from our glorious God and Creator, and they have. Please consider this illustration:

At the time of this writing Barack Obama is the president of the U.S.. When he dresses each morning, he is dressing the one and only president of the United States, commander-in-chief of our armed forces, the most powerful man in the world. His signature on a document carries the weight of that office because the presidency today is embodied in one person, Barack H. Obama. Whether or not you voted for him or approve of his policies, he alone deserves the respect, honor, and glory of that position!

But suppose you and I started a rumor or a political doctrine that in fact the presidency of the United States is actually made up of three persons, Barack Obama, Hillary Clinton, and John McCain. The president is not **one person**, but actually **three persons**. What would we have just done to Barack Obama in our doctrine? We would have reduced his position, honor and glory by **two thirds,** and made him one-third of who he really is!

That is exactly what Satan has done to the One Most High God in the minds of billions of people, and Christianity has been complicit in it!

> *"Hear O Israel, the Lord our **God is one Lord**"* [Moses speaking] *(Deut. 6:4)*.

> *"Hear O Israel, the Lord our **God is one Lord**"* [Jesus speaking] *(Mark 12:29)*.

> *"And this is life eternal that they might know **thee** [not "me"] **the only true God**, and Jesus Christ, whom **thou** hast sent"* [Jesus speaking] *(John 17:3)*.

> *"...there is none other God but **one**. But to us there is but **one God, the Father**...and one Lord Jesus Christ"* [Paul speaking] *(I Cor. 8:3, 6)*.

*"**One God** and **Father** of all, who is above all..."* [Paul]
(Eph. 4:6).

*"For there is **one God** and **one mediator** between **God** and
men, the **man** Christ Jesus" (I Tim. 2:5).*

Note: The above verses are the words of our Lord Jesus and two other
great men of God. They are written in plain English so a child
can understand them. If you refuse to believe these verses you
have become part of Christianity's problem, rather than part of the
solution!

Filth In The Water System

In the summer of 2008 the small town of Ridgetop, Tennessee, about eight
miles from where we live, began to experience a problem. About one
thousand homeowners started to find particles and trash in their sinks and
faucets. This continued for a period of several months while they complained
to the city officials. Finally someone discovered the problem at the city's
water treatment plant. Months before, a plumbing company hired to do
work at the plant, had mistakenly hooked up the *sewer line* to the *water line*,
gotten paid and gone on their way. There was much consternation at this
discovery, and the City Fathers called in the experts to make their analysis.
Their conclusion: *"Yes, the sewer was hooked up to the water line, and yes
there is bacteria in the water system! **But it is still at an acceptable level.**"*

Here is the analogy. Centuries ago the sewer of *Greek philosophy* was
attached to the water line of *Christian doctrine*, and the *experts* who see and
acknowledge it (including the Pope) want us to believe that *"the bacteria is
still at an acceptable level!"* I for one am not buying it! Paul said:
> *"Know ye not that a **little** leaven leaveneth the **whole lump**.
> Purge out therefore the old leaven, that ye may be a **new
> lump**" (I Cor. 5:6-7).*

When we do, we will have the purity, power, and purpose that we should have as the Church of Jesus Christ. The Church will no longer have a higher divorce rate than the world does. The Southern Baptist Convention will no longer have 9,000 churches that go a full year without baptizing one convert, as was true in 2007. Our churches will be revived and filled, our children and grandchildren will find God and be delivered from alcohol, drugs and illicit sex, and the Church world-wide will begin to affect the world for Christ, more than the world is affecting the Church. It was said of the Apostles:

> *"These* [Christians] *that have **turned the world upside down** are come here also" (Acts 17:6).*

But today, as Viola and Barna say in *Pagan Christianity?:*

> *"We have elders, we meet in a house, we do have a hired clergy, we take up a collection every Sunday and we preach the gospel. **But there is no rushing mighty wind!**"*

The Scene Of The Crime

In 399 B.C. the man whose name is in the title of this chapter was tried before a jury of five hundred of his peers, found guilty of crimes (which we will study as we go forward) and sentenced to death. However, the crime which he committed along with others against Christianity, is far greater than those he committed against the city of Athens.

I am asking you to serve as a jury of one and decide if my statement regarding fraud is true. As jurors are often taken to the place where a crime was perpetrated for better understanding of the event, I have studied this history carefully and would like for you to go with me to the scene of the crime.

I should say at this point, I am not a historian. I enjoyed the study of history in school and understand its importance. As Churchill said, *"Those who do not learn the lessons of history are destined to repeat it,"* and history has important lessons to teach. In the next several chapters we will rely heavily on historians. Since they sometimes disagree we will consider what is *"commonly reported."* Paul says in I Corinthians 5:1, *"It is commonly*

reported that there is fornication among you," and then proceeded to deal
with it on that basis.

Who Was Socrates?

Who was Socrates, this man who is quoted by Popes and scholars, and whose
name crops up so often in the study of the origins of the doctrine of the
Trinity? The man of whom Benjamin Franklin said, *"Regarding humility,
imitate Socrates and Jesus."*

Socrates *(469-399 B.C.)* was born in Athens, Greece, the son of a stone mason
father and a mother who was a midwife. He received the regular elementary
education in literature, music and gymnastics. Later he familiarized himself
with the rhetoric and teachings of the Sophists, the traveling teachers of his
time, who were notorious for their clever reasoning and arguments. Also at
a young age he was introduced to philosophy and studied science under the
teacher Archelaus. [1]

Initially, Socrates followed the craft of his father, but soon decided that he
was more suited for talk than manual labor. It is said that he did create
statues of *"the three Graces,"* which stood at the entrance of the Acropolis
in Athens until the second century A.D.

He served as an infantryman in the army of Athens and fought with bravery
in three of its battles with Sparta, between 432 and 422 B.C.

The Strangeness Of Socrates

One thing that is always mentioned when studying Socrates in history is the
oddity of his physical appearance. Lest you think I am being unkind to the
man, I will quote from the *Stanford Encyclopedia of Philosophy:*

> *"The extant sources agree that Socrates was profoundly
> ugly, resembling a satyr more than a man. He had wide-
> set, bulging eyes that darted sideways and enabled him, like
> a crab, to see not only what was straight ahead, but what
> was beside him as well; a flat, upturned nose with flaring*

*nostrils; and large fleshy lips like an ass. Socrates let his hair grow long, and went about **barefoot** and **unwashed**, carrying a stick and looking arrogant. **He didn't change his clothes** but efficiently wore in the daytime what he covered himself with at night. Something was peculiar about his gait as well, sometimes described as a swagger so intimidating that enemy soldiers kept their distance. He was impervious to ["not affected by"] the effects of alcohol and cold, but this made him an object of suspicion to his fellow soldiers on campaign."* [2]

Socrates was short in stature and by his own admission had a large pot belly. Historian Will Durant says, *"At Delium he was the last Athenian* [soldier] *to give ground to the Spartans, and seems to have saved himself by glaring at the enemy; even the Spartans were frightened."* [3]

Socrates' Demon

Not only were Socrates' fellow Athenians disturbed by his personal appearance, lack of hygiene, and that he could drink large amounts of alcohol without becoming dizzy, and walk through snow and ice barefoot with no effect, but the fact that Socrates acknowledged being guided by an inner *"daimon"* (demon) was unsettling to his fellow citizens. Socrates spoke often of this strange personal phenomenon, this **demon** or internal voice that prohibited his doing certain things, some trivial and some important, often unrelated to matters of right and wrong, ***"thus not to be confused with the popular notions of a conscience"*** *(Stanford Encyclopedia of Philosophy).*

Socrates claimed that this *"daimon"* had been with him since his youth and its presence in him is mentioned repeatedly in historical accounts. Regarding this, the *Encyclopedia Americana* says under the subject *"Demonology:"*

*"In classical times there was also a concept of a personal daimon - **Socrates**, for example, spoke of his daimon."* [4]

The early Roman church father, Tertullian *(160-230 A.D.)*, mentions Socrates' demon several times in his writings. For example:

> *"The philosophers acknowledge there are demons; Socrates himself waited on a demon's will. Why not? For it is said that an **evil spirit** attached itself to him even from his childhood, no doubt turning his mind from what was good"* *(circa 197 A.D.).* *"Socrates in contempt of the gods, was in the habit of swearing by an **oak**, a **goat**, or a **dog**"* *(circa 197 A.D.).* *"Socrates, as no one can doubt, was actuated by a **different spirit**. For they say that a **demon** clung to him from his boyhood"* *(circa 210 A.D.).* [5] [Note: circa means *"about"*]

The Immorality Of Socrates

Another troubling characteristic of Socrates that one encounters in the study of his life is his absolutely gross moral behavior! However, some modern philosophers (even Christians) try to justify this by saying he should not be judged by the standards of Christianity or of the twenty-first century. While this argument may have some small merit, what we see of Socrates in this area is reprehensible under **any standards** of human decency. Socrates was a *pervert*, and likely a *pedophile*!

An Immoral Culture

The morals of fifth, fourth, and third centuries B.C. Athens, and in fact Greece in its entirety, could hardly be called anything less than "rotten." As A.W. Tozer said, *"A society cannot rise above its religion, and a religion cannot rise above its view of God."* [6] [For example, consider the violence of modern Islam]. Regarding this lack of morals Will Durant says:

> *"The Athenians of the fifth century are not exemplars of morality; the **progress of the intellect** [philosophy] has loosened many of them from their ethical traditions, and has turned them into almost **unmoral individuals**...conscience rarely troubles them, and they never dream of loving their neighbors as themselves."* [7]

The Athenians act out the character of their gods! Among that considerable number of gods was Ares (Mars) the god of war, and it is said that nothing could compare with *"the thrill that came to him from lusty and natural killing."* Homer called Ares *"the curse of men."* Following the example of Ares, the Greeks show little restraint in their treatment of those they defeat in war. It is a regular matter, even in civil wars, to sack the conquered city, to finish off the wounded, to slaughter or enslave all unransomed prisoners and all captured noncombatants, to burn down the houses, the fruit trees, and the crops, to exterminate the livestock, and to destroy the seed for the future sowings. [8]

The Greeks, including Socrates, speak a lot about "virtue" and extol its importance, but this in no way pertains to sexual purity. As Durant says: *"To the Greek, virtue is man-liness. Knowledge is the highest virtue, which means excellence, rather than sinlessness."* To them virtue **is** knowledge, because according to Socrates *"no one knowingly does what is bad."* [False!]. In their sexual behavior also, the Athenians follow their gods. In a previous chapter I mentioned the temple of Aphrodite, *"the goddess of love,"* and the 1000 *"sacred temple prostitutes"* that were used in the *"worship"* of her. (Enough said about that). However, another god the Athenians worshiped was Hermes (Mercury) *"god of fertility,"* and from the cult of sacred stones his cult is derived. His is the tall stone placed upon graves, as he is the **demon**, or spirit in these stones. His is the stone or its god marking highways and roads out of the city, or marking boundaries and guarding fields. Because his function is also to promote fertility, the phallus became one of his symbols. His "herm" or pillar featured a carved head, an uncarved body, and a prominent male member, which was placed in front of all respectable houses in Athens. [9] Large stone carvings of the phallus of Hermes marked the boundaries of the city.

Homosexuality and Pedophilia
The entire subject of the Greeks and their gross immorality is sickening to consider, so we will not go into their behavior with women. (The word *"orgy"* comes from the Greek word *"ergon,"* which describes some of their

practices). Suffice it to say that prostitution was rife and public sex was not illegal. Most Athenians considered their wives as only keepers of the home and the bearer of children, and most had concubines. The Greeks considered romantic love to be a form of "possession" or "madness," and would smile at anyone who would use it as a fit guide in the choice of a marriage mate. [10]

I will discuss homosexuality and pedophilia in Athens just enough to discover the character of Socrates and that of his young student, the now famous Plato. Stranger than the prevalence of prostitution and obsession with philosophy in Athens, is what Durant calls *"the placid acceptance of sexual inversion"* [homosexuality]. The chief rivals of the female prostitutes were the boys of Athens. Merchants imported handsome **lads** to be sold to the highest bidder, who used them **first** as concubines and **later** as slaves, and only a negligible minority of the adult males of the city found this practice offensive. Athenian law took away the rights of those who engaged in homosexual acts, but the law was seldom enforced and public opinion tolerated the practice humorously. In the rival city of Sparta no stigma of any kind was attached to it and when Alcman wished to compliment some girls he called them his *"female boy-friends."* [11]

The women and girls of Athens had little education outside of household matters, and therefore the men considered them their intellectual inferiors, and had little desire for their company. Demosthenes says, *"We have courtesans* [mistresses] *for the sake of pleasure, concubines for the daily health of our bodies, and wives to bear us lawful offspring and be the faithful guardians of our homes."* [12]

Because the men of Athens, especially the aristocrats, seldom find mental companionship at home, and the lack of education among women creates a gulf between the sexes, they seek elsewhere the charms that they have not permitted their wives to acquire.

The Plague Of Pederasty
Thus the development of the wide-spread practice in Athens called

"pederasty." Webster's dictionary says this means *"a lover of boys, sodomy between male persons, especially as practiced by a man with a boy."* It is similar to our word *"pedophilia"* which *Webster's* describes as *"an abnormal condition in which an adult has a sexual **desire** for children."* The *Sanford Encyclopedia of Philosophy* says of pederasty in Athens:

> *"The socialization and education of males often involved a relationship...in which a youth approaching manhood, fifteen to seventeen, became the beloved of a male lover a few years older, under whose tutelage and through whose influence and gifts the younger man would be guided and improved. It was assumed among Athenians that mature men would find **youths** sexually attractive, and such relationships were conventionally viewed as beneficial to both parties."* [13]

What About Socrates?

We should note at this point that Socrates wrote nothing of which there is any record. He believed that his concepts and teachings could not be adequately conveyed by writing, so what we know of him we learn from the writings of others. The three primary sources are the playwright Aristophanes, who knew him in his early years, and the philosopher Plato and the writer Xenophon, who knew him as youths in the last ten years of his life.

Aristophanes wrote comic plays about Socrates which were performed in Athens in his lifetime, featuring an actor wearing the mask of Socrates, sometimes in a basket hanging in the air and speaking philosophical nonsense. Socrates was angered by these plays and considered Aristophanes dangerous; therefore his accounts of Socrates must be weighed in this light. Plato and Xenophon are considered more reliable sources regarding Socrates, but the views of Aristophanes must also be taken into account. For example he portrays Socrates as making fun of the traditional gods of Athens (which he was known to do), teaching dishonest techniques for avoiding the repayment of debt, and encouraging young men to beat their parents into submission. [14]

While young, Socrates studied under the teacher Archelaus, and the philosopher Diogenes *(412-323 B.C.)* says that, as a boy, Socrates was loved sexually by that teacher. This is confirmed by Prophyrius who says that Socrates did not disdain the love of Archelaus, *"because he was then very sensual."* However, Socrates later claimed that all he knew about erotic love, he learned from Diotima, a **witch** and priestess from Mantinea. [15]

About 318 B.C. Aristoxenus of Taruntum reported, on the testimony of his father who claimed to have known Socrates, that he was a person without education, *"ignorant and debauched."* [16]

Socrates first married Xanthippe, who bore him three sons, but since he did not work, she berated him for neglecting his family. He acknowledged the justice of her complaints and defended her to his sons and his friends. Socrates for sure was poor and showed no interest in acquiring anything of material value. He inherited a house from his father, his wife had come into the marriage with a sizeable dowry from her father, and some of his wealthy friends gave him money, but otherwise his family went lacking. But, when Athens temporarily legalized polygamy, because there was a shortage of husbands due to the high number of men killed in the wars, Socrates took a second wife. [17] (Yes, sometimes men who do not bathe, change clothes or work, can attract two!).

Plato and Xenophon agree in describing his habits and character. He was content with one simple and shabby robe throughout the year, and liked bare feet better than sandals or shoes. Durant says:

> *"All in all he was fortunate: he lived without working, read without writing, taught without routine, drank without dizziness, and died before senility."* [18]

But his morals were atrocious! Socrates is known to have had sex with his young boy students, a trait he supposedly learned as a boy from his own teacher-lover Archelaus. In Plato's dialogue *Phaedrus,* **Socrates** describes **ideal pederasty** as a relationship inspired by **"divine madness,"** a madness which *"is given us by the gods to ensure our greatest good fortune."* He describes a man falling in love with a beautiful boy as *"the best and noblest of all the forms that **possession by a god** can take."* [Sickening!]

Socrates' desire for the handsome boy Alcibiades is commented upon in several texts. In Plato's *Gorgias*, **Socrates** asserts that he is *"in love with two objects - Alcibiades, son of Clinias, and philosophy,"* and Plato describes him as *"in chase of the fair youth."* [19] Cornelius Nepos writes of Alcibiades: *"**As a boy** he was loved by many men, one of them **Socrates**; as an adult he himself loved not a few boys."*

The Athenian schools of martial arts often had a statue of the god Eros, and boys exercised there undressed. There was a law that prohibited grown-up men from staying near the dressing rooms, but it is stated that Socrates disregarded this prohibition. It is claimed that he frequented **boy brothels,** [20] and in the dialogue *Charmides*, Plato says he *"**took fire**"* with erotic intoxication upon glimpsing the naked body of the boy *Charmides* beneath his open tunic. He was also not above giving advice to homosexuals and prostitutes on how to attract lovers. [21]

As we go forward we shall see that this and other bad behavior will finally be his undoing. Consider this comment by the Roman church father Tertullian:

> *"If we challenge you to a comparison in the virtue of chastity, I turn to a part of the sentence passed by the Athenians against **Socrates**, who was pronounced a corrupter of youth. In contrast, the Christian confines himself to the **female sex**" (circa 197 A.D.).* [22]

The Gadfly Of Athens

Here is a question that has challenged philosophers and thinkers for the past twenty-four centuries. How did Socrates, a man such as the one we have described, who left no writings, who did not like to travel and seldom left Athens, a teacher who claimed no knowledge and established no school, a philosopher who called himself an *"amateur in philosophy,"* and who was condemned to death at the age of 70 by 500 of his peers, come to be known

as **the father of Western philosophy**? This is called the *Socratic problem.*
Though some will dispute my conclusion, I believe the answer lies in the
"daimon" that he spoke so much about and by which he was *"possessed"*
[his word]. He believed he was on a *"divine mission"* to act as a *"gadfly"*
(I have seen it written *"horsefly"*), to bite the men of Athens and disturb
them from their mental and intellectual sluggishness, in search of ultimate
truth. He believed he was given this *"divine"* assignment when he visited
the oracle (voice) of the god Apollo at Delphi. Oracles were the mediums or
fortunetellers by which the ancient Greeks and Romans consulted the gods,
and these oracles did at times exhibit super-human knowledge. The apostle
Paul and his helper Silas encountered one of these in the Macedonian city of
Philippi *(Acts 16)*, and cast the evil spirit out of the soothsayer.

> *"And it came to pass, as we went to prayer, a certain damsel*
> *possessed with **a spirit of divination** met us, which brought*
> *her masters much gain by soothsaying. The same followed*
> *Paul and us, and cried, saying, These men are the servants*
> *of the most high God, which show us the way of salvation.*
> *But Paul, being grieved, turned and said **to the spirit**, I*
> *command thee in the name of Jesus Christ to come out of*
> *her. And **he** came out the same hour" (Acts 16:16-18).*

And Peter says to ministers:
> *"If any man speak, let him speak as the **oracles** of God" (I*
> *Peter 4:11).*

But Socrates was flattered and taken in by this **demon spirit** of the oracle
at Delphi, and mentions the oracle often. Years later Chaerephon visits the
oracle and asks her the question, *"Is any man wiser than Socrates?"* To
which she replies, *"No one."* [23] Socrates always sought to *"**obey** the oracle*
at Delphi, which, when asked how one should worship the gods, answered,
'According to the law of your country'." Even his most famous saying,
"Know Thyself," came from Delphi. Consider the following conversation
between Socrates and a friend:
> *"Tell me, Euthydemus, have you ever gone to Delphi?"*

*"Yes, twice." "And did you observe what is written on the temple wall - **Know thyself?**" "I did." "And did you... examine yourself, and ascertain what sort of character you are?"* [24]

It is without question that Socrates made many appeals to oracles and dreams, as messages from the gods. And what did this *"divine mission from heaven"* produce in Socrates? It made him a driven person!

In his youth he had studied **science** with Archelaus, but in his maturity, turned from it as a **plausible myth** and interested himself no longer in **facts** and **origins,** but in values and ends. Xenophon says:

*"He discoursed always of human affairs. I was never acquainted with anyone who took greater care **to find out what each of his companions knew.**"* [25]

The *Encyclopedia Americana* says of Socrates turning from science:

*"He **abandoned all effort** to find out why things are as they are by examining nature itself. He turned instead to the examination of **logoi** [singular "logos"], that is, **statements, arguments,** or in general, **words** - as a way of **discovering something true.**"* They continue, *"The distinctive feature of Socratic inquiries is that they took as their object not some phenomenon in the **natural world,** but **some person and his ideas. Socrates hoped that by methodically and repeatedly examining someone's idea's, it might ultimately lead him to the discovery and establishment of the truth.**"* [26]

The Logos Doctrine

Please be patient as we go through this material, as its importance to Christianity, and our proper understanding as to who the One Most High God of the Bible is, can hardly be over-stated! What we have just witnessed in the foregoing is the birth of the so called *"divine Logos doctrine"* in a demon possessed man who acknowledged repeatedly his guidance by the spirit of the Greek god Apollo.

True, some fifty years before Socrates, the Greek philosopher Heraclitus was the first to use the term *"Logos"* in a metaphysical sense. The word *logos* has its root in the Greek verb lego, *"to say,"* and its earliest meaning probably was *"connected discourse."* Heraclitus asserted that the world is governed by a *"firelike"* Logos, **a divine force** that produces the order and pattern discernable in the flux of nature. He believed that **this force** is similar to **human reason** and that **his own thought partook** of the **divine Logos**. Heraclitus urges us to pay attention to the Logos, which *"governs all things"* and is something we *"encounter every day."* According to Martha C. Nussbaum, Heraclitus

> *"...**made logos a central concept**. We should probably emphasize the **linguistic** connections of logos when interpreting Heraclitus' thought...and **look to our language** and the **order embodied in it**, rather than to scientific or **religious views** that neglect this."* She continues, *"By the classical period* [the time of Socrates, Plato, Aristotle, etc.,] *it already had a wider variety of meanings: 'argument,' 'rational principle,' 'reason,' 'proportion.' "*

> *"In the 3rd century B.C. the proponents of **Stoicism** borrowed the idea of **logos**...and used it for the immanent ordering principle of the universe-represented **at the level of language** by humankind's **ordered discourse**. Nature and **logos** are often treated as one and the same..."* and *"humans are urged to 'live consistently with logos'."* Be patient with me but I must repeat this: She says, *"**Later Christian thinkers clearly did incorporate the Stoic logos doctrine; logos was associated particularly with Christ**."* [27]

The Pope and "Logos"

Nussbaum's quote from the 3rd century B.C. doctrine of the Stoics, where human beings are urged to *"live consistently with logos,"* sounds familiar. In Pope Benedict's afore mentioned speech he refers several times to *"logos"* in interesting terms. Benedict is an immanent theologian of the Catholic church, and before he became pope he was Cardinal Joseph Ratzinger. He was featured on the cover of *Newsweek* magazine, May 2, 2005, and the accompanying article says, *"In 1981 John Paul II named him Prefect of the congregation for the Doctrine of the Faith,* [defender of the faith] *a position that formerly went by the title Grand Inquisitor.* **In Ratzinger's time**, *of course,* **torture wasn't part of the agenda**. *But in the realm of ideas,* **Ratzinger was ruthless.**" [28]

Listen to Benedict the theologian:

> *"...***biblical faith***, in the* **Hellenistic** *period, encountered the best of* **Greek thought** *at a deep level, resulting in a* **mutual enrichment**...*"*

> *"The encounter between the* **Biblical message** *and* **Greek thought** *did not happen by chance."*

> *"***The mysterious name of God***, revealed from the burning bush...* 'I Am,' *already presents a challenge to the notion of myth, to which* **Socrates'** *attempts to* **vanquish** *and transcend* **myth, stands in close analogy.**" Note: Please read this statement closely, **"What God did at the burning bush"** stands in close analogy to what Socrates did. Wow!

The Pope continues:

> *"***Not to act 'with logos'*** *is contrary to God's nature."* *"The truly divine God is the* **God who has revealed himself as logos** *and, as logos, has acted and continues to act lovingly on our behalf."* He says love *"continues to be love of the* **God who is Logos.**"

May I respectfully say that this is religious mumbo-jumbo and doctrinal nonsense, and has no basis in Holy Scripture, Old or New Testaments. But he is right when he gives Socrates the credit for it!

Socrates and The Pursuit of Logos

Now we can better understand Socrates' drive to, and way of, pounding people with questions that is called the *"Socratic method."* He believed that **divine reasoning** was in every person (but not animals), and by causing them to **speak their minds** he could **dispel myth** and **arrive at ultimate truth** (logos). Will Durant says:

> *"It became his habit to rise early and go to the market place, the gymnasiums or the workshops of artisans and engage in discussion any person who gave promise of a stimulating intelligence or an amusing stupidity. 'Is not the road to Athens made for conversation?' he asked. His method was simple: he called for the definition of a **large idea**; he examined the definition, usually to reveal its incompleteness, its contradictions, or its absurdity; he led on, by question after question, to a fuller and juster definition, which, however, **he never gave.**"*

> *"So he went **prowling** among men's beliefs, **prodding** them with questions, **demanding** precise answers and consistent views, and **making himself a terror** to all who could not think clearly. He protected himself from a similar cross-examination by announcing he knew nothing; he knew all the questions, but none of the answers."* [29] And he always managed to dominate the discourse. Socrates was so driven in this pursuit of Logos that he even proposed that someday in Hades [hell] he would be a gadfly, and *"find out who is wise, and who pretends to be wise and is not."* [30]

His opponents objected that he tore down but never built, that he rejected every answer but gave none of his own, and that the results demoralized morals and paralyzed thought. In many cases he left the idea that he had set out to clarify **more obscure than before.**

The *Stanford Encyclopedia of Philosophy* says:

> *"Socrates was usually to be found in public areas, conversing*

*with a variety of different people, young and old, male and female, slave and free, rich and poor; that is with anyone he could persuade to join with him in his question-and-answer mode of probing serious matters. Socrates pursued this task single-mindedly...and he did this regardless of whether his respondents wanted to be questioned **or resisted him**.*"
Note: He is searching for *"logos!"*

To the charge that he always asked questions, but never gave answers, Socrates replied:

> *"The reason is that **the god** [demon] **compels** me to be a midwife, but **forbids** me to bring forth."*

Somehow Socrates had an unexplainable appeal to the youth of Athens. With all his irritating faults, his boy students loved him deeply. *"Perhaps,"* he says to one of them, *"I may be able to assist you in the pursuit of honor and virtue, from being mutually disposed to love; for whenever I conceive a liking for persons I devote myself with ardor, and with my whole mind, to love them and be loved by them in return, regretting their absence and having mine regretted by them, and longing for their society while they long for mine."* [31]

It is evident from reading the accounts of Plato and Xenophon that Socrates came to the point where he could *"subjugate"* his sexual desire for boys by substituting for it mental *"intercourse,"* **taking power over their minds** by teaching them the ideas of philosophy. He frequently compares ideas with children, and says *"ideas are the produce of the intercourse that men have with their beloved disciples"* (*Plato's Symposium*). For example, the dialogue *Lysis* deals extensively with the bond of affection between him and two boys of about 11 years of age *(Encyclopedia Americana; Vol. 22; p. 227)*. And I should point out once again, in *Plato's Gorgias*, Socrates asserts that he is *"in love with two objects - **Alcibiades**, son of Clinias, **and philosophy**."* But in *Symposium* it comes out that despite his love for this boy, and despite the fact that Alcibiades wishes to have Socrates as a lover in every sense of the word, Socrates spends the night in bed with the youth, without satisfying the desires, and their mutual love remains "chaste." [Can this be believed?] This sexually restrained form of Greek pederasty has since been called *"Platonic love."* Author T.K. Hubbard writes that *"Platonic love"* as articulated in *Plato's Symposium* and *Phaedrus*, *"attempts to **rehabilitate pederastic desire by sublimating** it into a higher, spiritual pursuit of Beauty in which the sexual appetite is ultimately transcended."* [32]

Corrupting Young Minds

Athens in Socrates' time was a democratic city, but he was known to despise democracy and argue that *"democracy is nonsense."* Also, instead of speaking of "gods" as all others in Athens did, Socrates usually spoke of "God" singular. *("Thou believest that there is **one God**; the devils believe also and tremble" James 2:19)..* And, he was corrupting the minds of their youth, so the majority of Athenians looked upon him with irritated suspicion!

Socrates' affect on the youths of Athens was varied and deep. They became the leaders of the most diverse philosophical schools and theories in Greece - Platonism, Cynicism, Stoicism, Epicureanism, and Skepticism.

There was the young **Phaedo**; Socrates *"loved the lad, and made him a philosopher."* There was **Xenophon** who testified that *"nothing was of greater benefit than to associate with Socrates, and to converse with him, on any occasion, on any subject."* There was **Plato**, upon whose vivid imagination the old man made so lasting an impression that the two are mingled forever in philosophical history.

There was the dashing young **Alcibiades**, who said:

> *"When we hear any other speaker, even a good one, his words produce absolutely no effect upon us in comparison, whereas the very fragments of your words, Socrates, even at second hand, and however imperfectly reported, **amaze** and **possess the souls** of every man, woman and child who comes within hearing of them. I am conscious that if I did not shut*

*my ears against him and fly from the voice of the **siren** ["one who snares, entangles"], he would detain me until I grew old sitting at his feet. I have known in my soul, or in my heart... the greatest of **pangs**, more violent in ingenious youth than any **serpents tooth**, the pang of philosophy. And you...and I need not say Socrates himself, have all had experience of the same **madness** and **passion** for philosophy."* [33]

Socrates referred often to the fact that his mother had been a midwife, and this is the role in which he saw himself. He was on a *"divine mission"* to birth ideas, reason, **Logos** from the minds of his pupils who were *"pregnant with thought" (Theaetetus)*. To this end he was driven and it was his greatest joy. But for him time was running out!

A Fatal Mistake

One of his pupils was **Critias**, who enjoyed Socrates' teachings against democracy, and helped to incriminate him by writing a play in which he described the gods as the invention of leaders who used them as night watchmen to frighten men into decency.

And there was the son of the democratic leader, Anytus, a lad who preferred to hear Socrates speak, than to attend his family's leather business. Anytus complained that Socrates had unsettled his son with skepticism, and that the boy **no longer respected his parents** or the gods. Anytus also resented Socrates' criticism of democracy and gave him a warning, *"I think you are too ready to speak evil of men; and if you will take my advice, I would recommend you to be careful!"* **And Anytus bided his time**. [34]

Athens was becoming more angry with Socrates and his skepticism that *"left reason itself in mental confusion unsettling to every custom and belief."* Even those like Aristophanes who had praised him in the past, now attributed to him the irreligion of the age, **the disrespect of the young for the old**, the **loosened morals** of the educated class, and the disorderly individualism that was consuming Athens.

Trouble For Athens and Socrates

The years from 412 B.C. until the death of Socrates in 399 B.C. were chaotic in Athens as the empire shrank because of revolts, and former allies refused to pay tribute any longer. There was war with Sparta and internal strife as this "disorderly individualism" consumed Athenian life. The *oligarchs*, advocating a form of government in which the ruling power belongs to a few people, began to arise in Athens. Though Socrates refused to support this faction, it was led by his pupil Critias and many of its other leaders were his pupils and friends. They were able to overthrow the democratic government in a rich man's revolution of ruthless terror, but eventually were defeated and democracy restored. But democrats like Anytus and a young poet named Meletus branded Socrates as the intellectual source of the oligarch uprising, and determined to remove him from Athenian life. [35]

In the spring of 399 B.C. Meletus composed a document charging Socrates with failure to show due piety to the gods of Athens, and corruption of the city's young men. He delivered this to Socrates in the presence of witnesses, instructing him to appear within four days to a chief magistrate for a preliminary hearing. As a citizen, Socrates had the right to simply leave the city and forgo the hearing, but this he refused to do. There was also a pre-trial examination before the same magistrate, and about thirty days later a trial.

The trial which lasted only one day, was conducted before a jury of 500 of Socrates' fellow Athenians. The accounts written by Plato do not provide Meletus' prosecuting speech or those of Anytus and Lycon, who had joined in the suit; or the testimony of the witnesses, if there were any, for the accusers or the defense.

The responses that Socrates gave to the questions raised can best be described as flippant. He was more serious in his response to the charge that he corrupted the young, insisting that, if he corrupted them, he did so unwillingly; and if unwillingly, he should be "instructed" (scolded), not prosecuted. The question concerning his **controlling demon** was raised and discussed. The demon had always warned Socrates if he was undertaking something harmful, but remained silent if he did good. Notable to Socrates was the fact that the demon made no sign of opposition to the recent circumstances, or during the trial that would condemn him to death. He took this to mean that death was not an evil to be feared, but was only the next journey of existence. Socrates addressed the court and said:

> *"O my judges - for you I may truly call judges - I should like to tell you of a wonderful circumstance. Hitherto the divine faculty to which the **internal oracle** is the source has constantly been in the habit of opposing me even about trifles. If I was going to make a slip or error in any matter; and now as you see there has come upon me that which may be thought, and is generally believed to be, the last and worst evil. But the oracle made no sign of opposition, either when I was leaving my house this morning, or when I was on my way to the court, or while I was speaking, at anything which I was going to say; and yet **I have often been stopped in the middle of a speech**, but now in nothing I either said or did touching the matter in hand has the oracle opposed me. What do I take to be the explanation of this silence? I will tell you, it is an intimation that what has happened to me is a good, and that those of us who think that death is an evil are in error. For the customary sign would surely have opposed me had I been going to evil and not to good."*

The jury found him guilty, and since these were capital crimes, he was sentenced to death. He stated that it might be a blessing, either a dreamless sleep or an opportunity to converse in the underworld. In his few remaining days he was visited in prison by friends, including the young Plato, who recorded the events in *Phaedo*, but who was not actually there on the day of the execution.

On his last day Socrates *"appeared happy both in manner and words as he died nobly and without fear."* Eleven prison officials met with him at dawn to tell him what to expect. When Socrates' friends arrived, Xanthippe and their youngest child was still with him. She reminded him that he was about to enjoy his last conversation with his companions, then went home in mourning.

Socrates spent the day in philosophical conversation and warned his friends not to restrain themselves in argument. *"Give little thought to Socrates but much more to the truth. If you think what I say is true, agree with me; if not, oppose it with every argument!"*

Though not known for usually doing so, Socrates did bathe himself at the prison cistern, so the women of his household would be spared from having to wash his corpse for burial. After meeting with his family again in the late afternoon, he rejoined his companions.

As his friends looked on, the executioner handed Socrates the cup of poison hemlock (a plant), and he cheerfully took the cup and drank. He was then instructed to walk around until his legs felt numb. After he lay down, the man who administered the poison pinched his foot and he could no longer feel his legs. The numbness slowly crept up his body until it reached his heart. **Socrates, the gadfly of Athens was dead!** [36]

Socrates In The Light Of Scripture

But was Socrates *really* dead? Consider! In the period shortly after his death, no less than fifteen writers and poets did works about him. The ideas which he passed down to Plato, and through him to Aristotle, became a system of logic so powerful that it remained unaltered for nineteen hundred years. **His focus on Logos, expanded by Plato and picked up by Philo, the Hellenistic Jewish writer, would flow through the *"Greek Church fathers"* into Christianity, and impact its doctrine beyond our ability to comprehend!** Although Socrates did injure science by turning students away from physical research, he became for Greek history both a martyr and a saint. Allusions to Socrates abound in literature, history, and political tracts, and he has been a subject for artists since ancient times. Benjamin

Franklin, a deist but a non-Christian, writes of using the Socratic method of disputing against Christians that he encountered. He wrote:

> *"I assumed the character of a humble questioner. Being a skeptic...to many of the doctrines of Christianity, I found Socrates' method to be both the safest for myself, as well as the most embarrassing to those against whom I applied it. It soon afforded me singular pleasure..."*

The poet Shelly 1792-1822 A.D., referred to **Socrates** as *"the **Jesus Christ** of Greece."* In his 1963 *"Letter from Birmingham Jail,"* Martin Luther King, Jr., wrote, *"To a degree, academic freedom is a reality today because **Socrates** practiced civil disobedience."*

Currently the old philosopher is an icon of popular culture and his name is used for all manner of different purposes. *"Socrates"* is a crater on the moon. *"Socrates"* is the name of an E.U. educational program. *"Socrates"* is the fifth movement of Leonard Bernstein's *Serenade*. *"Socrates"* is a sculpture park in New York City. **A life-size painting of him is included in Raphael's *"School of Athens"* at the Vatican, and there also his bust is given a place of honor.** When internationally known preacher R.C. Sproul on his radio program *"Renewing Your Mind,"* taught a recent series on Western Philosophy and its effects on Christianity, Socrates was included, along with Plato, Aristotle and others. Not one negative thing was said about him, his message, or his morals, but rather he is credited with *"saving Athens and possibly Western civilization."* (The question of *"how?"* is not addressed). At the end of each broadcast the announcer offered the entire series on C.D. *"for a donation of any amount, that we might know and better serve **the God of theology."*** [37]

The Teacher Who Did Not Learn

On the day of Socrates' death he said, *"If you do not agree with me, **oppose it with every argument."*** This I will endeavor to do, and mostly with **Holy Scripture**.

Considering all, Socrates might have been a master teacher, but he should have been a better pupil, a student of the truths that even **nature** teaches.

Perhaps he gave up on the study of creation too soon. Listen to the great apostle Paul:

> *"Doth not even **nature itself teach you**, that, if a man have long hair, it is a shame unto him?" (I Cor. 11:14).*

Paul is speaking here of a God given natural endowment of conscience or instinct, which guides even the heathen in proper conduct. For example, it is **not unusual** to find primitive peoples who believe in **one creator God**, and where adultery and murder are punishable by death. Some native American tribes believed in one God whom they called *"The Great Spirit,"* and knew He had created all and ruled over all, this before they encountered Christianity! Listen to Paul again:

> *"For when the Gentiles, which **have not the law**, do **by nature** the things contained in the law, these, **having not the law**, are a law unto themselves: Which show the work of the law, **written in their hearts**, their **conscience** also bearing witness, and their thoughts the meanwhile **accusing** or **excusing** one another" (Rom. 2:14-15).*

Therefore, the argument by some that Socrates' behavior should not be judged by modern or biblical standards is not really valid. Paul was speaking of those who practice homosexual acts when he says in Romans chapter one:

> *"Because that which may be known of God is manifest in them; for God hath showed it unto them. For the invisible things of him from the creation of the world are clearly seen, being **understood by the things that are made**, even his eternal power and Godhead [deity]; **so that they are without excuse**" (v. 19-20).*

> *"Professing themselves to be wise, **they became fools**. Wherefore God also gave them up to uncleanness, through the lusts of their own hearts, to dishonor their own bodies between themselves" (v. 22, 24).*

> *"...for even their women did change the **natural** use into that which is **against** nature: and likewise also the men, leaving the natural use of the woman, **burned in** their lust one toward another; **men with men** working that which is unseemly..." (v. 26-27).*

> *"Who knowing the judgement of God, that they which commit such things are **worthy of death**, not only do the same, but have pleasure in them that do them" (v. 32).*

Therefore, as Paul said in Athens at the Acropolis, perhaps standing near the statues of the three Graces that Socrates himself had carved, (it is said that they stood there until the 2nd century A.D.):

> **"God...commandeth all men everywhere to repent"** *(Acts 17:30).*

Consider this. There were many men in Athens who did not engage in pederasty and homosexuality. In fact there were laws against it, and those found guilty were not allowed to hold public office. This proves that even to these gentiles, conscience taught them that this was immoral; therefore, Socrates' lust for, and behavior with young boys, is inexcusable!

Socrates' Concept Regarding Words

From the time the oracle of Delphi told his friend Chaerephon that there was none wiser than Socrates, he was driven to find *"logos"*, i.e. divine reason and ultimate truth, in the **speech** of everyone that he met. He believed the wisdom of the ages **dwelt in the minds of people,** if it could only be retrieved through verbal discourse. This was the basis for his belief that he was a *"mid-wife"* for the birth of **ideas**, and thus his dying words *"warning his companions **not to restrain themselves in argument.**"* [38]

But is wisdom *really* found in a multitude of words?

> *"The fear of the Lord is the beginning of wisdom" (Ps. 111:10).*

270

"For God giveth to a man that is good in his sight wisdom, and knowledge, and joy" (Eccl. 2:26).

"If any man lack wisdom, let him ask of God that giveth to all men liberally" (James 1:5).

"In the multitude of words there wanteth [lacks] *not sin: but he that refraineth his lips is wise" (Prov. 10:19).*

"A fool's voice is known by a multitude of words" (Eccl. 5:3).

*"But I say unto you, That **every idle word** that men shall speak, they shall give account thereof in the day of judgement. For **by thy words** thou shalt be justified, and by thy words thou shalt be condemned"* [Jesus speaking] *(Matt. 12:36-37).*

*"We beseech you, brethren...that you **study to be quiet**, and do your own business" (I Thess. 4:10-11).*

Listen to the apostle James:

> *"**This wisdom** descendeth not from above, but is **earthly, sensual, devilish.** But the wisdom that is from above **is first pure**, then peaceable..." (James 3:15, 17).*

Remember this: Being careful with words is one mark of wisdom, and "the gift of gab" is not one of the nine spiritual gifts!

More About Socrates' Demon.

Socrates said of the demon that possessed him: *"The favor of the gods has given me a marvelous gift, which has never left me since my childhood. It is a voice which, when it makes itself heard, deters me from what I am about to do, and never urges me on."* He spoke familiarly of this demon, joked about it and obeyed blindly the indications it gave. According to Plato,

"He would always listen to its wisdom - sometimes standing motionless for a full day," barefoot, unaffected by a hard frost, listening to the demon's recommendations. Eventually, his friends never took an important step without consulting it. But the demon had its own will, and when it was unfavorable to the questioner, it remained silent; in that event it was impossible for Socrates to make it speak.

Any serious Bible student knows immediately upon reading the above that his *"daimon"* or *"inner oracle"* is not a *"marvelous gift"* from God! This is a foul, tormenting, demon spirit which the New Testament calls a *"devil."*

Our Messiah Jesus was famous for preaching the *"gospel of the kingdom,"* healing the sick, **and casting out devils**.

> *"And his fame went throughout all Syria: and they brought unto him all sick people that were taken with divers diseases and torments, and those which were **possessed with devils** and those which were lunatic...and he healed them"* (Matt. 4:24).

> *"And when the even was come, they brought unto him many that were **possessed with devils**: and he cast out the spirits with his word"* (Matt. 8:16).

> *"...there met him two **possessed with devils**, coming out of the tombs, exceeding fierce, so that no man might pass by that way. And they cried out saying, What have we to do with thee, Jesus, thou Son of God? Art thou come to torment us before the time? So the devil's besought him, saying, If thou cast us out, suffer us to go away into the herd of swine. And he said unto them, Go. And ...they went into the herd of swine: and the whole herd ran violently down a steep place into the sea, and perished in the waters"* (Matt. 8:28-32).

> *"Then he called his twelve disciples together, and gave them power and authority **over all devils**, and to cure diseases" (Luke 9:1).*

> *"Go ye into **all the world** and preach the gospel...and these signs shall follow **them that believe;** In my name shall they **cast out devils**..."(Mark 16:15, 17).*

Our Personal Experience

About fifteen years ago we were called upon to minister to a woman living in the Nashville area who was possessed with demons. Her deliverance was a process that involved much prayer over a space of time. When we were away on trips, she knew what time of day we prayed for her, even from 500 miles away, because the demons would become very agitated. Behold the power of prayer to the Father, in Jesus' name!

Much of the wanton violence and terror we are seeing in the world today is caused by demon possession. Several years ago we were attacked by a woman, twenty-eight years old, college educated, at the end of a very spiritual gospel concert. She tried to hit us with her fists and pull our hair, but happily we were shielded by the Holy Spirit and she could not touch us! This took place outside the auditorium near our tour bus, and as we invoked the name of Jesus, she fell on her back in the gravel, screaming. We put a large Bible under her head and began to cast out the evil spirits. When she was delivered to the point that she could speak rationally, she opened her eyes and said, *"I have to make a decision, don't I?"* When I answered in the affirmative she said, *"I want them all out!"* She was gloriously delivered, and now she and her husband have a successful family, business and lay ministry. Her demon possession came about, she later told us, through *transcendental meditation* and New Age studies. She had reached the point, before her deliverance, where she would see a large cobra during meditation, and her re-occurring fantasy was to take a machine gun and blow people away. This sounds a lot like some things we are hearing on the news! It is for sure that these problems will not be dealt with successfully as long as society and medical science deny the existence of demons, and the Church has no power to cast them out.

The Legacy Of Socrates

Here is a good question. Did the demons that Jesus permitted to go into the herd of swine, that caused them to *"run violently"* down the steep hill and drown in the sea, perish with the swine? It is for sure that they did not. No more than the terrible demons that possessed Hitler and his Nazi regime, died with them at the end of WWII. The proof that those demons survived and are still active in the world today, is the great number of youths from various nations (the U.S., Europe, etc.), sometimes called "skin-heads," that wear Nazi symbols and regalia, advocate Nazi, fascist, and racist policies, and engage in hostile and violent behavior. Most of these Hitler-loving youths come from parents who weren't even born when Hitler was alive, a sure sign of continued demon activity!

And the time of judgement for these demons has not yet come. (Notice their words in *Matt. 8:29, "before the **time**")*. Listen to the statement of Jesus regarding what happens when demons leave a person:

> *"When the unclean spirit is gone out of a man, he walketh through dry places, **seeking rest**; and finding none, he saith, I will return unto my house whence I came out. Then goeth he, and taketh to him seven other spirits **more wicked than himself**; and they enter in and **dwell there**: and the last state of that man is **worse than the first**" (Luke 11:24, 26).*

We learned in chapter nine from the Pope's own words that Roman Catholicism has fully embraced the "Greek spirit." Would it then be surprising if some of the characteristics of that Greek spirit that were evident in Athens, should be manifested today in the Catholic priesthood? For example, homosexuality, pedophilia, or man-boy love?

Need I remind you of some recent shocking disclosures that have shaken the Catholic Church world-wide: the troubling exposé by the secular media (the *Boston Globe, New York Times*, and *U.S.A. Today* newspapers; *Time* and *Newsweek* magazines) of the decades-long sexual abuse by priests from various dioceses, of literally thousands of innocent children, **mostly boys**. It has been proven, and admitted by the Catholic Church, that hundreds of priests pursued this pattern of abusive behavior, while bishops and church leaders knew, but looked the other way. Some molesting priests were transferred from parish to parish for years before the church finally *"defrocked"* them. (I have heard of none who were excommunicated, however, priests are excommunicated for marrying).

Since the *Boston Globe* first broke this sordid story in January, 2002, molestation of children by priests has been uncovered in such varied places across the U.S. as Boston, Fall River and Plymouth, Massachusetts; Manchester, New Hampshire; Portland, Maine; Philadelphia, Pennsylvania; Dallas, Texas; Lafayette, Louisiana; and West Palm Beach, Florida; causing people to ask, "What is going on with the Catholic Church?"

The *USA Today* newspaper, February 25, 2002, carried a large article titled, ***Abuse Response Varies By Diocese***. The sub-title read, *Catholic Church structure tends to complicate reform efforts*. The article said:

> *"**Boston** - year after year since 1985, Catholic dioceses across the nation have been forced to come forward with the same ugly confession. Some priests have committed acts of **pedophilia**. **Worse yet**, church leaders knew but did little to prevent it."* The article continued, *"Many of the nation's 194 dioceses are struggling to come to terms with a cultural change from a time when allegations of pedophilia were handled privately."*

An article from *The* (Nashville) *Tennessean*, January 6, 2003 was titled, ***Study Puts More Heat On Bishops***. It was sub-titled, ***Two-thirds*** *kept accused priests on job*. The article read:

> *"**Dallas** - roughly **two-thirds** of the top U.S. Catholic leaders have allowed priests accused of sexual abuse to keep working, a practice that **spans decades and continues today**. Church spokesmen did not dispute the results of the study."*

Newsweek magazine; March 4, 2002, featured as its cover story an article titled, ***Sex, Shame, and the Catholic Church***. The sub-title was, *80 Priests accused of child abuse in Boston and new soul searching across America.* A few enlightening excerpts:

> *"The cases the church is grappling with now involve two phenomena that are psychologically distinct:...**pedophilia**, defined as intense or recurrent sexual desire for prepubescent children; and sexual advances on sexually mature, but **underage**, boys and girls."* It continues, ***"But some researchers think the priesthood may hold a dangerous attraction for pedophiles."*** Then this troubling question: *"Is the failure of the **church** to confront the problem of sex abuse **bred in its bones?"***

Under lawsuits and public pressure, the Boston Archdiocese paid out $85 million in funds to 552 victims of molestation by priests there. And in July, 2007, a judge approved a $660 million settlement between the Los Angeles Archdiocese and 508 victims of sexual abuse by clergy there.

But no amount of money can repair the damage done to a child by being molested by a person who is supposed to represent God in their lives! Such molestation is not just a violation of the body and mind, but is a rape of the very soul, from which it is almost impossible to recover. The lawyer for the victims in the Los Angeles case asked for a moment of silence in court, for victims who had died during the years of negotiations, while the Roman Church dragged its feet. He said that he knew of nine who had committed suicide in the last five years, and several others who had died of drug overdoses.

As *Newsweek* said, *"But **secrecy** and **silence** has always characterized the Catholic Church, and in many of these cases the church does all it can to prevent the charges from coming to light."*

Instructions issued from the Vatican in 1962 stated that in cases of sexual abuse, *"those same matters be **pursued in a secretive way**, and...be **restrained*** *by a perpetual silence.*" Cardinal Ratzinger, now Pope Benedict, **endorsed this view** in a letter sent out to all bishops on May 18, 2001.

By July, 2007 it was reported that these abuse cases across the U.S. had cost Roman Catholic Churches around 2.1 billion dollars. By then at least four dioceses had gone bankrupt paying abuse victims.

Lest you think this problem is all in the past for the Roman Church, the results of a three-year probe by the government of Ireland into the abuse of children by priests in the Dublin Archdiocese was released in November 2009. The investigation, led by a judge and two lawyers, issued the 720-page report, and said they had no doubt that 46 priests were responsible for abusing **many more than 320 children**. The Commission found that three successive Archbishops of Dublin did not tell police about abuse cases involving more than 170 priests, instead opting to avoid public scandals by shuttling offending priests from parish to parish.

And *The New York Times* included (February 10, 2010), an article with this headline, *German Church Faces Child Abuse Charges*. They quoted an article by the German magazine *Der Spiegel* which said that nearly 100 Catholic clerics and lay people had been suspected of abusing children nationwide since 1995. *Der Spiegel* was quoted as saying, *"Already a tremor is shaking the church, which could be **the beginning of an earthquake.**"*

One other thing should be noted regarding the molestation by the Catholic priests in Ireland. It was stated that 100 percent of the **abusers** were male priests and **90 percent of the victims were boys**. To my mind that makes absolutely no sense. Therefore my next question must be, is this perverted pursuit of man-boy love by these priests part of the legacy from Socrates to the Roman Catholic Church that holds him in such high honor? (Remember Plato's statements that Socrates *"took fire"* at the sight of the boy Charmides, and that he was *"in chase of the fair youth"* Alcibiades, his *"lover"*).

Listen to Jesus:

> *"But whoso shall offend one of these little ones which believe in me, it were better for him that a millstone were hanged about his neck, and that he were drowned in the depth of the sea.* **And if thine eye offend thee, pluck it out**, *and cast it from thee: it is better for thee to enter into life with one eye than having two eyes* **to be cast into hell fire**. *Take heed that ye despise not one of these little ones; for I say unto you, That* **in heaven** *their angels do always behold* **the face of my Father which is in heaven** *" (Matt. 18:6, 9-10).*

Was Socrates A Christian?

Wait! Before you toss this book aside in disgust, let me explain why I would ask such a ridiculous question. It is because of the statement by the early church father Justin Martyr, quoted at the beginning of this chapter:

> **"Christ was known by Socrates, for Christ was and is the Logos who dwells in every man. It may be asserted that all who have lived with the Logos were Christians. Among the Greeks, this specially applies to Socrates and Heraclitus.** *"* [39]

Justin *(100-165 A.D.)* was himself a philosopher who converted to Christianity and became a tireless evangelist and writer. He greatly influenced Christian thinking after the death of the Apostles, and wrote more concerning Christianity than any other person up until his time. Sadly his teachings were very detrimental to those who followed him in the next several centuries, because he retained much of Greek philosophy in his belief system. He is a prime example of the devastating effects of the Socrates and Plato-promoted doctrine of the *"divine Logos."* His blindness is very evident when he says, *"Christ was known by Socrates...".* In another place he represents Christ as *"the Socrates of the barbarians."* [40]

278

There was a serious struggle among the so called "early Church fathers" for the next three centuries after the apostolic age, between those who believed and followed Greek philosophy, and those who thought it was **demonically inspired**. Compare Justin's statements with the following:

"However, not only do poets and philosophers contradict each other, nay many contradict themselves. Not a single one of the so-called philosophers is to be taken seriously; they have devised myths and follies; everything they have set forth is useless and godless. But God knew before hand the drivillings of these hollow philosophers, and made His preparations. Revelation is necessary because this wisdom of the philosophers is really **demon wisdom, for they were inspired by devils.**" (Theophilus; 2nd century Bishop of Antioch).* [41]

"We see that philosophers are neither lowly nor meek. Rather, they greatly please themselves" (Cyprian; Church father; circa 250 A.D.).* [42]

"It has been handed down to us in the sacred writings that the thoughts of the philosophers are foolish. Therefore, there is no reason why we should give so much honor to philosophers" (Lactantius; Church father; circa 304 A.D.).* [43]

"Heresies are themselves instigated by philosophy. The philosophers are the patriarchs of all heresy. **The apostle** *[Paul],* **so far back as his own time, foresaw indeed, that philosophy would do violent injury to the truth. So then, where is there any likeness between the Christian** *and* **the philosopher? Between the disciple of Greece and the disciple of heaven? Away with all attempts to produce a mottled Christianity of Stoic, Platonic,** *and dialectic composition!"* (Tertullian; 160-230 A.D.; Christian writer from Carthage, North Africa).* [44]

279

These words that Tertullian wrote some 1800 years ago express my sentiments very well! *"Away with all attempts to produce a mottled Christianity!"* The wisdom of his words will be seen more clearly as we go forward.

Please consider these facts:

• The **spirit** and **doctrine** of Jezebel was still corrupting the Church of Thyatira, 1000 years after her death *(Rev. 2:20)*.

• The **spirit** and **doctrine** of Balaam was still corrupting the Church of Pergamas, 1500 years after his death *(Rev. 2:14; II Peter 2:15; Jude v. 11)*.

• The **spirit** and **doctrine** of Socrates is still corrupting the Christian Church today, 2400 years after his death *(I Cor. 1:18-24)*.

Closing This Chapter

As difficult as this material is to wade through, and as disturbing as some of these disclosures are, this demonic Greek influence must be exposed, and I willingly accept the call to help do it. And I will not be satisfied until all God-fearing, Bible-believing, truth-loving people rise up with one voice and shout, *"Get the Hellenism out of here!"*

"Herein lies the root and stem of contemporary Christian education. It is built on the Platonic idea that knowledge is the equivalent of moral character. Therein lies the great flaw. Plato and Aristotle (both disciples of Socrates) are the fathers of contemporary Christian education. To use a biblical metaphor, present-day Christian education, whether it be seminarian or Bible college, is serving food from the wrong tree: the tree of the knowledge of good and evil rather than the tree of life."

Frank Viola and George Barna
Pagan Christianity? - Exploring The Roots of Our Church Practices; p. 215-216

Chapter Eleven

Who Was Plato?

*"We have observed that the specific metaphysical vehicle used to express **the classical doctrine of the Trinity** as originally formulated was a **Greek metaphysics** that was viable in that time but no longer makes a great deal of sense to most persons today. While it is customary to assume that the **major philosophical influence** on the Greek* [church] *fathers was **Plato** and the **Stoics**,* [Michael] *Durrant believes the influence of **Aristotle** should not be overlooked"* (Trinitarian scholar Millard J. Erickson; Southern Baptist).[1]

*"**The Bible does not teach the doctrine of the Trinity**. Neither the word 'trinity' itself nor such language as 'one-in-three,' 'one essence' (or 'substance'), and '**three persons**' is biblical language. The language of the doctrine is the language of the ancient church **taken from classical Greek philosophy**"* (Trinitarian professor Shirley C. Guthrie, Jr.; Christian Doctrine).[2]

*"**Plato** himself, the gentlest and most refined of all...in the first place declared, with truth, **a God** exalted above every **essence**, but to **him he added also a second**, distinguishing them numerically as **two**, though **both** possessing one perfection, and the being of the **second Deity** proceeding from the **first**. Thus far then **Plato's** sentiments were sound"* (The Roman Emperor Constantine; Addressing the Nicean Council; 325 A.D.).[3]

"Therefore, you [God] *procured for me certain **books** of the **Platonists** that had been translated out of **Greek** into*

*Latin. In them I read, not indeed in these words, but much the same thought...that before all times and above all times your only-begotten **Son** remains unchangeably **coeternal with you**; these truths are **found in the books**" (Trinitarian Church father Augustine; The Confessions of Augustine; circa 400 A.D.)* [4]

*"Christian men...are beginning to suspect that a vast amount of current **theology** has **human philosophy as its source**. Figures in the field of religious thought, which they used to think figures of Christ, His prophets, and His apostles, **they are beginning to suspect are figures of the evil spirit**, figures of **Plato**, and of various fathers who **derived their theology in a great measure from him**" (Trinitarian minister and author C.H. Constable; circa 1893).*

*H*ere is a challenge made in love. Pull any book from the shelf that deals with the doctrine of the Trinity, be it encyclopedia, Bible dictionary or work by a trinitarian scholar. Turn to the subject index and look up *"Logos doctrine"* or *"divine Logos doctrine,"* and it will likely refer you to Plato, Philo, and Greek philosophy. That fact does not bother most theologians, and it might not bother you, but to me it is totally unacceptable!

Someone wrote a book several years ago titled, *The Death of Outrage!* I did not read it but I do understand the concept. Most Americans, even Christians seem to have lost our ability to look at foolish and hurtful deeds and situations, and be stirred to action, or to take a stand. For example: a helpless little six-year-old girl, was mauled to death last week in Mississippi by a neighbor's pit bulldog **while playing in her own yard**. People should be outraged! (Note: the word *outrage* means; *1. An extremely vicious or violet act; 2. A deep insult or offense; 3. **Great anger; indignation, aroused by such an act or offense**. I am not using the word *enrage*, which means *"to put into a rage"*).

Please consider. Since the Supreme Court case *Roe v. Wade* in 1973, there have been over 50 million "legal" abortions in the U.S., as some people use the killing of the unborn as a lousy form of birth control. It is said that today, the most dangerous place that a baby can be in America, is in its mother's womb, and people should be outraged!

Please consider. Hollywood continues to pour out a foul stream of profanity, vulgarity, and violence to our youth in movies, video games, and on T.V., desensitizing them to human suffering, and turning some into killers without consciences. We have sown the wind and we are reaping the whirlwind, and people should be outraged!

Please consider. For past decades, even to now, the borders of this nation have been virtually unprotected, allowing over 10 million people as of today to be here illegally and undocumented. True, most of those are well intentioned people seeking a better life for themselves and their families, but what about any number who have come with evil intent? We have no idea who or what is here for our harm! Last week the top five security officials of our country told a Senate hearing, *"It is **certain** that Al-Quida will attempt a major strike in the U.S. in the next six months."* A former vice-President said on the news in the past week that this attack could be *"nuclear."* A former Speaker of the House told a gathering of Jewish leaders, a few months ago, that there is a good chance that in the next one to five years, the U.S. could lose one of our major cities and as many as one million people to a nuclear attack from within. People should be stirred and outraged!

Now to the subject of this chapter. **For some 1700 years, since the Council of Nicea,** Christianity has followed Plato in his demon-inspired beliefs that "God" exists as **three persons**, *"the Glory equal, the Majesty co-eternal,"* the Blessed Trinity. This we will prove as we go forward!

In 325 A.D. the Roman emperor Constantine, to settle a troubling dispute over the person of Jesus Christ, between the bishops of two important cities of his empire, Alexandria and Antioch, called a council at his palace in Nicea

(Turkey). He presided over the gathering of 300 bishops from an exalted place on his golden chair, and dominated the one month long meeting and its conclusions. The *Encyclopedia Americana* says of Constantine and Nicea: *"The Emperor became more than a referee in these disputes; when he took sides, as he had to, **he defined orthodoxy** [proper Christian doctrine]. **Constantine himself** proposed the formula of homoousion, the consubstantiality [equality, "of one and the same substance, essence, or nature"] of the son and the Father, which was inserted in the Nicean Creed. The union of church and state meant that **political considerations would influence definitions of orthodoxy."* They go on to say that although Constantine promoted Christianity, he was *"lacking more than one of the Christian virtues, he was on occasion **cruel, ruthless, and even inhumane"*** (end of quote). [6] Although Constantine is considered by much of Christianity as one of its heros, it is doubtful that he ever really became a Christian. He murdered his relatives to ensure that his three sons would be his successors, [7] he continued to build pagan temples after his "conversion," and it is doubtful that he ever abandoned sun-worship. He also declared himself to be the thirteenth Apostle! [8]

In essence, the conclusion of this council under pressure from Constantine, was that Jesus is God, just as the Father is God. And where did he get his information? I have a large history book in my library titled *"The Nicene and Post-Nicene Fathers"* that contains the speeches and arguments of that gathering. About twenty pages are devoted to Constantine's speech before the council. In it he makes no appeal to Holy Scripture as to the personhood of Jesus Christ, but rather appeals to human reason and Hellenistic doctrine, including the quote at the beginning of this chapter. Notice again:

> *"**Plato** himself, the gentlest and most refined of all...in the first place declared, with truth, **a God** exalted above every **essence**, but to **him** he **added also a second**, distinguishing them numerically as **two**, though **both** possessing one perfection, and the being of the **second Deity** proceeding from the **first**. Thus far then **Plato's** sentiments were sound"* [9]

Please study these words carefully, for outside of Holy Scripture itself, you will likely not read words more important to understanding how the Christian doctrine of "God" came to be corrupted! *"**Plato**...declared, with truth, **a God**...but to **him** he **added** also a **second**, distinguishing them numerically as **two**, though **both**...and the being of the **second Deity** proceeding from the **first**...**Plato's** sentiments were sound."*

So with Plato's doctrine firmly embedded in his mind, he dictated to the Council of Nicea that they adopt this statement:

> *"We believe in one God, Almighty Father, Maker of all things seen and unseen and in one Lord Jesus Christ, the Son of God, **eternally begotten** of the Father and only begotten. That is, **from the essence of the Father, God** from **God**, Light from Light, **True God** from **True God**, Begotten, **not made**, of **one substance with the Father**."*

At the end of the creed, the council attached a written condemnation and "decree of banishment" against anyone denying its conclusion, especially those who believed that Christ did not exist in all eternity. The fourth century church father, Athanasius, a moving force at Nicea, summed it up with these words, *"**God was made man that we might be made gods**."* [10] This is not biblical doctrine, but Greek and Roman thinking!

Please understand that the Council of Nicea did not declare a belief in a deity consisting of *three* persons. That did not happen until fifty-six years later when the Council of Constantinople *(381 A.D.)* expanded Nicea with these words:

> *"We believe in the Holy Spirit, the Lord, the giver of life, who proceeds from the Father and the Son. With the Father and the Son **he** is **worshiped** and **glorified**."* [11]

Thus the doctrine of the Trinity came into being, and it remains the view of "orthodox Christianity" to this day. However, for the next several hundred years after Constantinople, the place of the Holy Spirit in the Trinity was still being fought over and defined, especially by Augustine *(circa 425 A.D.)*, and John of Damascus *(circa 700 A.D.)*. Respected **trinitarian** professors Roger Olson and Christopher Hall, writing in their book, *The Trinity,* make a revealing statement regarding this fact.

> *"John of Damascus (650-749 A.D.)* **added his own trinitarian reflections** *to the church's treasury,* **especially in regard to the Spirit's role in the Trinity.** *Phillip Carey notes that John's 'Exact Exposition of the Orthodox Faith'....is the most comprehensive brief statement of* **Greek trinitarian doctrine.** *John's work demonstrates how* **the church's understanding of the Holy Spirit had matured** *since Nicea (325) and Constantinople (381). Whereas* **the Spirit had appeared almost as a footnote to the Creed of Nicea,** *John writes richly of the Spirit's* **person** *and work."*

Note their reference to *"Greek trinitarian doctrine."* Pardon me, but did they say, *"Greek trinitarian doctrine?"* Please consider again these facts concerning the true **biblical** doctrine of God.

- There are 31,000 verses in the Holy Bible and **not one of these verses** has the words "two" or "three" next to God.

- Jesus spoke 1,865 verses in the New Testament, and in **not one** of those verses did he claim (or even hint) that he is "God," a "second God," "God incarnate in flesh," or that he and God the Father are "one person."

- The New Testament says *"God"* over 1,300 times when it is clearly speaking of the Father, not Jesus. When Jesus himself says *"God,"* 184 times in the New Testament, he is **always** speaking of the Father.

- Paul said *"God"* 513 times in his thirteen epistles and **not once** can it be proven that he was speaking of Jesus Messiah; it was **always** the Father.

- Peter said *"God"* 46 times in his two epistles and **not once** was he referring to Jesus; it was **always** the Father.

- James, the half brother of Jesus, said *"God"* 17 times in his epistle and **not once** was he referring to Jesus; it was **always** the Father. (Note: The focus of this book isn't who Jesus Christ is not, but who God the Father is).

The only Bible verse that ever had the word *"three"* in reference to God was I John 5:7:

> *"For there are **three** that bear record in heaven, the **Father**, the **Word**, and the **Holy Ghost**: and these three are one."*

This verse has been proven by scholars (even trinitarians) to be a forgery, inserted sometime **after** the fifteenth century by someone determined to have at least one trinitarian Scripture. That explains why I John 5:7 **cannot be found** in the *NIV*, the *NCV*, the *NRSV*, the *NASB*, the *ESV*, the *Holman CSB*, or the *New Living Translation*.

The Most High God of the Bible is **one** entity, being, person. In spite of Plato and Constantine there is no "second God" or "second Deity," "numerically two!" Listen to Moses:

> *"Hear, O Israel: The Lord our God is **one Lord**"* (Deut. 6:4).

Notice: God is not "two Lords," or "three Lords" but *"**God is one Lord!**"* When the scribe asked Jesus in Mark chapter twelve, "What is the greatest commandment of all?" Jesus by-passed the obvious ten and went directly to Moses' statement above, and said:

> *"Hear, O Israel; The Lord our God is **one Lord**"* (v. 29).

Listen to Jesus. The greatest commandment in the world is, *"**Listen...God is one Lord!**"* With that in mind, would you please say this over several times with Moses and Jesus:

> *"The Lord our God is **one Lord**."*
> *"The Lord our God is **one Lord**."*
> *"The Lord our God is **one Lord**."*

If you will say this over until it gets deep into your spirit, then you will be a follower of Jesus, and not of Plato! Christianity has allowed Satan, through the doctrine of Plato, to put a veil over our thinking, and caused us to give God our Father's, love, worship, prayers, throne, act of creation, and glory to another. And with that realization people should be outraged!

Some thinking people down through the centuries who were Christians and who loved deeply the Lord Jesus Christ, came to this understanding and found it hard to deal with. They also found themselves hated, persecuted and attacked as heretics, atheists, deists, Anti-christs, etc.

Trinitarian Millard Erickson makes this strong admission:

> *"In fact, history suggests that the doctrine of **the Trinity has been part of a great doctrinal system that has been used to justify oppression and exploitation.** Whether this doctrine was actually correlated with oppression, **it has certainly accompanied such oppression"** [13] [emphasis mine].*

Christianity Has Wronged God

If you look closely at Jesus' words to the scribe in Mark chapter twelve, you will see that the *"greatest commandment"* has two parts, *"listen"* and *"love."* (Note: The word *"Hear"* in Deuteronomy 6:4 and Mark 12:29 is the Hebrew word *"shema,"* and it means *"listen!").* The second part as stated by Moses and Jesus is:

> *"And thou shalt love **the Lord thy God** with **all thy heart**, and with **all thy soul**, and with **all thy mind**, and with **all thy strength"** (Mark 12:30).*

Here is a good question. How in the world can people obey this greatest of all commandments, if they have no clear understanding as to who *"the Lord thy God"* is? I have met people who are fretting over the neglect of the fourth commandment, who had no idea they were breaking the one Jesus said is the **first** and **greatest!** If this seems unimportant to you, there is no need to proceed further with this book. Likewise with the Bible. If you do not believe the first verse on page one, why proceed further?

> *"In the beginning **God** created the heaven and the earth"* *(Gen. 1:1).*

And He did it with the breath of His mouth!

> *"By the **word** of the Lord were the heavens made; and all*

> the host of them **by the breath of his mouth**. *For he spoke*
> *and it was done; he commanded and it stood fast" (Psalm*
> *33:6, 9).*

Now to the last book of the Bible where *"the Lord God Almighty"* sits on **one** throne:

> **"Thou** *art worthy, O Lord, to receive* **glory** *and* **honor** *and*
> **power:** *for* **thou hast created all things,** *and for thy pleasure*
> *they are and were created" (Rev. 4:11).*

Do you believe those clear and simple statements regarding creation or do you look for other verses to try to offset them. Several months ago, one of the most famous evangelists in the world spoke the beliefs of multiplied millions of Christians when he tried to tell me that Jesus Christ is the creator of all. That is non-biblical, doctrinal nonsense! Jesus' part in creation is that he redeemed all of creation by shedding his sinless blood on Calvary's cross. But he is not the Creator! That kind of teaching dishonors God the Creator.

Have you ever been neglected, rejected, disrespected, unappreciated or dishonored by your own children whom you have given birth, raised, loved and provided for? There can be nothing more hurtful or harder to bear!

Listen to the cry of God our Father's heart:

> *"Hear, O heavens, and give ear, O earth: for the Lord hath*
> *spoken,* **I** *have nourished and* **brought up children,** *and*
> *they have rebelled against me" (Isa. 1:2).*

> *"A son honoreth his father, and a servant his master: if then*
> **I** *be a* **father, where is mine honor?.....saith the Lord of**
> **hosts"** [God the Father speaking] *(Mal. 1:6).* Please note: I
> have a ten thousand dollar reward for anyone who can show
> me one Scripture where Jesus Messiah is called "the Lord
> of hosts."

Hosea Learned Empathy For God

Why would the all-wise God of heaven give one of His beloved prophets a command such as He gave the prophet Hosea?

> *"And the Lord said to Hosea, Go take unto thee a wife of* ***whoredoms"*** *(Hosea 1:2).*

Yes, you read correctly. God told Hosea to go and marry the harlot Gomer. And the reason is found in the second half of the above verse.

> *".....for the land* [of Israel] *hath committed great whoredom."*

So God was experiencing rejection and "spiritual harlotry" from His "wife" Israel, and he needed someone to understand the pain of His heart and have empathy for Him. And Hosea was that man. But Hosea's book also teaches God's total forgiveness of *"scarlet sin,"* and His restoration of sinners.

Elijah Had Empathy For God

Elijah lived about 125 years before Hosea, but it also was a time when Israel was straying from God. And his empathy for God and indignation were stirred. Notice his prayer in I Kings 19:10:

> *"And he said,* ***I have been very jealous*** *for the* ***Lord God*** *of hosts: for the children of Israel have forsaken thy covenant, thrown down thine altars, and slain thy prophets with the sword."*

And he said again in verse fourteen:

> *"I have been* ***very jealous*** *for the* ***Lord God*** *of hosts."*

Is it not idolatry to give God our Father's love, worship and honor to another, even His awesome Son, the highly exalted *"man Christ Jesus?"* And Jesus himself must be saddened to see so many mis-guided Christians give to him, his Father's glory and honor. Much the same as Mary must be greatly grieved, if she is permitted to observe that hundreds of millions of Catholics look to her for protection, call her *"Queen of Heaven,"* and offer prayers to her!

We are told to honor Jesus, and we should, **but he sought and received only the honor that comes from God his Father**. Trust Jesus when he says in John:

> *"I receive not honor from men"* *(John 5:41)*.

> *"If I honor myself, my honor is nothing:* ***it is my Father that honoreth me"*** *(John 8:54)*.

Could Jesus have imagined while he performed his mission on earth, that his followers would some day be led astray in their understanding and worship, by a Greek philosopher named Plato who lived and died in Athens some 350 years before he was born in Bethlehem? I must say now weeping, I think not!

> *"All we like sheep have gone astray."*

Who Was Plato?

Plato *(424-347 B.C.)* was born in Athens to aristocratic parents, both of whom belonged to old and important Athenian families. His mother was the sister of Charmides and the niece of Critias, whom we met in the last chapter as students of Socrates. His father died when he was young and his mother remarried, to a man who was very active in the political and cultural life of Athens.

Originally named Aristocles (meaning *"best and renowned"*), Plato soon distinguished himself in almost every field. He excelled in the study of music, mathematics, rhetoric (speech), and poetry. He was nicknamed Plato, meaning broad, because of his robust frame, and it is said that *"he charmed the women, **and doubtless the men**, with his good looks."* [14] Very athletic, he wrestled at the Isthmian games, and in the military he fought in three battles and won a prize for bravery.

At a young age he showed a flair for literature and wrote witty poems, amorous verses and a series of dramas. He was deciding between poetry and politics as a career when, at the age of twenty, he succumbed to the fascination of Socrates. He knew him previously as an old family friend and teacher of his relatives, but somehow at this point he became charmed by the spirit of the old gadfly. As the historian Durant says:

> *"He **burned** his poems, **forgot** Euripides* [a Greek writer of tragedies], *athletics, and women, and **followed the master** as if under a **hypnotic spell**."* [15]

But three years later came the oligarch uprising and terror (led by his own relatives, Charmides and Critias), that ended with their deaths and the restoration of democracy to Athens. And then the final blow, the trial and death of his beloved teacher Socrates, in 399 B.C.

Perhaps fearing for his own safety and embittered, the world collapsing around this youth of twenty-five, he fled from Athens as if it were a haunted city. He visited the Greek city of Megara, then on to Cyrene in North Africa, and from there he went to Egypt and studied mathematics and the historical lore of the priests. About 395 B.C. he was back in Athens, and a year later fought for that city against Corinth. About 387 B.C. he set out again, visited briefly in two Greek cities and made his way to Sicily. In the Greek city-state of Syracuse he ran afoul of king Dionysius I and was imprisoned. About to be sold into slavery, his wealthy friend Anniceris supplied the 3000 drachmas to secure his freedom, and by 386 B.C. he was back safe in Athens.

By this time Plato was ready to teach. Some of his Athenian friends raised the money to reimburse his ransomer, but when Anniceris refused it, the money was used to purchase an olive grove on the suburbs of Athens, named for its local god Academus. And there Plato founded the university called the *"Academy,"* that was destined to be the intellectual center of Greece for the next nine hundred years, until it was closed by the Byzantine emperor Justinian I in 529 A.D., who saw it as a threat to Christianity. [16]

*"The Academy was technically a religious fraternity (or thiasos), dedicated to the **worship** of the Muses; the **spirits** that are thought to inspire poets or other artists"* (Durant). [17] Wow! Please look at that again. The Academy was *"dedicated to the worship of"* spirits.

Both young women and men were admitted as students and they paid no fees, but wealthy parents were expected to make substantial donations to the institution. Suidas says, rich men *"from time to time bequeathed in their wills, to the members of the school, the means of living a life of philosophic leisure,"* and king Dionysius II is reported to have given Plato eighty talents ($480,000).

Plato and his assistants taught, by lecturing and dialogue, the chief subjects: mathematics and philosophy, likely including arithmetic, geometry, music, literature, history and law. The lectures were technical and sometimes dry, but pupils like Aristotle, Demosthenes, Eudoxus, Heracleides, Lycurgus, and Xenocrates, were deeply influenced by them. Plato never wrote *technical* works, and Aristotle referred to the teaching in the Academy as Plato's *"unwritten doctrine."*

But Plato did write, and those writings are what he is most famous for. Plato wrote *dialogues*, a style of writing wherein two or more people engage in conversation regarding various subjects. Scholars still question why he chose this style over plays or dramas, but in all, he wrote thirty-six of these, all of which are still available complete, and studied today.

The Spirit Of Socrates Is Upon Plato

But there was and is a spirit (or spirits) behind all of this, and it is the famous spirit of Socrates. Please be patient and follow as I provide proof.

Consider this analogy. When the mighty prophet Elijah was about to be taken up to heaven, God instructed him to anoint Elisha to be prophet in his place. And Elisha had an awesome request, *"let a double portion of thy spirit be upon me" (II Kings 2:9).* Of course he referred to the supernatural power of God that rested upon his mentor, called in Luke 1:17, *"the spirit and power of Elijah."* Sure enough he received his request as recorded in II Kings 2:11-15:

> *"And it came to pass as they still went on and talked, that*
> *behold, there appeared a chariot of fire, and horses of fire,*

> *and parted them both asunder; and Elijah went up by a*
> *whirlwind into heaven. And he took up the mantle of Elijah*
> *that fell from him, and went back, and stood by the bank of*
> *Jordan;* **and he took the mantle of Elijah, and smote the**
> **waters** *and said,* **Where is the Lord God of Elijah?** *And*
> *when he* **also** *had smitten the waters* [as Elijah had done],
> *they parted hither and thither: and Elisha went over. And*
> *when the sons of the prophets...saw him, they said,* **The**
> **spirit of Elijah doth rest on Elisha***. And they came to meet*
> *him, and bowed themselves to the ground before him."*

And how did these young men know that the spirit of Elijah was now on Elisha? Because Elisha spoke his words and carried on his work! For instance, look at Elijah's unusual statement in I Kings 17:1 and 18:15: *"As the Lord God of Israel liveth, before whom I stand."* Following his example, Elisha is also recorded as making this statement twice *(II Kings 3:14; 5:16)*. And the Bible records that he did twice the number of major miracles as Elijah, while carrying on his work.

As we well established in the previous chapter, Socrates was guided and driven by a **demon spirit,** or spirits, that possessed him. It is my opinion that the reason the demon made no protest as Socrates made his descent toward death (a fact that had his attention and caused him to wonder) was, the demon had found a new home in his star pupil, Plato. Look at Durant's words again:

> Plato *"burned his poems, forgot athletics and women, and*
> *followed the master as if under a hypnotic spell."*

Please consider the following facts: The *World Book* encyclopedia says of Plato: *"The unjust execution of his teacher, Socrates, embittered him."* [18] Of the thirty-six literary works that Plato created over a period of about forty years, **only one**, *Laws*, does not have Socrates speaking in it. Of the thirty-six, only one, *Apology* cannot be truly called a dialogue, but purports to be the speech that Socrates gave in his defense at his trial (the Greek word *apologia* means *"defense"*). [19] In many of the thirty-five works that include the voice of Socrates, he dominates the conversation as he did in life, in the streets, markets, and gymnasiums of Athens. In fact, the spirit of Socrates is so prominent in these dialogues that Plato is half way through his long career as a philosopher before scholars who study them can begin to discern any distinction between his ideas and those of his dead teacher. (In all of his writings, **Plato never speaks** to his audience directly and **in his own voice**). [20]

And very little truth is derived. Will Durant says of the dialogues:

> *"There is no design unifying the whole, except as the continuing search of a visibly **developing mind for a truth that it never finds**. There is no system in Plato. Because he is a poet he has most difficulty with logic; **he wanders about** seeking definitions, and **loses his way** in perilous analogies; 'then we got into a labyrinth* ["confusing paths"]*, and when we thought we were at the end, came out again at the **beginning**, having still to see as much as ever' ."* Durant says Plato [or Socrates] concludes: " *'I am not certain whether there is such a science as logic at all' ."*

So the spirit behind these dialogues intends to bring darkness rather than light, and confusion rather than clarity. The *Encyclopedia Americana* says regarding this fact: *"In Lysis a discussion of friendship...ends **inconclusively**. In Charmides an inquiry into temperance...ends **inconclusively**. In Laches a discussion of education...ends **inconclusively**."* [21]

And there is more. The *Stanford Encyclopedia of Philosophy* says that some of the dialogues *"contain little or nothing in the way of positive philosophical doctrine, but are mainly devoted to portraying the way in which Socrates **punctured**"* the ideas of the other speakers, *"and forced them to realize that they are unable to offer satisfactory definitions of the **ethical terms they used**, or satisfactory arguments for their **moral beliefs**. In some of his works, it is evident that one of Plato's goals is to create a sense of **puzzlement** among* *his readers, and the dialogue form is being used **for this purpose**."* They say that especially in *Parmenides,* Plato *"rubs his reader's faces in a baffling series of **unresolved puzzles** and **apparent contradictions**."*

The foregoing quotes are definite proof that these dialogues were inspired and promoted by the **evil one**. Compare them with the Holy Bible, a book of light, truth, answers, and revelation, and you will see that they were designed by opposing powers. Please look with me at two Scriptures.

> *"For God is not the author of **confusion** but of peace, as in all churches of the saints" (I Cor. 14:33).*

> *"For where envying and strife is, there is **confusion and every evil work**" (James 3:16).*

Early Church Fathers

Some of the *"early church fathers,"* church leaders after the death of the Apostles, discerned that the teachings of philosophers, including Plato, were the work of demon spirits to bring confusion. Consider:

> *"Great is the **error** that the philosophers among them have brought upon their followers" (Aristides; circa 125 A.D.).*

> *"**Heresies** are themselves instigated by philosophy. What indeed has **Athens** to do with Jerusalem? What agreement is there between the **Academy** and the church? Away with all attempts to produce a mottled Christianity of Stoic, **Platonic**, and dialectic composition!" (Tertullian; circa 197 A.D.).*

> *"The philosophers are the patriarchs of **all heresy**" (Tertullian; circa 200 A.D.).* [22]

> *"Not a single one of the so-called philosophers, **including Plato**, is to be taken seriously......this wisdom of the philosophers and poets is really **demon wisdom**, for they were **inspired by devils**" (Theophilus; circa 180).* [23]

296

The Morals Of Plato

The measure of the character of an individual or a society is their treatment of the young, the weak, and those less fortunate. Athens and Plato fail this test. Please consider. In Athens every citizen was expected to have children, but at the same time law and public opinion accepted the killing of infants, to guard against over population and the dividing up of the land by the poor. The killing of the newborn was done by "exposing," leaving the infant in a large earthen vessel in the area of a temple, or in some other public place where it could soon be rescued if someone wished to adopt it. Any father may "expose" a newborn to death if he doubted it was his, or saw it as weak or deformed. The children of slaves were seldom allowed to live, and girls were more often subjected to "exposure" than boys, because at marriage she would need a dowry and would be leaving the family that raised her. The parental right to "expose" reflects the vigorous competition to make the Greeks a strong and healthy people. [24]

But what about Plato? Regarding him Durant says:

> *"The philosophers almost unanimously approve of family limitation:* **Plato will call for the exposure of all feeble children, and of those born of base or elderly parents.** *On or before the tenth day after birth the child is formally* **accepted** *into the family with a religious ritual around the hearth, and receives presents and a name. Once the child is accepted into the family it cannot be lawfully exposed."*

Compare this with the story of David fasting and weeping over the sickness of his newborn child *(II Sam. 12:15-23)*, and you will see how perverted the thinking of Plato and his fellow heathens really was. To me this sounds scarily like Hitler and Nazi Germany. Also like the rabid promoters of abortion in our day. A hen will flog you for her chicks and a dog will bite you over her pups, but these followers of demons have no such instincts.

Plato Regarding Love

It is remarkable that in all of Plato's writings that deal with "**love**", he puts in the mouths of the speakers, words that strongly suggest that *love* itself is homosexual. Of course this reflects his own feelings, since he himself was a homosexual. His writings leave the strong impression that most heterosexual people are unfaithful, and even sinful. He did not believe that women were capable of the deepest kind of love ("Celestial Love"), therefore the dialogues very rarely mention women in love with men or men in love with women, nor women loving or being loved at all. This is obviously no accident.

It is known that Plato never married, and some of his writings celebrate the relationships between older men and pubescent boys as young as eleven or twelve. The *Symposium* especially is a glorification of male homoeroticism and pederasty, and Plato himself is said to have loved boys, including Agathon, Dion, Alexis and Aster. He learned this sick and sickening behavior from his old teacher Socrates.

Kwasi Kwarteng, a researcher in history at Cambridge University, has written a work titled, *Was Plato The Only Greek Gay?,* and in it he makes these statements:

> *"In Plato's Symposium, homosexual love is discussed as a more ideal; more perfect kind of relationship than the heterosexual variety. This is a highly biased account because Plato himself was homosexual and wrote very beautiful epigrams to boys expressing his devotion. Behind Plato's contempt for heterosexual desire lay an aesthetic, highly intellectual aversion to the female body."*

Plato writes in *Symposium*:

> *"For I know not any greater blessing to a young man who is beginning in life than a virtuous lover, or to a lover than a beloved youth. For the principle, I say, neither kindred, nor honor, nor wealth, not any motive is able to implant so well as love."*

There are those of our day, even Christians, who believe that these philosophers are some of the greatest thinkers of all time. But take it from me, this is *stinking thinking*. King David expressed my sentiments well in the Psalm:

> *"Therefore I esteem all thy precepts concerning all things to be right; **and I hate every false way**" (Ps. 119:128).*

Listen to the early church father Theophilus *(circa 180 A.D.)*.

> *"And regarding **lawless conduct**, those who have blindly wandered into the choir of philosophy have, almost to a man, spoken with **one voice**. Certainly Plato did. He seems to have been the most respectable philosopher among them. Yet, he expressly legislates in his first book, entitled 'The Republic,' that the wives of all should be held in common"* [shared]. [25]

With the foregoing in mind, it is easy to see why massage parlors and places of immoral behavior are often given such names as *"Plato's Palace,"* *"Plato's Retreat,"* or *"Plato's Hideaway."* Such is the moral legacy of the philosophic hero!

The Impact of Plato

Here is an example of the influence of Plato on our world. Plato's university was named *"Academy"* because it was established in an olive grove on the hill of Academus, named for its local god. [26] Therefore every military academy, Christian academy, or school of higher learning in the world that uses *"Academy"* in its name, has borrowed it from the name of Plato's university, and the god Academus. However innocent this might be, it shows clearly his influence on our everyday lives.

Several years ago *Atlantic Monthly Press*, a secular book publisher from New York decided to publish a series of ten *Books That Changed The World*. It is interesting to note that this publisher considered the *Bible* to be **number two**, Darwin's, *Origin of Species,* to be number four, and *The Qur'an* to

299

be number six. In 2005, they persuaded Simon Blackburn, a professor of philosophy at the University of Cambridge, to write a biography of the book they consider to be the **number one** book *"that changed the world,"* Plato's *Republic*. Blackburn is the author of ten books on philosophy and is an eminent scholar in that field.

The book was published in 2006, and I became aware of it in 2007 through a review in our Nashville *Tennessean* newspaper. The review included some strong statements. Consider:

> *"Simon Blackburn, a professor of philosophy at the University of Cambridge, calls Plato's 'Republic' the greatest and most fertile single book of the Western philosophical cannon. It's a statement that's hard to dispute: Not only did Plato influence the direction of modern philosophical discourse, he also played an **immeasurable role in the development of Christianity**."* The review continues: *"...in his new book, 'Plato's Republic: a Biography,' the author offers a searing critique of the philosopher, arguing that Plato's writings marked a **fatal turn** that has corrupted clear thinking for millennia. A secular humanist, Blackburn has no great love for Christianity. He says, '**this faith owes more to Plato than it does to the Judaic Old Testament**, with its passion for social justice.'"* [27]

While reading the book I found many more informative and shocking statements from this authority on philosophy. He begins by questioning whether any book *"shakes the world,"* then says, *"Religions shake the world, and in practice a religion is just a fossilized philosophy."* He sees in Christianity many of Plato's ideas, and *"**Ideas work on minds**. That, after all, is what they are for: We could not be adapted for **thought** if it was useless. An idea is just a staging post to action."* He quotes Ralph Waldo Emerson regarding Plato's influence:

> *"**Plato is philosophy, and philosophy, Plato**, - at once the glory and the **shame** of mankind, since neither Saxon nor*

*Roman have added any idea to his categories. No **wife**, no **children had he**, but the thinkers of all civilized nations are his **posterity**, and are **tinged with his mind**. How many great men nature is sending up **out of night, to be his men**, - Platonist! The Alexandrians...Calvinism is in his Phaedo: Christianity is in it. Mahometanism draws all its philosophy...from him."*

He quotes St. Augustine as saying:

*"'It is well known that Socrates was in the habit of concealing his knowledge, or his beliefs; and Plato approved of the habit'." "One way of taking this is that Plato, and presumably Socrates, **really did have doctrines to teach**, but that for some irritating reason they preferred to unveil them only partially, one bit at a time, in a kind of intellectual striptease. **Socrates remains the great educator**..."* [28]

Blackburn says reading Plato *"is far from a light game of tennis with **ideas**. It is impossible to read it without again and again feeling that we are confronting **deep and serious doctrines**."* Doctrines that affected *"religion and literature for the last two thousand years or more,"* inspiring books on *"Plato and Christianity, Plato and the Renaissance, Plato and the Victorians, Plato and the Nazis, Plato and us."* He says, *"Anyone writing on this topic must be conscious of an enormous and **disapproving audience**, dizzying ranks of **ghosts overseeing** and **criticizing** omissions and simplifications."* [29]

Blackburn gives us an enlightening quote from Lord Macaulay *(circa 1837)*:

*"Assuredly if the tree which Socrates planted and Plato watered is to be judged by its flowers and leaves, it is the noblest of trees. But if we take the homely test of (Sir Frances) Bacon, if we judge the tree by its **fruits**, our opinion of it may perhaps be **less favorable**. We are forced to say with Bacon that this celebrated philosophy ended in **nothing but disputation**, that it was neither a vineyard nor*

*an olive ground, but an intricate wood of **briars** and **thistles,*** *from which those who lost themselves in it brought back many scratches and no food."* [30]

Blackburn delivers some of his harshest criticisms of Plato regarding the part his writings might have played in bringing about the horrible totalitarian regimes of the past century. In *Republic*, Plato, a known hater of democracy (following his teacher Socrates), puts forth the **idea** of a *utopian society,* ruled over by a wise philosopher-king, a person such as himself. And yes, it included the killing of deficient and unwanted babies to produce a strong master race. Blackburn says, *"In Republic the liberal Socrates has become the spokesman for a **dictatorship."*** [31]

Ideas carry weight! Especially the demon-inspired ideas of Plato. Blackburn writes: *"The view that 'Republic' is little more than an apology for a totalitarian state was voiced in Britain in the 1930's and 1940's when the rise of Hitler's Germany and Stalin's Soviet Union made totalitarianism a matter of some anxiety."* This charge was made mainly by two British statesmen in books, one in 1937 and another in 1945. In these books Blackburn says, ***"Plato is seen as the direct ancestor of Nazism, Stalinism**, and any other system that subordinates the individual to the collective. He is also seen as the **dangerous, utopian social engineer, providing blueprints... ."***

Of course the modern Platonists rose up to defend their beloved hero, but to them Blackburn replies *"**Ideals can motivate us."*** Therefore he says:

> *"Look what happens when you are inspired by the totalitarian, authoritarian, collectivist ideal. **You get Hitler and Stalin, either of whom might themselves have invoked Republic as their blueprint. Even movement toward Plato's ideal state tramples on values of democracy, egalitarianism and freedom.** Far from providing an ideal, **Plato has provided the road to a nightmare."*** [32]

302

The Immediate Future

What is even more disturbing than the memory of Hitler and Stalin is that the final chapter regarding Plato's vision of a utopian dictatorship has not been written. Very soon, a demon-empowered man will appear on the world's stage, and using Plato's demon-inspired "blueprint" will set up his Antichrist kingdom on planet earth. Seen in Daniel's vision, he is called *"the prince that shall come:"*

> *"And he shall magnify himself in his heart, and **by peace shall destroy many:** he shall also stand up against the **Prince of princes**; but **he shall be broken** without hand. **And I Daniel fainted, and was sick certain days...**" (Daniel 8:25, 27).*

Plato and Christianity According To Blackburn

Blackburn makes some strong statements regarding how much of Plato he sees in Christianity, but since we were told in the *Tennessean* review that he is *"no great lover of Christianity,"* his comments will be considered in that light. However, we are mistaken if we totally ignore the opinions of our critics; we need them for balance. Sometimes your critics will speak truth to you that your admirers will not. I make it a point not to allow my detractors to define who I am in God, or what I am called to do, but I weigh it out on my knees before Him, and receive His direction, correction, instruction and assurance.

Since Simon Blackburn is an authority on philosophy and philosophic ideas, his opinions on Plato in Christianity should be considered. He writes:

> *"In Raphael's famous painting in the **Vatican**, known as The School of Athens, **Plato** and **Aristotle** together hold center-stage, but while Aristotle points to the earth, Plato points upwards to the Heavens" (p. 9).*

> *"It was (the dialogue Timaeus) especially that came down through antiquity to influence **Christian thought**, the*

Neoplatonist (church fathers) *of the third century A.D.,* **St. Augustine, Boethius, the Renaissance Platonist...**" *(p. 14).*

"**Plato**, *together with* **his vulgarization in Christianity**, *was something that had to be overcome in order for the Enlightenment to win" (p. 19).*

Calling *Republic* "*the first book to shake the world*" Blackburn says: "*So* **Plato himself, Christianity**,...*and* **many others** *can find themselves* **cheek by jowl** *in any section" (p. 21).*

Plato and The Doctrine Of The Trinity

We should understand that Blackburn is only one of many secular scholars to see Plato strongly embedded in the doctrines of Christianity, and be turned off by that fact. In reality, anyone with a passable knowledge of history, who is not first grounded heart and mind in Holy Scripture, is subject to fall into that trap.

For example, Edward Gibbon *(1737-1794 A.D.),* the English historian who wrote the awesome work, *The Decline and Fall of the Roman Empire,* dealt much with the way in which Christianity, and its development, affected Rome and the later "Holy Roman Empire." He especially saw the influence of Plato in the early fourth-century fight over the doctrine of "God,"and the Doctrine of the Trinity at which they arrived. He writes regarding this:

> "*The more diffusive mischief of the* **Trinitarian controversy** *successively penetrated into every part of the Christian world...and was a high and mysterious argument, derived from* **the abuse of philosophy***. From the age of Constantine... the* **temporal interests** *of the Romans and barbarians were deeply involved in the* **theological dispute** *of Arianism. The* **historian** *may therefore be permitted respectfully to withdraw* **the veil of the sanctuary***, and to deduce* [see] *the progress of reason and faith, of error and passion,* **from the school of Plato** *to the decline and fall of the empire.*"

304

*"**The genius of Plato**, informed by his own meditation **or by the traditional knowledge of the priests of Egypt, had ventured to explore the mysterious nature of the Deity.**"* **His difficulties with these thoughts** *"might induce **Plato to consider this divine nature under the threefold modification**-of the first cause, the reason or **Logos**-and the soul or **spirit of the universe.**"* **In his *"poetical imagination, the three archical or original principles were presented in the Platonic system** as **three God's**, united* with each other by a mysterious and ineffable **generation, and the Logos was particularly considered under the more accessible character of the Son** of the **Eternal Father,** and the **Creator and Governor of the world. Such appear to have been the secret doctrines which were cautiously whispered in the gardens of the Academy."* [33] [Remember, this was over 350 years before Jesus].

Gibbon is right to this point. The doctrine of the Trinity originated with Plato and made its way into Christianity **after** the death of the **last Apostle**. This agrees with statements by some evangelical Christian scholars which we have already quoted, but that bear repeating.

Adolph Harnack *"finds the Christian community **borrowing heavily from Greek philosophy. It was from these foreign sources, not from Jesus himself, that the doctrine of the Trinity, the incarnation, and related conceptions grew.** While it is customary to assume that the major philosophical influence on the Greek fathers was **Plato**, and the **Stoics**,* [Michael] *Durrant believes the influence of **Aristotle** should not be overlooked"* (Trinitarian Millard J. Erickson; Southern Baptist theologian). [34]

*"**The Bible does not teach the doctrine of the Trinity.** Neither the word 'trinity' itself nor such language as 'one-in-three,' 'one essence' (or substance), and three 'persons'*

*is biblical language. The language of the doctrine is the language of the ancient church, **taken from classical Greek philosophy**" (Trinitarian Prof. Shirley C. Guthrie Jr.).* [35]

And this from trinitarians Frank Viola and George Barna, writing in their book, *Pagan Christianity?:*

> *"Exposing the heart of the problem: The Greek philosophers **Plato** and **Socrates** taught that knowledge is virtue. Good depends on the extent of one's knowledge. Hence, the teaching of knowledge is the teaching of virtue. **Herein lies the root and stem of contemporary Christian education.** It is built on the **Platonic idea** that knowledge is the equivalent of moral character. Therein lies the great flaw. **Plato** and **Aristotle** (both disciples of Socrates) **are the fathers of contemporary Christian education.** ...present day Christian education, whether it be seminary or Bible college, is serving food from the wrong tree: **the tree of the knowledge of good and evil rather than the tree of life.**"* They say of current *"Christian theological education," "**Athens is still in its bloodstream.**"* [36]

Back To Gibbon

With this understanding from his knowledge of history, that the doctrine of the Trinity originated with Plato, Gibbon made a serious mistake! A mistake for which we might forgive him, since it is one that has been made by far more biblically learned men than he. He misunderstood John chapter one, and believed that John the Evangelist had endorsed Plato's doctrine of the **divine Logos** in verse one, *"In the beginning was the word* (Greek - "logos"). As we have seen from Scripture, John's use of *"logos"* was *"speech, God's utterance, something said,"* which produced a virgin-born child in the womb of Mary, not an incarnation but **a creative act of the Holy Spirit**. Look at the following mistaken but enlightening statement from Gibbon.

> *"The theology **of Plato might have been for ever confounded** with the philosophical visions of the Academy...*

*if the name and divine attributes of the Logos **had not been
confirmed** by the celestial pen of the last and most sublime
of the Evangelists* [John]. *The Christian Revelation...
disclosed to the world the amazing secret, that the LOGOS,
who was with God from the beginning, and was God ...**was
incarnate in the person of Jesus of Nazareth**. Educated in
the school of **Plato**, accustomed to the **sublime idea of the
Logos**, they readily conceived that **the brightest Emanation
of the Deity, might assume the outward shape and visible
appearances of a mortal.*** 37

Plato died some 350 years **before** the birth of Jesus, and the *"divine Logos
doctrine"* was not officially adopted as a part of Christianity until 325 A.D.
(Nicea), so we will deal with some of the steps to that adoption in the next
chapter. But we should note at this point that one of those steps was a school
at Alexandria, Egypt, established by the Hellenistic Jew, Philo, **before** Jesus
began his ministry.

Gibbon says of that school, *"**the theological system of Plato was taught**,
with **less reserve**, and perhaps with some improvements, **in the celebrated
school of Alexandria"** (p. 302). "The same subtle and profound questions
concerning the **nature**, the **generation**, the **distinction**, and the **equality** of
the **three divine persons of the mysterious Triad**, or **Trinity, were agitated
in the philosophical and** [later] **in the Christian schools of Alexandria"** (p.
306).

Gibbon continues:

*"The **divine sanction** which the Apostle had **bestowed
on the fundamental principles of the theology of Plato**
encouraged the learned proselytes* [Christian Platonists]
*of the second and third centuries to admire and study the
writings of the **Athenian sage**, who had thus **marvelously
anticipated** one of the most surprising discoveries of the
Christian revelation. The respectable name of **Plato** was*

*used by the **Orthodox**, and abused by the heretics, **as the common support** of truth and error."* [38]

One important question: Was it the *"Athenian sage,"* Plato himself, that *"marvelously anticipated"* the acceptance of his *"Logos"* and *"Triad"* doctrines, **by the Christians** of the second, third, fourth (and yes twenty-first) centuries, **or was it the demon spirit that possessed Socrates, Plato and Philo** (next chapter) that anticipated and conceived a way to delude Christians, and rob God the Father of His glory? And rob Edward Gibbon of his only hope of eternal salvation! Turned off by what he saw of Plato in Christian doctrine, and some "Christians'" determination to make *"the man Christ Jesus"* **divine**; something Gibbon referred to as *"**violating the unity and sole supremacy** of the great Father of Jesus Christ, and of the Universe,"* **he rejected Jesus totally,** and as far as is known, **died unsaved!**

Thomas Jefferson

One person who saw and understood this mistake by Gibbon, and was deeply saddened by it, was his famous contemporary, Thomas Jefferson *(1743-1826)*. He believed that a man as intelligent as Gibbon should have distinguished better than he did between Christianity itself, **and the corruptions of it.** Gibbon knew enough history to **see** these corruptions, but not enough of Scripture to **see though them.** Jefferson wrote:

> *"They* [the Christian followers of Plato] *are mere usurpers of the Christian name, teaching a counter-religion made up of the 'deliria' of crazy imaginations, as foreign from Christianity as that of Mahomet. **Their blasphemies have driven thinking men to infidelity** [unbelief], with the horrors so falsely imputed to him [Jesus]. **Had the doctrines of Jesus been preached always as pure as they came from his lips, the whole civilized world would now have been Christian.** But much I fear, that* [believers] *will fall into the fatal error of **fabricating formulas of Creed and confessions of faith**...which destroyed the religion of Jesus, and made of Christendom a mere Aceldama* [field

of blood]; *that they will give up morals for mysteries, and Jesus for Plato."* [39]

I would not attempt to defend all of the religious beliefs of Jefferson, but he certainly was no atheist, or worse, as has been claimed by some of his enemies. Because he was strongly anti-trinitarian, these enemies, while honoring him as the author of the *"Declaration of Independence,"* and as the third President of the United States, set out to assassinate his religious character. But the twentieth century scholar Henry Wilder Foote, believed that Jefferson's *"knowledge of and admiration for the teachings of Jesus have never been equaled by any other president."*

Please consider the following statements by one of his biographers, Charles B. Sanford.

> *"He and his family were baptized, married and buried by the Anglican church. He attended church services regularly, using his own well-worn prayer book...Jefferson believed that **the symbol of the country's seal should contain a public profession of Christianity by the nation.** Both Jefferson and his father were elected vestrymen* [elders] *of their local Episcopal church. He was always generous in contributing to churches* [Episcopal, Presbyterian, Baptist]. *Jefferson not only referred to God frequently in his public addresses and studied the Bible in private but took pains to attend services in the House of Representatives. After his retirement to Monticello, Jefferson continued to attend church services, riding into town on horseback... . He described these services in a letter to Thomas Cooper: here Episcopalian and Presbyterian, Methodist and Baptist, meet together, join in hymning their Maker, listen with attention and devotion to each other's preachers and all mix in society in perfect harmony."* [40]

Cooper concludes:

> *"From the evidence of his life, we may safely conclude that Jefferson remained a member in good standing of his local Episcopal church all his life."* And he says, *"When he was dying, Jefferson was heard by his family to pray from the Bible, 'Lord, now lettest thou thy servant depart in peace.' He was buried with the Episcopal service by his own parish minister."*

So what made Jefferson so hated and reviled by some of his "Christian" enemies? He saw through their pagan doctrine of the Trinity and understood that Plato was its source. He referred to the Trinity as *"an unintelligible proposition of **Platonic** mysticisms that **three are one**, and **one is three**; and **yet one is not three**, and **the three are not one**."* He wrote, *"**I had never sense enough to comprehend the Trinity,** and it has always appeared to me that comprehension must precede assent* [agreement].*"* He saw Trinitarian Christianity as a relapse from the true *"religion of Jesus founded in the Unity of God* [one God] *into unintelligible polytheism."* Jefferson argued that Jesus taught *"that the world was created by the **supreme, intelligent being.**"* But later Christians, in order to make sense out of their "mistranslation" of Logos, *"undertook to make of this articulation **a second pre-existing being, and ascribe to him,** and **not to God, the creation of the universe.**"* [41]

Biographer Cooper says Jefferson was *"heated"* in condemning *"**Platonic Christianity.**"*

> *"**Plato, he declared sarcastically, was the 'saint' of such Christians** 'because in his foggy conceptions, they found a basis of impenetrable darkness whereon to rear delirious fabrications of **their invention** fathered blasphemously on Him* [Jesus] *whom they claimed as their Founder'."* [42]

Cooper says the difference between Jefferson's beliefs and *"traditional Christian theology is the use made of the concept of God's 'Word,' the Logos, to explain the creation of the universe. The early philosopher **Philo of***

*Alexandria, using the theories of **Plato**, had developed the idea of the **Logos** as an intermediate reality by means of which the immaterial, immortal, perfect God could have contact with the material, mortal, crass universe. The author of the Gospel of John personified this concept of the 'Word' of God and **applied it to the divine Christ**. Such a deification of the 'Word' of God, Jefferson maintained, **was based on a 'mistranslation of the word logos and a perversion of the doctrine of Jesus'**.*" [43]

Whether or not Thomas Jefferson was or is saved eternally is not for me to say. I can say this: I hope so. But if not, it certainly will not be for failure to believe in the doctrine of the Trinity, since Jesus our Savior himself was not a trinitarian! Jefferson (and Jesus) were thinking men, and the Trinity is not a "thinking man's" doctrine. This is illustrated well by the statement made often by one of my "preacher heros," the late Adrian Rogers, who was only partly correct when he said often:

> **"Define the Trinity and lose your mind**, *deny the Trinity and lose your soul."* [44]

Plato's Concept Of God

We saw in a previous chapter that the Greeks of the fifth and fourth centuries B.C. worshiped **three** main gods: **Zeus** (the sky), **Poseidon** (the sea) and **Hades** (the bowels of the earth). However, they believed in a hierarchy among the three, with Zeus *"enthroned as Father God over all gods."* Under these three they worshiped a "swarm" of lesser gods that may be divided into seven groups: sky-gods, earth-gods, fertility-gods, animal-gods, subterranean-gods, ancestor or hero-gods, and Olympians. [45]

So Socrates seemed even more strange to his fellow Athenians when he often referred to God, singular. We saw that the belief that God is one being, entity, person is not that unusual, even in primitive cultures, and Paul attributed it to the "conscience" that God has placed within all men *(Romans 1:19-20; 2:14-15).*

But somehow Plato came to a deeper than *primitive*, but still very *deficient*, understanding of who God is. He came to the belief in one Creator God, which he called the *"first cause"* or the ultimate *"Good."* This of course is truth, so the next question is, given the culture in which he lived, how did he arrive at this conclusion? Let us explore two possibilities: **Number one**. I believe that he, like his teacher Socrates, was demon-possessed, therefore he could have learned it from the demon, or demons. Demons surely know the truth that **God is one**.

> *"Thou believest that there is **one God**; thou doest well: **the devils also believe, and tremble**" (James 2:19).*

Number two: Plato traveled to various countries (including Egypt) from the time of Socrates' death in 399 B.C., until he founded his Academy in Athens in 386 B.C., so it is very possible that he encountered the Hebrew Torah and the teachings of Moses somewhere on his journeys. If he did, our question is answered, since Moses' writings are filled with the doctrine of "One God." Moses' foundational creed is:

> *"**Hear O Israel: The Lord our God is one Lord**" (Deut. 6:4).*

Did Plato encounter the teachings of Moses? There is strong evidence that he did. Consider. Moses wrote Deuteronomy 6:4 around 1450 B.C., about 1000 years **before** Plato, so there is no problem with the time factor. In 586 B.C., some 160 years before Plato was born, God allowed king Nebuchadnezzar of Babylon to destroy Jerusalem, and He began to scatter the Jews, along with their Torah, to *"every nation under heaven"* (Acts 2:5). By the year 20 B.C. there were some 250,000 Jews living in the city of Alexandria, Egypt alone! (Didn't Plato travel to Egypt?). The great Jewish historian Josephus *(37-95 A.D.)* taught that Plato studied the teachings of Moses while in Egypt. [46] According to a recent *History Channel* special, *"Decoding The Exodus,"* followers of Moses sailed to a port near Athens, within 100 years after the Exodus, which happened about 1490 B.C..

The *"early Church Fathers"* (after the deaths of the Apostles) believed that Plato derived some of his teachings from Moses. Consider the following quotes from them:

*"**Plato** says, 'The blame is on the one who chooses, and God is blameless.' However, he took this from the prophet **Moses** and uttered it"* (Justin Martyr; circa 160 A.D.).

*"Moses was older than the ancient heroes wars, and demons. And we should believe him...rather than the Greeks, who without being aware of it, **drew his doctrines as from a fountain**"* (Tatian; circa 160 A.D.).

*"**Plato** the philosopher was aided in his legislation by the books of **Moses**. On the plagiarizing of the philosophers from the Hebrews, we will address a little afterwards. **The philosophers of the Greeks are called thieves**, inasmuch as they have taken their principal dogmas from **Moses** and the Prophets, without acknowledgment. The Philosophers, having heard it from **Moses**, taught that the world was created"* (Clement of Alexandria; circa 195 A.D.).

*"Nor do we need to wonder if the speculations of philosophers have **perverted the older Scriptures**. Some of their brood, with their opinions, have even adulterated our new-given Christian revelation, and **corrupted it** into a system of philosophic doctrines...**the philosophers seem to have investigated the sacred Scriptures**...yet, because they have interpolated these deductions, they prove that **they have either despised them wholly or have not fully believed them**"* (Tertullian; circa 195-197 A.D.).

*"It is not very clear if **Plato** fell in with these stories by chance, or if...he met during his visit to **Egypt** with certain individuals who philosophized on the Jewish mysteries. Learning some things from them, he may have **preserved a few of their ideas and thrown others aside**"* (Origen; circa 248 A.D.).* [47]

So with the foregoing in mind, we should probably agree that Plato received his understanding that there is one Creator God from reading the Holy Scriptures written by Moses. But as Tertullian said, he *"perverted,"* *"adulterated,"* and *"corrupted it into a system of philosophic doctrines,"* an act that would be devastating to hundreds of millions (perhaps billions) of Christians' understanding, who would inadvertently follow him in an erroneous view of God. And how did he (and the demon that possessed him) accomplish this? Listen to **Emperor Constantine** who at Nicea helped to set Plato's mistaken doctrine in concrete for future generations of misguided Christians:

> *"Lastly, **Plato** himself....in the first place declared, with truth, **a God exalted above every essence**, but **to him he added also a second**, distinguishing them numerically as **two**, though **both** possessing one perfection, and the being of the **second Deity** proceeding from the **first**. For he* [the first] *is the creator and controller of the universe, and evidently* **supreme**: *while the **second**...refers the origin of all creation to him as the **cause*** [Remember that word, Plato's *"first cause?"*]*...but the **Word** being God himself is **also** the Son of God. For what name can we designate him except by this title of the Son, without falling into the most grievous error? For the Father of all things is properly considered the Father of his own Word* [Himself?]. *Thus far, then, **Plato's** sentiments were sound"* (Emperor Constantine; Addressing the Nicean Council; 325 A.D.). [48]

Plato's sentiments were sound? No! No! No! Ten thousand times "no," Emperor Constantine. You have followed Plato into a doctrinal jungle, and are as confused as a termite in a yo-yo! (Remember, he is quoting Plato, a known homosexual, and a demon inspired man). The following statements by Jesus himself and Paul are "sound" doctrine.

> *"**The one and only God**...the **Father*** [Jesus speaking] *(John 5:44-45 NASB).*

*"Father...this is life eternal, that they might know **thee the only true God**, and Jesus Messiah, whom thou hast sent"* [Jesus] *(John 17:1, 3).*

*"Why callest thou me good? There is none good but **one**, that is **God**"* [Jesus] *(Matt. 19:17).*

*"Hear, O Israel; The Lord our **God is one Lord**"* [Jesus] *(Mark 12:29).*

*"For there is **one God**; and **there is none other** but he"* [the scribe speaking]. *"And when Jesus saw that he **answered discreetly**, he said unto him, Thou art not far from the kingdom of God"* *(Mark 12:32, 34).*

*"To us there is but **one God**, the **Father**..."* [Paul speaking] *(I Cor. 8:6).*

*"**One God** and **Father** of all, who is above all..."* [Paul] *(Eph. 4:6).*

*"For there is **one God**, and **one mediator** between God and men, the **man** Messiah Jesus"* [Paul] *(I Tim. 2:5).* Note: If you do not say a hearty "Amen!" in agreement with the above Scriptures, you are likely a follower of Plato.

The Doctrinal Confusion Of Constantine

It is remarkable that in a speech that takes up twenty pages in a large history book, made before a council of 300 bishops who would decide for Christianity for the next 1700 years, the question of who Jesus is, the man who dominated that council and determined its conclusion, Emperor Constantine, **did not reference one Scripture** as to the answer to that awesome question! Not one quote from Moses, Peter, Paul or Jesus himself. He perhaps thought he was quoting John with one statement, *"even God the Word, who has ordered all things; but the Word being God himself is also the Son of God."*

But he loves Plato! He refers to Plato's doctrine as *"the admirable doctrine,"* and again as, *"a doctrine not merely to be admired, but profitable too"* (p. 567). So, thoroughly grounded in his pagan hero, he presses on to speak of *"**Christ**, the author of every blessing, **who is God, and the Son of God.** Is not the worship of the best and the wisest of the nations of this world **directed to that God?"** (p. 568).*

Thank God Christianity itself is based on solid Scripture from His Holy Bible, however the doctrine of the Trinity and the Incarnation are based on such fraudulent nonsense as we have just chronicled. After this speech and in this atmosphere, the delegates decided that Jesus is coequal, coeternal with the Father *"very God of very God,"* *"of one essence with the Father,"* and made the Nicean Creed, by their votes, **official church doctrine.** The *Encyclopedia Americana* says of Constantine's influence on Nicea:

> *"**Although Constantine was not baptized a Christian until he lay on his deathbed,** he undoubtedly considered himself **in some manner** a member of the sect, and certainly played a major role in the affairs of the church. Inevitably, the Emperor became more than a referee in these disputes; **when he took sides,** as he had to, **he defined orthodoxy** (accepted Christian doctrine). **Constantine himself proposed the formula of homoousion, the** [equality] **of the Son and the Father, which was inserted in the Nicene Creed.** In the long run, the union of church and state meant that political considerations **would influence definitions of orthodoxy"** (Vol. 7; p. 649).*

Church historians Robert Baker and John Roberts state:

> *"Everyone knew that the decision of the Council had been arbitrary. **Constantine had determined what the Council should decide,** yet the decrees of the Council were recognized as **authoritative Christian pronouncements.**"* They say also, *"the development*

> *that began with the first world council at Nicea in 325* **led directly to the Roman Catholic Church.** *Such a development would have been impossible without the friendly attitude and* **strong arm of the secular power.**" [49]

This is the troubling legacy of Constantine, and it is past the time that it should be recognized and repudiated! Authors Viola and Barna see this influence of Constantine in modern Christianity and write: *"Constantine is still living and breathing in our minds."* [50]

The Plague Of Plato

Without taking time to elaborate, I will state a fact that is provable and beyond dispute. Not only Christianity, but also Islam and Hinduism are plagued with the concepts of Plato. I invite you to look into this for yourself. However, my focus in this book remains his impact on Christian theology. The word *"theology"* means, *"the study of God and of God's relations to the universe."* His views about God have absolutely **permeated** Christian thinking. Please look at the following statements from credible sources.

> *"It is impossible to overestimate the importance of* **Plato's continuing influence** *on Western thought. The Academy, after going through a period of skepticism, developed Neo-Platonism, a combination of philosophy and religion... . Until the 13th century* **most areas of medieval thought** *were inspired by works in the* **Platonic** *tradition:* **theology followed the Platonist St. Augustine. In the Middle East too, Plato's works, in Syriac, Arabic, and Armenian** *versions, played an important part in the history of philosophy"* (Encyclopedia Americana; Vol. 22; p. 230). Note: The young Islamic extremists that are blowing themselves up for a trip to Paradise, are reflecting the influence of Plato's teaching that the body is the vile prison of the soul from which we should seek to escape. This is not a biblical concept! According to Paul our bodies are the temple of the Holy Ghost, not to be defiled *(I Cor. 6:19)*, in which we should *"glorify God" (v. 20)*, while we

await *"the redemption of our body" (Rom. 8:23)*. Behold the plague of Plato!

*"It was only from the second half of the fourth century (A.D.) that **the West was invaded by the Platonic theology** ["study of God"] which Hippolytus, Tertullian, and Novation had cultivated...**the recognition of Christ as the** [Greek] **Logos forced upon the West the necessity of rising from faith** to a **philosophical** and a **distinctively Neoplatonic dogmatic"** (Historian Adolph Harnack; Vol. 3; p. 79).*

*"**Plato's** impact on Jewish thought is apparent in the work of the 1ˢᵗ century Alexandria philosopher **Philo** Judaeus. The Theologians **Clement of Alexandria, Origen,** and **St. Augustine** were early **Christian** exponents of a **Platonic** perspective, and **Platonic ideas have had a crucial role in the development of Christian theology.** Medieval **Islamic thought** also was strongly influenced by **Plato"** (Funk and Wagnalls New Encyclopedia; Vol. 21; p. 74).*

*"**Religious thought** in the West, **particularly Christian thought,** has swung back and forth between **Plato** and **Aristotle** even to **modern times.** Later **Platonists**...developed a synthesis of **Plato, Aristotle,** and the **Stoics,** called **Neoplatonism,** which **heavily influenced the philosophy of early Christianity,** the Middle Ages, and much of modern philosophy. **Christian leaders in the development of Neoplatonism were Augustine** (circa 400 A.D.), **Pseudo-Dionysius** (circa 500 A.D.), **Thomas Aquinas** (circa 1250 A.D.)... . **The thought of Church Fathers from the Cappadocians** and **Pseudo-Dionysius** in the East to **Augustine** and **Boethius** in the West turned **Neoplatonic themes to Christian use** and served to transmit a **Christian-Neoplatonic** synthesis to the Middle Ages"* (The Harper-Collins Encyclopedia of Catholicism; p. 911, 1007).

*"In the period of Middle Platonism (1ˢᵗ century B.C. to 2ⁿᵈ century A.D.) interest centered on **Plato's thought on God** and the supersensible world [beyond our senses]. Subsequently the philosophers of **Alexandria** creatively systematized these and other aspects of **their forerunner's work** in Neoplatonism. Works of **Platonic** character produced by such writers as St. Augustine, Boethius and Macrobius, **transmitted Platonism** to the medieval West. Despite modern science's final debunking of Platonic cosmology, elements of **Platonism still permeate western thought** in areas as diverse as realist logic and **Christian ethics"** (New Webster's Universal Encyclopedia; p. 782).*

*"The full development of **Trinitarianism** took place in the West, in the Scholasticism of the Middle Ages, when **an explanation was undertaken** in terms of **philosophy** and **psychology**, especially of the recovered **Aristotelianism** of the 13ᵗʰ century. The **Classical exposition** [of the Trinity] is found in the works of St. Thomas Aquinas (1225-1274 A.D.)* [Catholic theologian] ***whose views on this subject have dominated most of later Christian theology, both Roman Catholic and Protestant"*** *(Encyclopedia Americana; Vol. 27; p. 117).*

When I read the preceding quotes, it is troubling to see that **Christian theology**, our view of God and how He relates to the universe, *"followed Plato,"* a demon-inspired, homosexual, pagan Greek! Mentally and spiritually I find myself applying my brakes. I am reminded of a large tombstone in an old cemetery with these words carved on it:

"Friend, where you are I once was, Where I am you shall be, So prepare to follow me."

On the white marble, someone had penciled this response:

"To follow you I'm not content, Until I see which way you went."

I refuse to follow Plato! *"Be ye followers of God, as dear children" (Eph. 5:1).*

Plato and The "Threes"

Just as sure as the Holy Scriptures are God-breathed for the restoration, wisdom, correction, instruction, and salvation of mankind, **the doctrines of Plato were breathed from hell,** to bring confusion and impart demonic ideas that seek to rob God of His glory and thwart His purpose for man.

Since Christianity followed Plato's concepts of God, in the teachings of the "Christian Platonists" of the second through fifth centuries A.D., (and every century since), we should take a closer look at those concepts. Plato was a pagan, from a pagan culture, that worshipped **three main gods.** The ancient Greeks even had a city named *"Hagia Triada"* - Holy Triad (Trinity). Therefore it is no surprise that he saw God as *three* entities, and was fascinated in general with the numeral "three." He was known to have been in the habit of drawing various triangles and studying them intently for hidden meaning. The historian Durant says of his *"Idea"* of triangles: *"Every individual triangle is only imperfectly a triangle, sooner or later passes away, and therefore is relatively unreal; but triangle - the form and law of all triangles is perfect and everlasting,"* whatever that means.

Look at the "threes" that fascinated him. In the defense of Athens, he fought in **three** battles. He saw **three** elements in nature, *fire, wind and water.* He saw **three** things at work in nature, *motion, creation* and a *soul* or principle of life. The soul or principle of life has **three** parts, *desire, will* and *thought.* Each *part* has its own *virtue* **[three]**, *moderation, courage* and *wisdom. Beauty,* like virtue lies in **three,** *fitness, symmetry* and *order.* A work of art should have **three** features, *head, trunk* and *limbs.* Love is the pursuit of beauty, and has **three** stages, love of the *body,* the *soul* or of *truth.* The soul of a man has **three** parts [in *Phaidros*], *mind, aspirations* and *sensations.* An ideal society has **three** parts, *productive* [workers], *protective* [warriors], and *governing* [rulers]. [51] I'm not making this up!

But his "three" that has permeated Christian doctrine and still troubles the understanding of millions of Christians today is, his **triune** view of God! It consists of: 1. The Good, or first cause - *"God."* 2. The changeless Ideas, Reason, Wisdom or Mind of God - the *"Logos."* 3. A soul or principle - the *"Spirit"* of all things.

This Platonic concept is the tap root of the Christian doctrine of the Trinity. To express his concept of "God," Plato created and used words such as *"essence, substance, generated, hypostasis,"* etc. As historian Durant says: *"He creates, even in these popular dialogues, technical terms - essence, power, action, passion, generation - which will be useful to later philosophy."* [52] Of course, this is a problem for those who love Biblical truth. The respected Southern Baptist (trinitarian) theologian Millard Erickson writes:

> *"Another reason for the importance of this* [Trinity] *doctrine is that it poses a continuing problem. Some doctrines...are worked out and thus cease to be major problems. This state has not been attained with respect to the Trinity, however. There is still **confusion** about just what the doctrine denotes. The formula was worked out quite definitely in the **fourth century**. **God is one substance or essence**, existing in **three persons**. The difficulty is that **we do not know exactly what these terms mean.** We know that the doctrine states that God is **three** in some respect and **one** in some other respect, but we do not know precisely what those two different respects are. We may not be much closer to being able to articulate just what we mean by this doctrine than were the delegates to the Councils of Nicea and Constantinople in A.D. 325 and 381. **The doctrine of the Trinity is a perennial problem, like the problem of evil. It therefore needs our continued attention."***

Brother Erickson is correct in his assessment of this trinitarian "problem," and I honor him greatly for his courage to say it. He continues:

> *"Another difficulty stems from the categories used by those who worked out the doctrine of the Trinity **that the church adopted**. They used **Greek categories** such as **substance, essence, and person**.... Over the years, questions have been raised regarding those concepts. One contention is that the Trinity is simply a product of those **Greek categories**. **It is not present in biblical thought**, but arose when biblical thought was pressed into this **foreign mold**. Thus, the doctrine of the Trinity goes beyond and even **distorts** what the Bible says about God. **It is a Greek philosophical, not a Hebraic biblical concept**."* [53]

Of course Professor Erickson is not the first modern biblical scholar to see the connection between Greek philosophy and accepted Christian doctrine, and speak up regarding that fact. Many is the number. Consider these words by William Inge *(1860-1954)*, a trinitarian professor of divinity at Cambridge, and Dean of St. Paul's Cathedral:

> *"There are some subjects, like philosophy and **religion**, which can hardly be understood apart from their history, and their history in both cases goes back to **Greece** through **Rome**. **Plato and Aristotle are as much alive as any modern philosophers**, and it is extraordinary how **modern thinkers go back to them for inspiration and enlightenment**.... The intelligent study of Christianity is impossible without a knowledge of **Greek and Roman religion**. We generally assume that there is an unbroken line of continuity **between the religion of the Jews and our own**, and that there is none between **paganism** and **Christianity**. **But the opposite is the truth**.* [54]

The evangelical Methodist minister, Dr. Norman H. Snaith *(1898-1982)*, caused a stir in his denomination in 1944 when he wrote:

> *"Our position is that the reinterpretation of Biblical theology in terms of the **Greek philosophers** has been both*

*widespread and **everywhere destructive to the essence
of Christian faith**. If these judgements are sound, and
we believe they are sound, then **neither Catholic nor
Protestant theology is based on biblical theology**. In each
case we have a domination of Christian theology by Greek
thought. What then is to be done with the Bible? Is it to
be regarded as the **norm**, and its distinctive ideas as the
determining factors of Christian theology? Or are we to
continue to regard **Plato** and **Aristotle** with their **pagan
successors as contributing the norm**, and the main ideas of
**Greek philosophy as the determining factors of Christian
theology**? We hold that there can be no right answer to the
question, 'what is Christianity? ,' until we have come to a
clear idea of the distinctive ideas of both Old Testament and
New Testament, **and their difference from the pagan ideas
which have so largely dominated 'Christian' thought.*** [55]

The Hindu Trinity

Dr. Snaith rightly referred to *"Plato and Aristotle with their **pagan
successors**"* and their ideas as *"**pagan ideas**."* Since the idea of *"three
persons in one God"* is not a biblical idea, its source for sure is pagan doctrine.
This is proven further by the fact that in Hinduism, a pagan religion, there is
also a "trinity" of gods. In their book, *The Great Religions By Which Men
Live*, authors Floyd H. Ross and Tynette Hills write:

> *"The Hindus use 'That' to refer to the supreme One,
> Brahman. They use the neuter pronoun to avoid any idea
> of a manlike God or Creator or First Principle. They
> believe that Brahman is the ultimate, behind and beyond all
> things...the supreme unity of 'That' (or 'that one') the All...
> out of a large number of gods, **three** are worshiped most
> by present-day Hindus. **The three together form a Hindu
> trinity: Brahma**, the Creator; **Vishnu**, the savior; **Shiva**,
> the destroyer and restorer" (p. 27). "All the creatures and
> creations of the earth are the same, bound up in inclusive*

Brahman. All are the same. **All are one**, *'It is Brahman' "*
(p. 29). **"Of the Hindu trinity**, *Shiva, the destroyer-restorer*
god, and Vishnu, the **savior** *god are especially revered.*
Vishnu is most often worshiped in one of his incarnated
forms, *Rama or Krishna" (p. 41).* [56]

There you have it! The pagan "Hindu trinity," with its *"creator god*
Brahman," and the *"incarnation"* as a man, of the second person of this
"trinity," the *"savior god,"* Vishnu. Deliver us! Would you please turn in
your Bibles to Exodus 20:1-3:

> *"And* **God** *spake all these words, saying,* **I** *am the* **Lord thy**
> **God**, *which brought thee out of the land of Egypt, out of the*
> *house of bondage.* **Thou shalt have no other gods before**
> **me**" [singular].

In Conclusion

Plato's focus on the *"threes"* reminds me of some of my trinitarian brethren,
whom I love. In their desperate attempt to make the Lord God *"three,"* they
seem to see *"threes"* everywhere. In the *world* they see *three*; land, sea and
air. In *man* they see *three*; spirit, soul and body. And any *"three"* in the
Bible will do. The fact that the *"four beasts"* say, "<u>**holy, holy, holy,**</u> **Lord**
God Almighty" to the *"one"* who sits on the throne, helps to convince them
that *"one"* is really *three*. This is a serious problem! God has declared in
His word that He is incomparable, beyond compare. Look at his humbling
words in Isaiah 40:9, 12, 17-18, 25:

> **"Behold your God!** *Who hath measured the waters in*
> *the hollow of his hand, and meted out heaven with a span,*
> *and comprehended the dust of the earth in a measure,*
> *and weighed the mountains in scales? All nations before*
> **him** *are as nothing; and they are counted to* **him** *less than*
> *nothing, and vanity. To whom then will ye liken God? Or*
> **what likeness** *will ye compare unto him? To whom then will*
> *ye liken me, or shall I be equal? Saith the* **Holy One**." ....
> Holy **One!** Holy **One!**

To this awesome question, to what can we liken God, some Oneness answer, *"H₂0; water, steam, and ice,"* and some Trinitarians answer, *"an egg; yoke, white, and shell."* [Perhaps we should pause for a moment of silence].

God has discouraged comparisons with Himself, with the rare exception of **our** *"fathers"* *(Isa. 64:8; Mal. 1:6; Luke 11:11-13; Rom. 8:15; Heb. 12:9).*

Listen to trinitarian professor Millard J. Erickson regarding the doctrine of *"three."*

> *"On the surface, the doctrine seems to present an outright contradiction. The contention is that God is both* **one** *and* **three**. *If he is* **one**, *how can he also be* **three**? *The usual response is that God is not* **one** *and* **three at the same time** *and in the same respect. If that is the case, what is the respect in which he is* **one** *and the respect in which he is* **three**? *That is where the vagueness becomes really serious....how do we know that it is the Son or the Spirit, rather than the Father that we encounter? How do we know them to be* **one**, *rather than* **letting the doctrine slip into tritheism** *[three Gods].* ***This is a major problem that neoorthodoxy never fully solved"*** *(p. 21).*

Erickson says of *"triad"* (Plato's word for God):

> *"He* (Theophilus - *circa 180 A.D.) was the* ***first*** *to use the term 'triad' with respect to the Godhead, stating that the* ***three days*** *that preceded the creation of the sun and the moon were* ***types of the Triad***, *that is, of God and of His Word and of His Wisdom"* *(p. 47).* [57]

Trinitarian professor Cyril C. Richardson, writing in his book, *The Doctrine of The Trinity*, makes these enlightening statements.

> *"In Paul, to be sure, the problem is not so simple as that, for he never calls the Son of God or Lord specifically 'God' "* *(p. 23). "The* ***'threeness'*** *of the Trinity is an arbitrary and*

*unpersuasive doctrine" (p.111). "But the variety of God's operations is such that **they can never constitute a genuine Trinity**" (p. 124). "My conclusion, then, about the doctrine of the Trinity is that it is an **artificial construct.** It tries to relate different problems and to fit them into an **arbitrary** and traditional **threeness.** It produces confusion rather than clarification... . It has posed for many Christians dark and mysterious statements... . Christian theology might be aided by abandoning such a procedure and by making clear the inadequacy both of the **ambiguous terms** and of the **threeness** into which its doctrines have been traditionally **forced.** But there is no necessary threeness in the Godhead" (p. 148-149).* [58]

Trinitarian professor Charles C. Ryrie, writing in his book, *Basic Theology,* makes these revealing statements:

*"A definition of the Trinity is not easy to construct. Some are done by stating several propositions. Others err on the side of **Oneness** or **Threeness.** The word "Persons' might be misleading as if there were **three individuals** in the Godhead, but what other word would suffice? (p. 61).*

*"In the **second half of the fourth century,** three theologians from the province of Cappadocia in eastern Asia Minor gave definitive shape to the doctrine of the Trinity..." (p. 65).*

*"It is fair to say that **the Bible does not clearly teach the doctrine of the Trinity**, if by clearly one means there are **proof texts** for the doctrine" (p. 89).* [59]

A Word Of Caution

I agree with Plato regarding this one thing. **Ideas are powerful things**, and I have decided that the mind is like a balloon; once it has embraced a certain knowledge or an idea, it is stretched, and it is almost impossible to return it to its former shape. God refers to this fact in Jeremiah chapter seventeen regarding the **memories** that the idolatrous Israelites had left in the **minds** of their children:

> *"The sin of Judah is **written with a pen of iron**, and with*
> *the point of a diamond: it is graven upon the table of their*
> *heart, and upon the horns of your altars; **while** [as long as]*
> *their children remember their altars and their groves by*
> *the green trees upon the high hills" (v. 1-3).*

My friend, if you have ever in your mind, embraced the pagan idea that God is three entities, beings, persons, in one, or that the eternal God became incarnate as a man or as *"a baby whose diaper Mary changed, and who had to learn to walk" (Lucado)*, please ask Him to forgive you and heal your mind of the wound of this error. I am only optimistic that you can recover from this damage to your understanding if you love truth more than tradition, and *"thus saith the word of God"* more than the philosophies of men. As someone has said, *"It is almost impossible to reason a person out of a belief, that they were not reasoned into in the beginning."* The doctrines of the Trinity and the Incarnation are not reasonable doctrines, and as the trinitarian scholars we have quoted say regarding the Trinity, it is *"troublesome," "confusing," "arbitrary," "ambiguous,"* a *"doctrine that is not likely to be held unconsciously."* [60] Yet Christians are encouraged to suspend their reasoning, give up on understanding, *"and just take it by faith."* **God gave you a good mind, use it!**

I am seeking God, that He will remove the doctrine of Plato from Christianity, that He might restore our unity and power and receive our worship, prayers, and praise.

> *"But the people **that do know their God shall be strong**..."*
> *(Daniel 11:32).*

> *"And this is life eternal, that they might know **thee the only**
> **true God**, and Jesus Christ, whom thou hast sent"* [Jesus
> speaking] *(John 17:3).*

*"That the **God** of our Lord Jesus Christ, the **Father** of glory, may give unto you the spirit of wisdom and revelation **in the knowledge of him**" (Eph. 1:17).*

Glory to God in the Highest!

*"Christian men...are beginning to suspect that a vast amount of current **theology** has **human philosophy as its source.** Figures in the field of religious thought, which they used to think figures of Christ, His prophets, and His apostles, **they are beginning to suspect are figures of the evil spirit**, figures of **Plato**, and of various fathers who derived their theology in a great measure from him."*

Trinitarian minister and author

C.H. Constable circa 1893

Chapter Twelve

Who Was Philo?

*"At stake is the loss of God: What is at stake in the **doctrinal hollowing out** of contemporary evangelism is the loss of God. And with him the loss of truth and beauty, **the loss of truly seeing God and savoring God**. Soon we may wake up and discover the evangelical king **has no clothes on**. And worst of all, our very reason for being may be lost - the capacity to know and love **the glory of God**. Then we lose our ability to reflect his truth and beauty in the world. **And the world loses God**. That is finally what is at stake."*

*"**Not to care about truth is not to care about God.** To love God passionately is to love **truth** passionately. What is not true is not of God. **What is false is anti-God. Indifference to the truth is indifference to the mind of God.** Our concern with the truth is simply an echo of our concern with God. And all this is rooted in **God's concern with God, God's passion for the glory of God"** (John Piper; God's Passion For His Glory).* [1]

*M*is-guided Christianity has robbed God of **the thing that is most important to Him, His glory!** Consider. God has declared that the sum of all *creation* He has designed for **His own glory** *(Isa. 43:1-7; 60:21; 61:3)*. God's *people* from all ages, were and are, for His glory *(Isa. 49:3; John 15:8; I Cor. 6:20)*. Our *faith* glorifies God *(Rom. 4:20; Phil. 2:11)*.. Our *repentance* glorifies God *(Joshua 7:19; Rev. 16:9)*. Our *praise* and *thanksgiving* give glory to God *(Ps. 50:23; Luke 17:18)*. Our *service* to Him glorifies God *(John 15:8; Phil. 1:10-11)*. His *grace* is a reflection of His glory *(Isa. 49:3; Eph. 1:5; II Thess. 1:11-12)*.

Our Savior Jesus Messiah himself is for **the glory of God the Father**. When Jesus was born in Bethlehem the heavenly host praised *"God"* saying, *"**Glory to God** in the **highest**, and on **earth** peace..." (Luke 2:14).*

> *"That ye may with **one mind** and **one mouth** glorify **God, even the Father** of our Lord Jesus Christ" (Rom. 15:6).*

> *"To **God** only wise, be glory **through Jesus Christ** for ever" (Rom. 16:27).*

> *"Unto **him** [God] **be glory** in the church **by Christ Jesus** throughout all ages, world without end" (Eph. 3:21).*

> *"After this manner therefore pray ye: **Our Father** which art in heaven...For **thine** is the kingdom, and the power, and the **glory**, for ever, Amen" [Jesus speaking] (Matt. 6:9, 13).*

Our Lord Jesus has great glory and *"the **brightness** of his coming"* will destroy the Anti-christ. But it is *"**his** glory"* *(John 2:11), "his **own** glory" (Luke 9:26), "the **throne of his glory**" (Matt. 19:28; 25:31).*

> *"Ought not Christ to have suffered these things, and to enter **into his glory**" [Jesus speaking] (Luke 24:26).*

John tells us what Jesus' glory is!

> *"...and we beheld **his glory**, the glory as of **the only begotten of the Father**" (John 1:14).*

Notice: Not the **glory** of being the eternal God incarnate in flesh, or of being the second person of a triune God, but *"the **glory** as of the **only begotten** of the Father."* The one and only time that God the Father has brought forth a child from the womb of a virgin, without the aid of a man, is Jesus Christ. What great glory! But Jesus' glory cannot compare with the glory of the Father. God's glory is innate, self-consistent and underived, and Jesus' glory is a "given glory," given to him by his Father! Notice his words to the Father:

> *"And **the glory which thou gavest me**, I have given them...*
> *that they may behold **my glory, which thou hast given me**"*
> *(John 17:22, 24).*

And Peter's words:

> *"Christ...who verily was **foreordained** before the foundation*
> *of the world...**God**, that raised him up from the dead, **and***
> ***gave him glory**; that your faith and hope might be in **God**"*
> *(I Peter 1:19-21).*

God our Father's glory is as the One Most High who created the universe with the breath of His mouth! *(Ps. 33:6, 9).* *"The heavens declare **the glory of God**; and the firmament showeth **his handiwork**" (Ps. 19:1).* God's glory is the Shekinah, the awesome radiance of His seldom seen presence *(Ex. 24:16-17; II Chron. 5:14; Ezek. 43:2; Luke 2:9; Rev. 21:23).* God's glory is His total goodness, awesome majesty, splendor, beauty, wisdom, magnificence, wealth, weightiness, greatness and moral perfection! We are commanded to give **God** glory *(Ps. 96:1-9; Isa. 42:12; Acts 12:23).* In fact *"the everlasting gospel"* to be preached at the end time, to the entire world is:

> *"Fear **God, and give glory to him:**....and **worship him** that*
> *made heaven, and earth, and the sea, and the fountains of*
> *waters" (Rev. 14:6-7).*

That is for sure **glory** and **worship** to God our Father, Creator of all. But we have robbed God the Creator of His glory, and in our sincere desire to exalt His Son, the Lord Jesus Christ, **have given it to him!** We have shamefully done what God Himself said He would not do! The first seven verses of Isaiah chapter forty-two are a prophecy concerning the coming Messiah, but God says in verse eight:

> *"**I am the Lord**; that is my name: and **my glory will I not***
> ***give to another**" (v. 8).*

*"...and **I will not give my glory** unto another" (Isa. 48:11).*

Trinitarians, who say the Father is **one of three persons of God**, have with that statement robbed God of two-thirds of His glory. As incredible as it may seem, I have recently had two prominent trinitarian ministers quote Genesis 1:1 to me as saying:

> *"In the beginning **Gods** created the heaven and the earth."*

Perhaps they did not know they were following Plato in his belief that God is more than one person. Both ministers expressed belief that the Hebrew word for God, *"Elohim,"* is plural. That is nonsense! In the Old Testament the word *Elohim* is used some 2700 times, but of those times, some 2300 times it speaks of the One God of Israel, and always takes a **singular** verb. That is a fact that cannot be disputed. The God of Israel is **One, singular!** Listen to trinitarian professor Charles Ryrie regarding the name *Elohim*:

> *"To conclude **plurality of persons** from the name itself is **dubious** [doubtful]."* [2]

The *NIV text notes,* regarding the name *Elohim*, say:

> *"The Hebrew noun "Elohim" is plural but the verb is **singular**, a normal usage in the O.T. when reference is to the **one true God**. This use of the plural expresses **intensification rather than number** and has been called the plural of **majesty**, or of **potentiality"** (NIV Bible; p. 6).*

What Christianity as a whole has done to God the Father in our doctrine, regarding His glory, is a crime! Some Christians have totally replaced the Father with Christ, making him the eternal God. Athanasius, who fought all of his life to see the doctrine of the Trinity accepted as orthodox Christian doctrine, admitted the serious implications of worshiping Jesus as God. He said:

> *"If Christians have worshiped and continue to worship Christ, he must be considered God. **To admit otherwise** would be to **accuse the church of continuous blasphemy***

> ***in its prayer and practice***, *from the first century onwards"*
> *(Olson and Hall; The Trinity; p. 19).* [2]

This reminds us of the letter that some of the delegates to Nicea wrote to Constantine after returning home with second thoughts regarding the creed they had endorsed. *"(We have)* *committed an impious act, Oh Prince, by subscribing to a blasphemy from fear of you."* We learned in the previous chapter that the Greeks worshiped three main gods, with Zeus (the Father god) being the creator and primary one. But historian Will Durant says there arose in Greek myth, the fascinating figure of a man named Orpheus, who *"in culture, music, and poetry, far surpassed all men"* of whom the Greeks had heard. He was pictured as a gentle spirit, tender, meditative, affectionate; a priest of the god Dionysus. This Orphic cult grew far superior to the cults of other gods, even Zeus, in doctrine, ritual and moral influence. But Durant, this secular historian, sees in this an analogy to Christianity. He says:

> *"Nevertheless there were in Orphism idealistic trends **that culminated in the morals and monasticism of Christianity**... and the mighty Zeus was slowly **dethroned** by the gentle figure of Orpheus, **even as Yahweh was** to be **dethroned by Christ.**"* [3]

Of course Durant means *"dethroned"* **in Christian doctrine.** But we can say for sure that Jesus had no part in Christians giving the Father's glory to himself. Jesus always pointed us to a **higher** and **greater.** He said *"God"* 184 times as recorded in the New Testament, and **not once** is he speaking of himself or the Holy Spirit; it is **always** the **Father** that is referred to. And he **never** reached for the Father's glory, as he was **more than content with his own!**

> *"My doctrine is not mine, but **his** that **sent me.** If any man will do **his** will, he shall know of the doctrine, **whether it be of God**, or whether I speak **of myself.** He that speaketh of himself seeketh **his own glory:** but **he that seeketh his glory that sent him**, the same is true, and **no unrighteousness is in him**"* [Jesus speaking] *(John 7:16-18).*

333

For Christianity to accuse Jesus of claiming to be *"God,"* is to charge him with *"unrighteousness."* Notice his words above, *"whether it be of God, or whether I speak of myself."* In the previous chapter of John, after the miracle of the feeding of the 5000, Jesus' popularity with the people was at an all time high. They began to say, *"This is of a truth that Prophet that should come into the world" (John 6:14).* But notice verse fifteen:

> *"When Jesus perceived that they would come and **take him by force, to make him a king**, he departed again into a mountain himself **alone**."*

Take him by force and make him a king? That sounds painfully similar to what Christianity has done! In spite of all of Jesus' protestations; *"Why callest thou me good? There is none good but one, **that is God"** (Matt. 19:17; Mark 10:18; Luke 18:19), "my Father is greater than I" (John 14:28), "that they might know **thee the only true God"** (John 17:3),* Christians have taken him by force, **to make him *"God!"*** Why?

1. A case of mistaken identity. He looks so much like the Father, we thought he was the Father. Jesus is *"**the express image of**[God's] **person"** (Heb. 1:3).* Note: An image is not the original; it is a representative likeness.

2. Like the people spoken of in John chapter six, we have been overwhelmed by the miracles of Jesus! They prove that he is the human Son of God (Messiah), but they were never meant to prove that he is **God.**

   > *"And declared to be **the Son of God**...by the resurrection from the dead" (Rom. 1:4).*

Here is a word of advice from your brother in Christ, a *Jesus* man. Let the biblically recorded miracles of Jesus inspire, encourage, and challenge you, but do not be overwhelmed by them. One clear statement from Jesus puts **all of his miracles** in perspective for us:

> *"Verily, verily, I say unto you, **He** that believeth on me, the works that I do shall **he** do also; **and greater works than these shall he do**; because I go unto **my Father"** (John 14:12).*

Look at Jesus' promise to "over-comers."

> *"And **he** that overcometh, and keepeth my works unto the end, **to him will I give power over the nations: And he shall** rule them with a rod of iron; as the vessels of a potter shall they be broken to shivers: **even as I received of my Father"** (Rev. 2:26-27). (Father, "the glory **which thou hast given me** I have **given them"** John 17:22).*

3. There is a big devil that has sought to rob God of His glory, as far back as the garden of Eden! And possessed by satanic power and inspired by him, some wicked and mis-guided men have led Christianity into a doctrinal swamp, and caused us to be complicit in it!

    > *"**Will a man rob God?** Yet ye have **robbed me**. But ye say, Wherein have we robbed thee...ye are cursed with a curse: for ye have **robbed me**, even this whole nation"* [God the Father speaking] *(Malachi 3:8-9).*

Of course God is speaking in these verses of *"tithes and offerings,"* but Christians have robbed God of something greater than these, His honor and glory. Hear the cry of His heart just two chapters back:

> *"A son **honoreth his father**, and a servant his master: if then **I be a father, where is my honor**...saith the Lord of hosts"* (Malachi 1:6). Who is this speaking? Look at Malachi 2:10: *"Have we not all **one father**? Hath not **one God** created us?"*

Since our Lord Jesus gave us an example of using parables and current events to illustrate lessons *(Luke 13:1-6),* perhaps I could use a little parable to illustrate my point.

Please picture a train traveling through the Old West. It is a large train, and the first car is a baggage car loaded with pure gold. The car is named "Creation," and the gold with which it is loaded is the glory of God. The next car is also a baggage car named "The Patriarchs," and it is loaded with this pure gold. The next two cars are named "Judaism," and "Christianity," and their purpose likewise is to bear this gold of God's glory. Following these rail cars are innumerable passenger coaches, loaded with innocent, smiling people. But as the train slows down near a town, about fifteen masked men on horseback, ride out of the sagebrush, accost the people, and rob the train of its precious cargo. Meanwhile, some misguided citizens of the town, viewing the robbers as *"Robin Hoods,"* cheer them on as they go about the evil deed. And saddest of all, some of these cheering citizens **are dressed as men of the cloth!**

But wait! That is not the end of the story! At the back of this train is a solid gold caboose, named "Millennium," that glistens in the Sonlight!

> *"**But as truly as I live**, all the earth shall be filled with **the glory of the Lord** [God]" (Num. 14:21).*

> *"For the earth shall be **filled with the knowledge of the glory of the Lord**; as the waters cover the sea" ("O Lord my **God**, mine Holy **One**") (Habakkuk 1:12; 2:14).*

> *"**God** came from Teman, and **the Holy One** from mount Paran. **His glory covered the heavens, and the earth was full of his praise**" (Habakkuk 3:3).*

> *"And behold, **the glory of the God of Israel** came from the way of the east: and **his voice** was like a noise of many waters: **and the earth shined with his glory**" (Ezek. 43:2).*

A Robber Named Philo

The group of bandits that robbed the train of its precious gold includes **only one Jew**, Philo Judaeus *(20 B.C. to 50 A.D.)*. We have already unmasked Socrates, Plato, and to some degree his most famous pupil, Aristotle. Now it is time to take a closer look at Philo.

Philo was born about twenty years before Jesus, in the city of **Alexandria, Egypt**, and became both a statesman and philosopher and **the most prolific author** of Hellenistic Judaism. He was born to a wealthy aristocratic Jewish family and received a thorough education in the Old Testament and in **Greek** literature and philosophy. He had an intimate knowledge of the works of Homer and of the **Greek** tragedies, **but his chief studies** were in **Greek philosophy**, especially the teachings of Pythagoras, **Plato**, and the Stoics. [4]

The *Harper Collins Bible Dictionary* says of Philo:

> *"Philo's writings are remarkably free of rabbinic concerns* [the teachings of the rabbis], ***and betray no awareness of any Christian person or event.*** *Philo **combined** a fierce loyalty to Judaism (i.e. the non-Palestinian branch of Judaism most influenced by **Hellenistic** culture), with a **profound love of Greek philosophy** to present a literary defense of Judaism to his racially troubled city and extensive allegorical interpretation of Scripture that made Jewish law consonant* [in agreement] *with the ideals of Stoic, Pythagorean, and **especially Platonic** thought. No New Testament writer owes a direct debt to Philo...His writings were preserved by **Christians**, and later his **philosophical ideas** and allegorical method **had a direct impact** on **Christian theology** [how we view God] through the writings of Clement of **Alexandria** and Origen."* [5]

Since our focus in this and the next chapter shifts from Athens, Greece to **Alexandria, Egypt**, there are a few things we should know about that city.

The City Of Alexandria

This capital city of Egypt on the Mediterranean coast near the Nile Delta, was founded in 332 B.C. by Alexandria the Great, and grew to be one of the largest cities of the Hellenistic world, second in size only to Rome, but first in industry and commerce. A major shipping port, famed for its 445-foot-high lighthouse and nine miles of wharves, Alexandria's merchant fleet wove a web of commerce over many seas. A manufacturing center, it produced thousands of articles including glass, paper, and linen on a large scale. Alexandria was the clothing and fashion center of the age, setting the styles and making the goods. It was also a tourist center, equipped with hotels, guides and interpreters for visitors coming to see the Pyramids and other majestic sights. The main avenue, sixty-seven feet wide, was lined for three miles with colonnades, arcades, and shops displaying the fanciest products of ancient crafts. Imposing structures adorned the central "Broadway," including a large theater, an exchange, and temples to Poseidon, Caesar, Saturn, and Serapis, god of the lower world. [6] There was a world famous university known as the *Museum*, with an unrivaled library of 400,000 volumes. [7] In the heart of the city, the body of Alexander the Great lay in a pretty mausoleum, preserved in honey and encased in glass.

The population of Alexandria in Philo's time was 800,000 to 1,000,000 and was at least twenty-five percent Jewish (Philo says 40%). It had a diverse culture, made up of Greeks, Egyptians, Italians, Arabs, Phoenicians, Persians, Ethiopians, Syrians, Libyans, Sicilians, Scythians, Indians, and Nubians. According to the historian Durant:

> *"They made a volatile and inflammable mixture, quarrelsome and disorderly, intellectually clever and irreverently witty, shameless in speech, skeptical and superstitious, loose in morals and gay in mood, fanatically fond of the theater, music, and public games. Dio Chrysostom describes life there as 'a **continuous revel**...of dancers, whistlers, and murderers.' The canals were alive with merrymakers in gondolas at night on their five-mile sail to the amusement suburb at Canopus."* [8]

The 250,000 to 300,000 Jews of Alexandria were employed in industry and trade, but some were in great poverty. Many were merchants, a few were money lenders, and some were rich enough to win important places in city government. Originally confined by law to one fifth of the city, they eventually overflowed to occupy two-fifths. They were governed by their own laws and elders, and Rome granted them the privilege to ignore any ordinance that conflicted with their religion. Their magnificent central synagogue was a basilica so huge that a system of signals had to be used to secure a proper response at proper times, from worshipers too distant from the sanctuary to hear the words of the priest. According to the historian Josephus, the moral life of the Alexandrian Jews was very good compared with the sexual looseness of the "pagan" population.

But as in all places where the Jews were scattered by God in the Diaspora (the dispersion of the Jews after the Babylonian Exile), they dealt with anti-Semitism and racial hostility. In 38 A.D. (when Philo was 58 years old) a mob of Greeks invaded the synagogues and insisted on placing in each of them a statue of the emperor Caligula as a god. The Roman ruler of Alexandria annulled the citizenship of the Jews and ordered those who lived outside the original Jewish section to return to it in a few days. When that time elapsed the Greek populace burned 400 Jewish homes and killed Jews outside the ghetto. Thirty-eight members of the Jewish senate were arrested and publically scourged in an open air theater. Thousands of Jews lost their homes, businesses, and savings. The matter was submitted to the Emperor, and two separate delegations, (five Greeks and five Jews) went to Rome in 40 A.D. to plead their causes before Caligula. He died before he could judge the matter, but his successor Claudius restored the rights of the Jews, and sternly ordered both factions to keep the peace. [8]

Philo Judaeus

The leader of the Jewish delegation to Rome was the philosopher Philo, whose brother was the manager of the Jewish export trade in Alexandria. We know hardly anything else of his life, but mostly we know him by the many works that he wrote to expound Judaism to the Greek world. Intensely loyal to his people, **and yet fascinated by Greek philosophy**, he made it the aim of his life to reconcile the Scriptures and customs of the Jews with Greek ideas, and above all with the philosophy of the man he called "the most holy", **Plato.**

In an earlier chapter we discussed the Pope's speech in which he mentions the blending of Greek and biblical ideas which he calls *"synthesis,"* a word which means *"combining"* or *"putting together."* Combining such as this must take place in the mind of a man or men, and regarding Greek philosophy and Judaism, this happened in the mind of **Philo.** In a later chapter we will see that regarding **Greek philosophy** and **Christianity,** this combining took place over a period of time in the minds of Justin, Origen, Athanasius, Constantine, Augustine, etc.

Durant says of Philo:

> *"He adopted for his purpose the principle that all **events,** **characters, doctrines,** and **laws** in the Old Testament have an allegorical* [a hidden or symbolic meaning] *as well as a literal meaning and symbolize certain moral or psychological truths; **by this method he was able to prove anything."*** [10]

Philo knew little Hebrew and like the other thoroughly Hellenized Jews of Alexandria, spoke and wrote in the Greek language. The Hebrew Bible had been translated into **Greek** *(the Septuagint)* several centuries before Philo, and this is the text which he studied and from which he wrote. His inefficiency in Hebrew created a serious disconnect between Philo and the concepts of the Old Testament, and also the God of the Old Testament, since he, like the Greek church fathers who followed him, **thought as Greeks.**

Philo's View Of God

The God of the Old Testament is high and exalted, but He has chosen to relate to men and women as our Father in heaven. From a careful reading of the Hebrew Scriptures it is clear that Adam, Abraham, Moses, Isaiah and others knew God and interacted with Him. This fellowship and interaction was initiated by God Himself and took nothing away from His awesome greatness.

However, Philo followed his hero Plato in the mistaken belief that God is **totally transcendent** and **unknowable**. The word *"transcendent"* means *"beyond the limits of possible experience"* or *"beyond human knowledge."* The word **transcendent** stands in opposition to the word *"immanent,"* which means that God is also *"present."* The concept of God's immanence is always a problem for **those who do not truly know Him**, because they thus believe that He is **unknowable!** God's "knowability" is such an important biblical concept that we need to establish it again.

> *"But let him that glorieth glory in this, that he **understandeth** and knoweth me, that I am the **Lord** which exercise loving-kindness, judgement, and righteousness, in the earth: for in these things I delight, saith the Lord"* [Almighty God speaking] *(Jer. 9:24).*

> *"And this is life eternal, that they might **know thee the only true God...**"* [Jesus Christ speaking to the Father] *(John 17:3).*

> *"Because that which may be **known of God** is manifest in them; **for God hath showed it unto them**. For the invisible things of him from the creation of the world are clearly seen...even his eternal power and Godhead [deity]; so that they are without excuse: Because that, when they **knew God**, they **glorified him not as God...**"* (Romans 1:19-21).

> *"That the **God** of our Lord Jesus Christ, the **Father of glory**, may give unto you the spirit of wisdom and revelation in the **knowledge of him"** (Eph. 1:17).*

> *"In flaming fire taking vengeance on them **that know not God**, and that obey not the gospel of our Lord Jesus Christ"* (II Thess. 1:8).

Note: It is a serious affront to God our Father to teach that He created human beings as His children and did not give us sense enough to know who He is! Philo, like Plato, believed that God is the Creator, and eternal, but **matter** is also eternal, and that God created all things by assembling **matter** into pre-existent *"forms."*. Plato's best known doctrine is the doctrine of *"Ideas"* or *"Forms."* Briefly this is the concept. Take for example the word **"table."** There are long and short *tables*. There are tall and small *tables*. There are wooden and stone *tables*. Plato taught that before there ever was a **table**, there already existed the **idea** or **form** of a **table**. One more example. Consider **chairs**. There are big *chairs* and small *chairs*. There are straight *chairs* and rocking *chairs*. There are wooden *chairs* and metal *chairs*. But before there ever was a **chair**, the idea or form of a chair already existed, according to Plato (Don't blame me!). Thus the Platonic belief that matter is co-eternal with God, and He only created by making things out of Ideas and Forms that already existed. This is some of the doctrinal nonsense that was loved, swallowed, and dispensed by Philo.

Listen to *Funk and Wagnalls New Encyclopedia* regarding Philo's view of God.

> *"He conceived of God as a being **without attributes**,......a being so exalted above the world that **an intermediate class of beings** is required to establish a point of contact between him and the world. These beings he found in the spiritual world of ideas - not merely ideas in the **Platonic** sense, but **real, active powers, surrounding God as a number of attendant beings**. All these **intermediate powers** are known as the **Logos**, the **divine image in which persons are created** and through which **they participate in the deity**."* [11]

Please study carefully these words concerning Philo's doctrine of *"real, active powers, surrounding God as a number of attendant beings," "intermediate powers known as the **Logos**, the **divine image** in which persons are created and through which **they participate in the deity**."* A more un-scriptural statement would be hard to find! First of all, that flies in the face of Genesis

1:26, *"So God created man in **his own image**, in the image of God created he him."* And then Philo builds a major doctrine on the idea of **Logos**, which was handed down to him by **Heraclitus, Socrates,** and **Plato,** a doctrine which would play a staggering role in corrupting Christian thought, through the "Hellenized Christian philosophers" which followed him there in **Alexandria, Egypt,** in the second, third, and fourth centuries A.D.

Philo and The Demon Spirit

When a man conceives and writes doctrines that lead multiplied millions of sincere people astray regarding the One Most High God, those doctrines cannot be Holy Spirit derived, so the next question is, "Where did they come from?" Remembering Paul's dire warning regarding *"seducing spirits, and doctrines of devils,"* we must conclude that there is a demonic source! Since Satan cannot long hide himself, all we need do is look for proof. For this we turn to a book by Professor Charles Bigg D.D., titled, *Christian Platonist's of Alexandria.* It is a large, enlightening, and well documented work and Professor Bigg describes how Philo's doctrines of *"the **Two Powers** and that of the **Logos"*** was *"given to him by **special revelation**."* Bigg quotes Philo:

> *"I will not be ashamed to relate what has happened to myself a **thousand times**. Often when I have come to write out **the doctrines of philosophy**, though I well knew what I ought to say, I have found my mind dry and barren, and renounced the task in despair. At other times, though I came empty, I was suddenly filled with thoughts **showered upon me from above** like snowflakes or seed, so that **in the heat of divine possession I knew not the place**, or the **company**, or **myself, what I said or what I wrote.**"* [12]

What are we to make of Philo's *"heat of divine possession?"* Did any writer of the Gospels or Epistles describe a time of inspiration when, *"I knew not the place, or the company, or myself, what I said or what I wrote?"* And of course the ultimate test of who his source was is in the content of his writing. Notice these biblical warnings:

> *"To the law and to the testimony: if they speak not according*

> *to this **word, it is because there is no light in them**" (Isa.
> 8:20).*

> *"Now I beseech you, brethren, **mark them** which cause
> divisions and offenses **contrary to the doctrine** which ye
> have learned; **and avoid them**" (Rom. 16:17).*

Since Philo's doctrine fails the *"biblical test,"* we must conclude that this
strange *"divine possession"* is in reality a demonic possession. Therefore,
whatever he writes must be considered suspect and *"avoided."* This includes
his view of God. Professor Bigg says of Philo's beliefs regarding God:

> ***"God has neither relations nor attributes. Hence He has
> no name.** Man in his weakness is ever striving to find some
> title for the Supreme. But, says Philo, 'names are symbols
> of created things, seek them not for Him who is uncreated.'
> Even the reverable and **scriptural** titles of **God** and **Lord**
> are inadequate.... . The phrases that Philo himself prefers to
> employ are 'the One,' 'He that is,' 'Himself.' **From all this
> it follows that God is incomprehensible."***

Bigg continues:

> *"It is evident that Philo was not prevented...from attributing
> the work of Providence, or even of Creation, to the Deity.
> There was however **a grave moral difficulty.** The world
> was created out of **pre-existing matter. And matter, though
> eternal**, was evil - 'lifeless, erroneous, divisible, un-equal.'
> It seemed impossible to bring the **Perfect being** into direct
> contact with the senseless and corruptible. Hence when
> Philo speaks of the royal or fatherly operations of the Deity,
> he is generally to be understood as referring **not to God
> Himself** but to **His Powers or Ministers** [i.e. the Logos].
> Though **He** [God] **be far off**, yet is he very near, keeping
> touch by means of His creative and regulative **Powers**,
> which are close to all, **though He has banished the things
> that have birth far away from His essential nature."** [13]*

Please study these statements closely. Although they may sound reasonable and good to the carnal mind, they are in no way scriptural. As Professor Bigg says: *"But in yielding thus to the fascination of **Greek wisdom**, the Jew stumbled on many difficulties."* There are two reasons Satan wants humans to believe that God is totally remote and *"far away."* 1. So the wicked will go about their wickedness, thinking that God does not notice, and that they will never have to answer to Him. 2. So Christians will perceive God as too removed to see and know their sorrows, or hear and answer their supplications. Both accounts are totally false! **The God of the Bible is not remote and *"far away."*** Consider:

> *"God is our refuge and strength, a **very present help** in trouble" (Ps. 46:1).*

> *"For thus saith the high and lofty **one** that inhabiteth **eternity**, whose name is Holy; I dwell in the high and holy place, **with him also** that is of a contrite* [repentant] *and humble spirit, to revive the spirit of the humble..." (Isa. 57:15).*

> *"**God that made the world** and all things therein, seeing that **he** is Lord of heaven and earth...And hath made of one blood all nations of men...That they should seek the Lord* [God], *if haply they might **feel after him, and find him, though he be not far from every one of us**" (Acts 17:24-27).* Note: Paul was speaking to **Greeks** on Mars Hill. Consider these other statements from Paul: *"...the world by **wisdom knew not God**...and **the Greeks seek after wisdom**" (I Cor. 1:21-22).*

> *"Humble yourselves therefore under the **mighty hand of God**, that he may exalt you in due time: Casting all your care upon **him**; for **he careth for you**" (I Peter 5:6-7).*

Philo and The Logos

Another famous doctrine of Philo's concerning which we should beware and *"avoid,"* is his Platonic doctrine of the *"divine Logos!"* Remember, the *"divine Logos"* was a Greek philosophic concept, mentioned first by the Greek philosopher Heraclitus *(circa 500 B.C.)* and picked up by Socrates some 50 years later, who believed it could be found in human reasoning, and sought for it fanatically through his *"Socratic method"* of intense questioning. To his student Plato, the Logos was a *"second God,'* a *"second Deity,"* one of the *"hypostasisses"* or representatives through which God relates to humans and controls the universe. This demonic doctrine found fertile soil in the mind of the Alexandrian Jew Philo, who became obsessed with it, and who came to use the terms *"Logos,"* or *"divine Logos"* some 1400 times in his writings. [14] (Yes, fourteen hundred times!). Crediting Plato and Greek philosophy with Philo's concepts, Professor Bigg says of his part in *"Hellenizing"* Christianity, *"But in truth even the Logos doctrine, **the keystone of the whole structure**, was already in place when he took up the work"* (p. 6).

As we go forward and study the statements that Philo made regarding the Logos, statements that the later Christian Platonists of Alexandria (Justin, Origen, Athanasius, etc.) took and applied to Jesus, it is important to remember that Philo wrote these **before the ministry of Jesus Christ!** The historian Gibbon says of this fact:

> *"The Platonism of Philo, which was famous to a proverb, is proved beyond a doubt by Le Clerc. [The historian] Basnage has clearly ascertained that the theological works of Philo **were composed before the death, and most probably before the birth, of Christ.** In such a time of darkness **the knowledge of Philo is more astonishing than his errors."***
> [15]

The *Encyclopedia Americana* makes this enlightening statement:

> *"Philo of Alexandria, a Jewish contemporary of Jesus of Nazareth, living in a center of **Hellenistic speculation**,*

*sought to work out a synthesis of the Jewish and Greek traditions. His thinking was largely **Neoplatonic,** and he frequently allegorized and **reinterpreted** the Biblical tradition. For Philo, 'logos' represented the Hebrew word of God, as colored by the **later idea of the divine Wisdom.** His concept also formed a bridge to **Hellenistic Stoicism.** It also had affinities with some **Neoplatonic conceptions,** wherein God...is so remote from...the experienced world that some intermediary or **some plurality within the divine unity** becomes a necessity. If the **logos** had these advantages for Philo, **his doctrine ran the risk of compromising Jewish monotheism"** (Vol. 17; p. 691-692).*

But here is the most serious and devastating problem in Christian doctrine: Christians are guilty of confounding the Logos of Plato with John's use of the word "*logos*" for God's utterance or speech in John 1:1, and making of it a "*second Deity,*" i.e. a second person in the Trinity! **No two things in the world could be more different than Plato's "*Logos*" and John's "*logos!*"**

The *Harper Collins Encyclopedia of Catholicism* says of the Platonic Christians who followed Philo:

*"The **Platonists** of **Alexandria** conceived of the **Logos** as the **divine intermediary** between God and the world. Integrating these views, Philo (20 B.C. - A.D. 50) spoke of the **Logos** as the divine intention operating at the heart of creation. It is the power of creation and **the means through which we know God.** The early Church writers Ignatius of Antioch, Justin Martyr, Clement of Alexandria, and Athanasius **employed the notion of Logos** to shed light on **the mystery of God's** self-revelation in Jesus Christ. But, as Irenaeus warned, **logos-language** can be pushed into Gnosticism."* [16] Note: *Webster's New World Dictionary* defines Gnosticism as *"stressing gnosis [knowledge] as essential to salvation, and variously **combining** ideas*

derived from mythology, **ancient Greek philosophy,** *ancient religions,* **and eventually Christianity.** *"* [This **combining** is documented in everything from encyclopedias, history books, dictionaries, and books by trinitarian scholars, as well as your local newspaper].

There is nothing more powerful or dangerous than **a lie that becomes mixed with truth.** If Plato had taught a doctrine of **ten God's** or **ten Deities,** there would be no need for this book I am writing, and as Jefferson said, *"the whole civilized world would now have been Christian."* As the skeptic Mark Twain said, *"a lie can make it half-way around the world, before the truth can get its boots on."* I agree with Twain but I say with godly confidence and biblical assurance, **God is ready for this truth that He is the One Most High God to be seen, and it is destined to shake and shape the world!**

Back to Philo.

Matthew chapter fifteen records that Jesus' disciples came and told him that the Pharisees were offended at his teachings. Jesus' response regarding these religious leaders was:

> *"Let them alone: they be blind leaders of the blind. And if the blind lead the blind,* **both shall fall into the ditch***" (v. 14).*

Philo is a blind guide, a follower of another blind guide Plato, and all who follow them have fallen into the ditch!

The *Encyclopedia Americana* says of Philo and those who followed him:

> *"He had little if any proficiency in Hebrew. Most of Philo's writings are preserved in the original Greek. As part of his endeavor to command respect for the acceptance of Judaism* **by the Greeks,** *Philo attempted to harmonize,* **indeed to fuse, Hebrew religion with Greek wisdom** *by means of allegory, which he learned from the Stoics* [Greek followers of Plato and Zeno]. *The* **Logos,** *which in Stoicism defined the*

> **Godhead** [Deity], *for Philo became **distinguished though not disconnected** from God; it constituted the **immanent** intelligence of the **transcendent** God. Here significant affinities exist to the Logos in the Gospel of John and **later Christologies**. The **Logos, as presented by Philo**, thus came to be construed as a **philosophical buttress** for doctrines of the Christ as mediator between God and humanity. In this fashion, while Philo's writings had but **minimal effect** on later Jewish thinking, **they became influential on the Church Fathers**, who preserved his writings for posterity."*[17]

As we go forward we will prove that Philo had no effect on the writings of the beloved disciple John, an **unhellenized Galilean**, but he did have a devastating affect on the writings of the so called "Church Fathers," who themselves were "converted" Greek philosophers.

The historian Will Durant writes of Philo's concept of God and the divine Logos:

> *"God, in Philo, is the essential being of the world, incorporeal, eternal, indescribable; reason can know his existence, **but can ascribe no quality to him**, since every quality is a limitation. God is everywhere...But he is not everything: **matter is also eternal and uncreated**; however, it has no life, motion, or form until infused with the **divine force**. To create the world by giving form to matter, and to establish relations with man, **God used a host of intermediary** [go-between] **beings**, called angels by the Jews, daimones by the Greeks, and Ideas by Plato. These, says Philo, may popularly be conceived as **persons**, though really they exist only in the Divine Mind, as the thoughts and powers of God. Together these powers [persons?] constitute what the Stoics called the **Logos**, or Divine Reason **creating** and guiding the world. Fluctuating between **philosophy** and **theology**, between ideas and personifications, Philo sometimes thinks*

of the Logos as a person; in a poetic moment he calls the Logos 'the first-begotten of God,' son of God by the virgin Wisdom, and says that through the Logos, God has revealed himself to man. Since the soul is part of God, it can through reason rise to a mystic vision not quite of God, but of the Logos."

These ideas from Philo have absolutely no basis in Old Testament Scripture. Remember, Philo told us he wrote these things *"in the heat of divine possession,"* when *"I knew not the place, or the company, or myself, what I said or what I wrote."* This is an attempt by a demon spirit to inject confusion into Jewish, and ultimately Christian, doctrine. And confusion it has brought. In Pope Benedict's speech, cited in an earlier chapter, he says, *"the truly divine God is the God who has revealed himself as Logos, and as Logos, has acted and continues to act lovingly on our behalf."* He speaks of the *"love of the God who is Logos."* But Benedict is correct on one point: *"The encounter between the Biblical message and Greek thought did not happen by chance."* One thing is for certain: **we will never have favor with God, our prayers answered, and apostolic power, until we truly "dehellenize" Christianity and rid ourselves of these Greek concepts and doctrines!**

The historian Durant continues:

> *"Philo's Logos was one of the most influential ideas in the history of thought. Its antecedents* ["going before in time"] *in Heraclitus, Plato, and the Stoics are obvious; presumably he knew the recent Jewish literature that had made a distinct person of the Wisdom of God as creator of the world; and he must have been impressed by those lines in Proverbs (8:22) where Wisdom says, 'The Lord possessed me in the beginning of his way, before his works of old. I was set up from everlasting...or ever the earth was.' Philo was a contemporary of Christ; he apparently never heard of him; but he shared unknowingly in forming Christian theology.*

> *The rabbis frowned upon his allegorical interpretations...*
> *they suspected the Logos doctrine was* **a retreat from**
> **monotheism** [belief in One God].... *But* **the Fathers of the**
> **Church** *admired the Jew's contemplative devotion, made*
> *abundant use of his allegorical principles to answer the*
> *critics of the Hebrew Scriptures, and joined with* **Gnostics**
> *and* **Neo-Platonists** *in accepting the* **mystical vision of**
> **God...** *Philo had tried to mediate between* **Hellenism** *and*
> **Judaism.** *From the Judaic point of view he had failed;*
> **from the historical point of view he had succeeded;** *and*
> *the result was* **the first chapter of the Gospel of John.** " [18]

Will Durant was a great historian! He received a Pulitzer Prize for this insightful and exhaustive, eleven-volume work. But here again we have a scholar who knows enough of history to **see** this infusion of Greek philosophy into Christian doctrine, but not enough of Scripture to **see through it!** We have proven and will continue to prove that the apostle John was not influenced in any way by Plato's and Philo's doctrine of the *"divine Logos."* It would be a major insult to John-and to the Holy God who inspired him to write-to believe otherwise!

The Word Of God In The Old Testament

Philo the Jew loved and followed Plato. When his friends and admirers wished to flatter him they said, *"Plato writes like Philo"* (yes, in that order). [19] If Philo had not been so blinded by his love for Plato and Greek philosophy, he might have seen clearer the God of his fathers, the One Most High God of the Old Testament. God has no like or equal; He is one, single, sole, unique Being, the only one in the God family. There is no *"second God"* or *"second Deity."* What is behind this attempt to find or produce, in or out of Scripture, another *"God"* than **God**?

Take for example the effort to make divine Wisdom another *"person"* of God. Job and Solomon when speaking of *"wisdom,"* to show its high value to man as a gift from God, often speak as if it were a person. For example

Proverbs 8:25 and 9:1:

> *"Before the mountains were settled, before the hills, was I brought forth."*

> *"Wisdom hath builded **her** house, **she** hath hewn out her seven pillars..."*

I must say one thing at this point. The Bible is a spiritual book that will never be understood by those with a carnal mind-set. If you do not truly know Almighty God the author, you will never truly understand His book. Much has been made of the above verses. But consider this question: Was Solomon asking for a *"person"* when he asked God for *"wisdom?"* *(I Kings 3:5-28; Eccl. 1:16-18).* Was James speaking of asking for a *"person"* when he said in James 1:5: *"If any of you lack **wisdom**, let him ask of God...?"* Some have even seen in Solomon's statements in Proverbs 8, a reference to the pre-existence of Jesus. But look again at 9:1 and ask yourself if Jesus is ever referred to in Scripture as *"her"* and *"she?"* The **trinitarian** professor James D.G. Dunn, writing in his insightful work, *Christology In The Making,* says correctly of these Old Testament writers:

> *"For them Wisdom never really became more than a convenient way of speaking about **God** acting in creation, revelation and salvation; Wisdom never became more than a personification of **God's own activity.**"* [20]

Given Satan's desire to rob God of His glory, and man's willingness to go along with it, it is a wonder to me that Christians, looking at the many references to *"wisdom"* in the Old and New Testaments, did not make *"Wisdom"* the *"fourth person of God,"* and turn the Trinity into a Quartet. (I say this with sadness).

Basically, this is what happened with the *"word"* of God. Anyone who has read much of the Jewish Scriptures which we call the *"Old Testament,"* is familiar with the phrase *"the word of God."* This occurs more than 240 times, and over 90% of these references describe a word of prophecy. The phrase is more or less a term for the prophetic claim that the prophet expresses the authoritative revelation and will of God in a particular situation. Thus we read again and again *"the word of the Lord."* Consider these examples:

> *"After these things **the word of the Lord** came unto Abram in a vision, saying, Fear not, Abram" (Gen. 15:1).*

> *"He that feared **the word of the Lord** among the servants of Pharaoh..." (Ex. 9:20).*

> *"If Balak would give me his house full of silver and gold, I cannot go beyond **the word of the Lord my God**" [Balaam] (Num. 22:18).*

> *"And the woman said to Elijah, Now by this I know that thou art a man of God, and that **the word of the Lord in thy mouth** is truth" (I Kings 17:24).*

> *"And it came to pass the same night, that **the word of Lord** came to Nathan, saying..." (I Chron. 17:3).*

So, in each of the above instances, and over two hundred more, *"the word of the Lord"* (or *"God"*), is His message to or through His chosen prophet. However, in a few verses in the Old Testament, God's *"word"* is spoken of in a way that seems to give it an independent existence of its own. Please consider the following:

> *"**He sent his word**, and healed them, and delivered them from their destructions" (Ps. 107:20).*

> *"**He sendeth forth his commandment** upon earth: **his word runneth** very swiftly" (Ps. 147:15).*

> *"**The Lord sent a word** into Jacob, and it hath lighted upon Israel" (Isa. 9:8).*

> *"So shall **my word** be that goeth forth out of my mouth: **it shall not return unto me void**, but it shall accomplish that which I please, and it shall prosper in the thing whereto **I sent it"** (Isa. 55:11).*

So the powerful *"word of God,"* once uttered, has as it were, a life of its own, especially as written down, when it functions as Torah or Scripture. But for these prophets the word they spoke under divine inspiration was no independent entity separate from God Himself. On the contrary, it was precisely the word of God, the utterance and breath of God, **God himself speaking**. Please notice:

> *"**By the word of the Lord** were the heavens made; and all the host of them by **the breath of his mouth**. For **he spoke, and it was done; he commanded**, and it stood fast"* (Ps. 33:6, 9).

As Professor Dunn says, *"It is an error to see in such personifications an approach to **personalization.** Nowhere either in the Bible or in the extra-canonical literature of the Jews is the word of God **a personal agent or on the way to become such."** * [21] So why did Philo, this famous Hellenistic Jewish writer from **Alexandria, Egypt,** not understand that? Again, he was blinded by his love for and fascination with, Plato and Greek philosophy. And he was just as obsessed with the *"divine Logos"* as Socrates and the Stoics before him. Listen to Professor Dunn:

> *"There can be no doubt of the importance of the word **logos** for Philo - he uses it more than 1400 times in his extant writings. Philo quite often speaks of the Logos as though a real being **distinct from God**, who acts as intermediary **between** God and the world."*

Dunn then cites these examples:

> *"To his **Word**, his chief messenger (highest in age and honour), **the Father of all** has given the special prerogative, to stand on the border and separate the creature from the*

*Creator. This same **Word** both **pleads with the immortal** as suppliant for afflicted mortality and acts as **ambassador** of the **ruler to the subject**"* [Philo].

[Therefore] *"of necessity was the **Logos** appointed as **judge** and **mediator**, who is called 'angel' "* [Philo].

*"The incorporeal world is set off and separated from the visible one by the **mediating Logos** as by a veil"* [Philo].

*"...follow the guidance of that reason (Logos) which is the **interpreter** and **prophet** of God"* [Philo].

*"It is reason (Logos) which has taken refuge with God and become his **suppliant*** [a person who supplicates]... " [Philo].

*"...the divine reason (Logos), the **ruler** and **steersman** of all"* [Philo].

*"...God's **firstborn**, the **Word**, who holds the **eldership among the angels**, their ruler as it were"* [Philo].

*"Nothing mortal can be made **in the likeness of the most high One** and Father of the universe, but only in that of the **second God**, who is his **Logos**"* [Philo]. [22] Note: This statement is a lie that flies in the face of Genesis 1:27, *"So **God** created man in **his own image.**"* **Philo is following Plato when he says: *"the second God, who is his Logos."***

*"This hallowed flock (the heavenly bodies) he leads in accordance with right and law, setting over it his true Word (Logos) and **firstborn Son**, who shall take upon him its government like some viceroy of a great king"* [Philo].

Please consider his statement above, calling the **Logos** the *"firstborn Son, who shall take upon him its government like some viceroy of a great king."* This is a prime example of Philo mixing the doctrines of Plato with the Hebrew Scriptures. God had said through the prophet Isaiah, some 700 years before Philo and 300 years before Plato, *"For unto us a child is born, unto us a son is given: and the government shall be upon his shoulders"* *(Isa. 9:6).* But there is no mention of a *"divine Logos,"* here, or any place else in God's Holy Bible!

In all of the above quotes from Philo, the Logos seems to be viewed as a wholly independent being who can act as a mediator between God and man. But since he endeavors to blend the doctrines of philosophy with his heritage as a Jew, Philo's writings are not consistent and are often in conflict. As Professor Dunn says, *"we have to pay special heed to a context of thought which is strange and difficult."* He speaks of Philo's *"strained and at times confusing or even contradictory particular allegories."* [23]

And Dunn leaves no doubt as to where he believes Philo's *"confusing or even contradictory"* ideas came from. He writes:

> *"What is sufficiently clear is that Philo's **thought**, not least his concept of the **Logos**, is what can fairly be described as a unique synthesis* [mixing] *of **Platonic** and **Stoic** world-views **with Jewish monotheism"** (p. 221).*

> *"In merging this **Platonic cosmology** with his Jewish faith Philo was of course greatly aided by.... The **Platonic** and Stoic elements do not of course remain unchanged within the Philonic system. In Philo the **Platonic ideas** are understood as thoughts in the mind of God" (p. 222).*

> *"It becomes evident that Philo was using the **Platonic** conception of a world of **ideas** to bridge the gulf between God and creation, between God and man. It is a gulf which Philo maintains is **ultimately unbridgeable: God is unknowable** in himself" (p. 228).* [24]

356

To confirm what I am saying, and add perspective to the writings of Philo, we should look at some statements from *The International Standard Bible Encyclopedia,* an exhaustive and authoritative, four-volume work. Under the topic *"Word,"* it states:

> *"In Greek philosophical writing* **logos** *takes on a special significance as early as the pre-***Socratic** *philosopher Heraclitus, 'the obscure' (circa 500 B.C.), who seems to have used the term for an underlying coherence or principle of the universe. Heraclitus' works survive only in short fragments...but Stoic philosophers of the Hellenistic Age looked back to his enigmatic words* **as the source of their logos doctrines.**
>
> *In the mid-5th century B.C. the Sophists used* **logos** *in a broad sense... Gorgias* [Socrates' lover] *in particular stressed* **the power of the logos,** *describing it in quasi-personal terms as a great ruler... .*
>
> *More important developments occurred among the Stoics, whose school of philosophy was founded at Athens by Zeno (circa 300 B.C.). Zeno, Clianthus, and others identified this* [logos] *with* **Zeus,** *the supreme god of the Greeks,* **and interpreted logos as a pantheistic world soul. Sometimes logos was also identified with Hermes the messenger God.**
>
> *A significant development in this literature is the vivid* **personification** *of Sophia or Wisdom, described* [in the non-biblical writings called "Wisdom"] *as the 'breath of the power of God' and the 'reflection of eternal light;'* **she** *is said to be with God, knowing His works, and to have come from the Most High to make* **her** *dwelling in Israel. Since* **Wisdom** *was closely associated with creation,* **it is easy to see how logos also became personified.** *This occurs most strikingly in Wisdom 18:15: 'Thy all-powerful* **word** *leaped*

*from heaven, from the royal throne, into the midst of the land that was doomed, a stern warrior carrying the sharp sword of thy authentic command, and stood and filled all things with death...'. It should be noted that here **logos** is the destructive agent of judgement, not the creative word."* [25]

This *Bible Encyclopedia* says of Philo and the Logos:

> *"An important figure for the development of **later Logos doctrines** is the Alexandrian Jew Philo Judaeus (circa 20 B.C.-A.D. 50), who uses the term **logos** over 1300 times in his extensive writings. Sometimes it is used simply for the spoken word, or for 'reason,' or in some other non-technical sense; but it is also used with the epithets **theios** ('divine') and hieros ('holy'), or with the dependent genitive **theoss** ('of God'), in a special religious sense for the manifestation of God's activity in the world. **This logos is said to be God's image** (eikon), and is sometimes described metaphorically in **personal terms** as His **first-born son**, or **High Priest**. Sometimes **logos** seems to be equated with the **whole world of Platonic 'ideas;'** elsewhere it seems to be used more in a **Stoic** sense for the ordered principle of the universe. We also see it used for the mind of God... .*
>
> *Philo's writings were composed on a wider variety of subjects, resulting in **no coherent doctrine of the Logos**. But his flexible and imaginative use of the term to express **Jewish and Greek** philosophical ideas **undoubtably influenced early** [post-apostolic] **Christian fathers**, and his influence has been postulated* ["to assume without proof to be true"] *on Hebrews and John."* [26]

Regarding the last statement I must say again: It is for sure that the Greek church fathers, after the deaths of the Apostles, followed this erroneous Platonic doctrine of the *"divine Logos,"* and applied it falsely to Messiah

Jesus. But to claim that **the apostle John, and the inspired writer of Hebrews** followed Heraclitus, Socrates, Plato, the Stoics and Philo in their understanding of the Creator and His dealings with the world, is a major insult to them and to the Holy God who anointed them to write!

The "Word Of God" In The New Testament
We will discuss later in this chapter the language in which the New Testament was written, but the fact remains that the two oldest known manuscripts are from about 350 A.D. and are in the Greek language. Therefore we will deal with it on that basis. The Greek word for *"word"* or *"utterance,"* as in the *"word"* of God is *"logos."* It occurs 331 times in the New Testament and its uses vary within the basic meaning.

Some examples of these uses are: *communication (Matt. 5:37), utterance (Matt. 12:32; 15:12; Luke 20:20), question (Matt. 21:24), command (Luke 4:36), report, information and rumor (Matt. 28:15; Mark 1:45; Luke 5:15; Acts 11:22), discourse (Matt. 15:12), wording (I Cor. 15:2), word of mouth (Acts 15:27; II Cor. 10:10), as apposed to the written word (Acts 1:1), mere words contrasted with power and action (I Thess. 1:5; I Cor. 4:19), a matter (Mark 9:10; Acts 8:21), words of Scripture (I Cor. 15:54), words of warning (Heb. 5:11), give account (Rom. 14:12), settlement of an account (Phil. 4:15), motive (Acts 10:29), proclamation, teaching, instruction (Luke 4:32; 10:39; John 4:41; 17:20); and also the word of God, the word of the Lord, the word of promise, of truth, of life, the word of Jesus, and the word concerning Jesus.* [27] In only **two** of these 331 occurrences of *"logos"* or *"word,"* do even trinitarian scholars think they see it *"incarnated"* as a **person** in Jesus Christ, as opposed to what the *"word"* or *"utterance"* of God produced or generated in the womb of the virgin Mary. Those two places are John 1:1, and 14.

Jesus and The "Word of God"
When Jesus preached or taught, **he spoke the "word of God."** You might ask, how can this be true if he was not God Himself? Let Jesus tell us:
> *"My doctrine is not mine, but **his that sent** me. If any man*

> *will do **his will**, he shall know of the doctrine, whether it be*
> ***of God**, or whether I speak of myself" (John 7:16-17).*

> *"...I do nothing of myself; but **as my Father hath taught***
> ***me**, **I speak** these things" (John 8:28).*

> *"For I have not spoken of myself; but the Father which sent*
> *me, **he gave me a commandment, what I should say, and***
> ***what I should speak**...whatsoever I speak therefore, **even***
> ***as the Father said unto me, so I speak**" (John 12:49-50).*
> Note: The above statements were recorded by the apostle
> John.

Jesus also spoke **about** the *"word"* of God. Please notice his words:
> *"The sower soweth the **word**. And these are they by the*
> *wayside, where the **word** is sown; but when they have **heard**,*
> *Satan cometh immediately, and taketh away the **word** that*
> *was **sown** in their hearts. And these are they likewise which*
> *are sown on stony ground; who when they have **heard the***
> ***word**, immediately receive it with gladness... . And these*
> *are they which are sown among thorns; such as **hear the***
> ***word**, and the cares of this world, and the deceitfulness, and*
> *the lusts of other things entering in, **choke the word**, and*
> ***it** becometh unfruitful. And these are they which are sown*
> *on good ground; such as **hear the word**, and receive **it**, and*
> *bring forth fruit..." (Mark 4:14-20).*

The above verses are very important to our understanding as to how Jesus
perceived himself in regard to the *"word"* of God. He cannot have seen
himself as the *"word incarnate."* To Jesus the *"word"* is something that is
"heard," is called *"it,"* and can be *"choked."* This can be God's *"words,"*
His *"gospel,"* and the *"preaching concerning Jesus,"* but it cannot be
"Jesus!" No New Testament writer, including John, quotes Jesus as saying
or even hinting that he himself is the *"word* [logos] *of God"* in fleshly form.

The noted James Dunn, Lightfoot Professor of Divinity at the University of Durham, England, and a scholar among scholars, in his afore mentioned book, studies closely the statements and claims of Jesus and writes his conclusion:

> **"Did the doctrine of the incarnation begin with Jesus?** *We find one who was conscious of being* **God's son,** *a sense of intimate sonship, an implication that Jesus believed or experienced this sonship to be something distinctive and unique; but the evidence did not allow us to penetrate further or be more explicit. We find one who claimed to be* **inspired** *by the Spirit of God, to be a* **prophet** *in the tradition of the prophets, but more than that, to be the* [endtime] *prophet, the one* **anointed** *by God to announce and enact the good news of God's final rule and intervention.* **But there is no indication that Jesus thought or spoke of himself as having pre-existed with God prior to his birth** *or appearance on earth.* [This is] *Christological thinking* **which cannot be traced back to Jesus himself. We cannot claim that Jesus believed himself to be the incarnate Son of God...**" [28]

Professor Dunn, himself a trinitarian makes a thorough search in his book for the doctrine of the incarnation in the New Testament. He comes to these enlightening conclusions:

> **Regarding Matthew**: *"There is no real indication that Matthew had attained a concept of incarnation, had come to think of Christ as a pre-existent being who became incarnate in Mary's womb or in Christ's ministry (as incarnate Wisdom). ...the thought of Christ's pre-existence or a doctrine of incarnation* **had not yet occurred to him**" *(p. 257).*

> **Regarding Mark**: *"So there is certainly nothing like a clear allusion to pre-existent glory here, and probably* **no implication of incarnation at all**" *(p. 48).*

Regarding Luke and Acts: *"There is certainly no thought of Jesus as a divine being called 'the Word' out of which arises the description of the gospel about Jesus as 'the Word'"* (p. 232).

Regarding the writer of Hebrews: *"...once again there is no real hypostatization of the word, and certainly no thought of Christ as the Word. What can be said with some greater confidence is that the identification of 'the word of God' as **the gospel**, was so firmly established in the earliest decades of Christianity that **the further equation of Christ as the Word** does not seem to have occurred to the writer of the Hebrews"* (p. 233).

Regarding James and Peter: *"There was no inherent logic in their understanding of their experience or in the language they used to describe it which made it necessary for them **to push the concept of the word beyond that of the impersonal power of God** to that of a hypostatization or divine being"* (p. 233).

Regarding the apostle Paul: *"It is clear from all this that Paul has no concept here of Christ as a pre-existent hypostasis, the Logos of God; it is simply that **Christ is so much the center and focus of the gospel** that to speak of the word is to speak of Christ - the good news is Christ, particularly his crucifixion and resurrection. **It is not that he identifies Christ with the divine Logos of Hellenistic Judaism or Stoicism** and goes on from that to **identify Christ, the Logos with the word** [logos] **of preaching;** it is rather that Christ is the heart and substance of the kerygma [preaching], not so much as the Word, **as the word preached"** (p. 231).

Concerning the question, "Did Jesus, 'the **last Adam** '*(I Cor. 15:45-47)*, exist before the first Adam?,*" Dunn says, *"Quite the contrary, for Paul makes it abundantly clear that Christ is **second**. Christ is not prior to Adam, either temporally or logically - **he comes after Adam, he is the last Adam**. Here in fact Paul deliberately and decisively distances himself from any potentially gnostic concept of redemption, for where the **logic** of Gnosis is that the redeemer must be first, Paul's logic is quite different. **Where Philo derived his exegesis** [explanation] **from a Platonic model** applied to Gen. 1-2,...**Paul derived his exegesis from the resurrection of Christ**" (p. 124).*

Dunn's conclusion in general: *"In Matthew and Luke Jesus' divine sonship is traced back specifically to **his birth or conception**: Jesus was the Son of David by his line of descent, but more important **he was the Son of God because his conception was an act of creative power by the Holy Spirit**" (p. 61).*

*"There is **no thought** in any of the passages we have studied of Jesus existing prior to his birth whether as an angel or archangel, a spirit or the Spirit. There is **no thought** whatsoever of Jesus on earth **as the incarnation** of angel or archangel, spirit or Spirit" (p. 159).*

*"This double refusal of the N.T. writers either to identify Christ as an angel or to understood Jesus of Nazareth as the incarnation of the Spirit shows us **just how far first-century Christology** is from both the speculation of **second - and third-century** Jewish Christianity and those of some more orthodox **patristic** [early Church Fathers] theology"* (p. 162).

*"In the early stages of this development at any rate it would be inaccurate to say that Christ was understood as **a pre-existent being become incarnate**, or that Christ himself was thought to have been present and active in creation"* (p. 211).

The One Exception, John. But professor Dunn and other trinitarian scholars who acknowledge the truth of the foregoing statements, think they see **one exception**, that is in the writings of the apostle John. Consider Dunn's following statements regarding John 1:1-14:

*"Here we have an explicit statement of incarnation, **the first, and indeed only such statement** in the New Testament"* (p. 241).

*"Here indeed we have a doctrine of incarnation clearly formulated. In short as the first century of the Christian era **drew to a close** we find a concept of Christ's real pre-existence **beginning to emerge, but only with the Fourth Gospel** can we speak of a full blown conception of Christ's personal pre-existence and a **clear doctrine of incarnation"** (p. 258).

"...only in the post-Pauline period [after Paul] *did a clear understanding of Christ as having pre-existed with God before his ministry on earth emerge, **and only in the Fourth Gospel** can we speak of a doctrine of the incarnation"* (p. 259).

But Professor Dunn has his own doubts and warns us before he makes these statements:

*"There is of course always the possibility that '**popular pagan superstition**' became **popular Christian superstition**, by a **gradual assimilation** and spread of belief at the level of popular piety; **we must beware** of assuming that all **developments in Christian thought** stem from the Pauls and the Johns of Christianity."* (p. 251) [29]

Some scholars believe that when John wrote his *"prologue,"* he drew from an earlier *"logos poem."* Alluding to this Dunn says correctly:

> *"But if we translated **logos** as **'God's utterance'** instead, it would become clearer that the poem did not necessarily intend the Logos in verses 1-13 to be thought of as a personal divine being"* (p. 243).

The Southern Baptist theologian Millard J. Erickson, himself a trinitarian, says of the apostle John: *"**He is, for example, the only Gospel writer to clearly identify the Son as divine.**"* Calling the prologue [introduction] to John's Gospel, *(John 1:1-14)*, *"one of the most theologically pregnant of all biblical passages,"* Erickson writes:

> *"The issue of the paradoxical relationship of the **Son** (or "Word") to the Father is faced immediately in 1:1: 'In the beginning was the Word, and the Word was with God, and the Word was God.' **Here is the seeming contradiction of the Word being God, and yet not being God.**"* [30]

Please study the above statement carefully. The reason John 1:1 seems contradictory to Professor Erickson is, in his mind he has substituted *"Son"* for *"Word"* before he even quotes the verse. The word **"Son"** is not in John 1:1, in fact it does not occur in John's prologue until verse **fourteen**! (More about this later).

We are alerted to error by the fact that many trinitarian scholars admit that the *"incarnation"* of Christ as *"the Word"* **occurs only in the writings of John**. The *International Standard Bible Encyclopedia* says of *"Word"* as a title for Christ, *"**In the New Testament this seems to be confined to the writings of John.**"* They continue:

> *"The Johannine doctrine would seem to relate closely to the Old Testament concepts of the creative **word** of God.... The author may well have been influenced also by developments in later Jewish thought, especially the personification or hypostatization of Sophia (Wisdom) and Torah (Law). Early*

> *Christian usage of 'the word' as a technical term for the*
> *gospel may also have facilitated the identification of Christ*
> *as the logos. Dependence on Philo has sometimes been*
> *suggested, but close examination of the parallels shows*
> *that the differences between John's 'logos' and that of*
> *Philo are substantial, and most scholars today think direct*
> *Philonic influence unlikely."* [31]

For additional context in which to consider John 1:1-14 (the Prologue) we should look at the words of the renowned trinitarian Bible scholar James Hastings. Writing in his respected work *Hastings' Dictionary of the Bible* he says:

> *"Some have held that John's Logos doctrine was derived*
> *entirely from the Judaeo-Alexandria philosophy, and*
> *specifically from the teaching of Philo. From early times*
> *there had grown up among the Greeks a conception of the*
> *Logos as the Divine Reason manifested in the universe,*
> *and explaining how God comes into relation with it. To this*
> *Logos philosophy Plato's doctrine of ideas had contributed,*
> *and afterwards the Stoic view of the Logos as the rational*
> *principle of the universe. In his efforts to blend Judaism*
> *with Hellenism, Philo adopted the term as one familiar*
> *alike to Jews and Greeks.... St. John cannot have derived*
> *his doctrine of the Logos from Philo. But he undoubtedly*
> *used the term because Philo had made it familiar to Greco*
> *- Jewish thought as a means of expressing the idea of a*
> *mediation between God and the universe."* [32]

My comment at this point is, I agree with Hastings, except I do not believe that the apostle John followed Philo (and Plato) if he actually did use the word *"logos"* (more on this later). Hastings continues:

> *"We must bear in mind that while the term 'Logos' was a*
> *new one to be applied to Christ, the place of dignity and*
> *power assigned to Him by John was by no means new. The*

*attempt has been made to distinguish between **the Logos doctrine of the Prologue** as **Hellenic**, and **the Gospel** itself as **Palestinian**; and it has been maintained that the influence of the Logos idea does not extend beyond the Prologue, and that it was merely intended to introduce to Greek readers the story of the Jewish Messiah with a view to making it more attractive and intelligible. **It is true that when we pass beyond the Prologue the word 'Logos' is not repeated. The author** [John] **nowhere puts it into the mouth of Jesus**."*

Please be patient and study these statements closely, as we will soon look at them in the light of Holy Scripture and come to clear biblical conclusions. Look at this final statement from Hastings:

*"**From the time of Justin** (circa 160 A.D.), **and ever since**, the Logos doctrine of St. John's prologue has served as the material of many a Christian metaphysic* [philosophy]. *It is no doubt inevitable that this should be the case; but **we must be careful not to make St. John responsible for the theological constructions that have been woven out of his words**. If an injustice is done him when his doctrine of the Logos is supposed to be nothing more than the fruitage of his study of Philo, **another injustice is committed** when it is assumed that he is setting forth here **a metaphysic of the Divine nature** or **a philosophy of the Incarnation**. It is plain, on the contrary, that in all he says, it is the religious and ethical interests that are paramount. He uses the Logos conception for **two great purposes** - to set forth Jesus (1) **as the Revealer of God**, and (2) **as the Savior of men**."* [33]

Sorting It Out

In this and the preceding chapters we have looked at statements from encyclopedias, historians, and trinitarian scholars, credible sources that can help us understand how Christianity has arrived at its erroneous doctrine about God: doctrine that preaches God as one-third of who He is, that preaches Christ to the exclusion of the Father, and gives the awesome Creator's glory to His virgin-born, human Son. It is time to sort out what we have seen and come to some biblically sound conclusions.

We learned in this chapter of Philo Judaeus, a man of gifts, talents and influence. A man who instead of using his God-given gifts to help prepare the world for the imminent birth of God's Messiah, yielded to a demon spirit and in the *"heat of divine possession,"* brought darkness rather than light, error rather than truth, and confusion rather than clarity. Remember Professor Dunn's warning that *"in Philo's writings we have to pay special heed to a context of thought which is **strange** and **difficult**...**strained** and at times **confusing** or even **contradictory**... ."* No such caution has ever been needed regarding men who write under the inspiration of the Holy Spirit.

Philo's greatest legacy of error to mankind is his promotion of the doctrine of the *"divine Logos."* He learned of the Logos from his study of Greek philosophy *(Heraclitus, Socrates, Plato, and the Stoics)* and became obsessed with it. He mentioned the *"Logos"* or *"divine Logos"* over 1300 times *(Dunn says 1400)* in his voluminous writings, calling it a *"person,"* the *"divine intermediary between God and the world,"* *"the first-begotten of God by the virgin Wisdom,"* *"His* (God's) *chief messenger,"* (God's) *"ambassador,"* the *"judge and mediator who is called 'angel,'"* *"the interpreter and prophet of God,"* *"the ruler and steersmen of all,"* *"God's firstborn who holds the eldership among the angels,"* and *"the second God, who is his Logos."* When he calls the Logos the *"firstborn Son, who shall take upon him its government like some viceroy of a great king,"* he is not referring to Jesus Christ. He was born twenty years before Christ, in Alexandria, Egypt, some 350 miles from Jerusalem, **and never in his life heard of Jesus.** He was about fifty years old when Jesus began his ministry in Galilee and was already a famous Hellenistic Jewish writer, impacting the world with his doctrines. As Erickson says of the concept of the divine Logos, *"It was found in **later** Judaism and Stoicism, **and through the influence of Philo it had become a fashionable cliche"*** **before Christ.** *(God In Three Persons; p. 43).*

Did Philo Influence John Of Galilee?

We learned in a previous chapter that Galilee in the Holy Land was the least Hellenized place in the Western world. They fought it fiercely, some even to the death. God must surely have chosen to birth His new movement there for this reason.

John the beloved apostle was a son of Galilee. Along with Peter and James, he was a poorly educated fisherman when Jesus called him to be a fisher of men. The high priest and his religious council according to Acts chapter four, *"saw the boldness of Peter and John, and perceived that they were unlearned and ignorant men" (v. 13).* John and Jesus spoke the language of Galilee, Aramaic, not Greek. Listen to the noted writer Philip Yancey:

> *"Speaking the common language of **Aramaic** in a slipshod way was a telltale sign of Galilean roots. The **Aramaic** words preserved in the Gospels **show that Jesus too, spoke in that northern dialect,** no doubt encouraging skepticism about him."* [34]

In What Language Did John The Apostle Write?

Before we go further with our study of whether John was influenced by Philo when he wrote the first fourteen verses of his gospel, we should attempt to answer the question as to in what language John wrote. This answer should go a long way toward establishing that this influence on John did not exist. I will make a statement at this point that cannot be successfully refuted. **There is no one on this planet who can prove that John ever took pen in hand and wrote the word *"logos."***

No copies of John's original gospel are known to have survived to the present. The oldest fairly complete manuscripts of the New Testament, including John, in existence today are Codex Siniaticus and Codex Vaticanus, and date to about 350 A.D. [35] They are both written in Greek. There is a fragment of John, also in Greek, that measures about two and a half by three and a half inches, containing five verses from chapter eighteen, that scholars have dated to about 150 A.D. [36] Since it is commonly believed that John wrote his gospel between 85 and 90 A.D., (some scholars place it before 70 A.D.), it went through several copying's and possibly more than one translation before the making of the copies now in existence.

John probably wrote in the language best known by him, Aramaic. The Old Testament was written in Hebrew. Modern Hebrew, the language spoken in Israel today, is similar to biblical Hebrew, with the addition of new words, such as telephone and automobile, and some changes in syntax. Aramaic, although a different language from biblical Hebrew, is also similar in that it uses the same alphabet, but much of the vocabulary and syntax are different.

Dr. Thomas McCall, Th. D., a noted theologian and authority on biblical languages, in his work, *The Language of The Gospel,* writes of the transition of the Jewish people from the Hebrew of the Old Testament to the Aramaic of New Testament times:

> *"The Jewish people learned to speak Aramaic in Babylon during the Babylonian captivity. The Book of Daniel illustrates this transition. The first part of the Book of Daniel was written in Hebrew, but as Daniel began to explain the prophetic dream of King Nebuchadnezzar, he switched to Aramaic. The next several chapters of Daniel...were written in Aramaic, and then the final chapters reverted to Hebrew. When the Jewish people returned to Israel, they carried back with them the language they had learned in Babylon. Hebrew was used in the synagogue when the Scriptures were read, but **the language of the street was Aramaic**. This continued through the time of **Christ**, and it is probable that **the language He most frequently used was the common Aramaic**."* Again Dr. McCall refers to *"the language of Aramaic that Jesus and most of the people of Israel in His time spoke."*

Regarding the Aramaic of the Gospel of John, Dr. McCall cites as an example John 19:13, 17:

> *"...in a place that is called the Pavement, but in the **Hebrew**, Gabbatha...in a place that is called the place of a skull, which is called in the **Hebrew** Golgotha."*

He says, *"Both Gabbatha and Golgotha are clearly **Aramaic** words, but John calls them Hebrew."* He explains that *"Aramaic had, by Jesus' day, become so identified with the Jewish people that it was commonly referred to as 'Hebrew,' as it is in the New Testament."* [37]

Concerning the language in which the Gospel of John is written, Professor Barry D. Smith of Crandall University states:

> *"The author seems to have written his gospel in **Aramaic** or a very Semitic type of Greek. The following is a list of grammatical features of John that most scholars agree suggest that the text is translated **Aramaic** or bears the influence of an author who **thought in Aramaic** but wrote in Greek."*

Smith then lists six distinct Aramaic - Hebrew features of the Gospel of John which lead him to the following conclusion:

> ***"These linguistic data suggest that the author's mother tongue was not Greek, but Aramaic."*** [38]

So, it is likely that the apostle John wrote his gospel in the Aramaic language. Therefore he would not have used the Greek word *"logos"* in John 1:1, but rather the Aramaic word *"memra."* This would match **the extensive use of "memra" in some of the Targums,** or Aramaic translations of the Old Testament (the Jerusalem Targum, the Palestinian Targum, etc.), commonly used in John's day by those Jews who spoke Aramaic. In reference to this, Martin McNamara, in his book *"Targum and Testament"* writes:

> *"....it is legitimate to assume that **John is very much under the influence of the targums** in the formulation of **his** doctrine of the Logos."* [39]

John Gill in his, *Exposition of the Entire Bible,* at John 1:1, indicates that the meaning of John 1:1 is based on the meaning of *"memra" from the Targums* **rather than from the writings of Plato or his followers.** Gill further states that it is much more probable that **Plato got his idea of the *"Logos"* from the *"memra"* of the Old Testament,** rather than supposing that John's ideas in John 1:1 **were derived from Plato.** The general meaning of the Aramaic word *"memra"* is *"speech," "utterance,"* or *"word."*

The *Pulpit Commentary,* a well known and widely used commentary says of these meanings:

> *"The New Testament writers never use the term* [logos] *to denote reason, or thought, or self consciousness, but always denote by it **speech, utterance, or word**..."* [40]

Notice how use of *"word"* or *"utterance"* in John 1:1 corresponds to the use of *"memra"* (speech, utterance) in Genesis chapter one in the Targum *(Aramaic translation).* In Genesis 1:3, the Targum reads, *"and there was light according to the decree of his memra."* Verses 3, 7, 9, 11, 15, 24 and 30 of the Targum read, *"and it was so according to his memra."* In many other places throughout the Old Testament, the word *"memra"* is used in the Targum for God's word, utterance or speech.

So it is possible, even likely, that John wrote in his common language the Aramaic word *"memra,"* and never in his life penned the Greek word *"logos."* **This of course makes moot** the discussion by some Christian scholars as to **why John chose to use "logos", a word that had already been given a meaning that is foreign to the Old Testament, the teachings of Jesus, and the writings of all of the New Testament writers.**

Trinitarian scholars Roger Olson and Christopher Hall, writing in their book, *The Trinity,* struggle with this possible use of the word *"logos"* in John 1:1, 14:

> *"How could the logos become a human being? **John wisely does not attempt to explain how such could be the***

case. *Apart from the events of the gospel narrative itself, **John would never have pictured God in such a complex manner***" (p. 7).

John As The Only Witness

We noted in a previous chapter that the Bible does not permit truth to be established by only one witness. Yet trinitarian scholars (Dunn, Erickson, Richardson, Bromiley, Hastings, encyclopedias, etc.) readily admit that John is the only clear witness to Jesus being the *"pre-existent Word."* The following Scriptures prove that God would not have allowed such a profound doctrine as that to be established by **only one witness**.

*"One witness shall not rise up...: at the mouth of **two witnesses**, or at the mouth of **three witnesses**, shall the matter be established"* [Moses speaking] *(Deut. 19:15).*

*"But if he will not hear thee, then take with the one or two more, that in the mouth of **two** or **three witnesses** every word may be established"* [Jesus speaking] *(Matt. 18:16).*

*"In the mouth of **two** or **three witnesses** shall every word be established"* [Paul speaking] *(II Cor. 13:1).*

Even Jesus Messiah himself was not permitted to establish truth **alone** without a witness. Notice his words as recorded by **John** in John 5:31-32, 37:

*"**If I bear witness of myself, my witness is not true.** There is **another** that beareth **witness** of me...the **Father himself,** which hath sent me, hath borne witness of me."* (Note: The Father is *"another"* than Jesus).

Jesus dealt with this issue again in John 8:16-18:

*"And yet if I judge, my judgement is true: for I am not alone, but **I** and **the Father** that sent me. It is also written in your law, that the testimony of **two** men is true. I am **one***

that bears witness of myself, **and the Father** *that sent me b>bereth witness of me."* (Note: This argument from Jesus would make no sense if he and the Father were **one person**).

So, John simply cannot be the only biblical witness that Jesus is the pre-existent *"Word of God"* incarnate. That could only be accepted as truth if there were one or two more clear scriptural witnesses. Of course there are none to be found!

If John Wrote The Word "Logos"

It has been over nineteen hundred years since John wrote his gospel, and again no original manuscripts of his are known to be in existence; therefore no one knows for sure if he wrote *"logos"* in his prologue. However, if he did, he for sure did not follow Socrates, Plato, and Philo in their Greek philosophic meaning of the word. That fact we have proven! Whichever word he used, *"memra"* or *"logos,"* he meant *utterance, speech, word.* Here are **three witnesses** from the Bible that prove it.

> *"By the* **word of the Lord** *were the heavens made; and all the host of them by the* **breath of his mouth**...*For* **he spoke**, *and it was done"* (Psalms 33:6, 9). Note: *"In the* **beginning God created**..." *(Gen. 1:1).* "*And* **God said**...*"* *(v. 3, 6, 9, 11, 14, 20, 24).*

> *"Through faith we understand that the worlds were framed by the* **word of God**" [something said] *(Heb. 11:3).*

> *"By the* **word of God**, *the heavens were of old, and the earth..." (II Peter 3:5).*

Every other verse in the Bible endorses the fact that John meant this:

> *"In the beginning* [some certain beginning] *was the word* [something said], *and the* **something said** *was with God, and the* **something said** *was God"* [the breath of His mouth] *(John 1:1).*

374

Remember the statement by the **trinitarian**, Professor James Dunn:

> *"But if we translated **logos** as **God's utterance** instead, it would become clearer that the poem* [John's Prologue] *did not necessarily intend the **Logos** in verses 1-13 **to be thought of as a personal divine being**."* [41]

If we make *"Word"* the pre-existent *being* of Greek philosophy, rather than God's utterance, the *"breath of His mouth" (Ps. 33:6)*, we create for ourselves many dilemmas. Listen to **trinitarian** Millard Erickson:

> **"Here is the seeming contradiction of the Word being God, and yet not being God."** [42]

My friend, the importance of understanding John 1:1 cannot be overstated. Because, upon a misunderstanding and misinterpretation of this verse a huge doctrinal structure has been built for 1700 years that is without foundation, and God is about to bring it down. Without inserting the Greek Logos into John 1:1, Christianity has no basis for its doctrine of the Trinity. Listen again to Professor Erickson:

> *"We would **seem to have** in this **one verse** possibly the strongest intimation* ["a hint; indirect suggestion"] *of the **Trinity** found anywhere in Scripture."* He continues, *"however, there are several other places where **at least subconsciously John appears to be wrestling** with issues that **eventually led the church to formulate the doctrine of the Trinity."*** [43] **Wow!** To put it in the vernacular, *"Go figure."*

Understanding John 1:3

But you may ask, if *"Word"* (properly "word") in John 1:1 is not a person, but *"God's utterance, the breath of His mouth,"* why does the KJV in verse three say:

> *"All things were made by **him**; and without **him** was not any thing made that was made."* (We addressed this briefly in a previous chapter).

That is a valid question and this is the truthful answer. In 1526 William Tyndale did the first translation of the New Testament from Greek into English. (For his labor he was burned at the stake by the Roman Catholic Church). Including his, there were at least ten Greek to English or Latin to English translations done by various translators, **before** the King James in 1611. Of these, **eight** (including Tyndale) rendered John 1:3, *"By it all things were made. Without it nothing was made."* **One**, the *Coverdale Bible* of 1550 says *"the same"* rather than *"it."* **None of these nine say *"him."***

In 1582 Gregory Martin did a Latin to English translation, the *Roman Catholic Douay-Rheims* version, in which he became the first to render John 1:3, *"All things were made by **him**."* When the King James translators, themselves trinitarians, approached John 1:3, although the Greek does not say this, they followed Martin and rendered it, *"All things were made by **him**."* This mistaken translation caused people to believe that the *"Son of God"* created the universe and was also *"God,"* causing the confusion that we have been dealing with throughout the pages of this book. From Tyndale's translation in 1526 until today, there have been at least **fifty notable translations** that did not follow Douay and the KJV in their serious error. Study carefully the following translations:

1. *"All things were made by **it**"* (Tyndale, 1526)
2. *"The worde...All things were made by **the same**"* (Coverdale, 1535)
3. *"All things were made by **it** and without **it** nothing was made"* (Matthews' Bible, 1537)
4. *"All things were made by **it** and without **it** was made nothing that was made"* (The Great Bible, 1539)
5. *"All things were made by **it**"* (Taverner NT, 1540)
6. *"All things were made by **it**"* (Whittingham, 1557)
7. *"All things were made by **it**"* (The Geneva Bible, 1560)
8. *"All things were made by **it**"* (Bishops' Bible, 1568)
9. *"All things were made by **it**"* (Tomson NT, 1607)
10. *"Nor can anything be produced that has been made without **it** [Reason]"* (John LeClerc, 1701)
11. *"The word...through **the same** all things were made"* (Mortimer, 1761)

376

12. *"In the beginning was Wisdom...All things were made by **it**"* (Wakefield NT, 1791)

13. *"The Word...All things were made by **it**"* (Alexander Campbell, founder of the Church of Christ, 1826)

14. *"The Word...All things were formed by **it**"* (Dickinson, A New and Corrected Version of the NT, 1833)

15. *"All things were made by **it**"* (Barnard, 1847)

16. *"Through **it** [the logos] everything was done"* (Wilson, Emphatic Diaglott, 1864)

17. *"All things through **it** arose into being"* (Folsom, 1869)

18. *"All things were made through **it**"* (Sharpe, Revision of the Authorized English Version, 1898)

19. *"All things were made by the Love **thought**"* (Goddard, 1916)

20. *"All things came into being in this God-conception and apart from **it** came not anything into being that came into being"* (Overbury, 1925)

21. *"All came into being through **it**"* (Knoch, 1926)

22. *"The word...the living expression of the Father's **thought**"* (Blount, Half Hours with John's Gospel, 1930)

23. *"The word was god"* (C.C. Torrey, The Four Gospels, 1933)

24. *"Through the **divine reason** all things came into being"* (Wade, The Documents of the NT Translated, 1934)

25. *"Without **it** nothing created sprang into existence"* (Johannes Greber, 1937)

26. *"**It** was in the beginning with God, by **its** activity all things came into being"* (Martin Dibelius, The Message of Jesus Christ, translated by F.C. Grant, 1939)

27. *"Through **its** agency all things came into being and apart from **it** has not one thing come to be"* (William Temple, Archbishop of Canterbury, Readings from St. John's Gospel, 1939)

28. *"The **energizing mind** was in existence from the very beginning"* (Crofts, The Four Gospels, 1949)

29. *"First there was the **Thought** and the **Thought** was in God...He, him"* (Hoare, Translation from the Greek, 1949)

30. *"At the beginning God expressed Himself. That **personal expression,** that word...ee"* (J.B. Philips, NT in Modern English, 1958)

31. *"All was done through **it**"* (Tomanek, 1958)

32. *"The Word was the **life principle** [in creation]"* (William Barclay, NT, 1969)

33. *"This **same idea** was at home with God when life began...He"* (Jordan, Cottonpatch Version, 1970)

34. *"All things became what they are through the Word"* (Dale, NT, 1973)

35. *"Within the Word was life"* (Edington, 1976)

36. *"**It** was his last werd. Ony **it** come first"* (Gospels in Scouse, 1977)

37. *"By **it** everything had being, and without **it** nothing had being"* (Schonfield, The Original NT, 1985)

38. *"All things were made through the Word"* (Inclusive Language Lectionary, 1986)

39. *"In the beginning was the Plan of Yahweh. All things were done according to **it**"* (Hawkins, Book of Yahweh, 1987)

40. *"All things happened through **it**"* (Gaus, Unvarnished NT, 1991)

41. *"In the beginning was the divine word and wisdom...everything came to be by means of **it**"* (Robert Miller, The Complete Gospels, Annotated Scholars' Version, 1992)

42. *"All things were made through the Word"* (Throckmorton, 1992)

43. *"In the beginning there was the divine word and wisdom, everything came into being by means of **it**"* (Robert Funk, The Five Gospels, 1993)

44. *"All things were made by the Word"* (NT in the Inclusive Language Bible, 1994)

45. *"Through the Word all things came into being"* (Inclusive NT, 1994)

46. *"All things came into being through the Word"* (Gold, NT and Psalms, 1995)

47. *"In the beginning was the **message**, through **it** all things were done"* (Daniels, The Four Gospels: A Non-Ecclesiastical NT, 1996)

48. *"All things through God were made"* (VanCleef, 1999)

49. *"That word of God was God...God's way of **speaking** and **acting**"* (Beck, NT, 2001)

50. *"In the beginning was the Word or the **expression** of divine Logic"* (Zeolla, Analytical-Literal Translation of the NT, 2001)

51. *"Nothing but God, and all that He means existed in the beginning of absolutely everything. There was no possible way to separate God from His meaning, for only by His meaning can He be identified as God. God's **intentions** and **purposes** existed with Him from the very beginning of everything. God, through His **intentions** and **purposes** created everything that has, or has had, existence in all of time"* (Junkins, A Fresh Parenthetical Version of the NT, 2002) [44]

The foregoing are fifty-one credible witnesses that the apostle John did not believe the *"word"* to be a person, the *"incarnate"* Son of God. With this in mind we are able to read what he wrote in verse fourteen with clear understanding.

> *"And the word-memra-logos* [utterance, speech, something said] *was made flesh* [Jesus]*, and dwelt among us, (and we beheld his glory, the glory as of the only begotten of the Father), full of grace and truth."* **What God said became flesh!**

John for sure did not write nor intend for us to believe that:

> *"In **eternity past** was the **Son**, and the **Son** was with God, and the **Son** was God."* **That is not what he says!**

Not only in John but throughout the New Testament there is no pre-existing Son. God spoke in Old Testament times *"unto the fathers by the prophets"* *(Heb. 1:2)*, not by a Son. Angels of God were not instructed to worship the Son until he was *"brought forth into the world" (Heb. 1:6)*. In reality there was no Son of God until that time, because the *"Son"* of God was to be a descendant of David *(II Sam. 7:14-16)*. Yes, Jesus Christ is the supernaturally conceived, virgin-born, sinless Son of God; savior, redeemer, Messiah, and the destined one-thousand-year ruler of planet Earth. But he never claimed to be *"God,"* or the pre-existent second person of a triune God that moved into the womb of Mary and came forth impersonating a baby. Neither did his chosen Apostles and the inspired Bible writers claim this for him. Listen to his apostle Peter to whom the *"Father which is in heaven"* had given special revelation on this subject:

> *"Thou art that **Christ** [Messiah], the Son of the living God"* *(John 6:69).*

> *"Christ...who verily was **foreordained** [Note: not "pre-existent"] before the foundation of the world, but was manifest in these last times for you..." (I Peter 1:19-20).*

Every other verse in the Bible is a witness to this truth, and these statements by Peter never were corrected or amended by Jesus, John, Paul or any other writer of Holy Scripture.

Conclusion

Based on these biblical as well as historical facts, it is time for Christianity to acknowledge the pagan origins of its doctrines of the Trinity and the Incarnation, repent, and purge itself of these demon-inspired and promoted teachings that diminish the work that Jesus did of condemning *"sin in the flesh,"* and rob God our Father of the glory He deserves and demands!

Listen to the *Harper Collins Encyclopedia of Catholicism* on Incarnation:

> *"This **notion** can be understood to refer to the moment when **God became a human being** at the conception of Jesus in his mother, Mary."* [45]

The pagan origins of *"incarnation"* through the divine Logos doctrine are stated well by historian Will Durant:

> *"Philo's Logos was one of the most influential ideas in the history of thought. Its antecedents [to precede] in **Heraclitus, Plato**, and the **Stoics** are **obvious**. Philo was a contemporary of Christ; he apparently never heard of him; **but he shared unknowingly in forming Christian theology."** [46]

Also by Professor Simon Blackburn:

> *"Philo allowed himself allegorical interpretations of the Judaic scriptures, bringing their message as closely as possible into harmony with this version of the* **Platonic** *world view.* **Platonism** *thereby became the* **background philosophical underpinning** *of the theologies of the monotheistic religions."* [47]

And in these shocking statements in the *Global Encyclopedia*:

> *"***Incarnation denotes the embodiment of a deity in human form.*** The idea occurs frequently in mythology. In ancient times, certain kings and priests, were often thought to be divinities. In Hinduism, Vishnu* [the second person of the Hindu trinity] *is believed to have taken nine incarnations. For Christians, the incarnation is a central dogma referring to the belief that the* **eternal Son of God**, *the second person of the Trinity, became man in the person of Jesus Christ.* **The incarnation was defined as a doctrine only after long struggles by early church councils.** *The Council of Nicea (325) defined* **the deity of Christ...**; *the Council of Constantinople (381) defined* **the full humanity of the incarnate Christ...**; *and the Council of Chalcedon (451) defined* **the two natures of Christ,** *divine and human" (Vol. 11; p. 73).*

I once was blind but now I see.

Glory to God in the highest!

*"We have observed that the specific metaphysical vehicle used to express **the classical doctrine of the Trinity** as originally formulated was a **Greek metaphysics** that was viable in that time but no longer makes a great deal of sense to most persons today. While it is customary to assume that the **major philosophical influence** on the Greek [church] fathers was **Plato** and the **Stoics,** [Michael] Durrant believes the influence of **Aristotle** should not be overlooked."*

Millard J. Erickson

Southern Baptist trinitarian scholar

Chapter Thirteen

The Church Fathers, Constantine and Nicea

*"**Steps to the Trinity**: The first is the identification of the preexistent Christ with the **Logos of Greek philosophy**. (2) **Origen's** doctrine of **eternal generation** of the Son. (3) The victory at Nicea of the **Athanasian formula 'of the same substance'"** (Trinitarian Dr. W.A. Brown; Outline of Christian Theology).*

*"The intelligent study of Christianity is impossible without knowledge of **Greek and Roman religion**. We generally assume that there is an unbroken line of continuity between the religion of the Jews and our own, **and there is none between paganism and Christianity. But the opposite is the truth**" (Trinitarian William Inge; Lay Thoughts of A Dean).*

*"**No responsible New Testament scholar would claim that the doctrine of the Trinity was taught by Jesus**, or preached by the earliest Christians, or consciously held by any writer of the N.T. It was in fact **slowly worked out** in the course of the **first few centuries** in an attempt to give an intelligible doctrine of God" (Trinitarian Professor A.T. Hanson; The Image Of The Invisible God).*

*"It must be admitted by everyone who has the rudiments of an historical sense that **the doctrine of the Trinity formed no part of the original message**. St. Paul did not know it, and would have been unable to understand the meaning of the terms used in the theological formula **on which the Church***

ultimately agreed." *(Trinitarian Dr. W.R. Matthews; God in Christian Experience).*

"*While it is customary to assume that the major philosophical influence on the Greek* [church] *fathers was Plato and the Stoics,* [Michael] *Durrant believes the influence of Aristotle should not be overlooked.*" *(Trinitarian Professor Millard J. Erickson; God In Three Persons).*

"*We will be disappointed if we expect to find developed trinitarian reflection in the early post-apostolic writers. It is simply not there. More time will be needed for the implications of early Christian thought and practice to ferment and mature. Thus, church historians and theologians often begin their treatment of the doctrine of the Trinity with the second century apologists.*" *(Trinitarians Roger Olson and Christopher Hall; The Trinity).*

$\mathcal{S}$ince we have proven conclusively in previous chapters, through Scripture, history and quotes from trinitarian scholars that Jesus and his chosen ministers of the first century knew nothing of a Trinity or an Incarnation, we will proceed to the end of the first, and then to the second century A.D. for understanding as to how Christianity came to embrace these errors. As has been noted earlier, humanity, aided by the "master deceiver," **has a tendency to go toward paganism and erroneous doctrine.** Jude wrote his epistle about 66 A.D., some thirty-three years after the birth of the Church, but he was already pleading for a return to *"the faith which was once delivered unto the saints" (v. 3).* Paul wrote II Thessalonians about 54 A.D., but he warned of a *"falling away"* from Christian doctrine that had already begun in his day *(2:3-12).* John wrote Revelation about 96 A.D., but to five out of the seven Christian churches addressed, the message from God through Jesus was *"repent."* Repent of what? False doctrines! Although these churches were commended for many good works, and by God's grace given awesome promises, they were scolded severely for embracing false doctrines! Notice the *"doctrine of Balaam" (2:14)*, the *"doctrine of the Nicolaitans" (2:15)*, and the *"doctrine of Jezebel" (2:20, 24)*. It is shocking to see that one of these churches, Pergamas, was so taken over by false doctrine that Satan had his own *"seat"* [throne] and dwelt there *(2:13)*. **And God hated these doctrines** *(2:6, 15)*! We do not know how long He had tolerated these devilish intrusions, but perhaps in His patience, a long time. Notice the warning by Jesus to Laodicea, *"I will spew thee out of my mouth" (3:16)*. I believe, as do many Bible scholars, that Laodicea is a type of modern Christianity, and its picture in Scripture is not good.

> *"So then because thou art **lukewarm**...Because thou sayest, I am rich, and increased with goods, and have need of nothing; and knowest not that thou art **wretched**, and **miserable**, and **poor**, and **blind**, and **naked**" (Rev. 3:16-17).*

And what were they commanded to do?

> *"I counsel thee to buy of me gold tried in the fire, that thou mayest be rich* [a type of God's glory]; *and white raiment, that thou mayest be clothed* [a type of God's righteousness]; *and that the shame of thy nakedness do not appear; and anoint thine eyes with eye salve* [a love for the truth] *that thou mayest see" (3:18).*

And the warning to all seven churches was:

> *"He that hath an ear, **let him hear** what the Spirit saith unto the churches."*

Here is a sobering thought to ponder. If God hated the doctrines of Balaam, the Nicolaitans, and Jezebel in these Christian churches of Asia Minor, He for sure hates the doctrines of Socrates (a pedophile), Plato (a homosexual), Philo (an errant Jew), and Constantine (a pagan emperor), that are found in modern Christianity, world-wide. (Note: The reference helps in the *Scofield* Bible say of Revelation 2:13: *"Pergamas, the church settled down in the world, **'where Satan's throne is,' after the conversion of Constantine, A.D. 316")*.

These false doctrines were assimilated over several centuries by Christians, through the teachings of a group of men variously referred to as the *"church fathers," "early church fathers," "Greek church fathers,"* or the *"post-apostolic fathers."* This assimilation of error, culminated in the fourth century in the doctrines of the Incarnation and the Trinity. That is why the *Harper Collins Bible Dictionary* says, *"it is only with the fathers of the church in the **third and fourth centuries**, that a full-fledged theory of the **incarnation** develops,"* [1] and trinitarian scholar Charles C. Ryrie writes, *"In the second half of the **fourth century**, three theologians from the province of Cappadocia in eastern Asia Minor **gave definitive shape to the doctrine of the Trinity**."* [2]

Trinitarian professors Roger Olson and Christopher Hall say of the development of this doctrine:

> *"Both the practices and documents of the church **finally led** early Christian leaders to propose **a trinitarian model of God**, but the formulation of this model took place over **many years** and in many contexts. What do we find in the writings of Christian leaders during roughly the first sixty years of the **second century** A.D.? As we might expect, **we do not find the developed trinitarian language or theology that will blossom from the fourth century on**."*

They continue:

> *"The early church fathers of the **second through the fourth centuries** realized this gradually* [the need to think of God as a trinity] *as they encountered opponents of Christianity... . They found it necessary to **invent terms such as Trinitas** [Trinity] and **homoousios** [of the same substance] to describe the relationship between the Father and his Son... when confronted with heretics who denied the deity of Jesus Christ. **Heresy is the mother of orthodoxy**. The doctrine of the Trinity developed gradually **after the completion of the New Testament** in the heat of controversy, but the church*

fathers who developed it believed they were simply exegeting [explaining] *divine revelation and not at all speculating or inventing new ideas.* **The full-blown doctrine of the Trinity was spelled out in the fourth century** *at two great ecumenical councils; Nicea (325 A.D.) and Constantinople (381 A.D.)."* [3]

The Progression Of Blindness

Clement 1 Bishop of Rome *(circa 40-101 A.D.)*. Clement of Rome, not to be confused with Clement of Alexandria who lived some one-hundred years later, was the first of the ecclesiastical writers whose works have survived till today. He is considered to be the third bishop (overseer) of the Christian churches at Rome. According to the second century theologian Irenaeus, Clement was personally acquainted with St. Peter and St. Paul, but modern scholars have largely discounted this claim.

Bishop Clement, writing in the last years of the first century A.D. repeatedly refers to the Father, Son, and the Holy Spirit. He correctly links the Father to creation. He writes in I Clement 35:1-3, The *"gifts of God,"* including *"immortality, splendor in righteousness, and truth with boldness,"* find their source in the *"Creator and Father of the Ages."* It is through *"his beloved servant Jesus Christ"* that *"the Creator of the universe"* keeps the elect of God *"intact" (I Clement 59:2).* In I Clement 16:2, he describes Jesus as the Creator's *"servant,"* the *"majestic scepter of God, our Lord Jesus Christ."*

But, in I Clement 42:1-4 and 46:6 he strikingly **joins together** the Father, Son, and Holy Spirit, and **groups** Father, Son, and Spirit in the context of mission and calling. Trinitarians Olson and Hall write:

> *"It is texts such as these that Basil the Great (circa 360) will later **recall** and **develop** in his own **trinitarian reflection**. In the late first century then, we have a Christian bishop **sprinkling nuggets of trinitarian ore** throughout his writing that will **later be mined and purified**."* [4] [In the Old West this was called *"salting the mine with ore"* to

make it appear that a vein of gold is there, when in reality it is not! Question: Why did Basil not mine the texts of Matthew, John, Peter, and Paul for *"nuggets of trinitarian ore?"* Because they are not there!].

Olson and Hall add:

> *"At this early stage in the tradition I Clement contains statements with startling **trinitarian implications. Firmer trinitarian affirmations will come later.**"* [5]

Ignatius Of Antioch *(circa 50-107 A.D.)*

Ignatius was bishop of Antioch, Syria, and is considered one of the Apostolic Fathers of the Church. On his way to martyrdom in Rome during the reign of Emperor Trajan, Ignatius wrote seven letters which have survived until today, five to churches in Asia Minor, one to Polycarp bishop of Smyrna, and one to the Christians of Rome, his destination.

Regarding his beliefs about God and Christ, Olson and Hall say, *"We have the same kind of sprinkling* [of the nuggets of trinitarian ore] *in the letters of Ignatius that are found in the writings of Clement."* [6] However, Ignatius was more resolute in declaring that Jesus is *"God."* In his letter to the church at Ephesus, he writes of *"the will of the Father and of Jesus Christ **our God.**"* Later in the same letter he describes Christ *"as the mind of the Father."* He makes reference to Christ as *"both flesh and spirit, **born and unborn, god in man,** true life in death, both from Mary and from God... ."* Olson and Hall write of *"the **trinitarian implications** of his language, **seeds that will later sprout** in the thought of an Athanasius or Basil."* [7] [Remember, we learned earlier that ideas are powerful].

These references in the letters of Ignatius led Christian theologian Rudolf Bultmann to a comparison with the reticence of New Testament writers to call Jesus *"God:"* *"Ignatius on the contrary speaks of **Christ as God** as if it were a thing to be taken quite for granted."* [8]

Although Ignatius, and the church fathers that followed him in the next two centuries often called Jesus *"God,"* there is no indication that he or they meant this in an absolute sense, as they always added qualifying words (i.e., *"god/God,"* but not *"the God"*). Christian historian A.C. McGiffert insists that such evidence as calling Jesus *God, "does not mean that Ignatius identified Christ with the supreme God."* [9] But after him, the progression toward trinitarian heresy took a major step forward about 160 A.D.

The Platonism Of Justin Martyr

Justin Martyr *(110-165 A.D.)* was born to pagan parents in Flavia Neapolis, a Roman city built on the site of the ancient biblical Shechem, in Samaria, and he was probably of Roman descent. **As a young man Justin devoted himself to the study of Greek philosophy**, notably the writings of **Plato** and the **Stoics**. His study of the Old and New Testaments caused him to convert to Christianity about 133, at which time he moved to Rome and began teaching as a **Christian philosopher**. Believing that Christianity is the true philosophy, Justin sought to reconcile Christian doctrine with Greek philosophy and pagan culture, and thus corrupted it. He accepted the doctrines taught at **Alexandria, Egypt,** that God is totally transcendent and otherworldly (Plato's influence was still alive and well). He believed God is incomprehensible and unapproachable. [10] But his most detrimental effect on Christian doctrine came through his teachings regarding the Logos. The *Encyclopedia Americana* states that Justin's writings *"give an exposition of Christian teaching and a view of its relation to **Greek philosophy. Justin's Logos theology stands at the beginning of early Christian attempts to define Christ."*** [11]

Justin's Christology centered strongly on a Logos concept as he equated **Logos** with the biblical use of the word *"Son."* He embraced the Gnostic belief that the Logos - Son only preexisted as a **power** or an **attribute** of God but that it later emanated from God to become the Son of God through whom He created the universe. Though Justin believed the Logos - Son preexisted, he did not hold that it was eternal, but had a beginning.

Concerning the man Christ Jesus, Justin wrote repeatedly that he was *"God."* One of his most famous works is *Dialogue with Trypho*, which purports to be a doctrinal discussion between himself and a Jew, Trypho. In it he says, *"Now I have proved that Christ is called God."* Though he often calls Jesus *"God,"* he does not mean this in an absolute sense, as he also sometimes refers to Jesus Christ as *"another God."* (Can there be more than one God?) Justin for sure sees Christ as subordinate to the Father, as he writes that Christians are *"holding Him in second place,"* after *"the true God Himself... we give to a crucified man a place second to the unchangeable and eternal God."* [12] He says of Christ, *"the first power after God the Father and Lord of all is the Word, who is also the Son."* (This is confusion!).

Although Justin was far from the belief in a triune God, he did somehow anticipate questions that would be hotly debated in the fourth century councils, such as the *"one essence"* of the Father and the Son. Straying from reliance on the Holy Scriptures alone for doctrine, Justin ushered Christianity along on the path of confusion, and this fact was recognized even by those who later adopted his view on the Logos. Of this, Roger Olson and Christopher Hall say:

> *"Justin's tendency to speak of the Son as an 'Angel' received a much cooler reception among later fathers. He was also less successful in his willingness to refer to the Son as 'another God besides the Creator...'. Still, even if Justin occasionally swerves off the path, his willingness to listen to the church at worship, in its prayers, liturgies, and creedal confessions, generally kept him moving in the right direction. Justin seemed to realize that if the church worshiped Father, Son, and Spirit, a trinitarian model of some kind must be forthcoming, and he provided important planks in its construction."* [13]

Sadly, here again we have an example of Christianity getting its doctrine from experience, rather than from God's Holy Bible! Regrettably, Justin was beheaded during the reign of Marcus Aurelius because he refused to offer sacrifice to the pagan gods. However, he left behind a legacy tainted by error. As trinitarian James Hastings says:

> *"From the time of Justin (circa 160 A.D.), **and ever since,** the **Logos doctrine** of St. John's prologue has served as the material of many a Christian metaphysic* [philosophy]." [14]

Remember, it was Justin who taught that **Heraclitus** and **Socrates** were *"Christians, for Christ was and is the Logos who dwells in every man,"* and *"The principles of Plato are not foreign to the teaching of Christ... ."* [15] Where did he get such non-biblical notions as this? Church historian Adolph Harnack tells us in his awesome work, *History of Dogma*:

> *"The fundamental idea from which **Philo** starts is a **Platonic** one...and has nothing more in common with the Old Testament conception. Philo's philosophy of religion became operative among Christian teachers from the beginning of the second century** [this includes Justin], *and at a later period actually obtained the significance of a standard of Christian theology, Philo gaining a place among Christian writers.* It can no longer, however, be shown with certainty how far the direct influence of Philo reached, as the development of religious ideas in the **second century** took a direction which **necessarily led to views similar to those which Philo had anticipated.**"* [16]

Considering the above facts, it is fair to say that Justin, this converted Greek philosopher and lover of Plato, did a serious dis-service to every Christian who came after him in the centuries that followed.

The Platonism of Clement of Alexandria

Clement of Alexandria *(circa 150-215 A.D.)*, is thought to have been born in Athens, as that is where he received his early education, to parents who were cultured pagans of considerable means. He developed a love for **Hellenistic philosophy** and **literature**, which was to show up in his writings, even after his conversion to Christianity. Soon after this conversion he moved to **Alexandria, Egypt,** where he studied in its school of religion under Pantaenus. He himself became head of this school about 200 A.D., but when the persecution of Christians ensued some two years later, he was forced to flee. Little is known about the remainder of his life until his death *(circa 215)*, however he possibly pastored in Jerusalem and Antioch.

The reason Clement is important to our study is the part he played in leading the Church along to doctrinal error by mixing his beloved Greek philosophy with the teachings of the Christianity that he had embraced. Historian Harnack writes of this confusion in him, and says that in spite of the fact that he *"plainly called Jesus a man, and spoke of his flesh...,"* he followed *"the old undisguised Docetism which only admitted the **apparent** reality of Christ's body. Clement expressly declared that Jesus knew neither **pain**, nor **sorrow**, nor **emotions**, and **only took food** to refute* [his critics]." [17]

Olson and Hall write:

> *"Clement of Alexandria sprinkles scattered references or illusions to trinitarian considerations in both 'The Instructor' and in the 'Stromata.'"* They say he speaks of *"the protection offered by 'the power of God the Father, and the blood of **God the Son** and the dew of the Holy Spirit' in his sermon... ."* [18] And what influenced Clement's doctrinal error? Olson and Hall say, *"**Clement speaks of the Trinity as reflected in Plato's Timaeus.** "* [19] They make reference in their book to *"**Greek trinitarian doctrine**"* [20] and *"**Greek trinitarian thought,**"* [21] and these trinitarian scholars make this strong admission: *"**Very early on** in the history of theology, reflection began to focus more and more on the **immanent Trinity** as church fathers became obsessed with Greek ideas of divine perfection and impassibility."* [22]

Although Clement's writings on this subject are sometimes contradictory, here are a few statements taken from *A Dictionary of Early Christian Beliefs* that reflect his feelings:

"Others think that philosophy was introduced into life by **an evil influence,** *for the ruin of men. But I will show... that evil has an evil nature. It can never turn out to be the producer of what is good.* **This indicates that philosophy is in a sense, a work of divine providence"** *(Clement of Alexandria; circa 195 A.D.).*

*"**Greek philosophy,** as it were,* **purges the soul** *and prepares it beforehand for the reception of faith, on which the Truth builds up the edifice of knowledge" (Clement of Alexandria; circa 195 A.D.).*

*"**Philosophy** is not, then, the product of vice, since it makes men virtuous. It follows then,* **that it is the work of God"** *(Clement of Alexandria; circa 195 A.D.).*

*"**For my part, I approve of Plato...** ."* *(Clement of Alexandria; circa 195 A.D.).* [23] [And there are more such statements].

There were many *"Church Fathers"* of the second and third centuries; Irenaeus, Ignatius, Tatian, Theophilus, etc., who by departing from the teachings of Jesus and his chosen Apostles while holding on to Greek philosophy, did their part in devastating the truth. However, I will not test your patience by dealing with the errors of each of them individually.

Please consider this fact: I have found in life that while traveling on a journey, for the first few miles after a wrong turn, you are not that far from the right road to your chosen destination. But the farther you go, the greater the distance between those two roads becomes, and the more lost you are. And the more lost others are who might be following you!

Now to Sabellius. As the third century began to take shape, a large majority of Christians still believed in the one true God as a single person, the one whom Jesus called *"my Father"* and *"your Father."* But they also believed that Jesus Christ was *"God,"* only to a lesser extent. However, there was a growing fear among church leaders of a possible mixture of heathen beliefs with their established, supposedly pure, doctrine. Some Christians were concerned that their religion could become polytheistic (a belief in multiple Gods), because they identified both the Father and Jesus as *"God,"* thus suggesting two Gods.

Consequently, *"modalistic monarchianism"* (called "Oneness" today), arose during the **third century**. It was an attempt to preserve the oneness of God in the form of a strict monotheistic belief. The chief spokesman for this doctrine was Sabellius, of whom little is known, except that he was from **Alexandria, Egypt**. Sabellius held to some important features of "orthodoxy," the virgin birth, the complete humanity of Jesus, and his being God. However, he viewed God as a monad (a one person monarch) who manifests Himself in varying modes, hence the term *"modalistic."* Sabellius identified three modes, *"Father,"* *"Logos - Son,"* and *"Spirit."* He deemed these modes merely as attributes or powers that resided in the one God. Thus, while modalistic monarchians like Sabellius solidly affirmed Jesus' humanity, they either obscured the personal distinction between the Father and the Son, or denied it altogether. Therefore, they came to be known mostly for identifying Jesus Christ as the Father.

About 260 A.D., the Catholic church officially condemned this teaching, which had become known as *"Sabellianism."* Ever since, both Catholic and Protestant orthodoxy have regarded Sabellianism as one of the worst heresies in church history. This teaching has resurfaced periodically, most significantly among Pentecostal Christians in the early 1900's, of whom most referred to their doctrine as "Jesus Only." They now prefer the labels "Oneness" or "Jesus Name."

Another mistaken doctrine that most "Oneness" hold to is the idea that Jesus had two distinct natures, both human and divine. **This doctrine was brought forth by Tertullian about 200 A.D.**, and promoted by Nestorius at the Council of Ephesus *(431 A.D.)*, which condemned it as heresy. Harnack says of Tertullian, *"on the other hand we owe to him the idea of the 'two natures'." (Vol. 2; p. 275)*. I wonder if those who embrace this doctrine, realize it came from a follower of Plato, about 200 A.D.! Question: If Jesus possessed both human and divine *"natures,"* how did those who traveled with him know which one they were dealing with at any given time, and which one was speaking when he spoke. Deliver us!

Although Sabellius and his followers avoided the trap of trinitarian doctrine toward which the Church was headed in his day, they embraced a doctrine that is equally as non-biblical, and added to the confusion regarding the One Most High God and His Son, the Lord Jesus Messiah! Note: One doctrinal advantage the "Oneness" do have over the "Trinitarians" is that they historically have baptized their converts *"in the name of Jesus Christ,"* following the example set by the Apostles in Scripture. [24]

The Platonism Of Tertullian

Tertullian *(circa 160-230 A.D.)*, was born in Carthage, the son of a Roman centurion. He was educated in law and became a lawyer in Rome, where in his own words, he *"drained the cup of lust to its dregs."* He converted to Christ in mid-life *(about 195 A.D.)* and soon after became a theologian.

As much as any other church father **before** Nicea, Tertullian is credited with developing the doctrine of the Trinity, especially its peculiar language. He coined over 900 new words, including *trinitas* (Trinity) to explain his belief that God is one *substantia* (substance), manifested by three separate and distinct *personae* (persons).

Although he was no fan of Greek philosophy and spoke out against it often, he followed the trend of his day, and unwittingly did much to further its false doctrines, especially the doctrines of the *"divine Logos,"* and the pre-existence of Christ as a distinct person of God. But Tertullian did not subscribe to the *"orthodox"* teaching of the *"eternality"* of the Son, and asserted that God *"could not have been a Father before the Son,"* and *"there was a time when there was no Son."* [25] When he did err, it can likely be explained by what the historian Harnack wrote: *"Tertullian when driven into a corner"* by his doctrinal critics, **would question or set aside Scripture.** [26] Harnack continues:

> *"He profoundly influenced the later Church fathers...and through them* **all Christian theologians** *of the West. He was the first writer in Latin to formulate Christian theological concepts,* **such as the nature of the Trinity. Having no models to follow,** *he developed* **terminology derived from many sources, chiefly Greek**... *. His legal turn of mind imprinted on this* **newly minted theological language** *of the West a legalistic character* **that has never been erased."** [27]

And the *Global Encyclopedia* says:

> *"At the end of the 2nd century Tertullian asserted that God was of one substance consisting in* **three persons.** *The language, and with it the* **ambiguity of Tertullian's formula prevailed.** *It became the official creed of the church, backed by the power of the newly Christian Roman emperor Constantine at the Council of Nicea in 325 A.D.,* **that the Son is one substance with the Father.** *No matter how deep were the disagreements on detail,* **the place of Jesus within the Trinity** *became a nearly universal feature of Christian faith."* [28]

The Platonism Of Origen

Origen *(circa 185-254 A.D.)*, was born into a Christian family in **Alexandria, Egypt**. He had a Christian upbringing which made him learned in Scripture, but he also received a **pagan education**. Perhaps this fact made him, as the record shows, a very confused young man, a confusion that was to remain with him for the rest of his life. For example, as a boy of 17, he was eager to follow his father, Leonides, in martyrdom during the persecution of Christians in 202, but was prevented by his mother, who hid his clothes. At the age of 19, taking Jesus' words in Matthew 19:12 to mean physical mutilation, he castrated himself to be a eunuch. [29] But this was only the beginning of his problematic thinking.

In 204, after teaching grammar in Alexandria, he was appointed head of the religious school there by Demetrius, the bishop. He remained active as a Christian teacher in Alexandria until 230, considering himself a lay-person rather than a member of the clergy. In addition to teaching, Origen wrote dogmatic treatises and lectured in churches.

But what did he teach and write? The noted church historian, Adolph Harnack has cataloged some of the strange and erroneous beliefs of Origen in volume two of his awesome work, *A History of Dogma*. They are:

- The devil's temporary estrangement from God, and the eventual return of him and all spirits, even evil ones, to the Creator *(p. 363, 366, 377)*.
- The pre-existence of **all** souls *(p. 364)*.
- Child baptism *(p. 365)*.
- An inherent evil in sexual union, even married sex; thus he castrated himself *(p. 365)*.
- The death of Christ is to be considered as a ransom **paid to** the devil. By his successful temptation of Adam, the devil acquired a right over men. This right cannot be destroyed, **but only bought off**; therefore God offers the devil Christs' soul in **exchange** for the souls of men *(p. 367)*.
- In all ages Christianity has ultimately had two objectives, a reconciliation with God and the **deification** [to make gods] **of men** *(p. 368)*.
- That Jesus Christ is the *"God-man" (p. 369)*.
- He taught that there is a system of **numerous** mediators and intercessors with God, such as **angels** and dead and living **saints**, and believed in **appealing to them** *(p. 377)*.
- At death, unpurified souls pass into a state of punishment, *"a penal fire"* [purgatory], which is to be thought of as a place of **purification** *(p. 377)*.

Christianity since ancient times has repudiated most of these outlandish doctrines, but today over 2 billion "Christians" world-wide, both Catholic and Protestant, hold firmly to his most serious error, belief in a triune God, which Harnack refers to twice as ***"Origen's doctrine of the Trinity!"*** [30]

And how did Origen arrive at these strange and erroneous beliefs? I believe the answer can be found in what we learned at the beginning of this section, i.e., that he was raised as a **Christian** and was learned in Scripture, but he also received a **pagan education**. His teacher was Ammonius Saccas, whom Durant calls *"a Christian converted to paganism, who was attempting to reconcile Christianity and Platonism"* [39] (A *Christian* converted to *paganism?*) I am not questioning Origen's sincerity or dedication since at seventeen he wished to offer himself as a martyr, and at nineteen he castrated himself in what he thought was obedience to Christ. However, it is dangerous to mix darkness with light and error with biblical truth. The apostle Paul expresses it well in Romans:

> *"For the wrath of **God** is revealed from heaven against all ungodliness and unrighteousness of men who **suppress the truth** in unrighteousness, because that which is known about **God** is evident within them; **for God made it evident to them**. For since the creation of the world **His** invisible attributes, **His** eternal power and **divine nature**, have been **clearly seen, being understood** through what has been made, **so that they are without excuse. For even though they knew God**, they did not honor **him** as **God** or give thanks, **but they became futile in their <u>speculations</u>**, and their foolish heart was darkened" (Rom. 1:18-21 NASB).*

Please notice carefully the word *"speculations"* in the verse above. Also notice these phrases, *"For even though they knew God, they did not honor **him** as God..."* but *"became futile in their speculations... ."* Paul says in verse eighteen that he is speaking of *"**men who suppress the truth**."* Now consider what the authoritative work, *A Dictionary of Early Christian Beliefs*, says about Origen:

> *"A pupil of **Clement of Alexandria** who took over the famous* [religious] *school in Alexandria after the departure of Clement. He has been called the '**father of Christian theology.**' Origen was also the **most prolific writer** of the pre-Nicean Church, **dictating around two thousand works**.*

*Many of his teachings reflect brilliant spiritual insights. On the other hand, some of his teachings exhibit **strained or unsound** theological __speculation__.* " [Wake up Christianity! This is the man you have followed.] [31]

Trinitarians Roger Olson and Christopher Hall say much the same things about Origen in their book, *The Trinity:*

*"Origen **sometimes strays in his musings** and constructions, **but his contributions to trinitarian thinking cannot be ignored**" (p. 24). "And yet Origen is not always successful or **consistent** in his attempt to **make sense of the nature of the Son and his relationship to the Father**" (p. 24). "Origen **fails to explain adequately** how there can be this kind of **proportionality within the shared divine nature** of Father, Son and Spirit, appearing to be **trapped by his Platonic background. Origen's thinking on the Holy Spirit is also a mixed bag**" (p. 25). "Origen serves as an apt model, perhaps because of **his creative, innovative mind**, of the **struggle** of the fathers **to say enough about the Trinity, but not too much**. At times he seems to violate his own advice. **He rightly observes,** 'human thought cannot apprehend how the **unbegotten God** becomes the Father of the only-begotten Son,' a **generation** Origen describes as 'eternal' and 'ceaseless.' Origen, though, exceeds his own advice, **proposing models rooted in his Platonic background** that will later be rejected as failing to preserve the **mystery of the Trinity** by trying to **explain too much**. In the effort to help us understand, **Origen ends up leading us away from the ineffable truth of the matter**" (p. 25-26).* [32] Remember: In the quote at the beginning of this chapter, trinitarian W.A. Brown listed three steps to the Trinity, the second of which was, ***"Origen's doctrine of eternal generation of the Son."*** Now, Olson and Hall tell us this idea was ***"rooted in his Platonic background."***

The fact that Origen was a follower of Plato and loved Greek philosophy is beyond dispute. The *Encyclopedia Americana* says of this fact:

> *"Origen, **Christian Platonist**, who was the **greatest theologian of the 3rd century** and whose **thought long remained important** as well as **problematic** for the established church. Problematic to the church were his belief in the **pre-existence** of souls, **theories about the Trinity**, apparent denial that 'this body' would be raised, a **succession of world orders** after the destruction of this universe, and a conviction that **all would be saved** at the end of this succession."* [33] Note: Origen had no problem with believing in the **pre-existence of Christ**, since he believed in the **pre-existence of everybody.** This proves again that when a person turns away from what *"thus saith the word of God,"* they are mentally like a ship without a rudder, and open to all sorts of *"futile speculations."*

Funk and Wagnalls New Encyclopedia adds to our understanding of **Origen** and his **Platonic errors** with these statements:

> *"Origen may well have been the most accomplished biblical scholar of the early church. **He was a Platonist and endeavored to combine Greek philosophy** and the **Christian religion.** He **developed** the idea of Christ as the **Logos,** or **Incarnate Word,** who is **with the Father from eternity,** but he taught also that the Son is subordinate to the Father in power and dignity."* [34]

The foregoing should be sufficient proof that Origen is someone whom Christianity should not have followed. But in case added proof is needed, here are some additional quotes from Harnack regarding his Platonic confusion.

> *"But the science of the faith, **as developed by Origen,** being built upon the appliances of **Philo's** science, bears unmistakable marks of **Neoplatonism** and **Gnosticism.** ...and the Christian doctrine is to him **the completion of Greek philosophy"** (Vol. 2; p. 335).

*"His outward life was that of a Christian and opposed to the law, but in regard to his views of things **and of the Deity, he thought like the Greeks**, insomuch as he **introduced their ideas** into the myths of other peoples" (Vol. 2; p. 341).*

*"The content of Origen's teachings about this **Logos** was not essentially different from that of **Philo** and was therefore **quite as contradictory**" (Vol. 2; p. 352).*

*"In general it must be said that Origen helped to **drag into the Church a great many ancient heathen ideas.... While he rejected polytheism**...he had for all that **a principal share in introducing the apparatus of polytheism into the Church**" (Vol. 2; p. 368).*

*"That such an acute thinker did not shrink from **the monstrosity his <u>speculation</u> produced** is ultimately to be accounted for by the fact that **this very <u>speculation</u>** afforded him the means of **nullifying all the** [scriptural] **utterances about Christ** and falling back on the idea of the divine teacher [i.e. the Logos] as being the highest one" (Vol. 2; p. 369).*

*"But while Gnosticism was completely ejected in two or three generations, **it took much longer to get rid of Origenism**. Therefore, **still more of Origen's theology passed into the 'revealed' system of Church doctrine**, than of the theology of the Gnostics" (Vol. 3; p. 106).*

*"But this [Apostle's] Creed was neither more nor less than **a compendium of Origen's theology**, which here, was thus introduced into the faith and instruction of the Church. After the Bishop has quoted extensive portions of it, which he describes as 'the whole pious **Apostolic doctrine'**... .*

401

*But these dogmas belong to Origen's theology. Finally, we perceive from the **Nicene transactions**, that many churches then possessed Creeds, which contained **the Biblical theological formulas of Origen**. We may assert this decidedly of the Churches of Caesarea, Jerusalem, and Antioch" (Vol. 3; p. 116).*

"We have already described in this volume the state of **Eastern theology** at the beginning of the **fourth century**. The theology of the Apologists had triumphed, and **all thinkers stood under the influence of Origen**. This endeavor was undoubtedly justified by an actual change accomplished before this and **promoted by Origen himself**, the incorporation of **the doctrine of the Logos** in the faith of 'the simple.' These simple Christians...." (Vol. 3; p. 132-133).

"...and **Origen** himself, **who in many points bordered on Polytheism**, on the other hand restored the **Logos** to the being of God, and united Father and Son **as closely as possible**" (Vol. 3; p. 135).

"Noteworthy, but not surprising, is the parallel capable of being drawn **between the history of theology and that of heathen philosophy** during the whole period from **Origen** to [Emperor] Justinian" (Vol. 3; p. 155).

"Origen's thorough-going principle that 'God can say and do nothing which is not good and just,' **by which he criticized and occasionally set aside the letter of Scripture,** was too bold for the Epigoni [fifth century believers] (Vol. 3; p. 200). [35]

Considering the above quotes, it is no wonder that Pope Benedict, upset over the *"dehellenization"* of Christianity, says that the ***"second stage in the process of dehellenization"*** began in the late nineteenth century with the writings of German historian ***"Adolf Von Harnack** as its outstanding representative."* The work of this great historian, weighed with sound reasoning in the light of Holy Scripture, **absolutely destroys** the **Platonic doctrines** of the Trinity and the Incarnation. And the most reliable and authoritative sources regarding history that can be found agree with him. Notice these statements by *The New Encyclopedia Britannica* regarding Origen:

> *"In the 3rd century, Clement of Alexandria and after him,* ***Origen*** *made* **Platonism** *the metaphysical* ***foundation** of what was intended to be a definitely **Christian philosophy."*** They say, ***"the platonizing tendency was continued*** *through the European Middle Ages under the influence of St. Augustine and Boethius."* [36]

The historian Durant, writing in his work, *Caesar and Christ*, says of Origen:

> *"In* [Stromata] *he undertook to demonstrate* **all Christian dogmas** *from the writings of the* **pagan philosophers.** *To lighten his task he availed himself of that* **allegorical method** *by which pagan philosophers had made Homer accord with reason, and* **Philo had reconciled Judaism with Greek philosophy.** *The literal meaning of Scripture, argued Origen,* **overlay two deeper layers of meaning,** *the moral and the spiritual, to which only the esoteric and* **educated few** *could penetrate.* ***He questioned the truth of Genesis*** *as literally understood:* **he explained away as symbols** *the unpleasant aspects of Yahweh's dealings with Israel; and he* **dismissed as legends** *such stories as that of Satan taking Jesus up to a high mountain and offering him the kingdoms of the world. Sometimes, he suggested,* **scriptural narratives were invented** *in order to convey some spiritual truth. As Origen proceeds,* **it becomes apparent** *that he is*

a Stoic, a Neo-Pythagorean [the belief that souls migrate from one body to another, as in re-incarnation], *a **Platonist**, and a Gnostic, **who nonetheless resolved to be a Christian**"* (p. 614).

Durant continues:

> "**God**, in Origen, **is not Yahweh**, he is the First Principle [Plato's idea] *of all things.* **Christ is not the human figure described in the New Testament,** he is the **Logos** or **Reason** *who organizes the world; as such he was created by God the Father, and is subordinate to him.* **In Origen the soul passes through a succession of stages and embodiments before entering the body; and after death it will pass through a like succession** *before arriving at God.* Even the **purest souls** *will suffer for a while in* **Purgatory**; *but in the end* **all souls will be saved.** *After the 'final conflagration'* **there will be another world** *with its long history;* **and then another, and another**...*each will improve on the preceding,* **and the whole vast sequence will slowly work out the design of God"** *(p. 615).* [37] Note: With the foregoing strange and erroneous statements in mind, one could conclude that Origen, whom Christianity followed, **was demon possessed!** [*"...giving heed to seducing spirits, and doctrines of devils" I Tim. 4:1*].

Origen, visiting in Palestine in 216 A.D. as a layperson, had been invited by the bishop of Jerusalem and the bishop of Caesarea to lecture in the churches on Scripture. About 230, the same bishops ordained him a presbyter without consulting Origen's own bishop, Demetrius of Alexandria. Demetrius objected, and two assemblies were held at Alexandria, the first forbidding Origen to teach there and the second depriving him of his priesthood.

Origen then settled in Caesarea and founded a school of literature, philosophy, and theology. During the persecution of the Christians in 250 under Emperor Decius, Origen was imprisoned and tortured. Released in 251, but weakened by his injuries, he died about 254, probably in Tyre.

In the fourth and sixth centuries the teachings of Origen, who wrote some 6000 books and brochures, [37] were re-examined by church leaders and many were declared to be heretical. However, to this present time Christianity, neither Catholic nor Protestant has renounced *"Origen's doctrine of the Trinity!"* Trinitarian professor T.E. Pollard admits, *"Perhaps Origen's greatest contribution to Trinitarian theology is **his** doctrine of **eternal generation**, yet **its primary source is his Middle-Platonist cosmology** [dealing with the origin of the universe].... ."* [38]

Origen, like all who have departed from this world, is in the hands of a just and merciful God (but for sure not in purgatory), so I will be careful in my judgement of him! However, Jesus said you can know a tree by its fruit and a fountain by its water. His fruit is rotten and his water is bitter. Sadly, as a young man of nineteen, Origen castrated himself, but even sadder, through *"futile speculations"* about God, he helped to castrate Christian doctrine!

Regarding the twin Platonic doctrines of the Trinity and the Incarnation, from Origen to Nicea it was all downhill. Other men of the third century aided it along, such as Origen's teacher **Ammonius Saccas**, Hippolytus, Novation, and the **pagan** philosopher and **mystic**, **Plotinus**, but after him, basically it was **established error**, waiting to be polished, fought over, and canonized. Like Origen, the Platonism of these men is beyond question. Of this fact Durant says:

> *"**Plotinus** was a culmination of this **mystic** theosophy. In his twenty-eighth year he discovered philosophy, passed unsatisfied from teacher to teacher, and found at last, in **Alexandria**, the man he sought. **Ammonius Saccas**, a Christian converted to paganism, was attempting to **reconcile Christianity and Platonism, as his pupil Origen would do.**"*

And what was this Plotinus' view of God? Durant tells us:

> *"**He is a triad, of unity**, reason and souls. Emanating from this Unity is the World Reason, **corresponding to Plato's Ideas**, the formative models... ."*

Durant continues:

> *"It was no accident that **Plotinus** and **Origen** were fellow*
> *pupils and friends, and that Clement developed a **Christian***
> ***Platonism** at Alexandria. Plotinus is the last of the great*
> *pagan philosophers,...**he is a Christian without Christ.***
> *Christianity accepted every line of him, and **many a page***
> ***of Augustine echoes the ecstasy of the supreme mystic.***
> *Through Philo, John, Plotinus, and Augustine, **Plato***
> *conquered Aristotle, **and entered into the profoundest***
> ***theology of the Church.*** [Durant is mistaken about John*
> the apostle]. *The gap between philosophy and religion was*
> *closing, and **reason** [sound thinking] for a thousand years*
> *consented to be **the handmaiden of theology.*** " [39]

A Tale Of Two Cities

As we know from Scripture, the Church of Jesus Christ was birthed at Jerusalem, and for several decades after, that city remained the center of its influence and outreach. However, after the persecution of Christians, and then the destruction of Jerusalem in 70 A.D., this influence began to be centered elsewhere, especially in Alexandria, Egypt, and Antioch, Syria. Regarding Antioch, we see this reflected in Acts 11:19-30. As we have seen, Alexandria was the second largest city in the Roman Empire and the intellectual center of the world, and Antioch was second.

In doctrine, these two theological centers differed remarkably. Perhaps because of the past influence of the Apostles, the Christians of Antioch focused on the importance of Scripture and its proper interpretation. On the other hand, the Christian theologians of Alexandria, because it was the center of Philo's teachings, were heavily influenced by Greek philosophy, with its metaphysics. They focused more on the Logos and its relation to both God and Jesus. They also viewed the Logos and the Son as having preexisted before Jesus' birth. Alexandria was to become the center of *"orthodox"* Christology. Their differing views regarding Christ resulted in these two centers of Christianity opposing each other.

A War Among Brethren

In 318 A.D. a controversy erupted in Alexandria, Egypt regarding the person of Jesus Christ, and his relationship to God the Father. It came to be known as the *"Arian Controversy,"* and it centered on the teachings of a church priest named Arius.

Arius *(circa 250-336 A.D.)* was tall, slender, an eloquent speaker, and nearly seventy years old when the dispute broke out. He pastored a church in the Baucalis district of **Alexandria**, near the **Great Harbor**. He wrote a book entitled *Thalia*, that contained his theology in rhyme and prose which the church later deemed heretical and banned.

Although Arius was from Alexandria, his beliefs about Christ were similar to those that were held by most Christians of Antioch. Like his orthodox opponents, Arius believed that Jesus preexisted as a complete Person as both the Logos and Son of God (he distinguished the two), and thus was a separate substance (Greek - *hypostasis*) from God the Father. Arius believed that Jesus was not God **absolutely**, so that only the Father is *"the one true God."* Arius was condemned by his opposers for teaching that Jesus was not fully God, but actually Arius believed like his and their predecessors, the Apologists (*"church fathers"*).

But the principle teaching of Arius that sparked fierce contention was when he asserted that, sometime prior to the creation of the world, God created His Son, basing this belief on the verses that say *"the firstborn of every creature" (Col. 1:15),* and *"the beginning of the creation of God" (Rev. 3:14).* Arius saw the Son as a God-made creature, though uniquely distinct from all other creatures. (This flew in the face of Origen's doctrine of *"eternal generation"*). He believed that Jesus had a divine nature that was *"like"* that of the Father but not the same. Since like his opponents, Arius had been influenced by the *"Greek church fathers"* and therefore his doctrine was not altogether scripturally sound, it was more biblical than that of his *"orthodox"* enemies.

The Arian Controversy broke out when Arius wrote a letter to his bishop defending his theology and that of his associates. But Bishop Alexander (of Alexandria) objected vehemently and denounced Arius' teaching as heretical. He alleged that it made Christ less than fully God and thus not God at all. He explained that God the Father generated the Logos-Son, but that in order for Christ to be fully God, there could never have been a time when the Logos-Son did not exist. The bishop opposed the apologists' teaching on this and affirmed **Origen's** contradictory doctrine of **eternal generation.**

This dispute between the priest Arius, and Bishop Alexander grew until it even became violent. Several assemblies were called by church leaders on both sides of the argument, to no avail. By 325 this Arian Controversy had escalated until it threatened the peace of the Roman Empire itself!

A Council Called Nicea *(325 A.D.)*

In 312 General Constantine *(272-337 A.D.)* had become emperor of the Roman Empire. He was propelled toward that office when he achieved a military victory in a war between differing Roman factions. How he came to win this victory caused him to convert to Christianity. As he and his troops marched toward Rome, they supposedly saw ahead of them in the sky a flaming cross on which was written in Latin, *Touto nika*, meaning, *"By this, conquer."* Constantine also claimed that on the previous night he had had a dream in which Jesus Christ appeared to him, showing him a cross, and commanding him to inscribe the sign of the cross on all of his soldiers' flags. The next day Constantine replaced his army's old flags, which had pagan symbols, with new flags, having a symbol of a cross. They then marched forth with courage and won the battle against the army of General Maxentius.

Up until that time the Roman world had never experienced freedom of religion. For any group of Roman citizens to legally practice a religion, Rome's authorities had to approve it, and Christianity had never been approved. But in 313 A.D. Constantine issued a decree acknowledging Christianity as a legitimate religion.

So, Constantine became the first emperor professing Christianity. He sought to unify both his empire and the church by intervening to settle the Arian Controversy. To do so, he sent a letter to each faction urging that they reconcile their differences. The identical letters stated that he had judged the *"cause to be of a truly insignificant character and quite unworthy of such fierce contention."* He believed that such discussions should be *"intended merely as an intellectual exercise."*

When this effort failed, early in 325 at the insistence of Constantine, Bishop Alexander called the regional bishops to a meeting in Alexandria to try to solve the matter. But those who gathered issued a biased, anti-Arian creedal statement that only worsened the conflict. Now, it seemed that stronger measures had to be taken. So, in the summer of 325 A.D., Emperor Constantine convened and presided over what came to be called the Nicean (Nicene) Council. It was so-named due to its location in the city of Nicea in Bithynia, Asia Minor, forty-five miles southeast of Constantinople (present day Istanbul, Turkey). Bishops were summoned from throughout the empire, and about 300 attended. But each bishop was accompanied by two presbyters and three servants, so perhaps in all, 2000 men attended. All were guests of the emperor at his expense, and the affair lasted one month. The importance of this *"first ecumenical council"* and its resulting creed can hardly be overstated. Dominated by Emperor Constantine, the result of this meeting would be to obscure the truth regarding the One Most High God from Christianity for the next seventeen centuries. **And ignorance allied with power is the most ferocious enemy that truth can have.**

Other writers, both past and present have done a good job of chronicling the details of this Nicean gathering with its bitter debate over concepts (*"substance," "being," "essence," "reality"*), and the Greek words (**homoousios** - *"Jesus is of the **same** substance as God,"* **homoiousios** - *"Jesus is of a **similar** substance with God'*) so I will not take time to do so here. [40] However, I will make two observations:

Number One - This was a tumultuous time of quarrelsome nitpicking in which a vocal **minority,** empowered by the presence of Constantine, overrode the better judgement of a fearful, less vocal **majority.** The historian Gibbon (a non-believer) in his highly-acclaimed seven-volume history of the Roman Empire, ridiculed this greatest of church councils for haggling over only one letter (i) in the alphabet. He famously stated, *"the profane of every age have derided the furious contests which the difference of a single diphthong* (speech sound) *excited between the Homoousians and the Homoiousians."* [41]

Number Two - The truth was not represented at this gathering. If any one of these 300 bishops understood the truth regarding the One Most High Creator God and His supernaturally conceived, virgin-born **human** Son, our savior Jesus Messiah, an account of him speaking up cannot be found. As the noted trinitarian writer Philip Yancey says in his book, *The Jesus I Never Knew,* regarding the Council of Chalcedon, a later council that quoted and fully endorsed Nicea:

> *"In church we affirmed Jesus as 'the only-begotten Son of God, begotten of his Father before all worlds...Very God of Very God.'* ***Those Creedal statements, though, are light-years removed*** *from the Gospel's account of Jesus growing up in a Jewish family in the agricultural town of Nazareth. I later learned that* ***not even converted Jews - who might have rooted Jesus more solidly in Jewish soil*** *- were invited to the Council of Chalcedon* ***that composed the Creed.*** *We Gentiles face the* ***constant danger*** *of letting Jesus' Jewishness* ***and even his humanity, slip away."*** [42]

Although God's truth, or a Jew who knew the truth **about** God, were not invited to these councils, I can tell you who was there. The godless, pagan, democracy-hating, homosexual, advocate for infanticide, Plato, was well represented! This was not a case of truth opposing error or light searching for more light. This was several hundred followers of Plato, meeting at the emperor's palace, on his dime, and arguing over their **Platonic differences.**

Consider Arius, whose teachings had stirred up this controversy. He attended these meetings but was not allowed to speak because he was not a bishop. So, his bishop friends presented arguments on his behalf. And the record shows that his Platonic credentials were well intact. The historian Durant says, regarding the teachings of Arius:

> *"We see in these doctrines the continuity of ideas from **Plato** through the **Stoics, Philo, Plotinus,** and **Origen** to **Arius;** **Platonism,** which had so deeply influenced **Christian theology....** "* [43]

And what about the young articulate deacon, **Athanasius** *(297-373 A.D.),* the protégé and assistant to the powerful Bishop Alexander, who was to play such a deciding role at Nicea, and who for the remaining fifty years of his life would so fiercely defend and promote its conclusions? There was not a more deeply devoted **Platonist** than he! Adolph Harnack expresses this well in his, *History of Dogma:*

> *"Certainly, as regards religion, a very great advance was arrived at, when **Athanasius,** by his exclusive formula of consubstantial **Logos,** negated both Modalism and subordinationist Gnosticism, but **the Hellenic foundation of the whole speculation was preserved...**No subsequent **Greek theologian** answered the question, **why God became man,** so decidedly and clearly as **Athanasius.** But all Fathers of unimpeached orthodoxy **followed in his footsteps,** and at the same time showed that **his doctrinal ideas could only be held on the basis of Platonism.** "* [44]

Even the word Homoousion, or consubstantial, making Jesus of the same *"substance"* with the Father, a word that Gibbon says was *"already familiar to the **Platonists,** "* was birthed by Athanasius and promoted by Constantine. [45] Regarding this, *Funk and Wagnalls New Encyclopedia* states, *"**Athanasius formulated the homoousion doctrine,** according to which the Son of God is of the same essence, or substance, as the Father."* [46]

Will Durant writes of Athanasius' part in forming the doctrine of Nicea:

> *"**Athanasius,** the eloquent and pugnacious archdeacon whom Alexander had brought with him as **a theological sword,** made it clear that if Christ and the Holy Spirit were not of one substance with the Father polytheism would triumph. **He conceded the difficulty of picturing three distinct persons in one God,** but argued that **reason must bow to the mystery of the Trinity.** [How many times have I heard that?]. All but seventeen of the bishops agreed with him, and signed a statement expressing **his** view."* [47] Note: Athanasius himself confessed that, *"**whenever he forced his understanding to meditate on the divinity of the Logos,** his toilsome and unavailing efforts **recoiled on themselves;** that **the more he thought, the less he comprehended;** and the more he wrote, the less capable was he of expressing his thoughts."* [48]

In addition to the doctrine of the Trinity, Athanasius was a life-long promoter of the Incarnation, the idea that God became a man. Notice this statement from *Collier's Encyclopedia:*

> *"Athanasius, known in his life-time as the **'Father of Orthodoxy,'** was the greatest champion of the Church's doctrine of the Incarnation. In his very first books...was evidenced the key concern of his life, **devotion to the Incarnation"** (Vol. 2; p. 367).*

In a book titled, *Athanasius and Constantius,* Timothy D. Barnes, a professor of Classics at the University of Toronto, states:

> *"**Athanasius appropriates the language and ideas of Greek philosophy without embarrassment,** and he expresses his position easily in the prevailing terminology of **Middle Platonism."***

In this large and well documented book, Barnes is candid as to what he sees in Athanasius. For example he says:

> *"Athanasius may often disregard or pervert the truth, but his is a subtler liar than* [author Eduard] *Schwartz realized. Paradoxically, Schwartz built much of his own interpretation of the fourth century upon Athanasius' largest and most successful perversions of the facts... ."* He speaks of *"Athanasius' misrepresentations, many of which have held sway for sixteen centuries... ."* [49]

Edward Gibbon says of the legacy of Athanasius, *"the immortal name of Athanasius will never be separated from the Catholic doctrine of the Trinity, to whose defense he consecrated every moment and every faculty of his being" (Vol. 2; p. 329).* Athanasius and his doctrine did prevail at Nicea, and somewhat in history, but the ups and downs of the rest of his life could fill many books. However, only one more paragraph in this one.

In 325 A.D., a council of over one hundred bishops met at Tyre, Lebanon, to hear charges of **terrorism, torture,** and **murder** lodged against Athanasius and his associates. It even sent a team of investigators to Alexandria. After the council received the report, it condemned Athanasius and advised the emperor to depose him of his office, and expel him from Alexandria. **Constantine immediately condemned Athanasius** and deported him far from Egypt, to the frontier of Gaul, where he remained until the emperor died two years later. So much for the friendship of these two Platonic collaborators!

The Platonism Of Emperor Constantine

The atmosphere at the Nicean gathering was euphoric. Christianity had suffered persecution by the Roman state throughout much of its history of three centuries. Several of the attendees bore scars from wounds received from prior torture for their refusal to recant their Christian testimony, especially in the *"Great Persecution"* of Christians from 303 to 311 A.D. Now, the emperor was a professing brother in Christ who was honoring his fellow Christians. Constantine's entrance to the meeting dressed in purple and gold is described by the historian Philip Schaff, quoting an attendee, Eusebius of Caesarea.

> *"The moment the approach of the emperor was announced by a given signal, they all rose from their seats, **and the emperor appeared like a heavenly messenger of God, covered with gold and gems**, a glorious presence, very tall and slender, full of beauty, strength and majesty."* [50]

The meetings were held in one of his magnificent palaces, called the Judgement Hall. He took his place to observe the debates on a sumptuous wrought - gold chair. When the time came the emperor gave his opening address to the council. Since he had just returned from a great victory in battle, he began, *"Discord in the church I consider more fearful and painful than any war.... . Delay not therefore my friends...put away all causes of strife."* [51]

In his words there seems to be a gentle nudge of political pressure! Like many politicians, Emperor Constantine had a hidden agenda. He was determined to form a Christian theocracy with an enforceable religious doctrine, under the slogan: *"One God, one emperor, one kingdom, one church, one faith."* But it never quite happened! He did produce a **temporary unity** in the empire, but sadly he produced what has been up until now a **permanent dogma!**

But was this man truly a Christian? Jesus said, *"By their fruits ye shall know them" (Matt. 7:20).* What were some of the fruits of Constantine?

It is highly doubtful that he ever truly abandoned sun-worship. After he professed Christianity, he built a triumphal arch to the sun god, and in Constantinople set up a statue of the same sun god bearing his own features. [52]

His actions made it evident that he was a statesman first and a Christian afterward. He continued to carry out the ceremonies required of him as *pontifex maximus* of the **pagan cult**. He restored **pagan** temples. He used **pagan** magic formulas in dedicating Constantinople. He used **pagan** magic formulas to protect crops and heal disease. He continued to mint coins with **pagan** images. He **murdered** his relatives to insure that his three sons would be his heirs to the throne. Though he had claimed conversion in 312, he was not baptized as a Christian until near the time of his death in 335 A.D. [53]

He declared himself to be the Thirteenth Apostle, [54] **and the place he prepared for his burial in Constantinople had marble statues of the twelve Apostles seated around his tomb**. [55]

Will Durant says that under Constantine's rule, *"**Christianity converted the world, the world converted Christianity, and displayed the natural paganism of mankind.**"* [56] Christianity can find better heroes!

But the important question for the thesis of this book is, "Was Constantine at heart a follower of the Greek philosopher Plato, more than of Jesus of Nazareth?" I think strong evidence for the answer to this question can be found in his major address to the council of bishops, just prior to their voting on the personhood of Jesus Christ. That speech said in part:

> *"Lastly, **Plato** himself...in the first place declared, **with truth, a God exalted above every essence**, but **to him he added also a second**, distinguishing them numerically as **two**, though **both** possessing one perfection, and **the being of the second Deity** proceeding from the **first**. For he [the first] is the creator and controller of the universe, and evidently **supreme**: while the **second**...refers the origin of all creation to him as the **cause** [Remember that word, Plato's "first cause?"]...but the **Word** being God himself is **also the Son of God**. For what name can we designate him except by this title of the Son, without falling into the most grievous error? For the Father of all things is properly considered the Father of his own Word. **Thus far, then, Plato's sentiments were sound.**"* [57]

These words of Constantine's are taken from a large history book titled, *The Nicene and Post Nicene Fathers,* and his speech takes up twenty pages in that work. It is remarkable that in a speech of this length, made before a council of 300 bishops who would decide for Christianity **for the next 1700 years** the question of who Jesus is, the man who dominated that council and determined its conclusion, Emperor Constantine, did not reference one Scripture regarding the answer to that awesome question! **Not one quote** from Moses, Peter, Paul or Jesus himself. He perhaps thought he was quoting John with one statement, *"even God the Word, who has ordered all things; but the Word being God himself is also the Son of God."*

But he loves Plato! He refers to Plato's doctrine as *"the admirable doctrine,"* and again as, *"a doctrine not merely to be admired, but profitable too" (p. 567).* So, thoroughly grounded in the doctrine of his pagan hero he presses on to speak of *"**Christ**, the author of every blessing, **who is God, and the Son of God**. Is not the worship of the best and the wisest of the nations of this world **directed to that God" (p. 568).*** Constantine continues:

> *"But since the world and all things that exist, and are preserved, their preserver* ["Christ"] *must have had a **prior existence**...for it needs must be that the **Creator** should care for his own works. But when the time came for **him to assume a terrestrial body,** and to sojourn on this earth, the need requiring, **he devised for himself a new mode of birth.** Conception was there, yet apart from marriage: childbirth, yet pure virginity: and **a maiden became the mother of God.** A radiant **dove**, like that which flew from the ark of Noah, **alighted on the Virgin's bosom: and accordant with this impalpable union**...were the results which followed. **From infancy possessing the wisdom of God.** Thus do we render thanks to thee, **our God and Savior, unto thee, O Christ, supreme Providence..**" (p. 569).*

Constantine continues:

> *"Likewise, we learn this truth from the victory of **God***

416

himself...*grievously insulted by the malice of the ungodly,* **yet passed unharmed through the sufferings of his passion**, *and gained a mighty conquest, an everlasting crown of triumph, over all iniquity"* [So, he believed "God" died] *(p. 572).*

At the birth of Jesus *"the power of the divine Spirit presents* **the very cradle of God**, *like fragrant flowers..." (p. 576).*

"For his Father is God, who is a **Power without sensible quality**, *existing,* **not in any definite shape**, *but as comprehending other beings..." (p. 578).*

This of course is pantheism! God the Father *"who is a Power without sensible quality,"* and *"existing not in any definite shape?"* I am sorry to say that many Christians have bought into this lie, even though Scripture clearly teaches us better. Please consider.

"So God created man in **his own image, in the image of God** *created he him" (Gen. 1:27).*

"...and the **similitude** ["form - shape - likeness"] *of the Lord shall he behold"* [God speaking regarding Moses] *(Num. 12:8).*

"...men, which are made after the **similitude** *of God" (James 3:9).*

"Blessed are the pure in heart: **for they shall see God"** [Jesus speaking, and they had already been blessed to see him] *(Matt. 5:8).*

*"**And they shall see his** [God's] **face"** (Rev. 22:4).*

Seeing God The Father

Our Father God is **a person** *(Job 13:8; Heb. 1:3)*, who has **a will** *(Luke 22:42; John 5:30)*, **a personality** *(Zeph. 3:17)*, **a shape** *(Num. 12:8; James 3:9)*, **a face** *(Matt. 18:10; Rev. 22:4)*, **a head** and **hair** *(Daniel 7:9)*, **eyes** *(Deut. 11:12; Prov. 15:3; Ps. 34:15)*, **ears** *(Num. 11:18; Isa. 59:1; James 5:4)*, **a mouth** *(Deut. 8:3; Matt. 4:4)*, **breath** *(Ps. 33:6; Gen. 2:7)*, **a voice** *(Gen. 3:8; Deut. 4:12; Heb. 12:25)*, **hands** *(Gen. 49:24; Ex. 15:17; Isa. 5:12)*, **back parts** *(Ex. 33:23)*, **and feet** *(Ex. 24:10; II Sam. 22:10; Isa. 60:13; Nah. 1:3)*. **He loves, laughs, sings, walks, stands, sits, feels** and **thinks. He is not in any way human,** but he has **a heavenly body** (as do angels - *Ps. 104:4; I Cor. 15:40, 44; Heb. 12:9; I Kings 22:19)*, and we are made in His image! Note: Do not be confused by the Bible verses that make reference to the Almighty's wings. This is speaking figuratively as the nations of Assyria and Moab are also said to have wings *(Isa. 8:8; Jer. 48:9;* and the Messiah, Jesus Christ is promised to *"arise with healing in his wings"* Mal. 4:2)*. **Come to know and love God our Father!**

More From Constantine

In this speech that would harm Christian doctrine greatly, Constantine was so determined to make Jesus the eternal God, that he grasped at any straw available. After Plato, he even invokes the testimony of a second demon spirit! Consider. As we learned in a previous chapter, there were, at the temples of false gods in ancient Greek and Roman cities, oracles, called *"sibyls,"* that spoke as the voice of those gods, and people went there to commune with them. That these are not just man-made gods but "devils," Paul affirms in I Corinthians 10:20.

> *"But I say, that the things which the Gentiles sacrifice, they sacrifice to **devils**, and not God: and I would not that ye should have **fellowship with devils**."*

There was one of these demonic *"sibyls"* at the temple of Apollo in the Greek city of Erythrea, and Constantine appeals to her as a witness to the Godhood of Jesus. The emperor's speech continues:

> *"My desire, however, is to derive **even from foreign sources** a testimony to the Divine nature* [Deity] *of Christ. For on*

> *such testimony* it is evident that *even those who blaspheme his name* must acknowledge that he is *God* , and the *Son of God... . The Erythrean Sibyl,* then who *herself assures us that she lived in the sixth generation after the flood,* was a *priestess of Apollo,* who wore the *sacred fillet* [a narrow ribbon of fabric] *in imitation of the God* [god] *she served,* who guarded also the tripod [a three-legged cauldron of fire] *encompassed with the serpent's folds, and returned prophetic answers to those who approached her shrine; devoted to this work by her parents, a work that produced nothing good or noble,* but only of *indecent fury,* such as we find recorded in the case of *Daphne."*

Please be patient and absorb this setting and what is taking place. Pressured by him, these delegates will **decide** and **vote on a document,** the Nicean Creed, that will determine for Christianity who Jesus is. And this document will be considered *"orthodox"* **Christian doctrine** down through the centuries, even to this day!

The editor of the history book quoted earlier, says of this wordy speech: *"The critical reader will not fail to mark occasional instances of inaccuracy and looseness of statement generally in the course of the oration."* [58] And worse the emperor invokes Plato and a demon inspired oracle. Notice his own description of her:

> *"A priestess of Apollo,"* who *"wore the sacred"* ribbon *"who guarded also the"* cauldron, covered *"with the serpent's folds,"* doing her work *"that produced nothing good or noble, but only indecent fury,"* such as *"Daphne."*

This *"Daphne"* that he compared her to was the oracle at Delphi (where Socrates received his "divine commission"), *"called Sibyl, on account of the wildness in her looks and expressions when she delivered oracles."* Obviously Constantine knows these oracles are possessed by evil spirits, but he continues:

*"On one occasion, however, having rushed into the sanctuary of her **vain superstition**, she became really filled with **inspiration from above**, and declared in **prophetic verses** the future purposes of God; plainly indicating the advent of Jesus by the **initial letters** of these verses, forming an **acrostic** in these words: Jesus Christ, Son of God, Saviour, Cross."*

An acrostic is a series of written lines or verses in which the first, last, or other particular letters form a word or phrase. The **first letter** of each word of the thirty-one line poem that Constantine now quotes, **read downward**, spells out *"Jesus Christ, Son of God, Savior, Cross."* Jesus Christ is for sure the Son of God, our brother, who saved us through his sinless blood on Calvary, but in this poem Jesus is referred to as *"God"* four times. It is notable that out of 1865 verses that **Jesus** spoke, **he never referred to himself as "God" once.** Who authorized Constantine to disagree with Jesus? After quoting (or reading) the poem he says:

*"It is evident that the virgin [oracle] uttered these verses under the influence of Divine inspiration. **And I cannot but esteem her blessed**, whom the Savior thus selected to unfold his gracious purpose towards us."*

Proceeding on, Constantine acknowledges that many people of his day considered the poem to be *"a forgery,"* but affirms that he and others had investigated and believed it was written long before the advent of Christ. But with the perspective of our day the editor notes: *"It can scarcely be necessary to observe that the acrostic...**must be regarded as the pious fiction of some writer**, whose object was to recommend the truth of Christianity to heathens by an appeal to the authority of an **alleged ancient heathen prophecy.**"*

In his desperation to make Jesus "God," Constantine goes on to invoke the Roman poet **Virgil**, the demon **oracle of Cuma**, and a poem by the orator **Cicero**. Of his use of Cicero's poem the editor says: *"Constantine takes **large liberty** with the poet here in order to make him say what he would like* *to have had him say."* But Constantine says: *"Those who search deeply for the import of the words, **are able to discern the Divinity of Christ.**"* [59] Please note: The word "divine" means *"Deity - God,"* or *"of God, from God, holy, sacred."* In the latter sense Jesus is *"divine,"* for he is for sure, *"of God, from God, holy, sacred,"* **but he is not God!** When Constantine says *"Divinity"* he means *"the eternal God."* He says of Jesus' birth, *"Indeed, the very joy of the elements indicates **the advent of God.**"* Constantine had no problem with making a man "God," as he had ordered that his own father be **deified** after his death.

Thank God Christianity itself is based on solid Scripture from the Holy Bible, however the doctrine of the Trinity and the Incarnation are based on such fraudulent nonsense as we have just chronicled. After this speech and in this atmosphere, the delegates decided that Jesus is coequal, coeternal with the Father and approved a dogmatic statement, about one page in length, called the Nicean (Nicene) Creed. (A creed is a statement of belief that often serves as a test of orthodoxy, meaning *"right opinion"*). The most important statement of this creed is that Jesus Christ is ***"very God of very God,"*** meaning *"fully God of fully God,"* or *"truly God of truly God."* Thus the Nicean Creed became official church doctrine. It reads as follows:

> *"We believe in one God, Almighty Father, Maker of all things seen and unseen and in one Lord Jesus Christ, the Son of God, eternally begotten of the Father and only begotten. That is, from the essence of the Father, God from God, Light from Light, Very God of Very God, [True God from True God] begotten, not made, of one substance with the Father."* [60]

The *Encyclopedia Americana* says of Constantine's influence on Nicea:

> *"Although Constantine was not baptized a Christian until he lay on his deathbed, he undoubtedly considered himself in some manner a member of the sect, and certainly played a major role in the affairs of the church. Inevitably, the Emperor became more than a referee in these disputes;*

*when he took sides, as he had to, **he defined orthodoxy*** [accepted Christian doctrine]. *Constantine himself proposed the formula of homoousion, the* [equality] *of the Son and the Father, which was inserted in the Nicene Creed. In the long run, the union of church and state meant that **political considerations would influence definitions of orthodoxy**" (Vol. 7; p. 649).*

Although none of the bishops dared to take a stand against this travesty of the truth, not all of them went home with peace of mind. According to Eusebius of Nicomedia, some of the delegates from Antioch who had signed the parchment later protested in a letter to Constantine that they had **"committed an impious act, Oh Prince, by subscribing to a blasphemy from fear of you."** [61]

This is the doctrine of Plato and Constantine, designed by Lucifer to lead even sincere people astray in their understanding of who the One Most High God is. Authors Viola and Barna see this influence of Constantine in Christianity after 1700 years and write: **"Constantine is still living and breathing in our minds."** But the Emperor is naked!

The Platonism Of The Three Cappadocians

Although when Nicea was ended, all of its bishops except Arius and two of his friends from Libya had signed the creed, agreement with its conclusion was far from unanimous. As the noted scholar J.N.D. Kelly says, *"only a comparatively small group...welcomed the language of the creed...*[the majority] *had no desire to be **saddled with an un-Scriptural term**."* [62]

And the work was not just about finished! One very important question that the Council of Nicea left unresolved was the place of the Holy Spirit in Christian dogma, and whether it (he?) proceeded from the Father, or Christ, or from both. The Nicean Creed began, *"We believe in one God, the Father, Almighty"* and ended *"And in the Holy Spirit."* As Olson and Hall say, *"the Spirit had appeared almost as a footnote to the Creed of Nicea... ."* [63]

And Nicea had not nearly settled the question of the person of Jesus Christ and his relationship to the Father. Following Nicea, the fires of this quarrel burned brightly for over fifty years. From 351 to 360 alone, Emperor Constantius (son of Constantine) convened and personally presided over no fewer than nine councils of bishops, for the sole purpose of trying to settle the Arian Controversy. And they made additional creeds, some of which omitted *homoousios*, and others that altered the phrase *"very God of very God."* But the controversy only intensified!

Yale history professor Ramsey MacMullen begins the preface of his book, *Voting About God In Early Church Councils,* thus:

> *"**How did Christians agree on their definition of the Supreme Being, Triune?** It was the work of the bishops assembled at Nicea in AD 325, made formal and given weight by majority vote and supported after much struggle by **later assemblies**, notably at Chalcedon (451) - likewise by majority vote. Such was the determining process. Thus agreement was arrived at, **and became dogma** widely accepted down to our own day."* [64]

MacMullen says the number of provincial and so-called *ecumenical councils* held between the years 325 A.D. and 553 A.D., and attended by clergy that numbered from 12 to 1000 of all ranks, cannot have totaled less than 15,000. (Only the names of some 250 of these councils are known today). One writer from that period said *"the highways were filled with galloping bishops"* going to this or that church council.

Many of these "Christian" councils were bitter and hate-filled fights. They, and the controversy they continued to stir, sometimes resulted in public riots, bloodshed, and even death, in the major cities. One non-Christian historian of that time named Ammianus observed, *"no wild beasts are such enemies of mankind as are Christians in their deadly hatred of one another."* [65] (What a terrible witness to the world!)

And still the doctrine of the Trinity was not developed. Please consider this fact. **In the year 350 A.D., there was no doctrine of the Trinity as later defined, anywhere in the world!** Note: This was 250 years after the death of the last Apostle.

Then along came three theologians from the province of Cappadocia in Asia Minor and figured it out. They were Basil *"the Great"* of Caesarea *(330-379 A.D.)*, Basil's younger brother Gregory, of Nyssa *(circa 331-395 A.D.)*, and their friend, Gregory of Nazianzus *(circa 330-390 A.D.)*. Together, they comprised what has come to be known as *"the three Cappadocians."* Notice this quote from the *Harper-Collins Encyclopedia of Catholicism*:

> *"**Trinitarian doctrine as such emerged in the fourth century**, due largely to the efforts of **Athanasius** and the **Cappadocians**... The doctrine of the Trinity **formulated in the late fourth century** thus affirms that the one God exists as three Persons. The purpose of this formulation was to profess that God, Christ, and the Spirit are equally responsible for our salvation, **thus each must be divine.**"* [66]

And this quote from *Collier's Encyclopedia*:

> *"Of the many who wrote on theology...**Basil** of Caesarea (fourth century), who, with his brother, **Gregory** of Nyssa, and their friend, **Gregory** of Nazianzus, **fixed the orthodox formulation of the doctrine of the Trinity**"* (Vol. 9; p. 41-42).

Consider this statement by the respected **trinitarian** scholar Charles Ryrie:

> *"**In the second half of the 4th century**, three theologians from the province of Cappadocia in eastern Asia Minor **gave definitive shape to the doctrine of the Trinity**..."* (Basic Theology; p. 65).

And this from Southern Baptist professor Millard Erickson:

> *"What Athanasius did was to extend his teaching **about the Word** to the Spirit, **so that God exists eternally as a***

> **Triad** *sharing one identical and indivisible substance. The* **Cappadocians** - *Basil, Gregory of Nazianzus, and Gregory of Nyssa* - **developed the doctrine of the Spirit, and thus of the Trinity, further.**" [67]

And what equipped this trio to develop this doctrine and answer the question that had so troubled Christianity throughout the second to fourth centuries? Listen to historian Adolph Harnack:

> *"The Fathers of orthodox dogma in the fourth and fifth centuries were* **Platonists**.... *The* **Cappadocians** *were still relatively independent theologians,* **worthy disciples and admirers of Origen,** *using* **new forms** *to make* **the faith of Athanasius** *intelligible to contemporary thought, and thus* **establishing them,** *though with modifications."*
> Harnack says of Gregory of Nyssa, *"Gregory was able to demonstrate the application of the* **incarnation** *more definitely than Athanasius could.... But he does so by the aid of* **a thoroughly Platonic idea** *which is only slightly suggested in Athanasius,* **and is not really covered by Biblical reference.**" [68] Note his words, *"the incarnation...a thoroughly Platonic idea...not really covered by Biblical reference."* Wow!

The following statements from the prestigious *Encyclopedia Britannica* confirm the **Platonism of the Cappadocians**, and also give an affirming overview of the truths I have brought forth in this chapter. Under the topic, *Christian Platonism,* they say:

> *"From the middle of the 2nd century A.D. Christians who had some training in* **Greek philosophy** *began to feel the need to express their faith in* **its terms,** *both for their own intellectual satisfaction and in order to convert educated pagans. The philosophy that suited them best was* **Platonism.** *The* **Platonism** *that the first Christian thinkers knew was of course* **Middle Platonism,** *not yet*

Neoplatonism. *Its relatively straightforward theism and high moral tone* **suited their purposes excellently;** *and the influence of this older form of* **Platonism** *persisted through the 4th century and beyond, even after the works of* **Plotinus** *and* **Porphyry began to be read by Christians.** *The first Christian to use* **Greek philosophy** *in the service of the Christian faith was* **Justin Martyr,** *whose passionate rejection of Greek polytheism, combined with an open and* **positive acceptance of the essentials of Platonic religious philosophy** *and an unshakable confidence in its harmony with Christian teaching,* **was to remain characteristic of the Christian Platonist tradition.** *This was carried on in the Greek-speaking world by* **Clement of Alexandria** *(c. 150 - 215), a persuasive Christian humanist, and by the greatest of the Alexandrian Christian teachers,* **Origen** *(c. 185-254). He produced* **a synthesis of Christianity and late Middle Platonism** *of remarkable originality and power, which is the first great Christian philosophical theology. In spite of subsequent condemnations of some of his alleged views,* **his influence on Christian thought was strong and lasting. The Greek philosophical theology that developed during the Trinitarian controversies** *over the relationships among the persons of the Godhead, which were settled at the ecumenical councils of Nicaea (325) and Constantinople (381),* **owed a great deal to Origen on both sides,** *orthodox and heretical. Its most important representatives on the orthodox side were the* **three Christian Platonist** *theologians of Cappadocia,* **Basil** *of Caesarea,* **Gregory** *of Nazianzus, and Basil's brother* **Gregory** *of Nyssa. Of these three, Gregory of Nyssa was the most powerful and original thinker (as well as the closest to Origen). He was the first great theologian of mystical experience,* **at once Platonic** *and profoundly Christian, and* **he exerted a strong influence on later Greek Christian thought.** ”

426

Collier's Encyclopedia confirms this Platonism when it says:

> *"During the **4th century**, ...the content of Christian dogma
> was developed in constructive and systematic manner by the
> very able men who have come to be known as the **Fathers
> of the Church**. Living in the eastern part of the Roman
> Empire, and writing in **Greek**, were St. Basil of Caesarea,
> St. Gregory of Nyssa, and St. Gregory of Nazianzus. **These
> men continued the <u>speculative</u> and Platonist tendencies of
> Clement and Origen....**" (Vol. 15; p. 318).*

**So, through these men we see clearly the fingerprints of Plato on the
doctrine of the Trinity!**

The Council Of Constantinople *(381 A.D.)*

In 379 A.D. the Roman general Theodosius became emperor of Rome.
He was a recent convert to Christianity and saw it as his task to stamp out
the still smoldering embers of the Arian Controversy. In 380 he declared
Christianity the official and only religion of the Roman Empire. He issued a
decree requiring that all Roman citizens confess the Nicene Creed or suffer
severe punishment. The next year **he confirmed this decree as law** by
summoning bishops to Constantinople for what the Catholic Church later
named *"the Second Ecumenical Church Council."*

This council was called the *"Council of Constantinople"*, and the creed which
it adopted is called *"the Creed of Constantinople,"* but since it accepted and
modified the Creed of Nicea, it is often called *"Nicene-Constantopolitan."*
Its main contribution to creeds is that it adds a statement which affirms both
the *"person"* and full **"deity"** of the Holy Spirit. **This represents the work
of the three Cappadocians whose view prevailed at this gathering.** The
concept, worked out and promoted vigorously by them is this: God is one
ousia, meaning substance, in three *hypostasis*, meaning subsistencies - the
Father, the Son, and the Holy Spirit - and these three are co-equal and co-
eternal. But this doctrine of three *hypostasisses*, called *"the Trinity,"* did not
escape the charge of tritheism (belief in three Gods). Later, Basil found it

necessary to publish a book titled *"Against Those Who Falsely Accuse Us of Saying That There Are Three Gods."* [69] Regarding the *"person"* of the Holy Spirit, the Creed, as approved by the 186 attending bishops, states:

> *"We believe in the Holy Spirit, the Lord, the giver of life, who proceeds from the Father and the Son. With the Father and the Son he is worshiped and glorified."* [70]

So after all the many decades of bitter wrangling, Platonic Christianity finally had a *"doctrine of the Trinity,"* although a *"primitive"* one, with much more work to be done. The *Encyclopedia Britannica* says of this fact:

> *"Although **Athanasius prepared the ground**, constructive agreement on the central doctrine of the Trinity **was not reached** in his lifetime... . The decisive contribution to the **Trinitarian argument** was made by a group of **philosophically minded** theologians from Cappadocia... . So far as Trinitarian dogma is concerned, the Cappadocians succeeded, **negatively**, in overthrowing Arianism....and **positively in a conception of God as three Persons in one essence that eventually proved generally acceptable."** [71]
> Note the word *"acceptable:"* They did not say *"Biblical,"* as that had been left behind long ago.

Here is a very good question. Should we be following these men and these councils? Southern Baptist theologian Millard J. Erickson makes these telling observations.

> *"Finally, **studying the doctrine of the Trinity is important**... because **the decision of a council at some point in church history carries little significance for us.** The number of those who would accord authority to bishops and official councils is greatly reduced from former times. **Perhaps the councils did not come to correct and final conclusions.** Since some councils **overruled** and **contradicted** earlier ones, **in principle not all of them could have been correct. It therefore becomes incumbent on us to scrutinize*

carefully the creeds formulated by the councils, to make certain they embody most fully the truth about the deity."

[72] [That is of course the purpose of this book].

In fact, Gregory of Nazianzus (one of the *"three Cappadocians"*), who presided over the Council of Constantinople, came to hold bishops and the work of their councils in very low esteem. Being a bishop himself, and a leader among bishops, he had an insider's view of the process to reach that office. He states that *"the highest clerical places are gained not so much by virtue, as **by iniquity; no longer the most worthy, but the most powerful, take the episcopal chair."*** [73] Sometime after this council, Gregory was summoned to another synod (assembly), but he declined to attend explaining in a letter, *"to tell the truth, I am inclined to shun every collection of bishops, **because I have never yet seen that a synod came to a good end, or abated evils instead of increasing them.** For in those assemblies (and I do not think I express myself too strongly here) **indivisible contentiousness and ambition prevail...Therefore I have withdrawn myself."*** [74]

And what about Emperor Theodosius, who convened the Council of Constantinople, and was largely responsible for this **first creed stating a doctrine of a *"Trinity?"*** His reputation is not good, and should be cause for alarm! For example, after the council he issued another decree requiring **the allegiance of all Roman citizens** to **its creed**, and declared that any dissidents were *"madmen"* and *"heretics."* This type of vicious name-calling is reminiscent of Athanasius, who used it against the Arian's, although they believed much the same as he did concerning many fundamental Christian teachings about Jesus. He said that Arians are like their *"father the devil,"* and that Arianism is a *"harbinger of Anti-christ."* He often called Arians *"Christ's enemies,"* and even *"atheists."* [75] In case you are wondering if that spirit is still alive today, **just question the man-made *"doctrine of the Trinity"* and you will see!**

In addition, in 394 A.D. Theodosius began **punishing pagans** for their refusal to adopt Catholic Christianity. Also troubling is his reaction to a riot in the city of Thessalonica that caused the death of one of his officials. He invited the entire unsuspecting Thessolonian population to be entertained in the city arena. About 7,000 attended, and **he had them all massacred** as punishment for the riot. [76] So much for *"Christian"* emperors!

The Council Of Chalcedon *(451 A.D.)*
As we learned previously, the number of *"church councils"* between Nicea and Chalcedon are far too numerous to mention. However, we should consider one, the *"Second Council of Ephesus" (449 A.D.)*. It was convened by the Emperor Marcian, at the insistence of Pope Leo *"the Great,"* because differing views had developed **over the question** as to whether there were **two separate and distinct natures in Jesus, or a single deified human nature.**

This *"Fourth Ecumenical Council"* consisted of only 135 bishops, and decided in favor of the latter, the group that believed that **God, as Christ, was born, suffered and died** and that Jesus was *"God crucified."* At the end of their statement of beliefs they added this appeal, *"May those who divide Christ be divided with the sword, may they be hewn in pieces, may they be burned alive" (Jenkins)*. Since this council contradicted several features of classical beliefs about God that had been adopted by its Hellenized Christian predecessors, it came to be known as *"the Council of Robbers,"* or the *"Gangster Synod."* So **Chalcedon,** *"the Fifth Ecumenical Council,"* was called to resolve the continuing dispute. It exceeded all previous councils in attendance (nearly 600 bishops) and it acted to: (1) annul the previous declarations of the *"Robber's Council,"* (2) affirm Mary as *"mother of God,"* and (3) adopt Pope Leo's view of Christ as having possessed both a human and divine nature. The Council's creed called, *"The Definition of Faith,"* states in part:

> *"Following then, **the holy Fathers**, we all with one voice teach that it should be confessed that our Lord Jesus Christ is one and the same Son, the Same perfect in **godhead**, the Same perfect in **manhood, truly God and truly man**....of the Virgin Mary, **the mother of God**; one and the same Christ, Son, Lord, Only-begotten, known in two natures*

[which exist] *without confusion, without change, without division, without separation...not parted or divided into two persons."* [77]

So, the Council of Chalcedon declared that Jesus had two natures, a divine nature, and a human nature, and that they are **distinct** while **united** in one person. It also declared that *"even the prophets....and our Lord Jesus Christ himself taught us"* these things. This declaration of Jesus' two natures, coupled with Nicea's description of Jesus as *"very God of very God,"* became the church's official explanation as to the **person of Jesus**, which has never been successfully challenged until the present time!

The emperor adjourned the Council with a prayer, thanking Christ for restoring peace to the church. Then he warned that anyone teaching contrary to the Council's declarations regarding Christ would suffer the dire consequences of imperial punishment. And so they did!

Throughout church history, Chalcedon has been regarded as second in importance only to the Council of Nicea. It is amazing that later non-Catholics (Protestants) accepted without question the conclusion of this **Catholic council**, that Jesus Christ is both man and God by possessing **two natures**, yet they vigorously opposed the same council's affirmation that Mary is *"the mother of God."* [As Grandma use to say, *"you might as well eat the devil, as to drink his broth"*].

The Jesus Wars

Chalcedon's assembly and resulting creed resolved little. Instead its assertions soon raised important questions never addressed before. For instance, if Jesus had two distinct and separate natures, yet he was not **two persons**, must he also have had two wills, both divine and human? And what about two consciences and two souls? The end result of the Council of Chalcedon was that it aroused more theological questions than it resolved! And more controversies were inflamed! (*"Saint"*) Hilary *(circa 400-468 A.D.)*, bishop of Poitiers, says of this time:

*"It is a thing equally **deplorable** and **dangerous**, that there are as many creeds as opinions among men, as many doctrines as inclinations, and as many **sources of blasphemy** as there are faults among us; because we make creeds arbitrarily, and explain them as arbitrarily. The Homoousion is rejected, and received, and explained away by successive synods. The **partial or total** resemblance of the Father and of the Son is a subject of dispute for **these unhappy times**. Every year, nay, every moon, **we make new creeds to describe invisible mysteries**. We **repent** of what we have done, **we defend those who repent**, we **anathematize** those whom we defended. We condemn either the doctrine of others in ourselves, or our own in that of others; and, reciprocally tearing one another to pieces, we **have been the cause of each other's ruin**."* [78]

Church historian Philip Schaff writes that these controversies:

*"**brought theology little appreciable gain, and piety much harm**; and they present a gloomy picture of the corruption of the church...theological **speculation** [remember that word?] sank towards barren metaphysical refinements; and **party watchwords and empty formulas were valued more than real truth**... . The external history of the controversy is a history of **outrages** and **intrigues, depositions** and **banishments, commotions, divisions,** and attempted reunions. **Immediately after the council of Chalcedon** bloody fights of the **monks** and the **rabble** broke out."* [78]

And It Was All Out War!

Author Philip Jenkins, a professor of history and religious studies at Penn State and Baylor Universities, has written a book titled, *Jesus Wars - How Four Patriarchs, Three Queens, and Two Emperors Decided What Christians Would Believe For The Next 1,500 Years*. In it he chronicles the *"wars"* that took place in the two centuries following Chalcedon. He says:

> *"in the fifth and sixth centuries, Christian monks served as private militias, holy head-hunters whom charismatic **bishops** could turn out at will to sack pagan temples, **to rough up or kill opponents**, and **to overawe rival theologies.** These were not rogue monks or clergy gone bad but **loyal followers of the churches**, doing exactly what was expected of them. When cities or regions divided along lines of **theology or faith**, rival bishops and monks literally fought for domination **in the hills and on the streets.** Between 450 and 650 A.D....**inter-Christian conflicts and purges killed hundreds of thousands, and all but wrecked the Roman Empire.**"* [80]

Jenkins continues:

> *"Arguably, fourth-century councils like Nicea marked the point **When Jesus Became God** - but that was the easy part. The fifth and sixth centuries had to tackle **the far more stressful task of preventing Jesus from becoming God entirely. Many lives would be lost in the process,** and at least one empire."* [81]

And exactly who were the thousands of *"heretics"* that were slaughtered by these zealous defenders of *"orthodox"* trinitarian doctrine? Were they Unitarians (believers that God is one person)? Or Binitarians (believers that God is two persons)? Absolutely not! These were Trinitarians (believers that God is three persons), killing other Trinitarians because they did not have it quite right!

Jenkins more than proves this fact in his book. He cites as an example an event that occurred in Constantinople around the year 511 A.D. He writes:

> *"The church of the day had a beloved hymn, the Thrice Holy, which praised, 'Holy God, Holy and Mighty, Holy Immortal.' But the emperor, Anastasius, [a trinitarian] wanted to revise it...by lauding this God 'Who was crucified*

for our sakes.' The new formula proclaimed that it was God alone who walked the soil of Palestine in the first century and suffered on the cross....'' [Note: This view is neither Unitarian nor Binitarian, but is in total agreement with the Trinitarian view of *"three in one"*]. *"So angry were the capital's residents that they launched a bloody riot: Persons of rank and station were brought into extreme danger, and many principal parts of the city were set on fire. In the house of Marinus the Syrian, the populace found a monk from the country. They cut off his head, saying that the clause had been added at his instigation; and having fixed it upon a pole, jeeringly exclaimed: 'See the plotter against the Trinity'!"* [82]

The poor man was a trinitarian, but in the view of his attackers he had missed one of its fine points. This reminds me of an observation by trinitarian professor Charles C. Ryrie. He acknowledges that *"the New Testament contains no explicit statement of the doctrine of the triunity of God,"* and adds, **"a definition of the Trinity is not easy to construct. Some are done** *by stating several propositions.* **Others err** *on the side of either* **oneness** *or* **threeness.** *Even with all the...delineation that we attempt in relation to the Trinity, we must acknowledge that it is in the final analysis a mystery."* [83]

Trinitarian professor Shirley C. Guthrie, Jr. addresses this same issue in his book, *Christian Doctrine.* He says, *"The doctrine of the Trinity is not found in the Bible..... ."* He then continues: *"Because* **everyone** *tends to emphasize either the unity -* **oneness** *or the distinction -* **threeness** *of God,* **we all tend toward** *one or another of these heresies.* **Which tends to be your heresy?"** [84] [So, whatever your *"tendency,"* the doctrine of the Trinity according to this eminent trinitarian scholar, **is a** *"heresy"!*]

The violence of the episode relayed by Jenkins brings to mind a statement by trinitarian scholar Millard Erickson. Referring to *"the doctrine of the Trinity, with its* **hair-splitting tendencies,** *"* he states:

> *"In fact, history suggests that **the doctrine of the Trinity has been part of a great doctrinal system that has been used to justify oppression and exploitation.** Whether this doctrine was actually correlated with oppression, **it has certainly accompanied such oppression.**"* [85] Note: This should tell us that there is something inherently wrong with this doctrine.

Jenkins says:

> *"Out-of-control clergy, religious demagogues with their consecrated militias, religious-parties usurping the functions of the state - these were the **common currency** of the Christian world just a few decades after the Roman Empire **made Christianity its official religion.**"* [86]

Jenkins says, *"Debates over the nature(s) of Christ were still vividly active in 650 or 800."* [87] And just to think that all of this pain, confusion, warfare and bloodshed could have been avoided if these *"Christians"* had only followed Jesus instead of Plato, and accepted the heaven inspired answer of Peter, to Jesus' simple question, *"But whom say ye that I am?"*

> *"Peter answering said, **The Christ** [Messiah - anointed] **of God"** (Luke 9:20).*

The Platonism Of (Saint) Augustine *(354-430 A.D.)*

Augustine, who became the Catholic bishop of Hippo, in North Africa, is considered a *"genius," the greatest of the doctors of the church,"* a thinker who *"remains one of the greatest and most influential figures in the history of thought."* [88] But he was a lover and follower of Plato to a shocking degree.

Augustine, like many of the other "fathers of the church," was before his conversion a Greek philosopher, and who when *"converted"* brought his Platonic doctrines into Christianity with him. Suppose Jesus had told the parable of the prodigal son this way. When the prodigal came to himself in the hog-pen, he gathered up several little pigs and took them home with him to his father's house. They grew and grew until they became big hogs, and took over the farm! In essence that is what happened with these Greek philosophers. The doctrines of Plato of which they should have repented and left behind, have taken over the farm.

Tertullian saw it happening in his day, about 195 A.D. He wrote:

> *"Nor do we need to wonder if the <u>**speculations**</u> of philosophers have **perverted** the older Scriptures. **Some of their brood**, with their opinions, have even adulterated our new-given Christian revelation, and **corrupted it into a system of philosophic doctrines**."* [89] Tertullian did not realize to what extent his own doctrines were influenced by these philosophic *"speculations."*

Of this Platonic influence on Augustine the historian Harnack says:

> *"In antiquity itself Neoplatonism influenced with special directness **one Western theologian**, and that the most important, **Augustine**. In the seven books of his confessions he has acknowledged his **indebtedness to the reading of Neoplatonic writings**. In the most essential doctrines, **those about God**, matter, **the revelation of God to the world**, freedom and evil, **Augustine always remained dependent on Neoplatonism**."* [90]

Stating that Augustine *"rightly belongs to the best tradition of Western thought,"* the *Encyclopedia Americana* says that Aristotle was one of his first influences, then adds:

> *"However, far greater than any Aristotelian influence on him was that of **Plato** and **Plotinus** [Origen's pagan-philosopher school-mate and teacher]. These **Platonic and Neo-Platonic** influences **united** with Augustine's religious beliefs, qualities of mind..., to place **mystical elements** in his work and **inspire him** to express them with eloquence and beauty. Among other Augustinian contributions are **his profound study of the incarnation**...."* [91]

436

This Platonic influence on Augustine, and his profound influence on Christian doctrine is attested to by the *Encyclopedia Britannica*. Regarding this they say:

> "But the Christian **Platonism** that had the **widest, deepest,** and most **lasting influence** in the West was that of St. Augustine of Hippo (354-430). Each of the great **Christian Platonists understood Platonism and applied it to the understanding of his faith** in his own individual way, and of **no one of them** was this truer than of **Augustine** with his extremely strong personality and distinctive religious history. Augustine's thought was not merely a subspecies of **Christian Platonism** but something unique - Augustinianism. Nonetheless, the reading of **Plotinus** and Porphyry [a disciple of Plotinus] had a decisive influence on his **religious** and intellectual development, **and he was more deeply affected by Neoplatonism than any of his Western contemporaries and successors.**"

They continue:

> "In his **anthropology** Augustine was firmly **Platonist....** In his **epistemology** Augustine was **Neoplatonic....**" [But this is what is most troubling to Christianity]. "In his **theology,** insofar as **Augustine's thought about God was Platonic**, he conformed fairly closely to the general pattern of **Christian Platonism**; it was Middle Platonic rather than Neoplatonic in that God could not be the One beyond Intellect and Being but was the **supreme reality** in whose **creative mind** were the **Platonic Forms**, the **eternal patterns** or regulative principles of all creation. **Perhaps the most distinctive influence of Plotinian Neoplatonism on Augustine's thinking about God was in his Trinitarian theology.**" What was that? "**Perhaps the most distinctive influence of Plotinian Neoplatonism** on Augustine's thinking about God was in his Trinitarian theology." Pardon me, but would you

repeat that again? *"Perhaps the most distinctive influence of Plotinian Neoplatonism on **Augustine's thinking about God was in his Trinitarian theology."* Shocking!

They continue:

> *"...and because he thought that **something like the Christian doctrine of the Trinity** was to be found in **Plotinus and Porphyry** [his pagan heros], he tended to regard it as a **philosophical doctrine** and tried to make philosophical sense of it to a greater extent than the Greek Fathers did."* Then they say again: *"**The widest, deepest, and most persistent Christian Platonist influence in the Latin West was that of Augustine."*** [92]

Since these sources repeatedly tell us that Augustine in addition to being a follower of Plato, was also a student of, and influenced by Plotinus, we should take a brief look at the latter's beliefs.

Plotinus *(205-270 A.D.)* was an Egyptian with a Roman name and a Greek education, who became a Neoplatonic Greek philosopher. His teachings greatly affected the mind of his friend Origen and later, Augustine. And what did he believe?

1. He had no care for his body, and was ashamed that his soul had a body.
2. He frowned upon and avoided **all** sexual relations.
3. The body is the prison of the soul from which it is longing to escape.
4. The trans-migration of souls from body to body.

But what about God? The historian Will Durant says regarding Plotinus' view of God, *"**He too is a triad - of unity, reason, and soul.** 'Beyond being there is the **One**.' Emanating from this Unity is the World Reason, corresponding to **Plato's Ideas**... ."* Durant says, *"**Christianity accepted nearly every line of him, and many a page of Augustine echoes the ecstasy of the supreme mystic.**"* And again this shocking statement from Durant: *"Through **Philo, John, Plotinus, Augustine, Plato conquered Aristotle, and entered into the profoundest theology of the Church.**"* [93]

438

Here is a good question. Do those who love Augustine and the doctrine of the Trinity (triad) which he embraced and perfected, realize that they are in fact following Socrates, Plato, and Plotinus, these *weird* men with their *weird* beliefs? Christianity is drinking water from polluted wells! We have not only drunk it but we have passed the cup to our young! And do trinitarian scholars realize this fact? Sure they do! Listen to trinitarian professors Olson and Hall:

> *"Augustine, the greatest of the Western Church fathers, has made his own unique contribution to the trinitarian thought of the church, particularly in the West. Augustine was influenced by Platonic thought, which inclined his trinitarian reflections in the direction of the unity of the Godhead."* They quote author Colin Gunton thus: *"Augustine's analogies of the Trinity can be more readily traced to Neoplatonic philosophy than to the triune economy... ."* [94]

Since the doctrine of the Trinity is derived, not from the Bible, but from *"Platonic thought"* and *"Neoplatonic philosophy"* it is therefore incomprehensible. Regarding this Olson and Hall say:

> *"Augustine reminds all theologians* [in *Confessions*] *that any attempt to comprehend the Trinity's mystery must be rooted in spiritual health and will still fall far short of the truth of the matter. 'Who can understand the omnipotent Trinity?'* Augustine asks. *'We all speak of it, though we may not speak of it as it truly is, for rarely does a soul know what it is saying when it speaks of the Trinity. This is a mystery none can explain, and which of us would presume to assert that he can?'"* [95]

It is shocking to read of the extent of Augustine's Platonism from modern trinitarian writers, but the most incriminating proof that he is a lover and follower of Plato is what he has written himself. And the volume of Augustine's writings is staggering. One translation of his surviving works fills sixteen large volumes, each volume containing approximately 1200 double-columned pages. Written over a period of four decades while he served as a priest and bishop, these works include his two best known, *Confessions* (actually thirteen books), and *The City of God* (twenty-two books). It is said that *Confessions* has been translated into more languages than any Latin writings except Virgil's. His *"Confessions"* are made directly to God, and he openly declares his Platonism. A distinguished translation by the noted Catholic scholar John K. Ryan is the one from which I will quote. In the introduction, comparing Augustine in his creative abilities as an artist and thinker to Plato, Ryan says:

> *"...the work contains some of the deepest findings of the philosophic perennis, as stated by* **Plato, Aristotle,** *and* **Plotinus,** *and the* **great Stoic thinkers,** *as well as* **St. Augustine's own development** *of earlier doctrines and his additions to them.* [96]

Ryan then goes on to give a brief summary of Augustine's life. He was born November 13, 354, in the town of Thagaste, near the eastern border of Algeria, to a pagan father and a devout Catholic mother. About the age of eleven he was sent to Madauros, twenty miles from Thagaste, for further studies, including pagan literature and the works of Plato. Madauros was a stronghold of paganism and the two or three years there likely had a bad effect on his moral foundation. In 370, at the age of seventeen, he moved to Carthage and enrolled in its schools of rhetoric. As he describes in *Confessions*, Augustine's moral corruption was made complete as a student at Carthage. He took a concubine, and when their first child was born, he named him Adeodatus, which in Punic is Iatanbaal, *"gift of Baal,"* a strong sign of his pagan leanings.

During his years in Carthage, Augustine was introduced to, and became a member of, the pseudo-Christian sect known as the Manicheans. This religion took its name from Mani, its founder, a Babylonian who lived from 215 to 277 A.D. Mani claimed to have had various revelations, including one in which he learned that he himself was the Holy Spirit, *"the third person of the Holy Trinity."* Manicheism had become a powerful force in the world, and Augustine became a missionary on its behalf and prevailed upon various friends to join also.

And its beliefs were as strange as its leader. It was a gnostic religion that claimed to have a special knowledge that led to salvation. It had its own *"sacred"* literature and **rejected the Old Testament**, and subjected it to detailed attack. It also attacked the New Testament, but did not reject it completely. It looked upon the body as evil and advocated vigorous self-denial. Augustine would eventually leave this sect in 384 and speak against it, but its doctrines would show up in his writings for the remainder of his life. For example, Augustine would share with Origen the non-biblical belief that all sex, including married sex, is unclean and evil, and is to be avoided.

What led Augustine to leave the perverted "Christian" sect that he was immersed in? Ryan tells us in his introduction that it was **books**. He writes:

> *"In the year 373 he became acquainted with Cicero's Hortensius, an exhortation in the philosophical life, based upon **Aristotle's** Protrepticus, and it had a profound effect upon him. ...his knowledge of philosophy grew in depth and extent. He became acquainted with the work of **Plotinus** [the pagan "Christian without Christ"] the last of the great **Greek thinkers**, and of **other Neoplatonist**, and their thought became a **most important part in...the formation of his mind** so that on the natural level **it would be ready for the acceptance of the gospel of Christ."** [97] Note: This would read much better if Ryan could say that Augustine read God's Holy Bible and found these heretical Manichean doctrines to be false.

And what did these **books** teach him? Ryan tells us.

> *"**The divinity is a graded triad or trinity**, of which the first hypostasis [Plato's word] **is the one**...the transcendent, the infinite, **the father. Its act**, or superact, is most perfect, and is therefore **thought**. This **thought** which...the **father***

> *thinks, is the **divine mind.... . Being good, this second
> hypostasis in the divine triad** produces good; **it is creative.***
> (That is why many trinitarians teach that the **second** person
> of the Trinity - Jesus - is the creator). *The **third hypostasis**
> is the all-soul, the eternal emanation from and image of the
> divine mind. **This divine triad is a unity.***" [98]

Ryan looks at the foregoing and concludes:

> *"Obviously, **the Plotinian system is essentially pantheistic**
> [the belief that God is a formless force, and in all] in
> character, but its tendency is away from pantheism and
> towards such a lofty theism as Augustine taught. Plotinus
> had his doctrine as to the nature, powers, and destiny of
> man, **and here too he influenced Augustine.***" [99]

Of course these are the doctrines of the pagan Plato *(circa 425 B.C.)*, taught
by the pagan Plotinus *(circa 250 A.D.)*, which became the doctrines of
Augustine *(circa 400 A.D.)*, *"Christianity's greatest thinker."* Ryan, the
Catholic scholar, acknowledges that the ultimate source of Augustine's
doctrines is **Plato**. He writes:

> *"In ethics, Augustine learned much from Seneca (circa 4
> B.C. - 65 A.D.) and other Stoic thinkers... . **He learned
> much from Plato, and much too from Aristotle**, although
> far less from **Aristotle** than from **Plato**. This knowledge was
> gained partly from **Aristotle's own works** and partly from
> other sources."* [100]

So Augustine learned his concept of God from **pagan "books."** And then
he had the blinded audacity to thank God in his *"confessions"* for bringing
those books to him! He says to God:

> *"Therefore by means of a certain man* [an unidentified
> acquaintance]*..., you procured for me certain **books** of the
> **Platonists** that had been translated out of Greek into Latin.
> In them I read, **not indeed in these words but much the***

> *same thought, enforced by many varied arguments, that 'In the beginning was the Word, and the Word was with God, and the Word was God'."* [101]

To help us understand the above statements by Augustine we will look to *Collier's Encyclopedia.* They say that his reading of Cicero's *Hortensis* at the age of nineteen caused him to seek a philosophy *"that would give meaning and purpose to his life."* They continue:

> *"He first turned to his mother's* [Catholic] *religion, **but on reading the Bible he was repelled** by the crudities of its style, and felt that **the teaching of the O.T. was in contradiction to that of the Gospels.** The sect of Manicheans...seemed to Augustine to offer a **more convincing explanation** of the source of unhappiness and of sin... ."*

So Augustine read the Bible but was *"repelled"* by it, and he turned to the perverted Christianity of the Manicheans. In 384, he moved to Milan, Italy, and came under the influence of the Catholic bishop, Ambrose. *Collier's* says:

> *"Augustine, listening to the bishop's sermons, was **charmed** by his Ciceronian* [Cicero] *eloquence and his **allegorical** interpretations of the Bible. At this time he also read the works* [those *"certain books"*] *of the **Neo-Platonic** philosophers,* [the pagans] *Plotinus and Porphyry,...and he was **through these influences brought to reconsider Christianity in the light of the Neo-Platonic doctrines of the immateriality of God** and the soul... . By 386 he was **intellectually converted...** ."* [102]

Notice, *"the immateriality of God."* This is the pantheistic notion (embraced by Hindus) that God is a formless force, and Augustine bought into it! And he learned it, not from God's Bible, but from *"those books."* Augustine continues in *Confessions*:

> *"**I found out in those books,** though it was said **differently**

and in many ways, that the Son, 'being in the form of the Father, thought it not robbery to be equal with God,' for by nature is he the same with him. That before all times and above all times your Only-begotten Son remains unchangeably coeternal with you...these truths are found in those books." [103]

It is shockingly apparent that Augustine quotes small portions of Scripture verses and adds his Platonic doctrines to it. For example no Scripture teaches that Jesus is *"by nature...the same with"* God. And not once does Scripture say that *"your Only-begotten Son remains coeternal with you."* This is a serious mixing of light with darkness, truth with error, and Platonic nonsense with the Holy Bible! This reminds us of what Southern Baptist scholar Erickson says of the historian Harnack:

*"He finds the Christian community **borrowing heavily from Greek philosophy. It is from these foreign sources, not from Jesus himself, that the doctrine of the Trinity, the incarnation, and related conceptions grew."*** [104]

And this statement by trinitarians Olson and Hall:

*"**Scripture, Plato, Aristotle**, and subtle **logical reasoning** all played **significant if not equal roles** in developing explanations and defenses of **doctrines such as the Trinity and person of Christ"*** [105]

Here is a good question. Does a person who is searching for truth, need to first read the writings of pagan scholars to come to love and understand Holy Scripture? Obviously Augustine thought so. He says to God:

*"At that time, after reading **those books** of the **Platonists** and being instructed by them to search for incorporeal **truth**, I clearly saw your invisible things which 'are understood by the things that are made.' Now I began to desire to appear wise. **When would those books teach it to me?** It is for this reason, I believe, that you wished me to come upon **those***

> *books before I read your Scriptures, so that the way I was*
> *affected by them might be stamped upon my memory."* [106]

Until Augustine read the pagan books, he says he thought the apostle Paul wrote *"difficult passages"* and *"he seemed to me to contradict himself,"* and *"to be at variance with the testimonies of the law and the prophets."* But this *"melted away,"* and he says, *"I made a beginning, and whatever truths I have read in those other works I have found to be uttered along with the praise of your grace... ."* [107]

Augustine might have learned his trinitarian doctrines from pagans but he learned it well. He says that previously, *"I did not hold fast to Jesus my God."* He speaks to God of *"Jesus Christ our Lord, whom you have begotten coeternal with yourself, and created in the beginning of your ways."* He says regarding the Trinity:

> *"Behold, there appears to me in a dark manner the*
> *Trinity, which is you my God, since you, the Father, in the*
> *Beginning of our Wisdom, because he is your Wisdom, born*
> *of you, equal to you, and coeternal with you, that is, in your*
> *Son, you made heaven and earth. And believing my God*
> *to be the Trinity, as I did believe, I searched into his holy*
> *words, and behold your 'Spirit was borne above the waters.'*
> *Behold the Trinity, my God, Father, and Son, and Holy*
> *Spirit, creator of all creation."* [108]

Yes, he bought into Plato's concept of God as a Trinity, but he doesn't even suggest that he understands it. He says to God in *Confessions*:

> *"Who among us understands the Almighty Trinity? Yet*
> *who among us does not speak of it, if it indeed be the Trinity*
> *that he speaks of? Rare is the soul that knows whereof*
> *it speaks, whatsoever it says concerning the Trinity. But*
> *whether there is a Trinity in God...who could conceive such*
> *things with any ease? Who could state them in any manner?*
> *Who could rashly pronounce thereon in any way?"* [109]

Regarding this, Ryan says:

> *"Since the Trinity is a mystery,* **the supreme mystery,** *Augustine indicates that it can neither be grasped by our minds nor expressed in words."* [110]

Perhaps Augustine's most famous statement regarding the Trinity is:

> *"So we say three persons, not in order to say that precisely, but in order not to be reduced to silence."* [111]

But, although he did not understand the doctrines of the Trinity and the Incarnation, believed that they could not be understood, and knew their origins were in pagan and Platonic teachings, **he did not remain silent!** If this failure to forbear to teach error to the world did not affect his **eternal destiny**, it will for sure affect his **eternal reward!** God does not take lightly those who speak falsely concerning Him. He refused to hear the prayers of Job's friends with this statement:

> *"...lest I deal with you after your folly, in that ye have not spoken of me the thing which is right"* (Job 42:8).

Collier's Encyclopedia says of the mix of Platonic doctrines and Christianity in Augustine's writings:

> *"The Cassiciarcum dialogues exhibit...an active, sensitive mind...exploring with optimistic enthusiasm the world of ordered perfections and beauties* **which his Neo-Platonic interpretation of Christianity had revealed."**

They continue:

> *"The De Trinitate is Augustine's principal work in systematic theology;...construed as the* **reflections of the infinite being of the Creator he gave great metaphysical development to the Athanasian doctrine of the Trinity."**

> *"In passing from* **Virgil** *and* **Cicero** *to* **Plotinus** *and* **Porphyry,** *and from these philosophers to the biblical and dogmatic viewpoint of his maturity,* **the earlier phases** *of Augustine's*

*life and thought were **absorbed and transformed into the later ones.*** [112]

Collier's says of Augustine's continuing influence on Christianity through the centuries:

> *"The theological Augustine dominated the earlier Middle Ages; the **Neo-Platonism embedded in his works became influential in the twelfth and thirteenth centuries**; and the literacy and rhetorical aspects of his writings made a fresh appeal to the humanists of the Renaissance. **With Luther and Calvin, the theological Augustine was again invoked....** Augustine's influence has been recurrently important, in one or another aspect of Western culture, **until the present time.**"* [113]

Summary of Augustine

We will use as a summary of the foregoing regarding the Platonism of Augustine, a statement from *Collier's*, and one from the Catholic scholar Ryan. *Collier's* states:

> *"It was chiefly from the **Neo-Platonists** that the Church Fathers drew the **philosophical conceptions** and **language** through which they formulated the dogmatic structure of **Christian theology** [i.e. view of God]. The voluminous writings of St. Augustine **had made known a substantial portion of the content of Hellenistic theology** and ...; the teachings of **Plotinus, especially, were worked deeply into Augustine's thought.**"* [114]

And Ryan says concerning *Confessions*, Book 7, Chapter 9:

> *"In this marvelous chapter Augustine tells of his introduction to **Neoplatonic philosophy,** compares it with certain scriptural doctrines, and indicates why and where it may be used. **Certain Neoplatonic doctrines parallel divine revelation with regard to the existence and nature of God, and some of them are relevant even to the doctrine of the Trinity.**"* [115]

Augustine was twenty-seven years old when the doctrine of the Trinity was birthed at Constantinople *(381 A.D.)*. He was not there, but he did much to further this error, to the serious detriment of Christianity's understanding of God for the following sixteen-hundred years.

Error Marches On!

It is amazing to read the history of the centuries that followed the deaths of the Apostles and realize that no man arose who successfully proclaimed a return to the God of the Bible. God who is One Great *"**King eternal, immortal, invisible, the only wise God**" (I Tim. 1:17)*, and who has a supernaturally conceived, virgin-born, human Son, *"the **man** Christ Jesus" (Luke 1:31-35; I Tim. 2:5)*. Considering the long line of mis-guided *"church fathers"* I am reminded of the words of the old poet, *"Solitary woes are rare - they love to go in a train - and tread on each others heels."* The *"Prince of darkness"* inspired and sent forth men who were followers and lovers of Plato, to further his erroneous, non-biblical views of God.

For example, about 525 A.D. there arose to prominence in the West a *"great scholar and thinker"* by the name of **Boethius**. He was a follower of Augustine and a promoter of the Trinity. Olson and Hall say of him:

> *"Boethius was one of the most influential of the early medieval period and wrote at least four...treatises on the doctrine of **the Trinity and person of Jesus Christ**. But known for his influential book 'On The Consolation of Philosophy,' the great Roman philosopher - statesman was also a major interpreter of the Augustinian tradition of **trinitarian thought who sought to use Aristotelian categories to explain it.** Boethius **and others like him** tended to make greater use of **speculation** [there is that word again] than did the earliest church fathers. The **medieval mind** of the Latin West **made little distinction** between philosophy and theology. **Scripture, Plato, Aristotle,** and subtle **logical reasoning** all played **significant if not equal roles** in developing explanations and defenses of **doctrines such as the Trinity and person of Christ.**"* [116]

Gibbon writes of him:

> "*Boethius, who was **deeply versed in the philosophy of Plato and Aristotle**, explains the unity of the **Trinity** by the indifference* [lack of difference] *of the **three persons**.* [117]

The *Encyclopedia Britannica* writes of the Platonism of Boethius:

> "*In the 4th century the **Christian** Calcidius prepared a commentary on Plato's **Timaeus**, which exerted an important influence on the medieval interpretation of the **Timaeus**. A **Christian Platonic theism of the type of which Boethius is the finest example thus arose**; based on a reading of the **Timaeus** with Christian eyes, it continued to have a strong influence in the Middle Ages... .*" They say also: "*In the 3rd century, Clement of Alexandria and after him Origen made **Platonism** the metaphysical **foundation** of what was intended to be a definitely **Christian** philosophy. ...the platonizing tendency was continued through the European Middle Ages under the influence of St. Augustine and Boethius.*" [118]

So, although you might have never before heard his name, Boethius was one of the pioneers of the doctrine of the Trinity, who helped to make it what most of Christianity holds to so dogmatically today. And what were his influences? Listen to *Collier's Encyclopedia*.

> "*Boethius' own philosophical ideas, which combine **Neo-Platonic, Stoic**, and **Aristotelian influences**, were expressed in his famous dialogue...in which he applied the distinctions of **Aristotelian logic to the dogmas of the Trinity and Incarnation**. The Pythagorean metaphysical of number, already present in **the Neo-Platonic sources that influenced St. Augustine**, was communicated to the Middle Ages in explicit fashion by Boethius' treatises... .*" [119]

Thus, again we see Plato's fingerprints on the doctrine of the Trinity! From Boethius until the present time, the names of those who **added their own particular "spin" to the doctrine of the Trinity** are too numerous to mention. There was Photius *(circa 890)*, the Byzantine patriarch who well represents **Eastern** trinitarian thought during his time. Olson and Hall say of him:

> *"Like Boethius, Photius was a great scholar who has been called a 'learned humanist' because he was steeped in the philosophy and literature of classical culture as well as in the biblical...sources of Christian thought. Photius offered the Eastern Church's definitive arguments against the Western doctrine of the Trinity as he saw it implied... ."* [120]

And the work on the Trinity continued in the second millennium A.D., called the Medieval times. There was Anselm of Canterbury *(1033-1109)*, of whom Olson and Hall say:

> *"Anselm attempted to correct heresies about the Trinity and shed some rational light on the mystery. Anselm picked up this Augustinian tradition of trinitarian reflection and added to it a decidedly scholastic 'spin.' Anselm's... reflections on the Trinity heavily influenced the Medieval Catholic Church's dogmatic defenses of the Trinity...as formulated officially at two councils; Latern IV in 1215 and Florence in 1438-1445."* [121]

There was Richard of St. Victor *(circa 1150 A.D.)*, *"who provided a new way of thinking about the unity of the trinitarian persons that some during his lifetime and since have considered almost heretical, but which is widely accepted in the modern world of Christian trinitarian reflection. Richard of St. Victor's subtle corrections and adjustments to the Anselm version of the Augustinian psychological model of the Trinity have been rediscovered and used in the twentieth century with the rise to prominence, especially among Protestants, of the social model of divine love."* [122]

And there was the darling of the Church, (Saint) Thomas Aquinas *(circa 1225-1274)*, the Italian born Dominican friar. Of him Olson and Hall write:

> *"Thomas Aquinas represents the pinnacle of medieval scholastic and **speculative** theology. He has been declared 'The Angelic Doctor of the Church' by popes, and **his theology baptized as normative for all Catholic thought by councils."***

Regarding his contribution to the doctrine of the Trinity they say:

> *"For...Thomas Aquinas, the doctrine of the Trinity provided wonderful grist for the philosophical-theological **speculative** mill. A complete account of Thomas Aquinas's **trinitarian contribution** would consume much more space than is permitted here. Almost without doubt, **Aquinas's version of the unity and multiplicity of the triune being of God** is closest to the **Augustinian - Anselm version**, but he tried to do justice to the **Victorine** [Victor] **version** as well."*

And what was the source of his philosophic influence? Olson and Hall tell us.

> ***"The philosophies of Plato** and **Aristotle both found expression in Aquinas's system of theology,*** as did the seemingly **competing trinitarian visions** of Anselm and Richard of St. Victor. Thomas Aquinas was a theological genius...."* [123] [Here are more of Plato's fingerprints on the doctrine of the Trinity!]

The *Harper Collins Encyclopedia of Catholicism* says, *"Thomas's great zeal to give to others what he had contemplated"* led him *"**to use extensively, even daringly, any authors who could lead him to truth, whether they were Christian or pagan."*** They say, *"from Augustine and the Pseudo-Dionysius he received **many elements of Neoplatonism.**"* But consider this statement: *"In December 1273, however, he had a mystical experience whose intensity **so overpowered him that he could no longer write."*** [124] Question: Would this be the Holy Spirit *"overpowering"* a man who is writing heretical doctrines learned from pagans? I think not!

Of Aquinas's pagan influences the *Encyclopedia Americana* states:
> *"He makes greater use of the writings of **Aristotle** and **St. Augustine**, but countless other men were quoted: **great Greeks** and **Romans** such as **Socrates, Plato, Plotinus, Cicero,** and **Seneca**... ."* [What about some Jewish men named Jesus, Peter, John, Paul, James? They are not mentioned!] They continue, *"**adding his own great contributions - he produced new syntheses** in both philosophy and **theology**."* [125]

But did Aquinas, by *"adding his own great contributions,"* over 900 years after the Council of Nicea, finally work out the doctrine of the Trinity, and lay it to rest? No way! Olson and Hall say:
> *"**Questions still remain about Aquinas's vision of the triunity of God. ...Aquinas seemed to deepen the problems of Trinitarian theology in the West.**"* [126]

And two hundred years after Aquinas' *"great contributions"* to the doctrine of the Trinity, councils were still being convened **to try and work it out.** Olson and Hall say regarding this:
> *"Two ecumenical councils that dealt with the **Trinity** met in the Latin West (not recognized by the Greek East) during the **high middle ages:** the Fourth Latern Council (1215 A.D.) and the Council of Florence (1438-1445 A.D.)."* [Note: They met for seven years!] *"**Both helped settle some debates over the details of the doctrine of the Trinity.** Overall and in general the high medieval era in Europe **was not a time of great creativity with regard to trinitarian reflection,** but it was a time when certain Christian thinkers **returned to rigorous examination** and **construction of the doctrine of the Trinity** using the tools of divine revelation and **human reason.**"* [127]

It is incredible that over **one thousand years** after the doctrine of the Trinity was formulated in Constantinople *(381 A.D.)*, these trinitarians still can't get their story straight! Perhaps one more meeting would have done the trick. Notice Olson and Hall's statement regarding *"the tools of divine revelation and human reason."* I trust divine revelation, but *"human reason"* can be deadly. I am reminded of the story of the lady who accompanied her husband to the doctor concerning his heart condition. The doctor told her to give him a small amount of strychnine. She asked him to be more specific and he said, *"about as much as you can heap up on a dime."* When they arrived back home she could not find a dime, but she **reasoned** that two nickels equal a dime, so she heaped it up on two nickels, gave it to him and became a widow! In doctrinal matters especially, beware of *"human reason"* that is not totally subjected to *"thus saith the word of God!"*

The Reformers and The Doctrine Of The Trinity
Of the time just prior to the *"reformers,"* Olson and Hall write:

> *"In general, the medieval era of theology in the West was a time of **tidying up trinitarian doctrine** within the Catholic-Orthodox tradition stemming from the early church fathers and especially Augustine. That is, **few major leaps in creative thinking about the Trinity were achieved**... . At the end of the medieval era and on the cusp of the great reformation of the 16th century, Renaissance humanist Christian thinkers of Europe like Erasmus of Rotterdam (1466-1536) **were fed up with** what they perceived to be **the over-fussiness** and **hairsplitting arguments** of the scholastic theology of the middle ages. Erasmus and other Renaissance **humanist reformers** of the church eschewed [avoided] **speculative construction of trinitarian doctrine** in preference for 'following Christ.' Out of **sheer disgust**...these Christian humanists seemed about to cast away **all theological reflection. It was into that milieu** [environment] **that Martin Luther and other Protestant reformers stepped.**"* [128]

453

The Protestant Reformers and The Trinity

Mostly, the **Protestant reformers** considered the doctrine of the Trinity a settled matter and refused to reconsider its essential content as expressed in the Nicean Creed, and worked out in the writings of Augustine. Their attitude is summed up in this statement by the *New International Encyclopedia*:

> *"At the time of the Reformation the Protestant Church took over the doctrine of the Trinity, **without serious examination**."* [129]

However, there were questions and doubts. The leading Protestant reformers were critical with varying degrees of harshness of what they considered the **overly speculative** and **too detailed** developments of the trinitarian dogma.

Martin Luther *(1483-1546)* is usually credited with being the main leader of the Protestant reformation of the sixteenth century. Before and after nailing his famous *"Ninety-five Theses"* to the church doors in Wittenberg, Germany, in 1517, he was arguing against the medieval theological tradition of emphasizing **logic** and **speculation** in doctrinal matters, but arguing also against his own followers and other Protestants who wished to discard every aspect of the church's tradition, **including the Nicean Creed and the doctrine of the Trinity**.

Luther had doubts about the work of the medieval theologians. He labeled scholastic metaphysics a *"seductress"* (sometimes translated *"whore"*) and expressed the desire that the entire science of metaphysics be *"boldly crucified"* **in the search for God**. And in his heart he knew better than to follow the theology of the Church Fathers. He said of them, ***"When the word of God comes to the Fathers, me thinks it is as if milk were filtered through a coal sack, where the milk must become black and spoiled."*** [130] He should have gone with his heart. Near the end of his life, when asked if he had any regrets about leaving the Roman Church, Luther has been quoted as saying he only feared he had not left it far enough. How right he was! While he was rescuing Protestant Christianity from the erroneous doctrines of Purgatory, worship of saints and angels, indulgences, etc., there is one more doctrine, that either for lack of courage or biblical understanding, he did not throw off! Christianity owes Luther a great debt of gratitude, but two things cause his legacy to shine less brightly, his shameful anti-Semitism and *"Origen's Platonic doctrine of the Trinity!"* Luther was a man of courage and reason as history attests. But regarding the Trinity, he was willing to suspend his God-given reasoning ability. He stated:

> *"**How this intertrinitarian relation is carried on** is something we must believe; for even to the angels, who unceasingly behold it with delight, **it is unfathomable. And all who have wanted to comprehend it have broken their necks in the effort.**"* [131]

But sadly, even with all of his doubts, Luther asserted that salvation depends on belief in the Trinity. He said of that doctrine:

> *"This is the faith; so the faith teaches; here stands the faith. Naturally, I mean the Christian faith, which is grounded in Scripture. But he who does not want to believe Scripture but runs after reason - why, let him run... . **This is a matter of either believing or being lost.**"* [132] [Question: "Where are those Scriptures?"]

These foregoing statements by Luther remind me of a comment made often by the late, respected Dr. Adrian Rogers, *"**Define** the Trinity and lose your mind, **deny** the Trinity and lose your soul."* Of course this is neither reasonable nor scriptural.

Ulrich Zwingli *(1484-1531)* and John Calvin *(1509-1564)* were the two major founders and leaders of the early *"Reformed"* branch of the Protestant reformation. Zwingli was the catalyst of the Swiss reformation and arrived at many of the same ideas as Luther around the same time that Luther was working in Germany. Like Luther, Zwingli affirmed the necessity of using **extra-biblical terms** to protect the orthodox teaching about God, and defended the authority of the early Christian creeds about God and Christ, and the dogma of the Trinity. **Warning:** Going outside the Bible for proof of doctrine is a prescription for error!

Trinitarian writers Frank Viola and George Barna say in their book, *Pagan Christianity*:

> "At no time did **Luther or any of the other mainstream Reformers** demonstrate a desire to return to the principles of the first-century church. **These men set out merely to reform the theology of the Catholic church**" (p. 55). "...Luther, Zwingli, Calvin contributed many positive practices and beliefs to the Christian faith. **At the same time, they failed to bring us to a complete reformation**" (p. 61).

Calvin, the reformer of the French-speaking Swiss city of Geneva, followed Luther and Zwingli by about twenty-five years and was greatly influenced by them. Regarding the doctrine of God, Calvin seemed to search for middle ground, but never found it. On the one hand he criticized deniers of the Trinity, accusing them of being responsible for nearly all heresies, but on the other hand scolding metaphysical speculators who were not content with the simple faith of the New Testament and early church, and wandered into vain, *"evanescent* **speculation,***"* trying to penetrate into a sublime mystery. **But influenced by the Platonists of the past, Calvin fell into the trap of the Trinity.** He quotes Gregory of Nazianzus approvingly and suggests that Augustine's *De Trinitate* provides all that is really needed in understanding the Trinity. Of this Olson and Hall say:

> "Calvin believed that attacks on the Nicene doctrine of the Trinity by anti-trinitarians...undermined the gospel itself. For him, the **trinitarian confession** is necessary in order to express and protect belief in salvation and Jesus Christ. **Calvin's exact formulations of the doctrine of the Trinity are often influenced by and reminiscent of Augustine...**" [a follower of the pagans Plato and Plotinus].

Trinitarian Charles Ryrie says of Calvin's beliefs:

> "Calvin seemed to find the idea of the **eternal generation of the Son difficult, if not useless,** though he did not deny it" (*Basic Theology; p. 66*).

456

However, there is one violent, un-Christian act of John Calvin that should make all of his teachings suspect. That is judicial murder!

During Calvin's time there arose several *"radical"* Protestant reformers, one of which was the young Spanish doctor, Michael Servetus *(1511-1553)*. Servetus was himself a trinitarian of a sort, whose view of the Trinity had evolved throughout his lifetime and was not entirely consistent. His formulation of the doctrine was a combination of Sabellianism and subordinationism. While some have labeled Servetus as anti-trinitarian, he was actually anti-Nicene, that is, he ***"did not propose to reject the doctrine of the Trinity** but rather to **correct the errors** of the scholastic and Nicene formulations."* [133]

Servetus published two books against the Trinity dogma in 1531-32. In 1553, he published his major work titled, *The Restoration of Christianity*. Throughout the fourth and fifth decades of the sixteenth century, Servetus traveled around the Protestant cities of Europe, trying to engage leading Reformed theologians in debates about the Trinity. His influence became so great that Calvin and others had serious concern for the future of the Protestant reformation's holding on to trinitarian orthodoxy.

Servetus tried on several occasions to get Calvin to hold a public debate with him on the dogma of the Trinity and specifically about whether it is biblical or reasonable. Calvin corresponded with Servetus and cautioned him very harshly and in no uncertain terms to stay away from Geneva. Seven years earlier Calvin had vowed in a letter to a friend that, *"if he comes here...I will never permit him to depart alive."* And Calvin had the power to carry out the threat. He had been made *"Master"* of Geneva, and it became the capital of the Reformed churches and a sort of model theocracy. Citizens were reprimanded and even punished for not greeting him with the title *"Master."* Although Calvin was small in stature, even frail and often sickly, he admitted to having a violent temper and absolutely no tolerance for criticism of himself.

For reasons unknown, on Sunday, August 13, 1553, Servetus showed up at the large church where Calvin pastored, and preached every Sunday. When he was recognized, Calvin ordered him arrested and held for trial. Earlier that year, on April 4, Calvin had summoned the Catholic Inquisitors to arrest him in Vienna, France, but Servetus outwitted his captors and escaped. This time there was no escape. During the next seventy-five days Calvin led Geneva's other **thirteen Protestant pastors**, called *"The Venerable Company of Pastors"* and members of the *"Little Council of Geneva,"* in an intense doctrinal interrogation of Servetus and his two main books. He was condemned to death for teachings that Calvin called, *"partly impious blasphemies, partly profane and insane errors, and all wholly foreign to the Word of God and the Orthodox faith."* And the civil authorities agreed.

Servetus was burned at the stake outside Geneva during midday on October 27, 1553. (Calvin tried to persuade the council of pastors to change the method of execution to beheading, but they refused). Author Marian Hillar describes the scene as follows:

> *"No cruelty was spared on Servetus as his stake was made of bundles of the fresh wood of live oak still green, mixed with the branches still bearing leaves. **On his head a straw crown was placed sprayed with sulfur.** He was seated on a log, with his body chained to a post with an iron chain, his neck was bound with four or five turns of a thick rope. This way **Servetus was being fried at a slow fire** for about a half hour before he died. To his side was attached copies of his (last) book by a chain. With a large crowd witnessing the proceeding, and in a moment of hushed solemnity, the executioner reached forth with his fiery torch and ignited the mass of kindling surrounding its victim. Flames quickly arose and engulfed his emaciated body. For a while, the accused heretic uttered painful shrieks and groans. Just before he expired...he cried out with a loud, penetrating voice, 'Oh Jesus Christ, **Son of the eternal God**, have mercy upon me."* [134] [He said this perhaps remembering that a

few hours prior, the pastors had offered him **hanging** if he would confess to them the words, *"Jesus Christ, **the eternal Son of God"**].

Upon his death the leading reformers of Germany and Switzerland congratulated Calvin and Geneva for ridding the Protestant cause of a nuisance. [132] John Calvin, the *"Master of Geneva,"* afterwards never recanted his participation in this dastardly deed. Despite an angry uproar against Servetus' execution when news spread like wildfire in much of Europe, Calvin remained stubbornly unrepentant for the rest of his life about this affair. In fact, the next year he published a book defending his actions saying:

> *"**Whoever shall maintain that wrong is done to heretics and blasphemers in punishing them makes himself an accomplice in their crime and guilty as they are.** There is no question here of man's authority; it is God who speaks,...Wherefore does he demand of us...to **combat** for His glory."* [135]

Those who are followers of Calvin and his non-biblical doctrines had best hope, for his sake, that God recognizes his doctrine of *"**unconditional** eternal security."* For, since when has **murder** been an acceptable way to deal with those who disagree with you, either doctrinally or otherwise. Nor was the Servetus affair just a blip on the radar screen of Calvin's life. Earlier, in 1547, a fellow Genevan, Jacques Gruet took a stand against the tyrannical power exercised by Calvin and the council of pastors. For this and the charge of being involved in a French plot to invade Geneva, at the behest of Calvin and the other pastors, Gruet was arrested, condemned, and beheaded. Another incident involved Jerome Bolsec, a former Roman Catholic monk, who had temporarily switched to the Protestant side and moved to Geneva. In 1551, **he spoke out against Calvin's doctrine of unconditional predestination**. For this he was arrested, imprisoned, and tried by the Geneva Council. **Calvin tried to get him condemned to death**, but he failed, only because other Swiss churches objected. There is no way to know, and only eternity will tell, how many good men through the centuries were trampled under the feet of such men as Athanasius, Theodosius, Calvin, etc.; men who could have helped them find their way to the truth if they had only listened! It was because of such diabolical acts as these from the past, that the editor of a Christian magazine of international scope said to me on the phone after reading my first book, *To God Be The Glory, "**Mister Hemphill, in another day and time, you would have been burned at the stake for writing this book.**"* Thank God for **this day** and **this time!**

Here is a historical note of importance. In 1903, on the 350th anniversary of Servetus' death, **a group of John Calvin's distant relatives and Geneva Calvinists** assembled at the site of Servetus' execution to ceremoniously denounce their forebear's role in the Spanish martyr's death. And, to Calvin's further disgrace, they erected a monument of block granite, measuring three meters in size, which still stands there today. On one side it reads, *"'On the 27 of October, 1553, died at the stake in Champel, Michael Servetus of Villeneuve of Aragon, born on the 29 of September, 1511','"* On the other side it reads, *"'As reverent and grateful sons of Calvin, our great Reformer, **repudiating his mistake, which was the mistake of his age**, and according to the true principles of the Reformation and Gospel, holding fast to the freedom of conscience, we erect this monument of reconciliation on 28 October, 1903'."* [136] And what was Calvin's *mistake?"* He murdered a Christian man, a fellow *"trinitarian"* who dared to disagree with him on some details! Was Servetus a Christian? Listen to historian Philip Schaff, himself a strong trinitarian, who writes, *"it is evident that he worshipped Jesus Christ as his Lord and Savior."* [137] Was Calvin a Christian? Listen to Jesus Messiah, *"By this shall all men know that **ye are my disciples**, if ye have **love one to another"** (John 13:35).*

From The End Of The Reformation Until Today

I will not take time in this book to go into great detail concerning all that transpired regarding the doctrine of the Trinity (pro and con) from the end of the Reformation until today. Others have done a good job of this and since it is not my focus, I will defer to them. [138] Regarding the work of trinitarians *"pro"* this doctrine, Olson and Hall make these interesting statements.

*"At the end of the reformation era the doctrine of the Trinity entered into a period of **neglect and decline**. ...the doctrine of the Trinity **languished** from severe neglect or satisfaction with traditional formulas. Here and there, occasionally, a Christian theologian wrote an article, tract, or treatise dealing with the doctrine itself or with some aspect of God's **triunity** that raised a new question or **hinted** at a **new or forgotten** perspective. By the dawn of the twentieth century the doctrine of the Trinity had fallen into such **severe decline** from either benign neglect or skepticism **that it was in danger of becoming a useless relic within the museum of dusty theology tomes** [books]."* [139]

There were many men in this period of time, non-trinitarians and anti-trinitarians, on the *"con"* side of the doctrine of the Trinity, and though at times it seemed as if they might gain a foothold, their efforts did not prevail. These have included the English poet John Milton *(1608-1674)*, the English educator John Biddle *(1615-1662)*, the English writer John Locke *(1632-1704)*, the renowned English scientist Sir Isaac Newton *(1642-1727)*, the beloved hymn writer *(Amazing Grace)* Isaac Watts *(1674-1748)*, the English theologian Samuel Clarke *(1675-1729)*, the third President of the United States Thomas *Jefferson (1743-1826)*, and the German theologian Freidrich Schleiermacher *(1768-1834)*. Regarding some of the English critics of the doctrine of the Trinity, they did present a serious challenge to it in the seventeenth and eighteenth centuries but were hindered by blasphemy laws under which *"heretics"* could be prosecuted. They gained some relief by the passage of, *"The Toleration Act,"* in 1689. While viewing the present state of Christianity I must agree with trinitarians Viola and Barna when they say, *"**Constantine is still living and breathing in our minds.**"* And when they say of Christian education, *"**Athens is still in its bloodstream.**"* [140] The reason being that Plato's **idea** of God as a triad or triune, is like a germ that keeps infecting the minds of men.

Trinitarians Olson and Hall end their work, *The Trinity*, with these statements:
"Discussion and explication of the Trinity may never truly

461

*cease... . The doctrine, **however difficult of exposition,** will continue to **fascinate theologians**. For **in it, in the very mystery of the Trinity,** the discussion may well come to embrace **the fullness of God's existence, and of our own.** "* [141]

These are noted scholars and I respect their opinions, however I have a different prediction. The Platonic doctrine of the Trinity will be so discredited biblically and historically, and its demonic source so exposed, that **Christians will run from it!** As the great Christian thinker and scientist Isaac Newton said to a friend *(circa 1725), "**the time will come, when the doctrine of the incarnation shall be exploded as an absurdity equal to transubstantiation**"* [142] [the notion that the bread and wine become the **literal** body and blood of Jesus in the Catholic mass].

There is a big devil behind the centuries' long attempts to rob God of His glory, but his days are numbered and so are the days of his doctrines!

Luther Regarding The Church Fathers

"When the word of God comes to the [Greek] Fathers, me thinks it is as if milk were filtered through a coal sack, where the milk must become black and spoiled."

Martin Luther-Christian Reformer

(Adolph Harnack; History of Dogma; Vol. 2; p. 7)

Chapter Fourteen

A Prophetic Call To Change

"If my people, which are called by my name, shall humble themselves, and pray, and seek my face, and turn from their wicked ways; then will I hear from heaven, and will forgive their sin, and will heal their land" (II Chron. 7:14.)

"Then they that feared the Lord spake often one to another: and the Lord hearkened [listened]*, and heard it, and a book of remembrance was written before him for them that feared the Lord, and that thought upon his name" (Mal. 3:16).*

"And Jesus increased in wisdom and stature, and in favor with God..." (Luke 2:52).

Diagnosing The Case

*I*f you read thoroughly and prayerfully the previous chapters, I believe you will agree with me that the Church of Jesus of today has a serious problem. Under the M.R.I. of Holy Scripture and the x-ray of the Holy Spirit the diagnosis is "cancer." And it is a cancer of **false doctrine**. The apostle Paul found a cancer *of false doctrine* in the Christian church at Corinth, caused by the teachings of two men, Hymenaeus and Philetus, and warned Timothy, *"And their word will eat as doth a canker" (II Tim. 2:17).* This cancer was not as severe as the one that afflicts present Christianity, for it concerned the *timing* of the resurrection (serious enough), but the current cancer concerns the most basic and important of biblical truths, **the identity of God!** The cancer at Corinth had two serious symptoms, *"they will increase unto more ungodliness" (v. 16),* and *"overthrow the faith of some" (v. 18).*

But you might ask, "Can Christianity be in such a serious condition?" The biblical answer is "Yes!" The Church of Laodicea, which most students of

Scripture agree is a type of end-time Christianity, appeared under the x-ray of God's vision thus:

> *"Because thou sayest, I am rich, and increased with goods, and have need of nothing; and knowest not that thou art **wretched**, and **miserable**, and **poor**, and **blind**, and **naked**"* *(Rev. 3:17).*

The population of Earth today is about six and one-half billion people, of whom one-third are considered to be "Christian." But notice what is said regarding the end-time in Revelation 12:9:

> *"And the great dragon was cast out* [of heaven], *that old serpent, called the Devil, and Satan, which deceiveth the **whole world**."*

It is significant that John did not say "two-thirds of the world," which is a strong indication that Christianity has also to some degree been *"deceived."*

Looking At The Symptoms

Just as there were symptoms of cancer in Corinth, there are symptoms of the doctrinal cancer in present Christianity. I love my Christian family and do not mean to paint with too broad a brush, but the Church of today has a serious illness. As Frank Viola and George Barna say:

> *"We have elders, we meet in a house, we do have a hired clergy, we take up a collection every Sunday, and we preach the gospel. **But there is no rushing mighty wind!**"*

Here are some of the symptoms that I see.

- Ministers leaving the ministry out of discouragement and frustration.
- Preachers drinking, using profanity and falling into moral sin.
- Churches that were once thriving, now half-filled on Sunday mornings and cancelling services at other times.
- Churches without power and conviction in their services, and where very little prayer is heard.
- Churches that have replaced anointed singing and Bible preaching with

entertainment. The General Superintendent and the Assistant General Superintendent of a large Pentecostal denomination resigned a couple of years ago, telling the huge crowd at the national conference that their church services reminded them of an *"American Idol TV show."*

- Christians who have lost their zeal for soul-winning and have very little concern for the lost. As a result, the Southern Baptist Convention reported that over 9,000 of their churches did not baptize even one convert in the year 2007. (At least they admitted it and set out to make a change, and have).

And these are the things that are seen in the *"fundamental," "Bible believing"* churches, not to mention the unspeakable things that are happening in the *"liberal"* denominations, that are ordaining gays and lesbians, etc. For example, a large front-page article in today's Nashville newspaper, *The Tennessean*, carries the title, ***Presbyterian leaders approve gay clergy policy*** (Leaders of the Presbyterian Church, USA). A.W. Tozer, twentieth-century American minister and author said, *"A society cannot rise above its religion, and a religion cannot rise above its **concept of God**."* Christianity has embraced the pagan concept that the eternal God was incarnated as a man, the lowly Nazarene, **a man that they do not fear!** Our worship of, and service for God must be based on two things: a heart full of *love* for Him, and a reverential *fear* of God that recognizes who He really is. That's why Jesus said the greatest commandment of all is to **know God as *"one,"*** and to **love Him** with *"all thy **heart**, and with all thy **soul**, and with all thy **mind** and with all thy **strength"** (Mark 12:29-30).* It is a fact that an abiding fear of God drives out sin, and a fervent love for Him produces worship and service.

Growing In Favor With God

Please look again with me at the last of the three verses at the beginning of this chapter. *"And Jesus increased in wisdom and stature, and in favor with God... ."* Two things are obvious from this verse. The first thing that is obvious is that Jesus did not increase in favor with *himself*. No more than he went out into a mountain, *"and continued all night in prayer"* to *himself*. He *"increased in favor"* with the one to whom he prayed, **his God!**

The second thing this verse should teach us is, if Jesus our Messiah *"increased in favor with God,"* then so can we. But we in Christianity must rid ourselves of Plato and his doctrine to do so. Look at Ephesians 5:2:

> *"And walk in love, as Christ also hath loved us, and hath given himself for us an offering **as a sacrifice to God for a sweet smelling savor*** [aroma]."

Now look at II Corinthians 2:15 in the NIV:

> *"**For we are to God the aroma of Christ.**"*

Now let me ask you a question. Would you accept intimacy from your spouse if he or she had on them the smell of another lover? Absolutely not! Neither does God accept intimacy from us as Christians, when we follow the teachings of Plato rather than Christ, and have the smell of the perverted Greek upon us! To the extent that He has, it is a testimony to His patience with our ignorance and self-will concerning these things.

The Address Of Revival

The ninth chapter of Acts begins, *"And **Saul**, yet breathing out threatenings and slaughter against the disciples of the Lord... ."* And verse ten tells us, *"there was a certain disciple at Damascus, named Ananias."* No doubt Ananias had heard of the great revivals at Jerusalem and Samaria that are told of in Acts chapters two through eight, in which thousands of people were saved. However, no revival is mentioned in Damascus. But I believe that, as most good Christians would, Ananias was praying for a move of God in his city. And God spoke to him in a vision and gave him an address *(v. 11)*, **the address of revival!** For through a *sovereign* act, God had struck Saul from his horse on the way to Damascus and brought change in his heart. Then God told Ananias that he was at a certain address, and *"behold he prayeth."* This address on *"Straight"* street was **the address of revival**, for Saul became the great apostle Paul, a *walking revival* and mighty soul-winner for God! The remainder of Acts tells of his travels from city to city where he either had *revival* or *riot* and *"turned the world upside down"* for Christ *(Acts 17:6)*. And yes, revival came to Damascus as Saul *"preached boldly at Damascus in the name of Jesus"* (Acts 9:27).

Notice that Saul was saved, and revival was brought, by a sovereign act of God. No one witnessed to Saul before his conversion, but through much prayer by the church, **God arrested him!** The revival that we need for this end-time will not come through promotion or entertainment. Neither will it be *"worked up"; it must be prayed down!* Consider what is said of the Apostles after Jesus' ascension, in the last verse of the book of Mark:

> *"And they went forth, and preached everywhere, the Lord working with them, and confirming the word with signs following."*

That is the desperate need of the hour for Christianity in a dying world today, *"the Lord working with"* us! But be advised, the Great Physician will not perform surgery with unclean instruments. Neither will He furnish His power to build *our kingdom* rather than His. God has given us the address of revival for all time in II Chronicles 7:14:

> *"If my people, which are called by my name, shall humble themselves, and pray, and seek my face, and turn from their wicked ways; then will I hear from heaven, and will forgive their sin, and will heal their land."*

This is the address of revival. This is what is required to bring the fire back to our churches, and turn the tide against Islam, Hinduism, Buddhism, New Age, violence and lawlessness that are enveloping the world. This is what it will take to win our lost relatives and friends to Christ, see our marriages healed and our children set free from alcohol and drugs. This being true, we should take a closer look at this verse.

Notice the words *"my people"* and realize that revival does not begin in the White House, courthouse, or school-house, but must begin in the **church house.** *"My people!"* There are those who are concerned about whether or not there is prayer in the White House, but who attend Christian churches in which there is *little prayer*. Listen to Jesus:

> *"It is written, My house shall be called the house of prayer..." (Matt. 21:13).*

467

Sadly, there are those who zealously fight for prayer in the school-house, who never take time to call their children to a family altar in the home.

Notice the words *"my name"* and realize that a majority of Christians today do not know the name of the eternal God. This is a serious problem, since many of God's promises are made to those who have **"known *my name,"*** and that *"**thought** upon his name."* Trust *"**The Lord God**"* when He says in Exodus 3:15: ***"...this is my name for ever, and this is my memorial unto all generations."***

Notice the words *"shall humble themselves"* and realize that pride has taken residence in the Church of the Living God. Not so much a pride of dressing up and looking nice, but a pride of **race, place, face,** and **faith**. It is damaging to our pride of *faith* to acknowledge to God and man that we have been mistaken in our beliefs and doctrinal teachings as to the most basic of religious questions, the identity of the One Most High God. Many people, especially ministers, simply do not have the humility and fortitude to do it!

Now notice the words *"pray and seek my face, and turn from their wicked ways."* These are things we have already addressed and they are of utmost importance. Jesus warns us in Matthew 24:12 that in the last days *"iniquity shall abound,"* and it certainly has. There are temptations for modern man that the ancient world never dreamed of. For example, the Internet and violent and sexually explicit movies. (How can Christians enjoy movies where the names of God and Jesus are taken in vain and profaned?) Because of such things, it is said that when a minister stands before a group to minister, on average, sixty percent of the men and boys in the congregation (and some of the women) are bothered by pornography. However, God loves us and is ready to forgive, hold, and help us. Nevertheless Paul says:

> *"Examine yourselves,* **whether ye be in the faith***; prove your own selves"* (II Cor. 13:5).

The Church Needs To Come Out Of Egypt
In 1986 when the God of Abraham, Isaac, and Jacob spoke to me (He also

identified Himself as the *"Lord God,"* the *"Lord God of the mighty host,"* and *"Elohim")* and promised to *"reveal"* Himself to me in His word and told me I would write books about His *"glory,"* He also said that He had *"delivered us from Egypt with the muscle"* of His mighty arm. I had very little understanding of that awesome statement until 2006 when I began to study the origins of the doctrines of the Trinity and the Incarnation. Delivered from *"Egypt"* is an analogy that is used again and again in Scripture. Consider these examples:

> *"...thou shalt carry me **out of Egypt** [Joseph]" (Gen. 47:30).* *"For with a strong hand hath the Lord brought thee* [Israel] ***out of Egypt*** *(Ex. 13:9). "Thou* [God of hosts] *hast brought a vine **out of Egypt** (Ps. 80:8). "I...called my son **out of Egypt**" (Hosea 11:1). "**Out of Egypt** have I* [God] *called my son* [Jesus] *(Matt. 2:15).*

But I have come to understand that the Church of Jesus Christ is **doctrinally in Egypt!** We have established in this book beyond question that the trinitarian concept of God that is held by a great majority of Christians, is Platonic. We learned in chapter eleven that Plato, after the death of Socrates, went to Egypt and studied there under the pagan priests. Even trinitarian scholars admit that many doctrines later embraced and absorbed by Christianity from Plato and the philosophers who followed him, **had their origins in Egypt.** The late professor Arthur Darby Nock in his book, *Early Gentile Christianity and Its Hellenistic Background,* writes of the doctrines of Hellenism being derived from Egyptian beliefs. He says:

> *"Nevertheless, the rapid diffusion of the Greek language in the Egyptian priesthood must have helped to make the Greeks more at home in beliefs partly new to them. A great impetus was therefore given...to the study and philosophic interpretation of **Egyptian tradition** and to the **worship of Egyptian** and other Oriental **gods**. In this, **Egyptian and Greek elements were combined**, and gods of all sorts were invoked."* [2]

469

Trinitarian James Dunn tells us that the belief that a *"god"* can be the *"son"* of another *"god"* by a *"human mother"* is an Egyptian idea.

> *"...Dionysus and Heracles were sons of Zeus by mortal mothers. Oriental rulers, especially Egyptian, were called sons of God. In particular, the Ptolemies in Egypt laid claim to the title 'son of Helios'..."* [3]

Of course, Alexandria, **Egypt**, was the home of Philo, Clement, Dionysius, Origen, Athanasius, Cyril and others, whose Platonic doctrine became the dogma of the Christian Church. In his work, *Jesus Wars*, historian Philip Jenkins refers to these Christian patriarchs as *"Alexandria's Pharaohs,"* who came to act as *"absolute rulers"* or *"Hellenistic god-kings."* He writes:

> **"Rather, the patriarchs saw themselves as effective rulers of Egypt within the context of a Christian empire... .** *They wanted to use their homeland as a secure base from which they could spread the* **historic truth of Egypt throughout the Christian world.**" [4]

Even Origen, as confused as he was in his Hellenism, acknowledged that to embrace these *"Greek"* doctrines was to *"take from Egypt"* only what is useful. [5]

Historian Will Durant confirms the fact that the idea of a *"divine trinity"* had its origins in Egypt. He writes:

> *"Christianity did not destroy paganism; it adopted it!* **From Egypt came the ideas of a divine trinity,**...*from Egypt the adoration of the Mother and Child, and the mystic theosophy that* **made Neoplatonism and Gnosticism, and obscured the** [biblical] **Christian creed... .**" [6] Wow! **"From Egypt came the ideas of a divine Trinity."**

Can you see the irony? Christian ministers have thundered from pulpits for centuries about how God delivered Israel from Egypt, and had no idea that they themselves were held captives by the taskmasters of *Egyptian doctrines.* **The Church needs to be delivered from Egypt!** But consider:

Deliverance did not happen for the Israelites until they recognized their plight and cried out to God for freedom from bondage. Also consider that it took only days to get the Israelites out of Egypt, but it took forty years in the wilderness to get Egypt out of them!

I must say again, the Church of Jesus Christ has been taken captive by the doctrines of Egypt, and they, along with the spirits that promote them, have become our taskmasters, our tormentors, and our oppressors! **The Church needs to come out of Egypt!** (Remember, trinitarian Erickson says, *"history suggests that the doctrine of the Trinity has been part of a great doctrinal system that has been used to justify oppression and exploitation." God In Three Persons; p. 23).*

Drastic Measures

When I was a boy of seven, my second grade teacher was a large imposing woman, a stern disciplinarian who knew how to keep order in a classroom. I smile now when I remember some of her statements, such as, *"Joel, you are a disturbing factor in this classroom, and I'm about to take drastic measures."* Sometimes it takes *"drastic measures"* to bring us to where we need to be with God!

The Reproach Of Egypt

In Joshua, chapter five, verse nine, God makes a wonderful declaration to Israel's strong young leader, Joshua.

> *"This day have I rolled away the reproach of Egypt from off you."*

Several days before, the Israelite host had stood looking at the river Jordan that was between them and the land for which they longed. And Joshua had said to the people, *"**Sanctify yourselves:** for tomorrow the Lord will do wonders among you" (Joshua 3:5).* Sure enough, when the priests put their feet into the water, mighty Jordan parted, and Israel marched over on dry ground. And God tells them (and us) why!

> *"That all the people of the earth **might know the hand of the Lord, that it is mighty: that ye might fear the Lord your God forever"** (Joshua 4:24).*

471

God had great plans for these people: Plans to drive out their enemies with hailstones and hornets. Plans to give them houses they had not built and vineyards they had not planted. Plans to make of them a *"kingdom of priests"* to impact the entire world for good, and teach them of the **One Most High God** of Israel!

But, one more *"drastic measure"* was required. While they were still rejoicing on the shore of Jordan, the Bible states:

> *"At that time the Lord said unto Joshua,* **Make thee sharp knives, and circumcise again the children of Israel** *the second time.* **And Joshua made him sharp knives...**" *(Joshua 5:2-3).*

There was pain and blood from this act that was not fully understood by them, but which they did in obedience to the voice of their God.

> *"And it came to pass, when they had done circumcising all the people, that they abode in their places in the camp, till they were whole* [well]. *And the Lord said unto Joshua,* **This day have I rolled away the reproach of Egypt from off you**" *(Joshua 5:8-9).*

And while they healed, they had time to reflect on their awesome Creator, and their obligation to Him!

Nehemiah's Drastic Measures

The book of Nehemiah tells the story of a godly man, Nehemiah, who was sent back to Jerusalem by the king of Persia to restore its gates, walls and temple. This work was accomplished through much prayer and toil, but not without great opposition and persecution. The enemies, Sanballat and Tobiah, were long-time residents and loved the *status quo*. They at first tried scorn, then persecution, then distractions, then out-right attack. They even hired a *"prophet"* to prophesy against Nehemiah and his efforts, to try to instill fear. But the work of restoration continued!

However, the greatest *restoration* that was needed was a *spiritual restoration* to bring the people back to a true worship of God. Tradition did not provide the answer; that was the *status-quo.* Nehemiah knew that the answer to a return to **favor with God,** as Moses, Joshua, Samuel, David, etc. had known, could be found only in **God's word.** So Nehemiah, and the scribe Ezra, gathered all the people into the streets of Jerusalem and read to them from *"the book of the Law of Moses,"* hour after hour, day after day, for seven days.

> *"So they read in the book* **in the law of God distinctly,** *and gave the sense, and caused them to understand the reading"* *(Neh. 8:8).*

And the people's response was:

> **"All the people wept, when they heard the words of the law"** *(v. 9).*

They wept because they realized how grievously they had failed God regarding the Feast of Tabernacles, the Sabbath, their tithe, inter-marriage with heathen neighbors, and neglect of the house of God! Even on one occasion, through the efforts of a back-slidden priest, the enemy himself, Tobiah, set up his dwelling and headquarters in **a wing of the Temple.**

> *And he had prepared for him* **a great chamber,** *where aforetime* **they** *[had]* **laid the** *...***offerings***" (Neh. 13:5).*

Nehemiah had been called back to Persia for a short stay, and when he returned, he was incensed that the Temple was defiled by this enemy of God. The Bible describes Nehemiah's response:

> *"And I came to Jerusalem, and understood of the* **evil** *that Eliashib did for Tobiah, in preparing him* **a chamber in the courts of the house of God. And it me grieved sore:** *therefore* **I cast forth all the household stuff** *of Tobiah out of the chamber. Then I commanded, and they cleansed the chambers" (Neh. 13:7-9).*

473

Eight Days Of Repentance, Bible Reading, and Prayer.

> *"And the seed of Israel separated themselves from all strangers,* **and stood and confessed their sins,** *and the iniquities of their fathers. And they stood up in their place, and read in the book of the law of the Lord their God* **one fourth part of the day;** *and another fourth part* **they confessed, and worshiped the Lord their God"** *(Neh. 8:18; 9:1-3).*

And on the eighth day was the greatest gathering of all.

> *"Also day by day, from the first day unto the last day, he read in the book of the law of God. And they kept the feast seven days; and on the eighth day was a solemn assembly, according unto the manner. Now in the twenty and fourth day of this month the children of Israel were assembled with* **fasting,** *and with* **sackclothes,** *and* **earth upon them"** *(Neh. 8:18; 9:1).*

A Timely Lesson For Us

About ten years after Nehemiah cleansed the Temple in Jerusalem by casting out Tobiah *(434 B.C.)*, a child was born not far away, in Athens, Greece. He was born to pagan parents, grew up in a pagan culture, and acquired pagan concepts of religion and God. Through the influence of a demon spirit, aided by some misguided people, he now occupies a place of prominence in the Church of the Living God! Pardon me, but I am incensed and am calling for **Plato** to be cast out, just as our Messiah Jesus plaited a whip of cords and drove the moneychangers from the Temple in his day! We need a twenty-first century reformation that goes all the way to true favor with God! Look at Nehemiah's statement again:

> *"**And it grieved me sore: therefore I cast forth all the ...stuff of Tobiah out of the chamber.**"*

The *"early church fathers"* loved Plato, and through them, and those who have blindly followed their error, he has taken up *"permanent"* residence in the doctrines of Christianity, world-wide. Listen to "Church father" Clement of Alexandria *(circa 195 A.D.)*:

> *"For my part, I approve of Plato." "For what is Plato, but Moses speaking in Attic* [ancient] *Greek."* [7]

Listen to historian Simon Blackburn:

> *"Augustine was joined by other churchmen who thought that Plato was 'but Moses in Attic Greek,' and clearly regretted that they had not been around to baptize him. He was, unfortunately, denied the Christian revelation. But Platonists, it was felt, could have become Christians with the change of a few words and phrases."* [8] [Not, repentance and forsaking their pagan ways and ideas].

Notice the words, *"and clearly regretted that they had not been around to baptize him."* Did they wish to baptize the Plato that we have been studying about? This pagan, homosexual, promoter of infant-killing and wife-sharing Plato? My one regret is that I was not around to cast the demons out of him, and change the course of Christian and secular history for the succeeding centuries to come. Who is this *"Christian"* Plato? Listen again to Blackburn:

> *"This is the Plato transmitted to Europe by so-called 'middle Platonists' such as the contemporary of Christ, Philo of Alexandria, then further by Plotinus in the second century, and that became folded into Christianity, notably by Augustine and Boethius, in the fourth and fifth centuries. It is the Plato of the renaissance philosopher Marcilio Ficino, who was president of Lorenzo de Medici's Florentine Academy and believed that Plato should be preached in the churches of Florence alongside the Bible. It is Plato of the so-called 'Cambridge Platonists' of the seventeenth century... ."* [9]

It is, I might add, the Plato of Dr. R.C. Sproul, whom I love and respect as a brother, who taught two lessons on his popular radio program regarding

Plato and never made a single negative comment about him, then offered the lessons on C.D. *"for a donation of any amount, **that we might know and better serve the God of theology.**"* It is the Plato of every mis-guided Christian minister who stands behind the sacred desk and preaches the Platonic doctrines of the Trinity and the Incarnation!

A Trumpet Call

God told the prophet Isaiah in chapter fifty-eight, verse one, to:

> *"Cry aloud, spare not, lift up thy voice like a trumpet, **and show my people their transgression**, and the house of Jacob their sins."*

Then the remainder of chapter fifty-eight is instructions from God regarding how to have His favor.

I am nobody from nowhere, but God has called me to sound a shofar of truth to my Christian family. The message He has given me is clear, distinct and biblical. I cannot be distressed or distracted by those who refuse to hear it; however, multitudes are hearing! This is not about me, it is about Him. And Rome wasn't torn down in a day! I know this truth of who He is, is important to God, as He says **seventy-seven times** in Scripture, *"**Then they shall know that I am God**"* (or *"the Lord,"* or *"the Lord God"*). When God spoke to me in 1986, and turned me in the direction that led to my current understanding of who He is, He said, *"**I speak of things that are important to me.**"* **And He knows how to make it important to you!** God also told me in 1986 to say to my *"large family,"* that many are careless and foolish, and their hearts are not turned toward Him, but they are turned toward the world and they are playing near the darkness." God said, *"**Return to me, and seek my face, and I will stretch forth my healing hand and heal your wounds, for if you do not return to Me I will soon stretch forth My hand in wrath.**"* God said, *"**The ground is hard! Plow it strongly, and plow it fiercely!**"*

God is not impressed by Christian churches where *Pablum* sermons of prosperity and positive thinking are preached to multitudes, and where career clergy have learned to operate *"successfully"* without the presence of God's spirit! A well known religion writer, who writes for secular publications, headlined an article recently, *"God May Have Decided To Pull Back From Earth."* He certainly did from Israel! He said:

> *"I will go and return to my place, till they acknowledge their offense, and seek my face: in their affliction they will seek me early" (Hosea 5:15).*

The prophet Hosea had already looked at their spiritual condition and said, *"he hath withdrawn himself from them" (v.6).*

The President of Israel, explaining that the leaders of that nation were doing the best they could in the conflict with their neighbors, said in an interview with the Jerusalem Post, in the May 6, 2005 issue:

> *"We have no prophet, or voice from Heaven or anyone connecting us directly to God and mediating between us."*

Sadly, when Jesus Christ (their mediator) was crucified about 32 A.D., and the veil of their temple was torn in two *"from the top to the bottom,"* signaling the departure of the Glory, instead of fasting and praying and seeking God for a return of His Spirit, they likely stitched it back together and **went on having church without the presence of God**. And in a very real sense, Christianity has done the same!

But Hosea made an appeal, with a promise:

> *"come, and let us return unto the Lord... . Then shall we know, if we follow on to know the Lord...and he shall come unto us as the rain, as the latter and former rain unto the earth."* Note: *"if we follow on to know the Lord."* This is about **knowing God!**

Because of ingrained tradition, this is not yet a popular message. But that will change and His truth will prevail! A.W. Tozer, twentieth-century American minister and author, saw the need for drastic change in Christianity, but knew that those who God used to bring it about would be unpopular and even hated. He wrote:

> *"If Christianity is to receive a rejuvenation it must be by other means than any now being used. If the church in the second half of the* [twentieth] *century is to recover from the injuries she suffered in the first half, there must appear a new type of preacher. The proper, ruler-of-the-synagogue type will never do. Neither will the priestly type of man who carries out his duties, takes his pay and asks no questions, nor the smooth-talking pastoral type who knows how to make the Christian religion acceptable to everyone. All these have been tried and found wanting. Another kind of religious leader must arise among us. He must be the old prophet type, a man who has seen visions of God and has heard a voice from the Throne. When he comes (and I pray God there will not be one but many) he will stand in flat contradiction to everything our smirking, smooth civilization holds dear. He will contradict, denounce and protest in the name of God and will earn the hatred and opposition of a large segment of Christendom."* [10]

A Response Is Required

If you have read this book with an open mind and a heart that hungers for the things of God, you know that it is a prophetic call to change. A call to change our doctrine, our worship, and our view of the eternal God. And as always when He brings light to a person, God requires of that person a response. If you are a minister and you preach a sermon where there is a sinner in the congregation, you know that he must give a response, a *"yes"* or *"no"* to the call of God. But we must **all** bow before biblical truth, and before God say to that truth, *"yes"* or *"no."*

478

I have always been amazed and blessed at the Gospels' accounts of the call of the *"twelve"* and their immediate and positive response to the Savior's call to sacrifice and service. Look at Jesus' call of Peter and Andrew.

> *"Now as he walked by the sea of Galilee, he saw Simon and Andrew his brother casting a net into the sea: for they were fishers. And Jesus said unto them, come after me, and I will make you fishers of men.* **And straightway they forsook their nets, and followed him"** *(Mark 1:16-18).*

Mark continues with the call of James and John:

> *"And when he had gone a little farther, he saw James the son of Zebedee, and John his brother, who also were in the ship mending their nets. And straightway he called them:* **and they left their father Zebedee in the ship with the hired servants, and went after him"** *(Mark 1:19-20).*

Notice also the call of Levi (Matthew):

> *"And as he **passed by**, he saw Levi...sitting at the receipt of custom* [tax collection], *and said unto him, Follow me.* **And he arose and followed him"** *(Mark 2:14).*

Notice their immediate heart response. They did not take six months to weigh it out, or even one hour to consider the opinion of the neighbors. Touched deeply by the Holy Spirit, their hearts gave a resounding *"yes!"* No wonder these are known as some of the greatest men who ever walked on this planet. No wonder Jesus said to them:

> *"And I appoint **unto you a kingdom, as my Father hath appointed unto me;** That ye may eat and drink **at my table in my kingdom,** and **sit on thrones** judging the twelve tribes of Israel"* *(Luke 22:29-30).*

Not everyone made this positive response to the call of our Lord Jesus. When the rich young man was offered the opportunity to be a part of this group, **"he went away sorrowful: for he had great possessions"** *(Matt. 19:22).* In 1986, God put my acceptance or rejection of this truth regarding who He is, on a strong basis. He said, *"Your reward is being weighed in regard to how you receive My word!"* And I received it gladly! It has been rightly said that when a man who is *"honestly mistaken"* hears the truth, **he either ceases to be mistaken**, or **he ceases to be honest**. Winston Churchill said:

> *"Most people, sometime in their lives, stumble across truth. Most jump up, brush themselves off, and hurry on about their business as if nothing had happened."*

I pray for you, that your response to this message of truth will be the proper one. Be aware that God is reclaiming His glory! He has risen up out of His holy place to take back to Himself what has been wrongfully given to others. Do not get in His way! God will tolerate blindness, or even sin, longer than He will **rebellion** against the truth.

Those Who Fight Against The Truth

Here is a note of caution. If you do not understand this thing that God is doing in our day, leave it alone, and for sure do not go to war against it! God was doing a new thing in the book of Acts, and some understood it and some did not. Some received it gladly, some left it alone, and some fought fiercely against it. A noted Jewish leader named Gamaliel gave them wise counsel:

> *"Refrain from these men, **and let them alone**: for if this counsel or this work be of men, it will come to nought: But if it be of God, ye cannot overthrow it, **lest haply ye be found even to fight against God"** (Acts 5:38-39).* [And as the old preacher said, *"Your arm is too short to box with God!"*].

The apostle Peter warned:

> *"But these...speak evil of the things that they understand not" (II Peter 2:12).*

A Proper Response

The response that God desires and requires from those who see that they have been in error, and the ones upon which He will shine His favor, can be summed up with one word: **repentance!** The response from Nehemiah's people, that brought God's favor, is told in one verse:

> *"**And they stood in their place**, and read in the book of*
> *the law of **the Lord their God** one fourth part of the day*
> *[three hours]; and another fourth part **they confessed, and***
> ***worshiped the Lord their God**" (Neh. 9:3).*

Now is a sifting time, much the same as when God sifted the followers of Gideon until He had three hundred men who were fearless, focused and full of faith. And on these He placed His favor to win the victory! This truth of the One True God is like a plumbline that God is placing in the midst of His people, and those who reject it will be left out of this final move of God on Planet Earth. None of us has an inborn entitlement to the favor of God. It comes only through obedience to His word.

Consider God's promise for end-time believers in Daniel 11:32:

> *"...the people that do know their God shall be strong, and*
> *do exploits."*

A Follower Of The Lamb

In Revelation, chapter fourteen, verse one, the apostle John is shown an awesome sight, Jesus Christ, the *"Lamb"* standing on mount Zion, *"and with him an hundred forty-four thousand, having **his Father's name** written in their foreheads."* Verse four says:

> *"These are they which **follow the Lamb** whithersoever*
> *he goeth. These were redeemed from among men, being*
> *the firstfruits **unto God** and **to the Lamb**"* [notice the
> distinction].

What does it mean to *"follow the Lamb?"* To follow the Lamb, is to believe what Jesus believed and taught, and to worship the God that he worships. Notice verse twelve, *"here are they that keep the **commandments of God** and the **faith of Jesus**."* I ask you an important question: Do you really believe what Jesus taught regarding God his Father?

> *"I go unto the Father: for **my Father is greater than I**"*
> *(John 14:28).*

[Father] *"this is life eternal, that they might know **thee the only true God**..." (John 17:1, 3)*.

*"Hear, O Israel; The Lord our **God is one** Lord" (Mark 12:29)*.

Remember, it was Plato who taught the doctrine of the *"second God,"* the *"second Deity."* Some are following Plato in these important matters and only *think* they are following the *"Lamb."*

Back to Revelation Chapter Fourteen

It is significant that the next thing John saw after he saw the *"Lamb"* and his *"followers"* was, a mighty angel flying in the midst of heaven with the *"everlasting gospel"* to preach to the entire world. And what was that end-time *"gospel"* message?

> *"Fear **God**, and **give glory to him**...and **worship him that made heaven, and earth, and the sea, and the fountains of waters" (Rev. 14:7)**.* Note: This is for sure speaking of God the Father!

His Truth Is Marching On!

One man with God and His truth, can effect great change. For example, in the early 1800's the disease of slavery was gradually infecting the whole U.S. Pro-slavery preachers, thinking they saw justification for this evil in the Bible, even preached it from some Christian pulpits. There were pro-slavery riots in the North and the disease was spreading. But a young minister, an associate of Charles Finney by the name of Theodore Weld, saw from Scripture the evils of slavery and in 1833, began to speak and write against it. His most famous book, *American Slavery As It Is (1839)*, greatly impacted Harriet Beecher Stowe's *Uncle Tom's Cabin*, and the tide began to turn. Weld preached so many anti-slavery sermons that he injured his voice, so he trained others, whom he called his *"seventy"* and sent them out. More people joined the fight and in just thirty years (1863), Abraham Lincoln put into law the *Emancipation Proclamation*, ending forever the scourge of slavery in America. And no one would dare teach the doctrine of pro-slavery today. Behold the power of a truth of God whose time has come!

Someone has rightly said, *"One man with God is a majority,"* but He is bringing **many** to this understanding. I am reminded of a story told by Abigail Adams in one of her letters to her husband John. They were facing the wrath and force of Great Britain, and the outcome of the *Revolutionary War* hung in the balance. A group of men were talking and one remarked that it seemed they had no help but God. An old fellow spoke up and said, that reminded him of what someone had said many years before about the Reformation. He said:

> *"The Catholicks have on their side the Pope, and the King of France, and the King of Spain, and the King of Sardinia, and the King of Poland, and the Emperor of Germany. But as for them poor Devils the Protestants, they have nothing on their side but God Almighty!"*

> *"If God be for us, who can be against us?"* (Rom. 8:31).

Thank you patient reader.

Glory to God in the highest!

Jesus' Greatest Lesson On Worship

*"Ye worship ye know not what: we know what we **worship**; for salvation is of the Jews. But the hour cometh, and now is, when the **true worshipers shall worship the Father** in spirit and in truth: for **the Father seeketh such to worship him**. God is a Spirit: And they that **worship him** must **worship him** in spirit and in truth. The woman saith unto him, I know that **Messiah** cometh, which is called Christ: when he is come, he will tell us all things. Jesus saith unto her, **I that speak unto thee am he**" (John 4:22-26).*

Question: Who authorized Christianity to disagree with Jesus on this most important subject?

Source Notes

Introduction

1. *The Hebrew-Greek Study Bible*; AMG International, Inc.; p. 1708-1709

2. Richard P. McBrien, ed.; *Harper Collins Encyclopedia of Catholicism*; p. 564-565

3. *The New International Encyclopedia*; 1916 edition; Vol. 23; p. 476, 477

4. Millard J. Erickson; *God In Three Persons*; Baker Books; Grand Rapids, MI; p. 19

5. Charles Swindoll; *Jesus: When God Became A Man*; IFL Publishing, Co.; Anaheim, CA; 1993; p. 4-5

6. Max Lucado; *God Came Near*; Multnomah Press; Portland, OR; 1987; p. 26

7. Philip Yancey; *The Jesus I Never Knew*; Zondervan; Grand Rapids, MI; 1995; p. 36

8. C.S. Lewis; *Mere Christianity*; Macmillan Publishing Co.; Collier Books; New York, NY; 1952; p. 155

Chapter One - While Jesus Was On Earth God The Father Was In Heaven

1. Dr. Colin Brown; *Trinity and Incarnation: In Search Of Contemporary Orthodoxy*; Ex Auditu; (7); 1991; p. 88-89

2. James D.G. Dunn; *Christology In The Making*; William B. Eerdmans Publishing Co.; Grand Rapids, MI; 1996; p. 259

3. Millard J. Erickson; *God In Three Persons*; Baker Books; Grand Rapids, MI; p. 193, 210

4. Millard J. Erickson; *God In Three Persons;* p. 40, 43

5. James D.G. Dunn; *Christology In The Making*; p. 221, 230

6. *Encyclopedia Americana*; Vol. 2; p. 603

7. Richard P. McBrien, ed.; *Harper Collins Encyclopedia of Catholicism*; 1995 ed.; p. 1271

8. Shirley C. Guthrie Jr.; *Christian Doctrine*; Westminister John Knox Press; Louisville, KY; 1994

9. Charles B. Sanford; *The Religious Life of Thomas Jefferson*; University Press of Virginia; Charlottesville, VA; 1988; p. 90

10. This oration may be found in *A Select Library of Nicene* and *Post-Nicene Fathers of The Christian Church*; 2nd series; ed. By Philip Schaff and Henry Wace; Oxford and NY; 14 Vols.; 1890-1916; p. 561-580; esp. p. 566

11. Ira V. Brown; *Joseph Priestly*; The Pennsylvania State University Press; University Park, PA; 1962; p. 285

12. Millard J. Erickson; *God In Three Persons*; p. 259

13. Douglas McCready; *He Came Down From Heaven*; Inter Varsity Press; Downers Grove, IL; 2005; p. 56

14. Charles C. Ryrie; *Basic Theology*; Moody Press; Chicago, IL; 1999; p. 89-90

15. Millard J. Erickson; *God In Three Persons*; p. 19-20

Chapter Four - God Our Father Is The One To Whom We Should Pray

1. James McGrath; *The Only True God*; University of Illinois Press; Chicago; 2009; p. 101

2. *A Dictionary of Early Christian Beliefs*; David W. Bercot, ed.; Hendrickson Publishing; 1998; p. 533

Chapter Five - The Holy Spirit Is The Spirit Of The Father

1. Shirley C. Guthrie Jr.; *Christian Doctrine*; Westminister John Knox Press; Louisville, KY; 1994; p. 76, 80

2. Charles C. Ryrie; *Basic Theology*; Moody Press; Chicago, IL; 1999; p. 89-90

3. Millard J. Erickson; *God In Three Persons*; Baker Books; Grand Rapids, MI; p. 11-12

4.   Douglas McCready; *He Came Down From Heaven*; Inter Varsity Press; Downers Grove, IL; 2005

5.   Cyril C. Richardson; *The Doctrine of The Trinity*; Abingdon Press; Nashville, TN; 1958

6.   Roger E. Olson and Christopher A. Hall; *The Trinity;* William B. Eerdmans Publishing Co.; Grand Rapids, MI; 2002

7.   Robert Baker and John Landers; *A Summary of Christian History*; Broadman and Holman Publishing; Nashville, TN; 2005; p. 62

8.   *Encyclopedia Americana*; Vol. 20; p. 310

9.   Ramsey MacMullen; *Voting About God In Early Church Councils*; Yale University Press; New Haven, Conn.; 2006; p. VII or Vii

10.   Yancey, Philip; Personal Correspondence

11.   Dr. Billy Graham; *The Holy Spirit*; W. Publishing Group; Nashville, TN; 1988; p. 7

12.   Roger E. Olson and Christopher A. Hall; *The Trinity;* p. 39-40

13.   Millard J. Erickson; *God in Three Persons*; p. 19

14.   Millard J Erickson; *God In Three Persons*; p. 28-29

15.   *The Harper Collins Encyclopedia of Catholicism*; p. 106

16.   Robert Baker and John Landers; *A Summary of Christian History*; p. 65

17.   Paul Johnson; *A History of Christianity*; Atheneum Press; New York, NY; 1976

18.   Millard J. Erickson; *God in Three Persons*; p. 23

19.   Quoted on a DVD of his memorial service that is in my library.

20.   Roger E. Olson and Christopher Hall; *The Trinity*

21.   Richardson, Cyril C.; *The Doctrine of The Trinity*

22.   For some of the material in this section I am indebted to the work of John David Clark, Sr; *The Influence of Trinitarian Doctrine on Translations of the Bible*; Pastor John's House; Burlington, NC; 2007.

23. *The Harper Collins Encyclopedia of Catholicism*; p. 565.

24. Charles C. Ryrie; *Basic Theology*

Chapter Six - Jesus Is Speaking. Listen!

1. J. Rodman Williams; *Renewal Theology*; Zondervan; Grand Rapids, MI

2. Millard J. Erickson; *God In Three Persons*; Baker Books; Grand Rapids, MI; p. 159, 166, 176, 181, 185, 201, 321

3. Frank S. Mead and Samuel S. Hill; *The Handbook of Denominations - 12th Edition*; Craig D. Atwood, ed.; Abingdon Press; 2005

Chapter Seven - The Influence Of Greek Philosophy

1. Will Durant; *Caesar and Christ*; Simon and Schuster; NY; 1950; p. 657

2. Charles C. Ryrie; *Basic Theology*; Moody Press; Chicago, IL; 1999; p. 91

3. Millard J. Erickson; *God In Three Persons*; Baker Books; Grand Rapids, MI

4. George O. Wood; *Living In The Spirit*; Gospel Publishing House; Springfield, MO; 2009; p. 64

5. *New International Dictionary of New Testament Theology*; Colin Brown, Gen. ed.; Vol. 2; p. 84

6. *Encyclopedia Britannica*; 11th Edition; Vol. 23; p. 963

7. Adam Clarke; *Adam Clarke's Commentary On The Bible*; p. 854

8. *Hastings' Dictionary of the Bible*; James Hastings, ed.; Hendrickson Publishers; 1994

9. *Encyclopedia International*; University of Glasgow; 1982 ed.; Vol. 18; p. 226

10. *Funk & Wagnalls New Encyclopedia*; 1986 ed.; Vol. 12; p. 175-176

11. Will Durant; *Life of Greece*; p. VII

12. Shirley C. Guthrie Jr.; *Christian Doctrine*; Westminister John Knox Press; Louisville, KY; 1994

13. Cyril C. Richardson; *The Doctrine of The Trinity*; Abingdon Press; Nashville, TN; 1957

14. Roger E. Olson and Christopher A. Hall; *The Trinity*

15. Millard J. Erickson; *God In Three Persons*

16. D. J. Constantelos; *Understanding The Greek Orthodox Church*; Hellenic College Press; Brookline, MA; 1998

17. Merrill D. Peterson, editor; *Library of America Edition Of Jefferson's Writings*; Chapter 6; p. 9

18. *Encyclopedia Americana*; Vol. 27; p. 28

19. Adolph Harnack; *History of Dogma*; Vol. 2; p. 184

20. Philip Yancey; *The Jesus I Never Knew*; Zondervan; Grand Rapids, MI; 1995; p. 56-57

21. William Barclay; Quoted in Malcom Muggeridge's, *Jesus The Man Who Lives*; Harper & Row; NY; 1975; p. 74

22. Philip Yancey; *The Jesus I Never Knew*; p. 57

23. *Funk and Wagnalls New Encyclopedia*; Vol. 13; p. 43

24. Philip Yancey; *The Jesus I Never Knew*; p. 60

25. Philip Yancey; *The Jesus I Never Knew*; p. 59

Chapter Eight - Enter The Apostle Paul

1. Will Durant; *The Life Of Greece*; Simon and Schuster; NY; 1950; p. 176

2. Will Durant; *The Life Of Greece*; p. 177

3. *My Dearest Friend: Letters of Abigail and John Adams*; The Belknap Press of Harvard University Press; 2007; p. 147

4. Will Durant; *The Life Of Greece*; p. 176

5. Adolph Harnack; *History of Dogma*; Vol. 2; p. 10

6. Will Durant; *Caesar and Christ;* Simon and Schuster, NY; 1944; p. 94-95

7. Will Durant; *The Life Of Greece*; p. 178

8. *NIV Text Notes*; p. 1851

9. *NIV Text Notes*; p. 1732

Chapter Nine - The Pope's Speech

1. *New International Encyclopedia*; 1916 ed.; Vol. 23; p. 476-477

2. *Life* Magazine; October 30, 1950; Vol. 29; No. 18; p. 51

3. Frank Viola and George Barna; *Pagan Christianity?*; Barna-Tyndale House Publishers, Inc.; Carol Stream, IL; 2008; p. XXIII

Chapter Ten - Who Was Socrates?

1. *Funk & Wagnalls New Encyclopedia*; Vol. 24; p. 77

2. *Stanford Encyclopedia of Philosophy;* (from their website)

3. Will Durant; *The Life of Greece*; p. 365

4. *Encyclopedia Americana*; Vol. 8; p. 700

5. *Dictionary of Early Christian Beliefs*; p. 621

6. A.W. Tozer writings.

7. Will Durant; *The Life of Greece*; p. 293

8. Will Durant; *The Life of Greece*; p. 295

9. Will Durant; *The Life of Greece*; p. 184

10. Will Durant; *The Life of Greece*; p. 303

11. Will Durant; *The Life of Greece*; p. 301

12. Will Durant; *The Life of Greece*; p. 304

13. *Stanford Encyclopedia of Philosophy*; (from their website)

14. *Stanford Encyclopedia of Philosophy*; (from their website)

15. Plato in *Menexenus*

16. Will Durant; *The Life of Greece*; p. 364

17. Will Durant; *The Life of Greece*; p. 365

18. Will Durant; *The Life of Greece*; p. 366

19. Will Durant; *The Life of Greece*; p. 366

20. Diogenes Laertires; *Lives of the Philosophers*

21. Will Durant; *The Life of Greece*; p. 366

22. *A Dictionary of Early Christian Beliefs*; p. 621

23. Will Durant; *The Life of Greece*; p. 367

24. Will Durant; *The Life of Greece*; p. 371

25. *Stanford Encyclopedia of Philosophy*; (from their website)

26. *Encyclopedia of Americana*; Vol. 25; p. 167

27. Martha C. Nussbaum drawing from; J. Carey, *Kairas and Logos*; 1978; and W. J. Ong; *Presence of the Word; 1967*

28. *Newsweek* Magazine; May 2, 2005

29. Will Durant; *The Life of Greece*; p. 367-368

30. Will Durant; *The Life of Greece*; p. 367

31. Will Durant; *The Life of Greece*; p. 369

32. Thomas K. Hubbard; *Homosexuality in Greece and Rome*; Berkley: University of California Press; 2008; p. 9

33. Will Durant; *The Life of Greece*; p. 370

34. Will Durant; *The Life of Greece*; p. 370

35. Will Durant; *The Life of Greece*; p. 373

36. Plato's *Phaedo*

37. R.C. Sproul; Ligioneer Ministries; www.ligonier.org

38. *Stanford Encyclopedia of Philosophy*; (from their website)

39. Adolf Harnack; Vol. 2; p. 184

40. Adolf Harnack; Vol. 2; p. 181

41. Adolf Harnack; Vol. 2; p. 194

42. *A Dictionary of Early Christian Beliefs*; David W. Bercot, ed.; Hendrickson Publishers, Inc.; 1998; p. 250

43. *A Dictionary of Early Christian Beliefs*; p. 520

44. *A Dictionary of Early Christian Beliefs*; p. 519-520

Chapter Eleven - Who Was Plato?

1. Millard J. Erickson; *God In Three Persons*; Baker Books; Grand Rapids, MI; p. 211, 258

2. Shirley C. Guthrie Jr.; *Christian Doctrine*; Westminister John Knox Press; Louisville, KY; 1994; p. 76-77

3. *The Nicene and Post-Nicene Fathers*; William B. Eerdmans Publishing Co.; Grand Rapids, MI; 1997; Vol. 1; p. 566

4. John K. Ryan, ed.; *The Confessions of Saint Augustine*; Image Books - Doubleday; New York, NY; 1960; p. 168-169

5. *Hades or The Intermediate State*; The Faith Press; Limited; London; p. 278

6. *Encyclopedia Americana*; Grolier, Inc.; Danbury, CT; 1992; Vol. 7; p. 649

7. Robert Baker and John Landers; *A Summary of Christian History*; Broadman and Holman Publishing; Nashville, TN; 2005; p. 65

8. Paul Johnson; *A History of Christianity*; Atheneum Press; New York, NY; 1976

9. *The Nicene and Post-Nicene Fathers*; William B. Eerdmans Publishing Co.; Grand Rapids, MI; 1997; Vol. 1; p. 566

110. *Newsweek* Magazine; March 28, 2005; p. 48

11. *Encyclopedia Americana*; Grolier, Inc.; Danbury, CT; 1992; Vol. 20; p. 310

12. Roger Olson and Christopher Hall; *The Trinity*; William B. Eerdmans Publishing Co.; Grand Rapids, MI; 2002; p. 39-40

13. Millard J. Erickson; *God In Three Persons*; Baker Books; Grand Rapids, MI; p. 23

14. Will Durant; *The Life of Greece*; p. 510

15. Will Durant; *The Life of Greece*; p. 510

16. Will Durant; *The Life of Greece*; p. 511

17. Will Durant; *The Life of Greece*; p. 511

18. *The World Book*; Vol. 15; p. 504

19. *Stanford Encyclopedia of Philosophy;* (from their website)

20. *Stanford Encyclopedia of Philosophy;* (from their website)

21. *Encyclopedia Americana*; Vol. 22; p. 227

22. *A Dictionary of Early Christian Beliefs*; David W. Bercot, ed.; Hendrickson Publishers, Inc.; 1998; p. 519-520

23. Adolph Harnack; Vol. 2; p. 194

24. Will Durant; *The Life of Greece*; p. 287

25. *A Dictionary of Early Christian Beliefs*; p. 519

26. Will Durant; *The Life of Greece*; p. 511

27. The *Tennessean*; July 22, 2007

28. Simon Blackburn; *Plato's Republic: A Biography*; Atlantic Monthly Press; New York, NY; 2006; p. 1

29. Simon Blackburn; *Plato's Republic: A Biography*; p. 7-8

30. Simon Blackburn; *Plato's Republic: A Biography*; p. 12

31. Simon Blackburn; *Plato's Republic: A Biography*; p. 17

32. Simon Blackburn; Plato's *Republic: A Biography*; p. 54-55

33. Edward Gibbon; *The Decline and Fall of The Roman Empire*; Everyman's Library; New York, NY; Vol. 2; p. 301

34. Millard J. Erickson; *God In Three Persons*; p. 123, 259

35. Shirley C. Guthrie Jr.; *Christian Doctrine*; p. 76-77

36. Frank Viola and George Barna; *Pagan Christianity?*; p. 215-216, 205

37. Edward Gibbon; *The Decline and Fall of The Roman Empire*; Everyman's Library; New York, NY; Vol. 2; p. 303-304

38. Edward Gibbon; *The Decline and Fall of The Roman Empire*; Vol. 2; p. 305

39. Thomas Jefferson; *A Letter to Dr. Benjamin Waterhouse From Monticello*; June 26, 1822

40. Charles B. Sanford; *The Religious Life of Thomas Jefferson*; University Press of Virginia; Charlottesville, VA; 1984; p. 4-5

41. Charles B. Sanford; *The Religious Life of Thomas Jefferson*; 1984; p. 88-89

42. Charles B. Sanford; *The Religious Life of Thomas Jefferson*; 1984; p. 113

43. Charles B. Sanford; *The Religious Life of Thomas Jefferson*; 1984; p. 148

44. Quoted at his memorial service, on a DVD in my library

45. Will Durant; *The Life of Greece*; p. 177-181

46. Edward Gibbon; *The Decline and Fall of The Roman Empire*; Vol. 2; p. 301

47. All of the *"Early Church Fathers"* quotes in this section are from *A Dictionary of Early Christian Beliefs;* Hendrickson Publishers, Inc.; David W. Bercot, ed.; 1998; p. 522-525

48. *The Nicene and Post-Nicene Fathers*; William B. Eerdmans Publishing Co.; Grand Rapids, MI; 1997; Vol. 1; p. 566

49. Robert Baker and John Roberts; *A Summary of Christian History*; Broadman & Holman Publishing; p. 66

50. Frank Viola and George Barna; *Pagan Christianity?*; p. 40

51. Will Durant; *The Life of Greece*; p. 510, 515-518

52. Will Durant; *The Life of Greece*; p. 515

53. Millard J. Erickson; *God In Three Persons*; p. 19-20

54. William R. Inge; *Lay Thoughts of a Dean*; 1926

55. Dr. Norman H. Snaith; *The Distinctive Ideas of The Old Testament*; 1944; p. 187-188

56. Dr. Floyd H. Ross and Tynette Hills; *The Great Religions By Which Men Live*; A Premier Book; Fawcett Publications, Inc.; Greenwich, CT; 1956

57. Millard J. Erickson; *God In Three Persons*

58. Professor Cyril C. Richardson; *The Doctrine of The Trinity*; p. 23, p. 111, p. 124, p. 148-149

59. Charles C. Ryrie; *Basic Theology;* p. 61, p. 65, p. 89

60. Millard J. Erickson; *God In Three Persons*; p. 18

Chapter Twelve - Who Was Philo?

1.   John Piper; *God's Passion For His Glory*; Crossway Books; Wheaton, IL; 1998; p. 82, 97

2.   Charles C. Ryrie; *Basic Theology*; p.58

3.   Will Durant; *The Life of Greece*; p. 191

4.   *Funk and Wagnalls New Encyclopedia*; Vol. 20; p. 351

5.   *Harper Collins Bible Dictionary*; Paul J. Achtemeier, Gen. ed.; Harper One Publishers; 1996; p. 849

6.   Will Durant; *Caesar and Christ*; p. 499-500

7.   *Harper Collins Bible Dictionary*; p. 23

8.   Will Durant; *Caesar and Christ*; p. 500

9.   Will Durant; *Caesar and Christ*; p. 501

10. Will Durant; *Caesar and Christ*; p. 501

11. *Funk and Wagnalls New Encyclopedia*; Vol. 20; p. 351-352

12. Charles Biggs (reprint); *Christian Platonists of Alexandria*; Kessinger Publishing; 1886; p. 22-23

13. Charles Biggs (reprint); *Christian Platonists of Alexandria*; p. 8-11

14. James D.G. Dunn; *Christology In The Making*; William B. Eerdmans Publishing Co.; Grand Rapids, MI; 1996; p. 220

15. Edward Gibbon; *The Decline and Fall of The Roman Empire*; Everyman's Library; New York, NY; Vol. 2; p. 303

16. *Harper Collins Bible Dictionary*; p. 792

17. *Encyclopedia Americana;* Grolier, Inc.; Danbury, CT; 1992; Vol. 20; p. 922-923

18. Will Durant; *Caesar and Christ;* p. 501-502

19. Will Durant; *Caesar and Christ;* p. 501

20. James D.G. Dunn; *Christology In The Making;* p. 210

21. James D.G. Dunn; *Christology In The Making;* p. 219

22. James D.G. Dunn; *Christology In The Making;* p. 220-221

23. James D.G. Dunn; *Christology In The Making;* p. 230

24. James D.G. Dunn; *Christology In The Making;* p. 221, 222, 228

25. *The International Standard Bible Encyclopedia;* Geoffrey W. Bromiley; Gen. Ed.; William B Eerdmans Publishing Co.; Grand Rapids, MI; Vol. 4; p. 1103

26. *The International Standard Bible Encyclopedia;* Vol. 4; p. 1103-1104

27. For some of the research in this section I am indebted to Geoffrey W. Bromiley; Gen. Ed.; *The International Standard Bible Encyclopedia;* Vol. 4; p. 1106

28. James D.G. Dunn; *Christology In The Making;* p. 253-254

29. James D.G. Dunn; *Christology In The Making;* p. 257, 48, 232, 233, 231

30. Millard J. Erickson; *God In Three Persons;* p. 199, 210

31. *The International Standard Bible Encyclopedia;* Vol. 4; p. 1105

32. *Hastings' Dictionary of the Bible;* James Hastings, ed.; Hendrickson Publishers; 1994; p. 550

33. James Hastings, ed.; *Hastings' Dictionary of the Bible;* p. 550-551

34. Philip Yancey; *The Jesus I Never Knew;* Zondervan; 1995; p. 60

35. Lee Strobel; *The Case For Christ;* Zondervan; 1995; p. 62

36. Lee Strobel; *The Case For Christ;* p. 61

37. Dr. Thomas S. McCall, Th. D.; *The Language of The Gospel;* This article appeared originally in the May, 1997 *Levitt Letter.* Dr. McCall holds a Th. M. in O.T. studies and a Th. D in Semitic languages, and the O.T.

38. Professor Barry D. Smith; *The New Testament and Its Context*; Crandall University; (from their website)

39. Martin McNamara; *Targum and Testament*; William B. Eerdmans Publishing Co.; Grand Rapids, MI; 1972; p. 104.

40. *The Pulpit Commentary: St. John* Vol. 1; ed. H.D.M. Spence-Jones; Bellingham, WA; Logos Research Systems, Inc.; 2004.

41. James D.G. Dunn; *Christology In The Making*; p. 243

42. Millard J. Erickson; *God In Three Persons*; p. 199

43. Millard J. Erickson; *God In Three Persons*; p. 201

44. I am indebted to Sir Anthony Buzzard for this list of translations. He personally copied them from the library of a friend who is a collector of Bibles.

45. *The Harper Collins Encyclopedia of Catholicism*; Richard P. McBrien; Gen. Ed.; p. 659

46. *Global Encyclopedia*; Global Industries, Inc.; Arlington, VA; 1986

47. Will Durant; *Caesar and Christ*; p. 502

48. Simon Blackburn; *Plato's Republic: A Biography*; Atlantic Monthly Press; New York, NY; 2006; p. 105

Chapter Thirteen - The Church Fathers, Constantine and Nicea

1. *Harper Collins Bible Dictionary*; Paul J. Achtemeier, Gen. ed.; Harper One Publishers; 1996; p. 453

2. Charles C. Ryrie; *Basic Theology*; Moody Press; Chicago, IL; 1999; p. 65

3. Roger E. Olson and Christopher A. Hall; *The Trinity;* William B. Eerdmans Publishing Co.; Grand Rapids, MI; 2002; p. 2, 15, 16

4. Roger E. Olson and Christopher A. Hall; *The Trinity;* p. 17

5. Roger E. Olson and Christopher A. Hall; *The Trinity;* p. 120

6. Roger E. Olson and Christopher A. Hall; *The Trinity;* p. 17

7. Roger E. Olson and Christopher A. Hall; *The Trinity;* p. 18

8. Rudolph Bultmann; *Theology of the New Testament* (1948-1953); Translated by Kendrick Grobel; London: SCM; 1951-55; Vol. 1; p. 129

9. A.C. McGiffert; *A History of Christian Thought*; Scribner's Sons; New York; 1954; p. 38

10. Kermit Zarley - Servetus the Evangelical; *The Restitution of Jesus Christ*; 2008; p. 38

11. *Encyclopedia Americana*; Vol. 16; p. 244

12. Kermit Zarley; *The Restitution of Jesus Christ* ; p. 39

13. Roger E. Olson and Christopher A. Hall; *The Trinity;* p. 22-23

14. *Hastings' Dictionary of the Bible*; James Hastings, ed.; Hendrickson Publishers; 1994; p. 550

15. Adolph Harnack; *History of Dogma*; Vol. 2; p. 184, 186

16. Adolph Harnack; *History of Dogma*; Vol. 1; p. 110, 113, 114

17. Adolph Harnack; *History of Dogma*; Vol. 2; p. 370

18. Roger E. Olson and Christopher A. Hall; *The Trinity;* p. 23

19. Roger E. Olson and Christopher A. Hall; *The Trinity;* p. 124

20. Roger E. Olson and Christopher A. Hall; *The Trinity;* p. 39

21. Roger E. Olson and Christopher A. Hall; *The Trinity;* p. 131

22. Roger E. Olson and Christopher A. Hall; *The Trinity;* p. 110

23. *A Dictionary of Early Christian Beliefs*; David E. Bercot, ed.; Hendrickson Publishers, Inc.; Peabody, MA; 1998; p. 521, 524

24. For some of the information in this section on *Sabellius*, I am indebted to Kermit Zarley, writing as *"Servetus The Evangelical"* in *The Restitution of Jesus Christ*; 2008; p. 40.

25. Kermit Zarley; *The Restitution of Jesus Christ* ; p. 41

26. Adolph Harnack; *History of Dogma*; Vol. 3; p. 201

27. *Funk & Wagnalls New Encyclopedia*; Vol. 25; p. 249

28. *Global Encyclopedia*; Global Industries, Inc.; 1986; Vol. 11; p. 406

29. *Encyclopedia Americana*; Vol. 21; p. 74-75

30. Adolph Harnack; *History of Dogma*; Vol. 3; p. 101

31. *A Dictionary of Early Christian Beliefs*; p. XIX

32. Roger E. Olson and Christopher A. Hall; *The Trinity;* p. 24-26

33. *Encyclopedia Americana*; Vol. 21; p. 74-75

34. *Funk & Wagnalls New Encyclopedia*; Vol. 19; p. 441

35. Adolph Harnack; *History of Dogma*; Vol. 2, p. 335, 341, 352, 368, 369; Vol. 3, p.106, 116, 132-133, 135, 155, 200

36. *Encyclopedia Britannica*; Encyclopedia Britannica, Inc.; Chicago; 2002; Vol. 9; p. 509

37. Will Durant; *Caesar and Christ*; p. 614-615

38. T.E. Pollard; *Johannine Christology and The Early Church*; Cambridge University Press; 1970; p. 95

39. Will Durant; *Caesar and Christ*; p. 608-611

40. One such detailed account is given by Kermit Zarley in his work *The Restitution of Jesus Christ*. Writing under his pen name Servetus The Evangelical, he has done an excellent job of research and writing and I am indebted to him for this information.

41. Edward Gibbon; *The History of The Decline and Fall Of The Roman Empire*; 7 Vol's.; Methuen; London; 1909; Vol. 2; p. 373

42. Philip Yancey; *The Jesus I Never Knew*; Zondervan; Grand Rapids, MI; 1995; 49-50

43. Will Durant; *Caesar and Christ*; p. 658

44. Adolph Harnack; *History of Dogma*; Vol. 3; p. 72-73, 295

45. Edward Gibbon; *The History of The Decline and Fall Of The Roman Empire*; Vol. 2; p. 314

46. *Funk & Wagnalls New Encyclopedia*; Vol. 19; p. 441

47. Will Durant; *Caesar and Christ*; p. 660

48. Edward Gibbon; *The History of The Decline and Fall Of The Roman Empire*; Vol. 2; p. 306

49. Timothy D. Barnes; *Athanasius and Constantius*; Harvard University Press; Cambridge, MA; 1993; p. 3, 12

50. Philip Schaff; *History of The Christian Church*; Eerdmans Publishing; Grand Rapids, MI; 1907-1910.

51. Kermit Zarley; *The Restitution of Jesus Christ* ; p. 47

52. Paul Johnson; *A History of Christianity*; Atheneum, NY; 1976; p. 141

53. Will Durant; *Caesar and Christ*; p. 656, 663, 664

54. Paul Johnson; *A History of Christianity*; p. 141

55. Various Sources

56. Will Durant; *Caesar and Christ*; p. 657

57. *The Nicene and Post Nicene Fathers*; William B. Eerdmans Publishing, Co.; Grand Rapids, MI; Vol. 1; p. 566

58. *The Nicene and Post Nicene Fathers*; Vol. 1; p. 574

59. *The Nicene and Post Nicene Fathers*; p. 575-577

60. Will Durant; *Caesar and Christ*; p. 660

61. Ian Wilson; *Jesus: The Evidence*; Harper and Row Publishing; 1984; p. 168

62. J.N.D. Kelly; *Early Christian Creeds*; 3rd Edition; Longman; Essex, England; 1972

63. Roger E. Olson and Christopher A. Hall; *The Trinity;* p. 40

64. Ramsey MacMullen; *Voting About God In Early Church Councils*; Yale U. Press; New Haven, Cy.; 2006; p. 7

65. Richard E. Rubinstein; *When Jesus Became God*; Harcourt Brace; NY; 1999; p. 194

66. *Harper Collins Encyclopedia of Catholicism*; p. 1271

67. Millard J. Erickson; *God In Three Persons*; p. 90

68. Adolph Harnack; *History of Dogma*; p. 151, 287, 297

69. Kermit Zarley; *The Restitution of Jesus Christ* ; p. 59-60

70. *Encyclopedia Americana*; Vol. 20; p. 310

71. *Encyclopedia Britannica*; Vol. 9; p. 319

72. Millard J. Erickson; *God In Three Persons*; p. 28-29

73. Philip Schaff; *History of The Christian Church*; Vol. 3; p. 252

74. Philip Schaff; *History of The Christian Church*; Vol. 3; p. 347

75. Athanasius; *Orations Against The Arians*; Vol. 1, p.1; Vol. 3, p. 37, 47, 50, 55-58, 64, 67

76. Richard E. Rubinstein; *When Jesus Became God*; p. 224

77. Kermit Zarley; *The Restitution of Jesus Christ* ; p. 63-64

78. Edward Gibbon; *The Decline and Fall of The Roman Empire*; Vol. 2; p. 317

79. Philip Schaff; *History of The Christian Church*; Vol. 3; p. 764

80. *USA Today*; April 19, 2010; p. 9A

81. Philip Jenkins; *Jesus Wars*; Harper One; New York, NY; 2010; p. 19

82. Philip Jenkins; *Jesus Wars*; p. 31

83. Charles C. Ryrie; *Basic Theology*; p. 60-62

84. Shirley C. Guthrie Jr.; *Christian Doctrine*; p. 80-81

85. Millard J. Erickson; *God In Three Persons*; p. 23, 26

86. Philip Jenkins; *USA Today*; April 19, 2010; p. 9A

87. Philip Jenkins; *Jesus Wars*; Harper One; p. 12

88. *Encyclopedia Americana*; Vol. 2; p. 687

89. *A Dictionary of Early Christian Beliefs*; p. 522

90. Adolph Harnack; *History of Dogma*; Vol. 1; p. 359-360

91. *Encyclopedia Americana*; p. 686, 687

92. *Encyclopedia Britannica*; Vol. 25; p. 903, 904

93. Will Durant; *Caesar and Christ*; p. 608-611

94. Roger E. Olson and Christopher A. Hall; *The Trinity;* p. 43, 45, 55

95. Roger E. Olson and Christopher A. Hall; *The Trinity;* p. 132

96. John K. Ryan; *The Confessions of Saint Augustine*; Image Books - Doubleday; New York; First Image edition published 1960; p. 18

97. John K. Ryan; *The Confessions of Saint Augustine*; p. 21-22

98. John K. Ryan; *The Confessions of Saint Augustine*; p. 22

99. John K. Ryan; *The Confessions of Saint Augustine*; p. 22

100. John K. Ryan; *The Confessions of Saint Augustine*; p. 23

101. John K. Ryan; *The Confessions of Saint Augustine*; p. 168

102. *Collier's Encyclopedia*; The Crowell-Collier's Publishing Co.; New York; 1961; Vol. 2; p. 453

103. John K. Ryan; *The Confessions of Saint Augustine*; p. 169

104. Millard J. Erickson; *God In Three Persons*; p. 102

105. Roger E. Olson and Christopher A. Hall; *The Trinity;* p. 52

106. John K. Ryan; *The Confessions of Saint Augustine*; p. 178

107. John K. Ryan; *The Confessions of Saint Augustine*; p. 179

108. John K. Ryan; *The Confessions of Saint Augustine*; p. p. 176, 180, 338

109. John K. Ryan; *The Confessions of Saint Augustine*; p. 342

110. John K. Ryan; *The Confessions of Saint Augustine*; p. 418

111. Douglas McCready; *He Came Down From Heaven*; Inter Varsity Press; Downers Grove, IL; 2005; p. 250

112. *Collier's Encyclopedia*; Vol. 2; p. 454

113. *Collier's Encyclopedia*; Vol. 2; p. 454

114. *Collier's Encyclopedia*; Vol. 15; p. 318-319

115. John K. Ryan; *The Confessions of Saint Augustine*; p. 390

116. Roger E. Olson and Christopher A. Hall; *The Trinity;* p. 51-52

117. Edward Gibbon; *The Decline and Fall of The Roman Empire*; Vol. 2; p. 313

118. *Encyclopedia Britannica*; Vol. 25; p. 904; Vol. 9; p. 509

119. *Collier's Encyclopedia*; Vol. 15; p. 319

120. Roger E. Olson and Christopher A. Hall; *The Trinity;* p. 53

121. Roger E. Olson and Christopher A. Hall; *The Trinity;* p. 55-57

122. Roger E. Olson and Christopher A. Hall; *The Trinity;* p. 55, 58

123. Roger E. Olson and Christopher A. Hall; *The Trinity;* p. 54, 63, 64

124. *Harper Collins Encyclopedia of Catholicism*; p. 84, 85

125. *Encyclopedia Americana*; Vol. 2; p. 142

126. Roger E. Olson and Christopher A. Hall; *The Trinity;* p. 64

127. Roger E. Olson and Christopher A. Hall; *The Trinity;* p. 55

128. Roger E. Olson and Christopher A. Hall; *The Trinity;* p. 66-67

129. *New International Encyclopedia*; 1916 ed.; Vol. 23; p. 477

130. Adolph Harnack; *History of Dogma*; Vol. 2; p. 7

131. Roger E. Olson and Christopher A. Hall; *The Trinity;* p. 68

132. Roger E. Olson and Christopher A. Hall; *The Trinity;* p. 69, 76

133. George H. Williams; *The Radical Reformation*; Westminister Press; Philadelphia; 1962; p. 322

134. Marian Hillar, with Claire S. Allen; *Michael Servetus: Intellectual Giant, Humanist, and Martyr*; University Press of America; Lanham, MD; 2002; p. 185

135. John Marshall; *John Locke, Toleration and Early Enlightenment Culture*; Cambridge University; 2006; p. 325

136. Kermit Zarley; *The Restitution of Jesus Christ* ; p. 85

137. Kermit Zarley; *The Restitution of Jesus Christ* ; p. 84

138. May I recommend Kermit Zarley's, *The Restitution of Jesus Christ*, in which he gives a good account of this period.

139. Roger E. Olson and Christopher A. Hall; *The Trinity;* p. 80-81

140. Frank Viola and George Barna; *Pagan Christianity?*; p. 40, 205

141. Roger E. Olson and Christopher A. Hall; *The Trinity;* p. 115

142. Stephen Snobelen; *Isaac Newton, Heretic;* British Society for the History of Science; 1999; p. 389

Chapter Fourteen - A Prophetic Call To Change

1. Frank Viola and George Barna; *Pagan Christianity?*; p. 238

2. Arthur Darby Nock; *Early Gentile Christianity*; Harper Torchbooks; New York; p. 8, 16

3. James D.G. Dunn; *Christology In The Making*; William B. Eerdmans Publishing Co.; Grand Rapids, MI; 1996; p. 14

4. Philip Jenkins; *Jesus Wars*; Harper One; New York, NY; 2010; p. 91, 97

5. *A Dictionary of Early Christian Beliefs*; David W. Bercot, ed.; Hendrickson Publishers; Peabody, MA; 2002; p. 520

6. Will Durant; *Caesar and Christ*; p. 595

7. *A Dictionary of Early Christian Beliefs*; p. 522, 524

8. Simon Blackburn; *Plato's Republic: A Biography*; Atlantic Monthly Press; New York, NY; 2006; p. 105

9. Simon Blackburn; *Plato's Republic: A Biography*; p.103-104

10. Frank Viola and George Barna; *Pagan Christianity?*; p. 243-244

Appendix A

Understanding John Chapter One

"In the beginning was the Word, and the Word was with God, and the Word was God" (John 1:1).

The wide spread misunderstanding of this verse among Christians is the source of much of the confusion that exists regarding who the One Most High God of the Bible is. It is a serious mistake for Christians to read John 1:1 as if it says: "In *eternity past* was the *Son*, and the *Son* was with God, and the *Son* was God," thus making Jesus the eternal God.

It should be read and understood as:
*"In the **beginning** [some certain beginning] was the **word** [Greek - logos - speech, something said], and the **word** was with God, and the **word** was God"* [the breath of His mouth].

Note: John uses the word *"beginning"* 23 times in his writings and not once does he mean *"eternity past."* It is always some certain *beginning*.

Note: The word *"word"* in John chapter one is not capitalized in the original Greek, and in many older translations.

Here are the proof texts:
*"By the **word** of the Lord were the heavens made; and all the host of them by **the breath of his mouth**....for **he spoke** and it was done" (Ps. 33:6, 9).*

*"Through faith we understand that the worlds were framed by the **word** of God" (Heb. 11:3).*

*"By the **word** of God the heavens were of old, and the earth...." (II Peter 3:5).*

*"These things saith the Amen, the faithful and true witness, **the beginning** of the creation of God"* [Jesus speaking] *(Rev. 3:14).* **Trust Jesus!**

Now please look at John 1:3.

> *"All things were made by **him**; and without **him** was not*
> *any thing made that was made."*

Is the word *"him"* in this verse translated properly? First of all it does not harmonize with a true understanding of the two prior verses. (The *"word"* - logos - *"something said"* is not a "him").

Second, it is important to note that of **nine prominent English translations that preceded** the King James Version of 1611, **not one** used the word "him." **Eight** of the nine rendered John 1:3, *"By **it** all things were made. Without **it** nothing was made" (Tyndale Bible, 1535; Matthew, 1535; Tavener, 1539; The Great (Cranmer's) Bible, 1539; Whittingham, 1557; Genera, 1560; Bishop's Bible, 1568; Tomson NT, 1607).* **One**, the famous Coverdale Bible of 1550 says *"the same"* rather than "it." **None of these eight say "him."** Why did the King James translators render *"it"* as *"him,"* as if it were a person? They were influenced by Greek philosophy through the *"logos doctrine"* which came from Plato and Philo, and made its way into Christian thought by way of Justin, Origen, Athanasius and Augustine, and was promoted by 1300 years of false Catholic tradition. Their error has helped to lead millions of sincere Christians astray in their understanding of who the one true God is!

A challenge made in love.
Go to your library and find any book, encyclopedia, Bible concordance or dictionary that deals with the doctrine of the Trinity. Look in the subject index under *"Divine logos doctrine"* and it will refer you to Plato, Philo, and other Greek philosophers. Thus our understanding was corrupted!

What John meant in John 1:14.

> *"And the word* [logos - something said] *was made flesh* [Jesus, the Son of God], *and dwelt among us, (and we beheld **his glory**, the glory as of the only begotten of the Father,) full of grace and truth."* **What God said became flesh!**

These verses in John chapter one are at the heart of the debate as to Jesus' deity, and the key to a true Biblical understanding of who he is.

Words of truth from Professor James Dunn.

The noted **trinitarian** scholar Professor James Dunn correctly states in his exhaustive study, *Christology In The Making:*

> *"There is no clear indication anywhere in Paul that he ever identified Christ (pre-existent or otherwise) with the Logos (Word) of God" (p. 39). "Similarly in Acts there is no sign of any christology of pre-existence" (p. 51). "In Matthew and Luke Jesus' divine sonship is traced back specifically to his birth or conception...he was **Son of God** because his conception was **an act of creative power by the Holy Spirit**" (p. 61). "In the earliest period of Christianity 'Son of God' was not an obvious vehicle of a christology of incarnation or pre-existence. Certainly such a christology cannot be traced back to Jesus himself with any degree of conviction...it is less likely that we can find such a christology in Paul or Mark or Luke or Matthew" (p. 64). **"There is no indication that Jesus thought or spoke of himself as having pre-existed with God prior to his birth or appearance on earth. We cannot claim that Jesus believed himself to be the incarnate Son of God"** (p. 254). "There is always the possibility that **popular pagan superstition became popular Christian superstition** by a gradual assimilation and spread of belief" (p. 251).*

Yet, after making these statements Professor Dunn closed out his book with a *"Trinitarian Confession"* (p. 268). This proves again that even though a doctrine is not taught in Scripture it does not bother some theologians. But is does bother me and it should trouble every Christian who loves the truth!

God Did Not Become A Man!

There is not one verse in the Bible that says God needed to, intended to, or did become a man!

*"For **I am God**, and **not man**; the **Holy One** in the midst of thee" (Hosea 11:9).*

*"**God is not a man**....neither the son of man...."* *(Num. 23:19).*

"For he (God) *is not a man...." (I Sam. 15:29).*

The eternal God has a human Son who is a man!

*"Ye seek to kill me, **a man** that has told you the truth, **which I have heard of God**"* (Jesus speaking) *(John 8:40).*

*"Greater love hath no **man** than this, that **a man** lay down his life for his friends. Ye are my friends...."* (Jesus speaking) *(John 15:13-14).*

*"If I had not done among them the works which **none other man** did....* (Jesus speaking) *(John 15:24).*

*"For there is **one God**, and one mediator between **God** and **men**, the **man Christ Jesus**" (I Tim. 2:5).*

Note: Jesus is called "son of man" 84 times in the Gospels. God called Ezekiel "son of man" 90 times in the book of Ezekiel. It means **a human being.**

Appendix B

Three Doubtful Verses

It has never been a practice of mine to support a doctrine which I hold by casting doubt on the authenticity of Bible verses that seem to disagree with it. God is the custodian of His word and I believe He has given us all we need in Holy Scripture for salvation and service. You will notice that I have used the authorized King James Version in this book. Some of the modern translations are good and I use them for study, but my preaching and writing are done mostly from the KJV.

However, there are three verses in the KJV that we should consider, the authenticity of which is questioned by some of the best modern scholars, on textural and historical grounds. It is remarkable that even Trinitarian scholars question these verses, because without their support the doctrine of the Trinity has absolutely no basis in Scripture.

The original texts of the O.T. and N.T. as breathed by the Holy Spirit are infallible and inerrant. However there has possibly been some tampering with the original texts in the ensuing centuries to support the doctrine of the Trinity. The following is mostly from Trinitarian sources.

I John 5:7
Author Lee Strobel in his book, *The Case for Christ*, (over 2 million copies sold) interviewed Bruce M. Metzger, PH.D., an 84 year old authority on the authenticity of the N.T., who has authored or edited fifty books relating to the subject. He puts the *"grand total of (early) Greek manuscripts at 5,664."* Metzger tells Strobel that if someone challenges the authenticity of I John 5:7: *"For there are three that bear record in heaven, the Father, the Word, and the Holy Ghost: and these three are one,"* saying *"that's not in the earliest manuscripts,"* his answer would be, ***"and that's true enough. I think that these words are found in only about seven or eight copies (manuscripts), all from the fifteenth or sixteenth century. I acknowledge that is not what the author of I John was inspired to write."*** Strobel and Metzger are both **trinitarian** in belief, but they have cast doubt on one of the main Scriptures Trinitarians use to support their doctrine.

The NIV quotes in its text **notes** the words *"the Father, the Word and the Holy Spirit, and these three are one. And there are three that testify on earth,"* and then explains why they are not in the **text** of the NIV. They say, ***"the addition is not found in any Greek manuscript or N.T. translation prior to the 16th century."*** These words are also not found in the *New Revised Standard Version*, the *New American Standard Bible*, the *English Standard Version*, the *Holman Christian Standard Bible* or the *New Living Translation*.

Respected **trinitarian** Biblical scholar Professor Charles C. Ryrie agrees. Writing in his well known work, *Basic Theology*, he states:

> *"The N.T. contains no explicit statement of the doctrine of the triunity of God (since 'these three are one' in I John 5:7 **is apparently not a part of the genuine text of Scripture**)" (p. 60).*

Trinitarian Millard J. Erickson (Southern Baptist) in his book, *God In Three Persons,* says that some oppose the doctrine of the Trinity because of:

> *"....the **apparent silence** of the Bible on this important subject. This contention notes that **there really is no explicit statement of the doctrine of the Trinity in the Bible**, particularly since the revelation by textual criticism of the **spurious nature** of I John 5:7. Other passages have been seen on closer study to be applicable **only under the greatest strain**."*

The *New Bible Commentary* says regarding I John 5:7:

> *"The whole of verse 7 of the Authorized Version is omitted in the Revised Version because it was not written by John. It first appeared in a Latin version three hundred years after John was dead, and not in any Greek manuscript till a thousand years later."*

So is this a forgery? Why would someone take it upon themself to insert a verse into God's Holy Bible as if it were written by the apostle John, several hundred years **after** the death of John? Look at I John 5:7 again:

> *"For there are three that bear record in heaven, the **Father**, the **Word**, and the **Holy Ghost**: and these three are one."*

Is this not an attempt to deceive people into believing that God is *"three"* persons in *"one"*? There is no other similar verse in the Bible. There are sixty-seven Bible verses that say God is *"one,"* and not a single authentic verse that says He is *two*, *three*, or any other number.

> *"Hear, O Israel: The Lord our God is **one** Lord"* [Moses speaking] *(Deut. 6:4).*

> *"Hear, O Israel: The Lord our God is **one** Lord"* [Jesus speaking] *(Mark 12:29).*

Please say this several times with Moses and Jesus:

> *"The Lord our God is **one** Lord."*
> *"The Lord our God is **one** Lord."*
> *"The Lord our God is **one** Lord."*

Matthew 28:19

Now to Matthew 28:19, another mainstay of those who hold the trinitarian view of God.

> *"Go ye therefore, and teach all nations, baptizing them in the name of the Father, and of the Son, and of the Holy Ghost."*

The *Interpreters Dictionary of the Bible* says:

> *"There is **grave doubt** whether they (the traditional words Father, Son and Holy Ghost) may be regarded as the actual words of Jesus."*

Encyclopedia Britannica says:

> *"Elsewhere in the New Testament the triune formula is not used. Some scholars thus **doubt the accuracy** of the quotation in Matthew. In the **oldest sources** it is stated that baptism takes place in the name of Jesus."*

Hastings' Dictionary of the Bible says:

> *"It has been customary to trace the institution of the practice [Christian baptism] to the words of Christ recorded in Matt. 28:19. But the authenticity of this passage has been challenged on historical as well as on textual grounds. **It must be acknowledged** that the*

formula of the threefold name, which is here enjoined, does not appear to have been employed by the primitive church, which, so far as our information goes, baptized 'in' or 'into the name of Jesus' (or "Jesus Christ" or 'the Lord Jesus': AC. 2:38, 8:16, 10:49, 19:5; of I Co. 1:13, 15) **without reference to the Father or the Spirit.***"* Hastings elsewhere holds up for the doctrine of the Trinity but must admit that it cannot be supported by Matthew 28:19.

The Harper Collins Encyclopedia of Catholicism **says:**

"While the explicit formula in Matthew might come from **the liturgy of the** [Catholic] **Church,** *the commandment to baptize and the central meaning of baptism come from Jesus" (p. 134).*

The *Encyclopedia Americana* **says:**

"The charge at the end of the Gospel of Matthew to the disciples to baptize all nations 'in the name of the Father and of the Son and of the Holy Spirit' (Matt. 28:19) - which modern critics regard as **reflecting not the words of Jesus himself,** *but a development that took place* **sometime after the Apostolic preaching began** *- provides* **the basis upon which the earliest creedal statements were built.***"* Please study these words closely, *"reflecting not the words of Jesus himself "but providing" the basis upon which the earliest creedal statements were built."* They are saying in essence the earliest creeds (Nicea, Constantinople, Chalcedon) were built on words that probably did not come from Jesus. Shocking!

Professor Millard J. Erickson (S.W. Baptist Theological Seminary) **says:**

"Whether one concludes that the **threefold** *pattern found at the conclusion of Matthew's Gospel* **is an authentic word of Jesus,** *it is apparent that the church used this formula from quite an early period."*

The great church historian Eusebius of Caesarea *(260-339 A.D.)*, is called the father of church history. His work, *Ecclesiastical History,* (10 volumes), is an account of the rise and triumph of Christianity. In this and his other writings done before the Nicean Council in 325 A.D., he quotes Matthew 28:19 some eighteen times writing, *"....disciple all nations **in my name,"*** with no mention of the Father and Spirit. Justin Martyr *(100-165 A.D.)* also quoted Matthew 28:19 in his writings as *"....disciples all nations **in my name,"*** as did other Christian writers (Hermas, Apharaates of Nisibis, etc.).

The highly respected *International Standard Encyclopedia* (4 volumes) says:

> *"The formula of Christian baptism, **in the mode that prevailed**, is given in Matt. 29:19: 'I baptize you in the name of the Father, of the Son, and of the Holy Ghost.' **But it is curious that the words are not given in any description of Christian baptism until the time of Justin Martyr, and there they are not repeated exactly but in a slightly extended and explanatory form.** In every account of the performance of the rite **in apostolic times** a much shorter formula is in use. The 3000 believers were baptized on the day of Pentecost 'in the name of Jesus;' and **the same formula** was used at the baptism of Cornelius and those who were with him. **Indeed it would appear to have been the usual one,** from Paul's question to the Corinthians: 'Were you baptized into the name of Paul?' (I Cor. 1:13). The Samaritans were baptized 'in the name of the Lord Jesus;' and the same formula (a common one in Acts of devotion) was used in the case of the disciples at Ephesus. In some instances it is recorded that before baptism the converts were asked to make some confession of their faith, which took the form of declaring that Jesus was the Lord or **that Jesus Christ was the Son of God.** The historian Socrates informs us that some.... 'corrupted' baptism by using only the name of Christ in the formula; while **injunctions** [orders] to use the longer formula and **punishments,** including deposition, [being banished] **threatened** to those who presumed to employ the shorter [formula] which meet us [in history] prove that the practice of using the shorter formula [Jesus' name] existed in the 5th and 6th centuries, **at all events in the East."***

The great Church historian **Dr. Adolph Harnack, in his exhaustive work,** *History of Dogma,* **(seven volumes) makes this strong statement:**

> *"Matthew 28:19 is not a saying of the Lord. The Trinitarian formula is foreign to the mouth of Jesus, and has not the authority in the Apostolic age which it must have had if it had descended from Jesus himself."*

Dr. Harnack brings up a good point. If Jesus' last command to his faithful followers before he ascended, was to baptize *"in the name of the Father, and of the Son, and of the Holy Ghost,"* why is there **not one instance** recorded in Scripture of the apostles using this formula? Seven days after Jesus' ascension Peter told the multitude:

> *"Repent, and be baptized every one of you in the **name of Jesus Christ**...." (Acts 2:38).*

Please consider these verses also:

> *"....they were baptized in the **name of the Lord Jesus**"* [Samaria] *(Acts 8:16).*

> *"And he* [Peter] *commanded them to be baptized in the **name of the Lord**"* [Cornelius' household] *(Acts 10:48).*

> *"When they heard this, they were baptized in the **name of the Lord Jesus**" (Acts 19:5).*

> *"Know ye not, that so many of us as were **baptized into Jesus Christ** were baptized into his death" (Rom. 6:3).*

One final point on this subject. Matthew 28:19 does not seem to harmonize with Jesus' last words on earth to his disciples as recorded by Luke:

> *"And that repentance and remission of sins should be preached **in his name** among all nations" (Luke 24:47).*
> Note: Compare this verse with Peter's words at Pentecost seven days later in Acts 2:38, *"....in the **name of Jesus Christ**...."*

I have addressed this subject dear reader because I believe you have a right to see the evidence and judge it for yourself. If you conclude that Matthew 28:19 was actually spoken by Jesus, there are several points that should be considered.

1. This verse says nothing about *three* co-equal, co-eternal persons in *one* God.

2. This verse says nothing regarding "God the Son," "God the Spirit," or a "second God." This is non-biblical terminology which Christianity should cease to use.

3. This is not a "Trinitarian commission" from Jesus as some noted Christian ministers assert.

4. The word *"name"* in this verse is **singular.** What **single name** would Jesus have had in mind that would refer to three separate and distinct persons of God? (Please note: Jesus' name is not "Son." *"And she shall bring forth a son and thou shalt call his name Jesus" Matt. 1:21).* The Fathers name in Scripture:

   "Thus shalt thou say unto the children of Israel, The ***Lord God*** *of your fathers....this is* ***my name for ever,*** *and this is* ***my memorial unto all generations....the Lord God*** *of your fathers...." (Ex. 3:15-16).*

   "And the Lord descended in the cloud, and stood with him there, and ***proclaimed the name of the Lord.*** *And the Lord passed by before him, and proclaimed, The Lord, The* ***Lord God....*** *" (Ex. 34:5-6).* Would you disagree with God?

   "Incline your heart unto the ***Lord God*** *of Israel" (Joshua 24:23).*

   "Thus saith the ***Lord God*** *" (Ezek. 2:4).* Note: God called himself *"Lord God"* over 200 times in the book of Ezekiel.

   "The ***Lord God*** *shall give unto him* [Jesus] *the throne of his father David"* [Gabriel to Mary] *(Luke 1:32).*

   "And denying the ***only Lord God,*** *and our Lord Jesus Christ" (Jude v. 4).*

*"And I saw no temple therein: for the **Lord God** Almighty and the Lamb [Jesus] are the temple of it" (Rev. 21:22).*

*"Holy Father, **keep through thine own name** those whom thou hast given me" [Jesus' prayer] (John 17:11).*

*"I will write on him **the name of my God**....and I will write upon him **my new name**" [Jesus speaking] (Rev. 3:12).*

I Timothy 3:16

The apostle Paul in his 13 epistles makes a clear distinction between God and Jesus over 500 times. However I Timothy 3:16 in the King James Version seems to blur this distinction.

"And without controversy great is the mystery of godliness: God was manifest in the flesh, justified in the Spirit, seen of angels, preached unto the Gentiles, believed on in the world, received up into glory."

Did Paul actually write that *"God was manifest"* in Jesus' flesh? It is possible for he said in II Cor. 4:11:

*"That the life also of **Jesus might be made manifest in our mortal flesh**."*

We of course are not Jesus and Jesus is not God. Look at how Paul opens this same epistle of I Timothy:

*"Paul, an apostle of Jesus Christ by the commandment of **God our Savior** [God is our Savior but He used His Son Jesus to save us], and **Lord Jesus Christ**, which is our hope; Grace, mercy, and peace, from **God** our Father **and Jesus** Christ our Lord" (I Tim. 1:1-2).*

To Paul they are not the same and only one is God. See verse 17:

*"Now unto the King **eternal immortal** ["deathless"], **invisible**, the only wise God, be honor and glory for ever and ever."* (The *"only wise God"* is the one who is *"eternal, immortal, invisible"*).

Many of the best Bible scholars of today, even those of the trinitarian persuasion, based on the most reliable manuscripts, have been forced to admit that Paul probably did not include the word "God" in this verse. The NIV says:

> *"Beyond all question, the mystery of godliness is great:*
> **He appeared in a body."**

The *NASB, The New English Bible, The Holman CSB, The English Standard Version* and *The Message* all agree using "He" or "He who" instead of "God." *The New Living Translation* renders it thus:

> *"Without question, this is the great mystery of our faith.*
> *Christ was revealed in a human body."*

Did Paul call Jesus "God"? Listen to James Hastings, noted trinitarian Bible scholar, writing in *Hastings' Dictionary of the Bible*:

> *"It may be that St. Paul nowhere names Christ "God."*
> *To a Jew the idea that a man might come to be God*
> *would have been an intolerable blasphemy."*

Please note also that the Godhead is not Paul's subject in I Tim. 3:16. The subject is the *"mystery of godliness."* This word *"godliness"* is the Greek word *"eusebeia" (Strongs #2150)* and means *"piety"* or *"holiness."* "*Great is the mystery of piety or holiness, Christ who was manifest in the flesh.*"

Three Cappadocians

*"Of the many who wrote on theology...Basil of Caesarea (fourth century), who, with his brother, Gregory of Nyssa, and their friend, Gregory of Nazianzus, **fixed the orthodox formulation of the doctrine of the Trinity**."*

(Collier's Encyclopedia under the topic "Greek Theology;" Vol. 9; p. 41-42)

This large painting by Raphael *(circa 1509)* is titled, ***The School of Athens***, and is in the Vatican's Apostolic Palace. It depicts *Socrates* (1), *Plato* (2), *Aristotle* (3), and other Greek philosophers *(Heraclitus - Zeno - Boethius, etc.)* who greatly influenced trinitarian Christian doctrine. *"The building is in the shape of a Greek cross...to show a harmony between pagan philosophy and Christian theology."*

This marble bust of **Socrates** has a place of honor in the Vatican.

This bust of **Plato** also has a place of honor in the Vatican.

519

About The Author

Joel Hemphill.....

- Has been married to his wife LaBreeska for fifty-three years.

- Has been a minister of Jesus Christ for over fifty years.

- Has written and recorded over 300 Gospel songs.

- Along with his family has received eight Dove Awards, and has received ten Dove nominations as Song Writer of the Year.

- Has been inducted into the Southern Gospel Music Hall of Fame and the Southern Songwriters Hall of Fame.

- Has ministered in Israel, Egypt, South Africa, the U.K., Germany, Austria, Honduras and throughout North America.

- Received a revelation in Holy Scripture in 2005 regarding the One Most High God, and wrote a revolutionary book on this subject titled "To God Be The Glory."

- Through his books, CDs, website and seminars is helping ministers of various denominations come to this Biblical understanding.

NOTES

For Music & Preaching CDs, Prayer,
Books by Joel & LaBreeska
or additional copies of this book
please write or phone:

Joel & LaBreeska Hemphill
P.O. Box 656
Joelton, Tennessee 37080
Phone: 615/299-0848
Fax: 615/299-0849

email: jhemphill@wildblue.net

www.thehemphills.com
www.trumpetcallbooks.com

**To hear Joel teach 7 lessons on the awesome subject of
the One Most High God
go to www.trumpetcallbooks.com**

NOTES

LaVergne, TN USA
23 December 2010
209979LV00004B/1/P